Guide to Egypt

by Michael Haag
Member, The Egypt Exploration Society

Author and publisher Michael Haag is able to organise and conduct tours to Egypt for individuals and groups. For a journey of special insight, adapted to your interests and with a personal touch, write to Michael Haag, PO Box 369, London NW3 4ER, England, or telephone 01-794 2647.

Michael Haag publishes a number of classic books about Egypt:

Egypt, Land of the Valley, by Robin Fedden
Flaubert in Egypt, translated and edited by Francis Steegmuller
Journey to the Orient, by Gérard de Nerval
Pharos and Pharillon, by E M Forster
Alexandria: A History and a Guide, by E M Forster with an introduction by Lawrence Durrell

Send for our complete list: Michael Haag Limited,
PO Box 369, London NW3 4ER

Guide to Egypt, second edition

Photo credits: all photos by Michael Haag, with the exception of St Anthony's Monastery and Chephren's Pyramid by David Hodson, and veiled bedouin girl © Lehnert and Landrock, Cairo

Cover illustration by Colin Elgie

Typeset by Witwell Ltd, 92 The Albany, Old Hall Street, Liverpool L3 9EJ

Printed in Great Britain by litho at the Bath Press, Lower Bristol Road, Bath BA2 3BL

Published by Travelaid Publishing (Michael Haag Limited), PO Box 369, London NW3 4ER, England

ISBN 0 902743 41 4

CONTENTS

Practical information sections follow most chapters and there are indexes at the rear.

ABOUT THIS GUIDE

The monuments of Egypt tell a story. The Pyramids created the Egyptian state; the monasteries of the Wadi Natrun transformed Christianity; the mosques of Cairo recount the struggles of Islam; the High Dam at Aswan is rolling back the deserts of northern Africa. Their stories are as awesome as the monuments themselves. It is not enough for a guide to describe, to list statistics of age and size. It must explain the significance of what is seen.

This Guide, therefore, is in large part a narrative. There are parts however — for example step by step descriptions of great temples — that may be rewarding only on the spot. But generally the Guide is meant to be read through at any time, or dipped into now and again. The main text of the chapters contain this narrative, and the descriptions. Descriptions of monuments are interwoven with their stories. An outline chronology is provided in the *Background* chapter to help you get your bearings.

At the end of most chapters there are *Practical Information* sections with details on accommodation, eating places, travel, etc, within the area. These sections make it easy for the traveller to plan his journey, get the most for his means, and enjoy his stay. The information is for all price ranges and degrees of adventurousness.

The *Background* chapter provides the information you need before you go; explains in general terms what you can expect when you arrive; and also serves as a reference section on the spot, with an Arabic vocabulary, railway timetables, an Islamic calendar, tables of weights and measures, a glossary of names and terms, and so on.

This is an entirely revised and expanded Guide to all aspects of Egypt, from boarding a bus in downtown Cairo to unravelling the mystery of the Pyramids. But while the Pyramids can be expected to remain unchanged for some time yet, the price of a hotel or finding a good place to eat can change from year to year. The *Background* chapter and the *Practical Information* sections were up to date when going to press, but inflation and changing circumstances can have their effect. The reader is asked, therefore, to help keep this Guide up to date by sending us any information that will help with the next edition. Please write to the *General Editor, Guide to Egypt, Travelaid Publishing, PO Box 369, London NW3 4ER, England.* Thank you.

BACKGROUND

In pharaonic times the people of Egypt believed the sun was daily born of the goddess Nut and travelled westwards across the heavens until swallowed by her at day's end, to be born once more the following dawn. And they believed the waters of the Nile rose from beneath the firmament, flowed through their country and out beyond the Delta where they sank to their source and then rose to run their course again.

The cycle and continuity of natural events was translated into the philosophical basis of ancient Egyptian politics and religion. In hieroglyphs the name of a pharaoh or god always appeared within a cartouche, an oval ring that represented the unbroken, unending, unchanging power of ruler or deity. The order of natural events in Egypt continues to impress a sense of timelessness upon the country.

Herodotus described Eygpt as 'a gift of the river', and Egypt's gift, like a great river of time, has been to carry within her the presence of the pharaonic, Hellenistic, Christian and Islamic periods, all embraced by the cartouche of the fellahin's millenial toil. Her endurance and stability in a region of conflict, flux and immense creativity has been her outstanding contribution to the world. She herself has not been exceptionally innovative; she did not give mankind mathematics, philosophy, science, medicine, Judaism, Christianity or Islam. But Egypt was essential to each, offering an impetus or a home, sometimes stamping them with the shape by which we know them today.

The Nile

About 10,000 years ago a dramatic change in climate caused the once fertile lands of northern Africa and the Middle East to turn to dust. Rock drawings in the Sahara depict ancient man hunting herbivors where now there is only sand. The inhabitants of this great belt of arid land migrated towards the few remaining rivers.

The Nile provided water and its annual flood covered the fields with rich alluvial soil. The ancient Egyptians called their country 'The Black Land', and the Nile Valley and Delta is still today the most fertile land in the world. Were it not for the existence of the Nile, no part of Egypt would be capable of agriculture.

Egypt is larger than any European country except Russia. However, about 93 percent of its area is dry and barren desert where only a few oasis-dwellers and nomadic bedouin can survive. Effectively, Egypt is no wider than the Valley and the Delta. In pharaonic times Egypt was likened to a lotus plant. The river was the stem, the Fayyum the bud, the Delta the flower. Within this figure of fertility today lives 95 percent of the nation's population.

The People

Egypt's population is approaching 50 million, and it is increasing by one million every year. The birth rate has been falling, but the death rate has fallen faster, a reflection of improved health services. The strain that rising population puts on Egypt's food supplies, housing and services is the country's greatest problem. Within its narrow cultivable area, Egypt is one of the most densely populated countries in the world, with about half its people now living in cities.

Egypt's hope lies in peace. 'In war', I was told by a Luxor doctor, 'if you win, you lose something; if you lose, you lose everything. We want peace to build. The Egyptian people are used to living on very little. But we want a future, we want something for our children'. Since the construction of the High Dam at Aswan the Nile no longer floods. Instead its water flows evenly throughout the year, the harvests have been multiplied, deserts brought to life. And Egypt gains the energy she needs to embark on wholesale industrialisation. A relaxation of ideology, a more liberal economic policy and the repair of relations with the West have also brought great benefits. Slowly the fellahin are being released from their drudgery, Egypt from her poverty.

Egypt's treasure is her people. They are warm, good humoured and tolerant, yet with extraordinary tenacity and a courage which they express in the ambition and love they feel for their country. Even after you have been greeted for the hundredth time by a stranger in the street with 'Welcome to my country!' you have to admit that beneath the pressing courtesy there is enthusiasm and genuine warmth. You pause in exasperation but then really must smile when you are asked, as if his life would hang upon your reply, 'Do you like my country?'.

Tourist Information

Tourist information may be obtained from **Egyptian State Tourist Offices abroad**. In Britain this is at 168 Piccadilly, London W1 (Tel: 493 5282). In the United States there are offices at 630 Fifth Avenue, New York, NY 10020 (Tel: 246-6960) and at 323 Geary Street, San Francisco, California 94102 (Tel: 433 7562). There are offices also in Montreal, Paris, Geneva, Frankfurt, Rome and Athens.

In Egypt, the headquarters of the Egyptian State Tourist Office is at 5 Sharia Adli, Cairo (Tel: 923000). There are offices also at Cairo Airport, the Pyramids, and at Alexandria, Luxor and Aswan. Another organisation worth contacting is **Misr Travel**, the state-run tourist company. They are in business for themselves and so their advice is not necessarily impartial, but they are the largest tourist company in Egypt, run hotels, operate coaches and limousines, and can make bookings for just about anything. In London they are at 40 Great Marlborough Street, W 1 (Tel: 734 0238). And they have offices in New York, Paris, Copenhagen, Stockholm, Frankfurt, Milan, Jeddah, Kuwait, Tokyo and Sidney. In Cairo they are at 1 Sharia Talaat Harb (Tel: 750010; telex 92035 MRSHIP UN).

When to Go

In the leisured days of travel it was often the custom to spend an entire winter, from November to May, in Egypt. This was 'the season', climatically, socially, and for those in search of

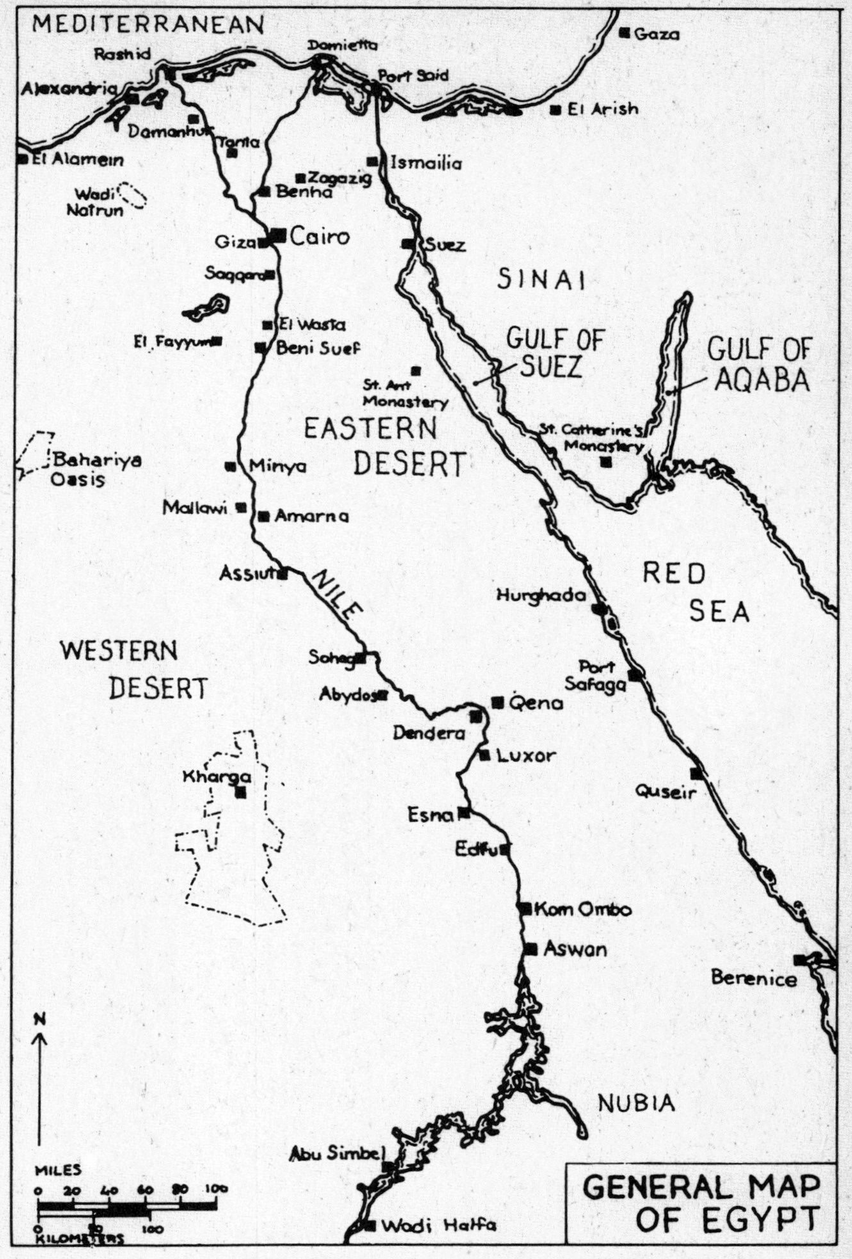
MEDITERRANEAN
Rashid
Damietta
Gaza
Port Said
Alexandria
El Arish
Damanhur
Tanta
El Alamein
Ismailia
Zagazig
Wadi Natrun
Benha
Giza
Cairo
Suez
Saqqara
SINAI
El Wasta
El Fayyum
Beni Suef
GULF OF SUEZ
GULF OF AQABA
St. Ant Monastery
EASTERN DESERT
St. Catherine's Monastery
Bahariya Oasis
Minya
Mallawi
Amarna
Assiut
NILE
RED SEA
Hurghada
WESTERN DESERT
Sohag
Port Safaga
Abydos
Qena
Dendera
Luxor
Kharga
Quseir
Esna
Edfu
Kom Ombo
Aswan
Berenice
N
NUBIA
Abu Simbel
MILES
0 20 40 60 80 100
0 50 100
KILOMETERS
Wadi Halfa
GENERAL MAP OF EGYPT

dry, mild conditions conducive to relief from asthma, chronic bronchitis, rheumatoid arthritis, gout, Bright's disease and other diseases of the kidneys. The late 20th C visitor is unlikely to come to Egypt for medicinal reasons, nor to stay so long, though late autumn through early spring is still the most comfortable period within which to visit, except that the reverse is true of Alexandria.

But not too much emphasis should be laid on season, for a variety of reasons. Cairo and Upper Egypt are most visited from November through April and there is pressure on accommodation. From May through September prices are lower in Upper Egypt. Air conditioning is general in the new hotels and in the better older ones — and in any case, hotels built in the pre-air-conditioned age will often have enormously high ceilings and louvred windows designed to dissipate the heat at any time of year. It can be very hot in Egypt, especially Upper Egypt, during the summer, but seeing the sights early in the morning and late in the afternoon, and the extraordinary dryness of the air the further south you go, can make your stay entirely agreeable. The proof is that Egypt has become a year-round destination.

Year-round destination

What to Take

The **clothing** you take will depend on the time of year. In winter you will need light woollens and sweaters; in summer light cottons. In spring and autumn, some combination of both is advisable against warm days and cool nights, and the possibility of changeable weather. Even in summer, however, at least one sweater or knit is likely to come in handy: at night the deserts can be cool, and Alexandria is freshened by strong sea breezes.

Clothes should be light in colour to reflect the sun, and should be easily washable and drip-dry. In summer, anywhere in Egypt except Alexandria, you can wash a suit at night and have it bone dry in the morning.

Conservative dress

Although far more liberal than most other Arab countries, Egypt is nevertheless conservative by Western standards and your dress should allow for this. Shorts on men and women, revealing blouses and very short skirts are becoming increasingly common in tourist areas, but are not always approved of. One solution, particularly in Upper Egypt, is for visitors, men and women, to wear a long flowing *galabiyya* — it happens to be ideal for the climate, day or night, warm or cool, and is both comfortable and graceful. Egyptians are not conservative on beaches, however, and bikinis are perfectly acceptable — not only on visitors, but on Egyptian women.

Bring sandals and also comfortable walking shoes. Sunglasses and a broad-brimmed hat will keep out the glare of the sun, intense in the desert.

Any items Egypt has to import will be expensive, and while a pharmacy or other stores will have Egyptian shampoos, soaps, toothpastes, razor blades and other **toilet items**, if you prefer your own brand, bringing it with you will save some money. **Batteries** are expensive and the range limited; if you are bringing anything that is battery-powered (do not forget camera and flash), bring also a supply of spare batteries.

Electrical current in Egypt is 220 volts; bring a converter if need be. **Film** is very expensive; bring plenty.

A few **other items** can be useful: insect repellent, especially if you are staying in a non-air-conditioned hotel; a water canteen for excursions (though a plastic bottle of local spring water can serve); salt tablets, not obtainable in Egypt, as an alternative to frequent water drinking; toilet paper, a rare commodity, sometimes even in the best of places; a flashlight, invaluable for exploring pyramids and tombs; binoculars, especially if you are cruising along the Nile, but also for examining details of gargantuan ruins.

Toilet paper and flashlight

Egyptian cotton is famous for its quality; clothes and shoes are inexpensive. Rather than overpack these things, it would be better to buy them once you are in the country.

Climate

Only a thin strip of the northern coastline shares in a Mediterranean climate, giving Alexandria an annual **rainfall** of 18 centimetres — most of this from December to March, when Alexandria experiences blustery, often stormy weather. This is true inland to Damanhur and Tanta in the Delta. Further south, Egypt is within the arid zone, with rainfall throughout most of the country well under 2.5 centimetres per year.

Temperatures increase as you travel south, though in Cairo during December, January and sometimes even February it can be chilly. Cairo can be very hot from June to September, though the heat is often relieved by a northerly breeze.

Table of Temperature °C	**January** min./max.	**February** min./max	**March** min./max.	**April** min./max.	**May** min./max.	**June** min./max.
Alexandria	9.3 18.3	9.7 19.2	11.2 21.0	13.5 23.6	16.7 26.5	20.2 28.2
Aswan	8.0 23.8	9.4 26.1	12.6 30.4	17.5 35.0	21.1 38.5	24.2 42.1
Cairo	8.6 19.1	9.3 20.7	11.2 23.7	13.9 28.2	17.4 32.4	17.9 34.5
Dakhla	4.6 21.5	6.1 23.9	9.7 27.9	14.4 33.0	19.6 37.4	22.4 38.8
Hurghada	9.6 20.6	9.9 20.9	12.3 23.0	16.1 26.0	20.7 29.6	23.5 31.4
Ismailia	8.2 20.4	9.1 21.7	11.0 23.9	13.6 27.6	17.3 32.1	20.2 34.8
Luxor	5.4 23.0	6.8 25.4	10.7 29.0	15.7 34.8	20.7 39.3	22.6 40.7
Mersa Matruh	8.1 18.1	8.4 18.9	9.7 20.3	11.8 22.7	14.5 25.5	18.2 27.8
Minya	3.9 20.6	5.4 22.5	7.8 25.4	11.7 30.2	16.7 35.4	18.8 36.3
Port Said	11.3 18.0	12.1 18.7	13.5 20.2	16.1 22.6	19.6 25.8	22.4 28.5
Siwa	4.1 19.7	5.7 21.8	8.2 25.0	12.1 39.9	16.8 34.3	19.2 37.1

Table of Temperature °C	**July** min./max.	**August** min./max.	**September** min./max	**October** min./max.	**November** min./max.	**December** min./max.
Alexandria	22.7 29.6	22.9 30.4	21.3 29.4	17.8 27.7	14.8 24.4	11.2 20.4
Aswan	24.5 41.2	24.7 41.3	22.2 39.6	19.3 36.6	14.5 20.2	9.9 25.5
Cairo	21.5 25.4	21.6 34.8	19.9 32.3	17.8 29.8	19.9 24.1	10.4 20.7
Dakhla	23.0 39.0	22.9 38.9	20.7 36.1	17.4 33.0	12.0 28.0	6.7 23.0
Hurghada	24.8 32.6	25.0 33.0	23.2 30.6	19.7 28.5	15.5 25.7	11.9 22.4
Ismailia	22.2 36.4	22.5 36.5	20.7 33.9	17.8 30.7	13.9 26.6	10.0 21.5
Luxor	23.6 40.8	23.5 41.0	21.5 38.5	17.8 35.1	12.3 29.6	7.7 24.8
Mersa Matruh	20.2 29.2	21.0 29.9	19.7 28.7	16.8 27.0	13.3 23.4	10.0 19.7
Minya	20.2 37.0	20.5 36.6	18.6 33.4	15.9 31.2	11.5 26.6	7.0 21.7
Port Said	24.1 30.4	24.9 30.9	23.9 29.2	21.8 27.4	18.4 24.0	12.7 19.9
Siwa	20.7 38.0	20.7 27.8	18.3 35.1	14.9 31.7	10.1 26.3	6.0 21.3

For conversion to Fahrenheit, see the *Weights and Measures* section below.

Though it is hotter yet in Upper Egypt and summer can be reckoned from May to October, peak temperatures are to a great extent compensated for by extremely low humidity. Also, everywhere in Egypt at any time of year, temperatures can fall off sharply at night.

Leaving aside the summer extremes from Cairo southwards and the winter extremes from Cairo northwards, the climate of Egypt can be described as mild.

Entry Regulations

Immigration documents and procedures

All visitors to Egypt require a **visa**. To obtain one, your passport must be valid for at least three months following your arrival in the country. Visas can be obtained in person (allow 24 hours) or by post (allow at least two weeks) from an Egyptian Consulate abroad. You will need to present your passport, one passport photograph, and pay the appropriate fee. Also, you may obtain a visa on arrival. Visitors visas are normally valid for one month. **Multiple-entry visas** can sometimes be obtained. Alternatively, a **re-entry visa** can be obtained once you are in the country (see below).

With the exception of those on pre-paid package holidays, anyone staying in Egypt longer than 72 hours must **purchase on arrival** $150-worth (or the equivalent) of Egyptian pounds at the disadvantageous rate of $1 = 82PT. In my experience this is not always enforced, and is more likely to be enforced in the case of visitors arriving without a visa. Egyptian currency may not be imported or exported. Visitors must **declare their currency** on Form D handed to them on arrival. Any sums declared on this form can be exchanged for Egyptian currency at authorised banks at the official exchange rate of $1 = 112PT. These transactions should be recorded on Form D or the banks' exchange receipts. Visitors are then allowed to leave the country with the amount of money they originally declared on Form D minus the sums they officially exchanged and used during their stay in Egypt. (See *Money*, below).

Visas may be extended by satisfying immigration officials that you are able to transfer sufficient additional funds into Egyptian pounds. Also, if you want to visit a neighbouring country and then return, you can obtain a re-entry visa. Both these things are done at the Ministry of the Interior, in the Mugamaa building, Midan el Tahrir, Cairo. Within seven days of your arrival you must **register your presence** in the country with the police, obtaining a triangular stamp in your passport (hotels do this for you automatically).

Car and health documents

To hire a car in Egypt you will need an **International Driving Licence**. This will also be needed, along with a **Carnet de Passage** (both obtainable from your motoring organisation at home), special **insurance** (obtainable on arrival) and either a **deposit** or some form of guarantee against road tax and customs duties. The deposit is refundable on departure. For further details, contact the Egyptian State Tourist Office or your motoring organisation. *Note that diesel vehicles are not allowed entry into Egypt.*

Cholera and yellow fever certificates are required if arriving from an infected area.

You may bring into Egypt, exempt from duty and other taxes, all personal effects, used or new, including camera equipment, radios, typewriters, recorders, jewellery, etc, provided these are listed on the customs declaration form. Also exempt are 400 cigarettes, or 250 grams of tobacco or 50 cigars, and one litre of alcohol.

Departure Regulations

When leaving Egypt you will be allowed (eg at the airport) to take with you the amount of money you declared on entry minus the sums officially exchanged and used during your stay. It has been known (very rarely) for travellers to have foreign currency confiscated because they have attempted to leave with more than they could possibly have under the above formula. More importantly, the amount of Egyptian pounds you will be allowed to **change into foreign currency** is based on the amount you first officially changed into Egyptian pounds and can show bank receipts for, minus an assumed daily spending rate at a fairly high level — double or triple what a low budget traveller might spend. The best thing to do is to have spent all your Egyptian pounds before you go and forget the nonsense of trying to convert them.

But be sure to keep LE5 spare to pay the **departure tax**.

Getting to Egypt

By air The most common and usually cheapest way of getting to Egypt is by air. All flights arrive at Cairo International Airport.

Regular air fares are extortionate and travellers should look for such deals as the **Advance Purchase Excursion** (APEX) fare or **discounted** (bucket shop) fares. Conditions may include having to pay for your ticket some weeks in advance, fixing the date of your return at the time of purchase and spending a minimum time away — but you can save around 50 percent on the normal roundtrip economy fare. Also look into **student** and **youth** fares.

Many travellers to Egypt take advantage of **package holidays** which combine flights with accommodation often at prices competitive with the roundtrip economy fare alone. These can be as brief as seven days, though longer ones, especially those including several days of cruising along the Nile between Luxor and Aswan, will be more expensive. Thomas Cook (45 Berkeley Street, London W1), Speedbird Holidays, owned by British Airways (152 King Street, London W6), Kuoni Travel (Kuoni House, Dorking, Surrey) and Thompson Holidays (Greater London House, Hampstead Road, London NW1) are some of the better operators offering a variety of Eyptian holidays. Similar packages are available in the United States and elsewhere: enquire at the Egyptian State Tourist Office.

For those serious about a **Nile cruise**, seeing everything between Cairo and Aswan in the company of an expert Egyptologist, both Swan Hellenic (Beaufort House, St Botolph Street, London EC3) and Bales Tours (Bales House, Barrington Road, Dorking, Surrey) are recommended. They are expensive, however, and are sometimes booked up as much as a year in advance. Shorter and less expensive cruises are operated by several of the major Cairo hotels and can be booked there or abroad (see Cairo, *Practical Information*).

By sea

Russia's Black Sea Shipping Company (agents: CTC Lines, 1-3 Lower Regent Street, London SW1) and Italy's Adriatic Line (agents: Sealink UK Limited, Victoria Station PO Box 29, London SW1) both sail to **Alexandria**. Adriatica sails from Venice and Piraeus and carries cars as well as passengers. Black Sea, sailing from Beirut, Istanbul, Larnaca, Latakia, Odessa, Piraeus and Varna, carries passengers only.

Alexandria and Port Said are ports of call for a number of **cruises**.

Two modern ferries operate in the **Red Sea** between Suez and Aquaba, Jordan, and Suez and Jeddah, Saudi Arabia (agents: Menatours, 14 Sharia Talaat Harb, Cairo).

Overland

Entry to Egypt overland from **Libya** is forbidden. The border between Egypt and **Israel** is open and it is possible to take a bus or taxi across via El Arish. From the **Sudan** there is a scheduled but notoriously unreliable train service between Khartoum and Wadi Halfa on the border, connecting with a twice weekly steamer plying between Wadi Halfa and Aswan. The last time I did this journey the steamer before mine caught fire and sank. Three hundred passengers were burnt to death or drowned or were eaten by crocodiles. When the steamer is afloat, it can also carry cars, minibuses and trucks. In Egypt, information on the steamer and rail service to and from the Sudan can be obtained from the Nile Navigation Company Limited, Ramses Square, Cairo (this is a tiny office in the train station); and the Nile Company for River Transport, 7 Atlas Building, Aswan.

Travel Within Egypt

By air

Egyptair is the principal carrier within the country, with a fleet of Beoing 727s and a few F27s for short hops. It is advisable in winter to make advance reservations to Upper Egypt, in summer to do the same for Alexandria. But even when flights are said to be full up, it can be worth standing by.

One-way fares in dollars (roundtrip is double):

Cairo to	Abu Simbel	$82	
	Alexandria	$18	(winter)
		$23	(summer)
	Aswan	$58	
	Hurghada	$45	
	Luxor	$41	
	New Valley (Kharga)	$45	
Luxor to	Abu Simbel	$41	
	Aswan	$17	
	Hurghada	$17	
	New Valley (Kharga)	$35	
Aswan to	Abu Simbel	$25	
	New Valley (Kharga)	$17	

Air Sinai is Egypt's other scheduled airline and from Cairo serves El Arish, Sharm el Sheikh and St Catherine's Monastery, as well as Tel Aviv. Aircraft are F27s. The roundtrip fare from Cairo to St Catherine's is $54.

By rail Air-conditioned rail travel in Egypt is comfortable and inexpensive, and still more inexpensive for students in possession of an International Student Identity Card and holders of a Youth Hostel membership card (50 percent discount). The latter should go to the Egyptian Youth Hostels Travel Bureau, 7 Sharia Dr Abdel Hamid Said, Maarouf, Cairo (Tel: 43799), where vouchers can be obtained. All first class and combined first and second class trains are air-conditioned; others are not. Local trains serving smaller stations are likely to be slow, crowded and uncomfortable, and they will not be air-conditioned — the experience can be interesting if it does not go on for too long. No matter what class of train you are travelling on, bring toilet paper.

Almost all air-conditioned trains require **reservations** and you should book at least a day in advance. You can try getting on a train at the last moment to see if there is any space. Note that when queuing for tickets, men approach the ticket window from the right, women from the left, taking turns. The women's queue is shorter and quicker.

From Cairo the **fare** to Alexandria is LE5 first class, LE2.50 second class, one way. To Luxor the fare is LE13 first class, LE6.50 second class; to Aswan LE14 first class, LE7 second class. From Cairo to the canal towns the second class fares are LE1.75 for Suez, LE2.50 for Ismailia and LE3.50 for Port Said.

There is a Wagons-Lits **sleeper service** between Cairo and Luxor/Aswan using well-appointed German rolling stock. You know it is deluxe when you discover the air conditioning is excessive and the Muzak seeps into your compartment even after you turn the loudspeaker off. Compartments are single and double, and meals are served in them. There are two club cars for drinks and socialising. The new rolling stock does not compensate for the still dreadful condition of the track between Cairo and Beni Suef when the carriages rock back and forth and your drink smashes to the floor. The one-way fare, inclusive of meals, is LE65 for a single-berth compartment and LE40 per person for a double-berth compartment. Reservations are essential. Abroad, you can book through Promint Paris, 8 Rue d'Athènes, 75440 Paris Cedex 09 (Tel: 268 2420; telex 643241 ARINT XVXV 53+) or a good travel agent; in Egypt, at Compagnie Internationale des Wagons-Lits Egypte Pour le Tourisme (CIWLET), 48 Sharia Giza, Cairo (Tel: 985764; telex 93005 WALIT UN). Their operations office is at Ramses Station, Cairo.

On all services, children under 4 travel free; those from 4 to 10 obtain a 50 per cent reduction and on sleepers are expected to share a berth with an adult.

Travelling aboard a non-air-conditioned train can be like sharing a room in an tenth-rate Arab hotel with scores of guests, the only difference between second and third class being the number of Egyptians per cubic metre. In third class they sit, stand and lie on one another — a few lucky ones stretched out on the luggage racks overhead. Second class under these conditions is quite all right on a short run, but third class is to suffer an intimacy one would prefer to do without.

At every station half a dozen vendors get on with bottles of soft drinks carried in buckets of ice on their shoulders, and with cigarettes, biscuits, cakes and magazines. Each one presses his wares on the passengers, it making no difference that just one pace and five seconds before him another has been selling soft drinks and cigarettes too.

The varieties of railway experience

A thin, gritty, invisible layer of sand enters the carriage. You feel it between your fingers and filling up the corners of your eyes. You sit in the corridor, a cockroach for the journey, stepped on and over by biscuit men and passengers.

On the Wagons-Lits sleepers of course you miss all this. More eventful and still agreeable is to travel first class on a non-sleeper. The carriage attendant, called the *raïs* like the captain aboard an Arab boat, shuffles about in his slippers and shabby grey uniform that fits him like a tent. You prime him with a little baksheesh and he calls you *cawadja* (foreign gentleman); he shows you how the seat reclines and produces a pillow, then disappears to the end of the carriage to smoke and eat watermelon. A white-jacketed waiter brings meals and snacks and drinks to your seat. You think how good it is not to be a cockroach after all. At sundown a newspaper is smoothed along the aisle or on the floor behind your seat and a man gets down on his knees facing east.

Outside, endless detail and intimacies. At Daraw, between Aswan and Kom Ombo, on the boundary between the Arab and Nubian languages, you draw in along a line of wagons full of reclining camels, their heads just looking over the sides. They too are travelling first class after their long walk across the Eastern Desert to be sold at the age-old camel market here every Tuesday. You pass by the meanest mudbrick houses, their doors open, brown and dark inside. It is the hour of darkness and the fellahin have abandoned the vignettes they present to cruise passengers along Nile-side fields. That universal dim blue glow illuminates their simple homes now; within bare rooms a television sits flickering on a table.

It is nearly impossible in Egypt to get your hands on a complete **railway timetable**; it is assumed that tourists want only to travel between Alexandria, Cairo, Luxor and Aswan, and then only on certain trains, so these are the only schedules readily available. But for the more adventurous traveller, a complete timetable for all but the minor stations and more tenuous services follows. It has been the same for several years past and is likely to remain so. Note that trains usually depart from main termini (eg Cairo, Alexandria) on time, but rarely arrive anywhere on time.

CAIRO – ISMAILIA – SUEZ – PORT SAID

23	23	23	23A	23				23	23A	23	23	23
6 25	1150	1530	1845	2140	dep.	**Cairo**	arr.	8 40	9 55	1710	2125	2350
7 06	1244	1610	1927	2228	dep.	Benha	dep.	7 56	9 17	1633	2048	2037
7 56	1324	1700	2015	2113	dep.	Zagazig	dep.	7 10	8 35	1552	2008	2223
9 15	1435	1825	2127	0 40	arr.	**Ismailia**	dep.	5 10	7 00	1430	1838	2105
1205	1715	2205	—	. .	arr.	**Suez**	dep.	. .	—	1035	1505	. .
1002	. .	. .	2212	. .	arr.	Qantara	dep.	. .	6 16	1345	1751	. .
1055	. .	. .	2305	. .	arr.	**Port Said**	dep.	. .	5 15	1250	1650	. .

CAIRO - SUEZ

23	23	23	23				23	23	23	23
5 50	1000	1535	1935	dep.	**Cairo**	arr.	9 00	1225	1805	2200
8 35	1305	1820	2240	arr.	**Suez**	dep.	5 50	9 40	1450	1915

CAIRO - FAYYUM

23	23	23	23	23				23	23	23	23	23
5 00	9 10	1120	1640	2125	dep.	**Cairo**	arr.	8 15	1025	1445	1655	2245
6 59	1055	1305	1830	2320	dep.	El Wasta	dep.	6 23	8 36	1232	1521	2053
8 00	1158	1358	1923	0 18	arr.	**El Fayyum**	dep.	5 14	7 30	1130	1415	1943

ALEXANDRIA - MERSA MATRUH

23	23	23A	23	23	23				23	23	23	23	23A
. .	. .	SUM 7 30	. .	D	F	dep.	Cairo	arr.	. .	. .	. .	. .	SUM 0 25
6 35	7 10	—	1010	1645	1855	dep.	**Alexandria**	arr.	7 35	1445	1920	2050	—
7 56	8 24	—	1129	1812	2024	dep.	El Amriya	dep.	6 17	1314	1752	1934	—
9 00	9 25	1138	1223	1915	2140	dep.	El Hammam	dep.	5 05	1150	1650		2019
9 48	. .	—	1318	. .		dep.	**El Alamein**	dep.	. .	1049	1546	—	
1055	. .	1316	1435	. .		dep.	El Dabaa	dep.	. .	9 45	1445		1843
. .	. .	—	1713	. .	23	dep.	Similla	dep.	. .	7 13	. .	23	—
. .	. .	1525	1725	. .	Su	arr.	**Mersa**	dep.	. .	7 00	. .	M	1630
. .	. .	. .	. .	. .	7 40	dep.	**Matruh**	arr.	. .	. .	. .	1615	. .
. .	. .	. .	. .	. .	8 10	dep.	Similla	dep.	. .	. .	. .	1555	. .
. .	. .	. .	. .	. .	1840	arr.	Sallum	dep.	. .	. .	. .	7 05	. .

1 — First class
2 — Second class
3 — Third class
12 — First and second class
23 — Second and third class

A — Air conditioning in first and second class; or where train has second and third class, air conditioning in second class. Reservations are required on all air-conditioned trains, with the exception of trains without a first class on the Cairo-Upper Egypt line.

S — Sleeper. Air-conditioned. Reservations necessary.
D — Daily except Fridays.
F — Fridays only.
Su — Sundays only.
M — Mondays only.
SUM — Summer only (July through September).

CAIRO — UPPER EGYPT

23	2A	23	23A	2A	23A	23	12A	23	S	12A	12A	23	23	3		
3 10	7 30	7 40	1000	1200	1225	1400	1610	1620	1900	1935	2000	2040	2105	2250	dep.	**Cairo**
4 34	-	9 21	-	-	1348	1553	-	1803	-	-	2123	2226	2251	0 14	dep.	Wasta
5 18	9 24	1005	1154	1355	1426	1637	1804	1846	-	-	2201	2310	2336	0 54	dep.	Beni Suef
7 31	1056	1224	1339	1534	1600	1847	1939	2057	-	-	2345	1 24	1 46	2 44	dep.	**Minya**
8 21	-	1317	1418	-	-	1935	-	2148	-	-	0 26	2 12	2 37	3 27	dep.	Mallawi
1010	1246	1502	..	1720	1745	2100	2129	2337	-	-	1 44	5 05	4 17	4 50	dep.	**Assuit**
1215	1413	1720	..	1840	1938	..	2310	2 07	-	-	3 22	8 05	6 20	7 00	dep.	Sohag
-	1455	1822	-	1925	2024	..	-	3 05	-	4 08	9 30	7 06		7 51	dep.	Girga
-	-	1900	-	1947	2047	..	-	3 27	-	4 31	1000	7 29		8 26	dep.	El Baliana
-	1556	2014	-	2052	2201	..	-	4 23	-	5 26	1115	8 50		9 45	dep.	Nag Hammadi
-	1705	2248	-	2203	2341	..	-	5 36	-	-	6 37	1309	1004	1059	dep.	Qena
-	1814	0 50	-	0 20	1 20	..	-	7 04	5 38	8 30	8 10	1457	1135	1235	arr.	
-	1830	..	-	..	..	..	-	7 35	6 06	-	8 25	1517	..	1255	dep.	**Luxor**
-	1954	..	-	..	..	..	-	8 48	-	-	9 47	1657	..	1430	dep.	Esna
-	2110	..	-	..	..	..	-	9 54	-	-	1049	1851	..	1600	dep.	Edfu
-	2223	..	-	..	..	..	-	1109	-	1235	1202	2112	..	1745	dep.	Kom Ombo
-	2320	..	-	..	..	..	-	1212	1000	..	1258	2235	..	1930	arr.	
-	..	..	-	..	..	..	-	1232	-	..	1327	..	..	..	dep.	**Aswan**
-	..	..	-	..	..	..	-	1300	-	..	1350	..	..	..	arr.	Sadd el Ali

		23	23	3	12A	12A	S	12A	23	23	12A	23A	23	2A	23	23A
Cairo	arr.	5 35	6 00	6 20	6 40	9 20	9 50	1130	1310	1330	1635	1730	2010	2055	2335	2400
Wasta	dep.	3 39	4 14	4 52	-	7 52	-	-	1110	1202	-	1602	1843	-	2209	-
Beni Suef	dep.	3 13	3 38	4 21	-	7 22	-	9 39	1033	1133	1446	1525	1809	1903	2133	2210
Minya	dep.	0 59	1 25	2 28	-	5 35	-	8 04	9 50	1311	1348	1558	1728	1921	2022	
Mallawi	dep.	0 08	0 29	1 42	-	4 47	-	-	6 58	8 56	-	-	1505	-	1825	1939
Assuit	dep.	2230	2258	0 32	-	3 42	-	6 24	6 24	7 27	1134	1205	1338	1545	1642	1830
Sohag	dep.	1943	2050	2229	-	2 10	-	4 30	4 30	5 32	1022	9 37	1147	1424	1440	..
Girga	dep.	1823	1930	2131	-	1 09	-	-	..	4 31	9 28	8 42	1035	1332	-	-
El Baliana	dep.	1749	1857	2107	-	0 45	-	-	..	3 53	9 06	8 20	1003	-	-	-
Nag Hammadi	dep.	1638	1805	2013	-	2353	-	-	..	2 18	8 15	7 29	8 50	1232	-	-
Qena	dep.	1433	1638	1856	2238	-	-	-	..	1 02	7 04	6 05	6 39	1126	-	-
	dep.	1242	1510	1719	1809	2114	2145	-	..	2336	5 15	4 15	4 25	1014	-	-
Luxor	arr.	1220	..	1655	-	2054	-	-	..	2317	..	..	..	9 54	-	-
Esna	dep.	1042	..	1526	-	1951	-	-	..	2213	..	..	..	8 49	-	-
Edfu	dep.	8 45	..	1345	-	1852	-	-	..	2108	..	..	..	7 31	-	-
Kom Ombo	dep.	7 00	..	1203	1405	1738	-	-	..	1949	..	..	..	6 15	-	-
	dep.	5 40	..	1015	..	1638	1745	-	..	1840	..	..	..	5 15	--	
Aswan	arr.	..	..	..	..	1623	-	-	1823	..	..	..	..	..	-	-
Sadd el Ali	dep.	..	..	..	..	1600	-	-	..	1800	..	..	..	..	-	-

ALEXANDRIA — THE DELTA — CAIRO

	23	3	2A	23	12A	12A	12A	23	12A	3	12A	23	2A	23	12A	12A	23	12A	3	2A	12A	12A	23	12A
Alexandria ....dep.	3 35	5 25	6 05	6 45	7 45	8 10	9 20	9 30	1030	1115	1140	1150	1240	1330	1415	1530	1540	1710	1745	1800	1825	1925	2000	2125
Sidi Gabir ....dep.	3 45	5 35	6 16	6 55	7 55	8 20	9 30	9 40	1040	1125	1150	1200	1251	1340	1425	1540	1550	1720	1755	1810	1835	1935	2010	2135
Damanhur ....dep.	4 41	6 29	7 02	7 55	-	9 03	1013	1037	1122	1209	-	1254	1337	1438	-	1622	1641	1801	1840	1852	-	2017	2106	2217
Tanta ....dep.	5 42	7 35	7 58	9 25	9 18	9 50	1057	1135	1207	1255	1313	1350	1426	1600	1547	1707	1746	1846	1926	1936	1958	2107	2206	2301
Benha ....dep.	6 35	8 23	8 45	1036	-	1027	1132	1221	1247	1337	-	1436	1504	1647	-	1742	1832	1922	2006	2017	-	2142	2253	2337
Cairo .... arr.	7 25	9 00	9 20	1125	1025	1100	1205	1315	1320	1410	1420	1510	1540	1730	1650	1815	1915	2000	2045	2050	2105	2215	2340	0 10

	23	3	2A	23	12A	12A	12A	23	12A	3	12A	23	2A	12A	23	12A	23	12A	3	2A	12A	12A	23	12A
Cairo ....dep.	3 15	6 05	6 55	7 00	8 00	8 55	9 30	1000	1120	1135	1220	1240	1340	1400	1420	1550	1640	1750	1810	1830	1905	2000	2025	2130
Benha ....dep.	3 59	6 45	7 33	7 56	-	9 31	1006	1054	1156	1217	-	1317	1349	-	1511	1626	1722	1826	1852	1908	-	2035	2107	2206
Tanta ....dep.	5 09	7 25	8 20	9 17	9 11	1005	1046	1142	1230	1254	13269	1400	1433	1505	1604	1700	1810	1901	1923	1954	2014	2110	2153	2241
Damanhur ....dep.	6 17	8 21	9 13	1022	-	1051	1132	1242	1316	1340	-	1459	1522	-	1706	1746	1914	1948	2015	2040	-	2202	2253	2327
Sidi Gabir ....dep.	7 18	9 03	9 57	1118	1033	1133	1213	1338	1358	1423	1453	1548	1607	1628	1758	1828	2008	2028	2058	2123	2138	2243	2348	0 08
Alexandria .... arr.	7 25	9 10	1005	1125	1040	1140	1220	1345	1405	1430	1500	1555	1615	1635	1805	1835	2015	2035	2105	2130	2145	2250	2355	0 15

For trains to **Damietta (Dumyat)** *from Alexandria and Cairo via Tanta and Zagazig, enquire locally.*

By road

To drive your own **car** or to hire one (unless you hire a driver too) you will need an International Driving Licence, obtainable from your motoring organisation at home (eg AA, RAC, AAA). Car hire is not expensive, and petrol is very cheap. The problem is that Cairo is a madhouse on wheels, agricultural roads in the Delta and along the Valley are often busy with trucks and donkeys and camels, and Egyptians are in any case very odd drivers. With little appreciation of the virtue of keeping to a lane or even to the right-hand side of the road, they meander and eddy about as though negotiating mudbanks in the Nile. The way to survive is to wander with them, which means needing eyes on the sides and the back of your head — or no eyes at all. But do not be put off: you soon get the hang of it, and having your own car gives you great freeedom and flexibility, especially in discovering the less beaten paths and trodden sites of Egypt. And the desert roads, eg from Cairo to the Fayyum, to the Suez Canal and to Alexandria, are good as well as free of most of the problems mentioned above.

You can still have the advantage of a car without any of the problems if you hire one with a **driver** (not expensive) or hire a **taxi** — among several people it can be quite reasonable to hire a taxi, say, from Cairo to Alexandria, stopping at Wadi Natrun along the way.

Long-distance buses can be fast, cheap and comfortable. From Cairo (and its airport) there are regular runs to Alexandria and to Upper Egypt. There are good services too from Cairo and the canal towns to Sinai and along the Red Sea coast, also from Qena to the Red Sea (Hurghada), and from Assiut to the Kharga and Dakhla oases in the Western Desert.

The joy of the open road

There are **local buses** and **service (shared) taxis** running just about everywhere, very cheap, and convenient for hopping from town to town, site to site, along the Nile. **Hitchhiking** is possible though uncommon and it can be difficult.

Or you could package yourself by taking a **tour**. Try to avoid the more standard coach tours (eg American Express) in favour of more personal arrangements (eg Thomas Cook).

Along the Nile

For *cruises* along the Nile between Cairo and Aswan lasting 10 to 21 days you must book well in advance (sometimes a year) with such companies as Swan Hellenic and Bales Tours. These are all-inclusive tours, including travel by air to Egypt (see *Getting to Egypt*, above).

Shorter cruises between Luxor and Aswan lasting four to six days are operated by Hilton, Sheraton, Oberoi and Marriott, and like the hotels themselves, all are in the luxury class. Bookings can be made through the respective hotels in Egypt, but it would be wise to book in advance through one of their hotels near you or through a travel agent. Hilton includes Abydos and Dendera in these short cruises, and in any case they are the best: the guides excellent, the ships not impersonally large, the atmosphere intimate. Expect to pay around LE600 for four nights per person in a double room.

Cheaper cruises of varying duration are also available. Contact your nearest Egyptian State Tourist Office or an

Egyptian travel agent, eg Misr Travel (see *Tourist Information*, above).

For the adventurous, sailing the Nile in a **felucca** is the thing. Sleeping bags may be necessary, though often blankets will be provided. Meals are included in the cost which varies with the number of people aboard and your bargaining powers, but count on around LE100 per boatload between Aswan and Luxor. The duration of the journey will depend on the strength of the winds.

Sailing with the wind

Further information on these various forms of travel — air, rail, road and river — will be found in the relevant *Practical Information* sections. It is sometimes said that it is impossible, or difficult anyway, to travel around Egypt under your own steam. This is complete nonsense; the country has excellent, varied and generally inexpensive travel facilities, and lots of friendly people to help you out. The best readily-available **map** of Egypt is the Kuemmerly & Frey 1:750,000. In Egypt it is published by Lehnert and Landrock and widely available.

Finding your way

Accommodation

Until recently the number of decent **hotels** in Egypt had not kept pace with the surge in tourism, and getting a room in the hotel of your choice during the winter high season in Upper Egypt, the summer high season in Alexandria, or year-round in Cairo was not easy. The situation has now improved greatly in the main centres, particularly at the upper end of the market, and new medium-priced hotels are opening in the Cairo suburbs. But outside these centres, eg along the entire length of the Nile between Cairo and Luxor, it is difficult to find a decent hotel — or sometimes any hotel — at all.

If you have your heart fixed on a particular hotel you should try to **reserve** in advance. An experienced travel agent should be able to help you, or you can try contacting the hotel directly — their addresses and phone numbers, and also their telex numbers if they have them, have been included in the *Practical Information* listings. The international chain hotels, eg Hiltons and Sheratons, can be booked by contacting one of their hotels in your own country. You can also book through Misr Travel (see *Tourist Information*, above).

Hotels in Egypt are **officially rated** from 5-star (luxury) to 1-star. The rating system is not always evenly graduated, and you may find that a 3-star hotel is just as good as a 4-star one, or that two 4-star hotels charge markedly different rates. Nevertheless, the official system has been used in this Guide, along with a description which should help you form your own preliminary judgement. As a rule of thumb, any 3-star hotel will do; below that you should have a look for yourself.

There are also hotels that have **no star rating**; very few of these have been included in this Guide as the standard is pretty low, though at a pinch they can be worth checking out. And there are **youth hostels** in Cairo, Alexandria, Luxor, Aswan, Suez, Port Said and Sharm el Sheikh, though they are often full and, though they cost around LE1 per night, it is often possible to find more congenial accommodation without damaging the most exiguous budget.

One of the glories of Egypt is its older hotels, cavernous

The good old days

places with louvred doors and mosquito nets over the beds, an atmosphere of worn elegance. Some have been well refurbished, others languish and too many are disappearing, replaced by modern nondescript hotels. I prefer the older hotels, whatever their condition; they are friendly, personal, and speak of Egypt. In case you are of the same mind, I will tell you my favourites: in Cairo the Windsor; at the Pyramids the old part of the Mena House; in Alexandria the Cecil; in Luxor the Savoy and the Old Winter Palace though the heart has been torn out of it by the New Winter Palace tacked alongside; and in Aswan there was the Grand, alas now burnt down, and the best of them all the Old Cataract, separate and at a distance from the soulless New Cataract Hotel.

Hotel rates

The rates that follow are all for double rooms with bath. To these must be added service and tax which put about another 15% on top. Also, breakfast is obligatory. Outside Cairo, in resort areas like Alexandria, Luxor, Aswan and Hurghada, some hotels make half-board obligatory too. Single rooms or single occupancy of a double room costs about 20% less than the doubles rate. Rates in Cairo are the same year-round; in Alexandria they are about 10% lower in winter; in Upper Egypt about 10% lower in summer. Lower category hotels will also have rooms without bath, and these will be cheaper; also other factors, eg a less favourable view, may mean a lower rate than indicated here.

Cairo's rates, category for category, are higher than in the rest of Egypt:

5-star: LE63 to LE103 per double room with bath
4-star: LE26 to LE63 per double room with bath
3-star: LE18 to LE42 per double room with bath
2-star: LE10 to LE33 per double room with bath
1-star: LE5 to LE16 per double room with bath

Rates in the rest of the country are:

5-star: LE44 to LE77 per double room with bath
4-star: LE22 to LE55 per double room with bath
3-star: LE11 to LE38 per double room with bath
2-star: LE8 to LE22 per double room with bath
1-star: LE4 to LE11 per double room with bath

Within the 5-star and 4-star categories it is the internationally-known chains, eg Hilton, Sheraton, that charge the maximum rates; foreign- or Egyptian-owned hotels lacking this high profile 'brand image' charge at the middle and lower end of their category range.

Food and Drink

Most Egyptian hotels, particularly the larger ones, cater to the tastes of foreign visitors by serving an international cuisine. In Cairo, as befitting a large cosmopolitan city, there are also many restaurants specialising in one or other national cuisines, eg French, Italian, Lebanese, Greek, Chinese, Indian. Alexandrian cuisine is Levantine.

Eating Egyptian-style

Though the classic **Arab-Turkish cuisine** of Egypt is best encountered in private houses, you should venture forth to Egyptian eating places, spanning the gamut in price and sophistication, for a taste of Egyptian cooking. Dishes are usually savoury, neither too oily nor too spicy, and as only fresh ingredients are used the menu varies with season. Except in the simplest eating places frequented exclusively by Egyptians, restaurant menus will be available in English and French as well as in Arabic, and the maitre d'hotel will speak English. In the simple Egyptian places, as at a Greek taverna, you can go into the kitchen, have a look, a taste, and then point to what you want.

The international hotels serve meals at the usual Western hours. Egyptians will take a large meal between noon and 2pm, though more often in the early evening, and restaurants are likely to be crowded at these times. At any time of day or evening, drinking water, mango juice, slices of coconut and other tidbits are sold in the streets. Street vendors are often landless fellahin who have left the countryside and have no other way of earning a living. The preparation of mint tea and coffee is a ritual. Thick and black, Turkish-style, coffee is ordered according to the amount of sugar: sweet (*ziyada*), medium (*mazboota*), bitter (*saada*).

There follows a list of some typical Egyptian foods.

The menu

Hors d'oeuvres and snacks:

Babaghanoug — a mix of taheena with mashed eggplant, flavoured with lemon, garlic and olive oil; it is served as a dip, or with salad, or as a first course vegetable dish.

Batarikh — Egyptian caviar; it is pressed, dried and preserved in salt and oil, and is served in thin slices with bread or biscuits.

Feteer — served at an eating place called a *fataran*, it is made of filo dough wrapped round a variety of fillings, eg onion, egg, meat, or, in its sweet variety, raisins with sugar and spices.

Gibna beida — a white cheese, equivalent to Greek feta.

Gibna rumi — literally 'Roman' cheese, a hard light-yellow cheese with a sharp flavour.

Leban zabadi — plain white yogurt to which honey, jam or mint can be added. It is recommended for stomach upsets.

Makarona — baked macaroni and white sauce, often served with gravy and ground meat.

Mashi — a cold mixed vegetable dish, usually of peppers, tomatoes, courgettes, eggplants. A light meal in itself.

Mish — a paste made from dry cheese and spices.

Shakshouka — of North African origin, chopped lamb and tomato sauce with an egg on top.

Taamiya — also known as *falafel*, these are patties of mashed *fool* with parsley, highly seasoned and fried in oil.

Taheena — an oil paste from sesame seed, combined with lemon, garlic and spices; sometimes an ingredient in other foods, but also served on its own as a dip.

Turshi — spicy mixed pickled vegetables.

Wara einab — grape leaves stuffed with rice, sometimes with meat or lentils, and flavoured with lemon juice; the equivalent of Greek dolmades.

Main courses:

Firakh — chicken; not so scrawny as they used to be. Grilled chicken is best.

Fool mudhammas — the national dish of Egypt, *fool* is fava bean cooked with spices, sometimes tomatoes, into a thick sauce; at breakfast it is served with an egg on top.

Hamam — pigeon, a great favourite with Egyptians. It is usually grilled.

Kebab — either grilled marinaded chunks of lamb or ground lamb (*kufta*) made into long patties, skewered and broiled.
Mouluqiya — a steamed green vegetable, often served with rice or as a viscous soup. Although common throughout the Middle East, Egyptian mouluqiya sets the standard. It is a heavy dish, not usually eaten late.
Roz bel khalta — fried rice with currants, nuts, liver and meat.
Samak — the generic term for fish; the particular type will usually be identified in English on the menu. Other seafoods include *gambari* (shrimp), *calamari* (squid) and *gandofli* (scallops).

Desserts:
Ata'if — a special sweet dessert during Ramadan.
Baklava — the well-known Levantine pastry of filo with honey and nuts.
Dondurma — a sherbet of sweet white milk ice.
Kanafa — as *baklava*, but made with shredded wheat instead of filo.
Mohallabiya — a thick cream (often creamed rice) confection with fruit, nuts (often pistachios) and a fruit syrup.

Beer, wine, arak...

Beer long antedates wine as the regional drink of the Mediterranean, so it is not so strange to find it reintroduced and very popular in Egypt. The commonest brand is *Stella*, in green litre bottles, unpredictable but usually very good. *Stella Export* is sweeter, of more consistent quality, more expensive and not as good. It is in smaller brown bottles. Both are lagers. *Aswali* is an excellent dark beer from Aswan, sometimes found elsewhere. Bock beer is available briefly in the spring and is referred to as *Marzen* (ie *Marzenbier*, March beer).

Egyptian **wines** are from ex-Greek vineyards around Alexandria and Lake Mareotis, 'mobilised' by the government. Red, white and rosé are available and pleasant enough. *Omar Khayyam* is a dry red, *Cru des Ptolemes* a dry white, and *Rubis d'Egypte* a decent rosé. All years are equally vintage years. In shops, these wines will sell for about LE2.50; at a hotel or restaurant the markup will be at least 200 percent.

Imported **liquors** are extremely expensive even in shops and the same order of markup makes them nearly prohibitive at clubs and restaurants. Egypt does make its own: the gin is undrinkable; the brandy compares with the Spanish variety and is satisfactory for punches and brandy sours; while *arak*, the Arab equivalent of Greek ouzo, Turkish raki, French anisette, and referred to in Egypt as *zibab*, is excellent, whether neat, on the rocks, or diluted with water, which turns it a characteristic milky colour.

and drinking from the Nile

Soft drinks, Egyptian-made or imported, are widely available, including Coca-Cola and 7-Up. Egypt scores well on fruit drinks and cane juice, delicious, cheap and variously available with season. Finally, it is said that if you drink water from the Nile, you will be sure to return to Egypt. You might think you would drop dead instead. But I have drunk it while sailing on the river at Aswan where boatmen assure me it is better than the ice-cold drinks favoured by tourists, its temperature more agreeable to the stomach. It is fresh if somewhat organic in taste. I have survived and have returned to Egypt to drink from the Nile again (see *Health*, below). Tap water is heavily chlorinated and entirely safe. Bottled spring water is available.

Health

Cholera and **yellow fever** vaccination certificates are required when entering Egypt from an infected area, but it would be a good idea to have these vaccinations anyway. Recently in Cairo there have been outbreaks of what the authorities euphemistically call 'the summer disease' and which bears a remarkable similarity to cholera, though this is not admitted. **Malaria** is a problem in the Sudan but only rarely in Egypt; nevertheless it is worth taking precautions against this and both **typhoid** and **polio**. The rich, damp soil of the Egyptian countryside offers a fine breeding ground for the **tetanus** bacteria; if you are going to tramp about here, get inoculated. Obtain the advice of your doctor beforehand.

Bites of all kinds need the immediate attention of a doctor. The bites of carnivores can be rabid, or at least can turn septic as can camel bites. Snakes may be encountered when you wander off the beaten path, and you should avoid turning over stones. Most Egyptian snakes are not poisonous (their bite is recognised by a double row of teeth), but some are, especially the cobra and the viper. The smaller Egyptian cobra (*Naja haje*), 120 to 200 cms long, is normally a sandy-olive colour and is found throughout the country. The black-necked cobra (*Naja nigricollis*), 200 cms long, is darker and is confined to southern Egypt. Both are capable of displaying the characteristic hood; the black-necked cobra has a dark band on the underside of the hood. Cobra bites display a single row of teeth plus fang-marks. It was *Naga hage* that appeared as the uraeus on the pharaonic crown. It was the viper that Cleopatra used to commit suicide. There are several kinds, from 34 to 150 cms long, varying in colour from sandy to reddish, or sometimes grey. The most dangerous snake in Egypt is the carpet viper (*Echis carinatus*), 72 cms long, with a light X on the head. Viper bite markings are simply the two fang punctures. It is helpful when seeing a doctor if you can describe the snake.

There are two diseases associated with Egypt, trachoma and bilharzia, though neither need unduly worry the visitor. **Trachoma** is a contagious infection of the eye, specifically the conjunctiva and cornea, and causes a cloudy scar and hence blindness. Unfortunately, many Egyptians have suffered from it. If you notice any inflammation of the eyes, you should at once consult an opthalmologist. **Bilharzia** (or schistosmiasis) is caused by a worm which enters the body, causing disorders to the liver, bladder, lungs and nervous system. The worm lives only in stagnant water, eg some irrigation channels and slow-moving parts of the Nile. The Nile is entirely safe for swimming and drinking between the Aswan High Dam and Esna where, except possibly along its banks, it runs swiftly. If you have ventured or fallen into stagnant water, you should get a check-up when you return home.

To repeat, there is little risk of the visitor contracting either disease. Both can be successfully treated.

Getting medical assistance

If you are unwell, you should first seek advice from your hotel. They will be able to refer you to a **doctor**, **dentist** or **hospital**, and may even have a doctor on call. Your embassy will also be able to recommend medical assistance. Particularly in the major centres, the standards of medical care are high. Many doctors will have trained in Europe or the United States and will speak English. More detailed information on medical care, and on pharmacists, will be found in the *Practical Information* sections.

Most likely the worst you will suffer will be a brief **upset stomach**. This is an entirely normal reaction to a change of diet and passes after a few days. There is no need suddenly to stop eating Egyptian food; on the contrary, after a pause, you should continue. An anti-spasmodic medicine can be taken; standard preparations are available at any pharmacy. The one rule you should observe when eating in Egypt is to be sure your food has been washed; provided even the simplest eating place has running water, there should be no problem. Drinking water is heavily chlorinated and safe, though you can always have bottled water if you prefer.

Protection against the climate

The **sun** can be hot at any time of year, and the temperature can fall off sharply at night. At both times it is wise to be appropriately covered. During the day you should wear a head covering and sunglasses. It is not advisable to drink spirits before sundown, nor to consume iced drinks during the heat of the day. Unless you do not mind drinking lots of water, it would be helpful to bring along a supply of salt tablets. These are not available in Egypt. Also **insect repellent** would be helpful.

And of course it can pay to be medically insured.

Money

The unit of **currency** is the Egyptian pound (LE) which is divided into 100 piastres (PT). There are coins for ½, 1, 5 and 10PT, and notes for 5, 10, 25 and 50PT, as well as for LE1, 5, 10 and 20. Also notionally, piastres are divided into 10 milliemes, so that there are 1000 milliemes to the pound. Apart from the ½PT coin which is really 5 milliemes, there is no millieme currency. However, prices may be expressed in pounds, piastres or milliemes, so that four pounds might be written LE4 or 400PT or LE4.000. This can get a bit confusing, as when a restaurant bill states, say, 843.7, meaning 843PT and 7 milliemes, or LE8.437. What is more, instead of using a decimal point, Egyptians follow the continental European practice of using a comma, so the bill would appear as 843,7. Usually, your own common sense will tell you what is meant.

At the time of going to press (and currency flunctuations can change these figures up or down) the official **rate of exchange** is $1 = LE1.12, or putting it the other way round, LE1 = $0.89. There is also a black market.

There are exchange banks at the airport and at major hotels throughout Egypt for converting to Egyptian currency. American Express and Thomas Cook also exchange money. You should hold onto your receipts in the event you need to change money back out of Egyptian pounds.

Credit cards have made an entry onto the Egyptian scene, but their use can only be counted upon in the more obvious tourist areas. All the major hotels take them, as do some restaurants and shops. Some shops will impose a surcharge on credit card purchases to counter the percentage they have to pay the credit card company. The most commonly accepted cards are American Express, Diner's Club, Carte Blanche, Visa and Master Charge (Access).

Baksheesh

Tipping is expected for all services, and often for no service at all. 25–50PT is a reasonable minimum, though do not be surprised if sometimes you are grumbled at — too often tourists are absurdly ignorant or generous, which has led some Egyptians to believe, often rightly, that if they pull a sour face, even vociferously complain, they can milk you for more. The Egyptian term for a tip is *baksheesh* which means literally 'share the wealth' and helps explain why sometimes an Egyptian is not at all abashed at wanting something for nothing: you have it, he does not but feels you should pass it round. Baksheesh can be a plague, and you may find yourself pestered for it in the streets. The rule is obvious: offer baksheesh only in return for a service, do not pay until the service has been performed, and do not pay too much. Never be reluctant, when appropriate, to tell someone to get lost (*Imshee!*).

Photography

Taking photographs is forbidden in most museums (cameras must be checked at the entrance) and all ancient tombs. This is an abuse, presumably for the mean purpose of protecting the post card industry. Using a flash will attract attention and you will have to face the consequences (being bawled out); or you can be discreet, using no flash but high-speed film (1000 ASA) instead. I have never experienced any objection to taking photos in mosques or other Islamic monuments, though one should be courteous and inobtrusive. By and large, people do not object to being photographed on the street; indeed, if you ask first, people often compose themselves into the most charming pictures. No doubt Egypt's enemies have more photographs of her airports, docks, bridges, dams, etc, than they know what to do with; nevertheless these can be sometimes sensitive subjects for tourists to poke their cameras at — look out for warning signs.

The skies are blue, the sun is bright, and there is much reflected light off sand and water: for the best outdoor results use low-speed film.

Electricity

Electrical current throughout Egypt is 220 volts. Sockets take the standard continental European round two-pronged plug. Plug adaptors and current converters, as well as dual voltage appliances, can be bought at home.

Communications

Detailed information on mail, telephones, telegrams and telexes will be found in the *Practical Information* chapters, particularly at the end of the *Cairo: Mother of the World* chapter.

Language

The language of the country is Arabic, but English is taught to every schoolchild and, with French a close second, is the foreign language most spoken by Egyptians. In particular, most staff at hotels, restaurants and travel companies catering to foreigners will speak English, probably French, and perhaps also German and Italian. So along the well-beaten tourist paths, language is unlikely to prove a great problem.

However, even the least adventurous will sometimes encounter incomprehension — Cairo taxi drivers, for instance, may prove to be multilingually loquacious or, just as likely, may know only Arabic. It is useful, therefore, to know a few Arabic words and phrases, and it is always appreciated.

Arabic Vocabulary

A basic Arabic vocabulary, expressed phonetically, follows. The consonantal sounds are all approximately as in English, though in Arabic a distinction is made between 'hard' and 'soft' consonants, not indicated here. Vowels and diphthongs are pronounced thus:

ay as in *fate*	*ii* as in *machine*
ee as in *feet*	*o* as in *social*
i as in *it*	*u* as in *put*

There is also the *ain*, a gutteral vowel sound, indicated here by the raised *c* as in *mat*^{c}*am* (restaurant), which is achieved by constricting the throat as far back as possible.

General Words and phrases

Hello/goodbye	*sa*^{c}*eeda*
Please	*minfadlak*
Thank you	*shukran*
No thank you	*la shukran*
Yes	*aywa*
No	*la*
I want	^{c}*aayiz* (m)/^{c}*ayza* (f)
Do you have?	*andak?* (m)/^{c}*andik?* (f)
What is this?	*ayda?*
There is/Is there?	*fee/fee?*
There is no	*mafeesh*
Give me/us	*id dee nee/id dee na*
This	*di*
That	*da*
Much/many	*ki teer*
Little	*a leel*
Very	*aa wee*
Good	*kuwayyis*
Bad	*mish kuwayyis*
Hot	*sukhn*
Cold	*baarid*
And	*wa*
Or	*walla*
Not	*mish*
Possible	*mumkin*

	Impossible	*mish mumkin*
	Never mind	*ma^{c}alish*
	Enough/stop	*bass*
	Go away	*imshee*
People	I	*ana*
	You (m,f, sing., pl.)	*enta*
	He	*howwa*
	She	*heyya*
	We	*ehna*
	They	*homma*
	Man	*ragil*
	Woman	*sitt*
	Boy	*walad*
	Girl/daughter	*bint*
	Son	*ibn*
	Mother	*oum*
	Father	*ab*
	Sister	*ukht*
	Brother	*akh*
Medical	Doctor	*doktor*
	Dentist	*doktor is si naan*
	Hospital	*mustashfa*
	Headache	*sooda^c*
	It hurts	*byu ga^c*
	My stomach hurts	*ba ta nee buy ga^{c}nee*
	Accident	*hadsa*
	Pharmacy	*say da lya*
	Medicine	*da wa*
Official	Post Office	*bosta*
	Embassy	*sefara*
	Ministry	*wizaara*
	Ministry of Culture	*Wizaaret el Sekafa*
	Ministry of the Interior	*Wizaaret el Dakhleyya*
	Ministry of Tourism	*Wizaaret el Seyaha*
Hotel	Hotel	*lookanda*
	Room	*oda*
	Bed	*soreer*
	Bathroom	*hamaam*
	Toilet	*twalit*
	Restaurant/dining room	*mat^{c}am*
	How much?	*bekaam?*
	Cheap	*rikhees*
	Expensive	*ghaali*
Restaurant and food	Restaurant	*mat^{c}am*
	Breakfast	*fetaar*
	Lunch	*ghada*

Dinner	*ᶜasha*
How much?	*bekaam?*
The bill	*el hesaab*
Bread	*ᶜaysh*
Butter	*zebdah*
Cheese	*gebnah*
Eggs	*bayd*
Olives	*zatoon*
Rice	*roz*
Tomatoes	*tamatem*
Potatoes	*batatis*
Onions	*baasal*
Lettuce	*khass*
Garlic	*tome*
Carrots	*gazzar*
Fish	*samak*
Chicken	*ferrakh*
Meat	*lahma*
Beef	*kandoos*
Lamb	*daani*
Oil	*sayt*
Vinegar	*khal*
Salt	*malh*
Pepper	*fifil*
Herbs	*aᶜhaab*
Spices	*buharat*
Sugar	*sokkar*
Milk	*laban*
Tea	*shaay*
Coffee	*bon*

Travel

Station/stop	*mahatta*
Train	*atr*
Airport	*mataar*
Plane	*tayyara*
Car	*otomobeel*
Bus	*otobees*
Taxi	*tax*
Map	*khareeta*
Street	*shariᶜ*
Square	*midaan*
Bridge	*kubri*
Timetable	*gadwal*
Ticket	*tazkara*
First class	*daraga oola*
Second class	*daraga tanya*
Sleeping car	*ᶜarabee yit nom*
Dining car/restaurant	*matᶜam*
Reserved	*mafooz*
What time does it arrive?	*yoosal is saa ᶜa kam?*
What time does it leave?	*yisaafir is saa ᶜa kam?*
(Two) o'clock	*is saa ᶜa (etnayn)*
...a.m.	*...bin na harr*
...p.m.	*...bil layl*
Hour/s	*saa ᶜa/sa ᶜaat*

I want a taxi	*^{c}aayiz tax (m)/^{c}ayza tax (f)*
Take me to (Ramses Station)	*waddiyni (Mahattat Ramses)*
Wait a little	*estanna shiwayya*
Where is?	*fayn?*
Straight ahead	*^{c}ala tool*
Right	*yemeen*
Left	*shemal*
Stop	*waaf*
Here	*hina*
There	*hinaak*
Far	*bi^{c}eed*
Near	*urayyib*
Now	*dilwaatee*
Later	*ba^{c}dayn*
Morning	*el sobh*
Noon	*el dohr*
Afternoon	*ba^{c}d el dohr*
At night	*bellayl*
Today	*enneharda*
Yesterday	*embareh*
Tomorrow	*bokrah*
Next week	*el esbou^{c} iggay*

Money and numbers

Money	*feloos*
Bank	*bank*
The bill	*el hesaab*
One	*wahed*
Two	*etnayn*
Three	*talatah*
Four	*arba^{c}a*
Five	*khamsah*
Six	*settah*
Seven	*sab^{c}aa*
Eight	*tamannya*
Nine	*tes^{c}aa*
Ten	*^{c}ashrah*
Eleven	*hedashar*
Twelve	*etnashar*
Thirteen	*talattashar*
Fourteen	*arbaa^{c}tashar*
Fifteen	*khamastashar*
Sixteen	*settashar*
Seventeen	*sabaa^{c}tashar*
Eighteen	*tamantashar*
Nineteen	*tessa^{c}tashar*
Twenty	*^{c}eshrin*
Twenty-one	*wahed we ^{c}eshrin*
Twenty-two	*etnayn we ^{c}eshrin*
Thirty	*talatiin*
Forty	*arbe^{c}iin*
Fifty	*khamsiin*
Sixty	*settiin*
Seventy	*sab^{c}iin*
Eighty	*tamaniin*
Ninety	*tes^{c}iin*

Hundred	*meiyah*
Thousand	*alff*
Million	*milyon*
Pound	*genayb*
Half pound	*nus genayh*
Piastre	*ersh*
Two piastres	*ershayn saagh*
Three piastres (to ten)	*talatah saagh (etc)*
Eleven piastres (etc)	*hedashar ersh (etc)*

The calendar

Day	*yom*
Night	*layl*
Week	*esbou*^{c}
Month	*shahr*
Year	*sana*
Sunday	*el had*
Monday	*el etnayn*
Tuesday	*el talaat*
Wednesday	*el arba*^{c}
Thursday	*el khamiis*
Friday	*el gom*^{c}*aa*
Saturday	*el sabt*
January	*yanayer*
February	*febrayer*
March	*maris*
April	*abriil*
May	*mayo*
June	*yonyo*
July	*yolyo*
August	*aghostos*
September	*sebtember*
October	*octobar*
November	*november*
December	*disember*

Numerals

Arabic, of course, has its own alphabet (read from right to left), so the above list can help you only in verbal communication. However, it is important that you learn to recognise the Arabic numerals (read from left to right, ie units at the right, preceded by tens, hundreds, etc) — this will prove a great help when shopping or catching numbered buses.

ARABIC NUMERALS

١	٢	٣	٤	٥	٦	٧	٨	٩	١٠
1	2	3	4	5	6	7	8	9	10

Transliteration

Note that there are several methods of transliterating Arabic into English. For example, the town of Minya can also be written as Minia, or as Minieh. Also, Sultan Qaytbay can be written as Kait Bay, Qaitbai, Qait Bey, etc. So first, I apologise for any inconsistencies; and second, in consulting the index, or looking for places on maps, bear in mind possible variant spellings.

Religion

The principal belief of Islam is the existence of one God, the same God worshipped by Christians and Jews, whom the Moslems call Allah. Islam means submission. Moslem means one who submits to monotheism as interpreted by the religion's founder, Mohammed (AD 570-632).

The message

Moslems must hold six **beliefs**: that Allah exists, is unique and is omnipotent; that the Angels of Allah are his perfect servants, and intercede for man and are his guardians; that there is only one true religion and the Koran is the only tangible word of Allah; that there have been many prophets of Allah, among them Ibrahim (Abraham), Nuh (Noah), Musa (Moses), Isa (Jesus) and Mohammed who was the last, his message uncorrupted; that everyone will live in eternity and will be judged; and that whatever has been or will come has been predestined by Divine Will and it is forbidden to question or investigate this point.

There are five **practical devotions**, the five Pillars of Faith, that all Moslems must perform: pronounce publicly that 'I bear witness that there is no god but Allah and Mohammed is His Prophet'; pray at five specific times of day (noon, afternoon, sunset, night and daybreak); pay a tithe, which is then dispersed to the poor, to needy debtors, for the ransom of captives, to travellers, and for the defence of Islam; fast during the month of Ramadan; and at least once in a lifetime make a pilgrimage to Mecca.

In addition, Islam is based on **laws** found in the Koran, in the *Sunna* (the actions of the Prophet), decided by the unanimous agreement of Moslem scholars (*Ijma*), and arrived at by reasoned analogy (*Qiyas*) — each of descending authority.

The Prophet

Mohammed was a merchant in Arabia. He often contemplated in the desert and at the age of 40 had a vision of the Angel Gabriel who commanded him to proclaim monotheism to the pagan Arabian tribes. In Arabic, 'to proclaim' is *Qur'an*, and so the Koran is the word of Allah as given to Mohammed. The merchants of Mecca, concerned by the unsettling effects of this new religion, drove Mohammed out of the city in 622. His flight (the *hegira*, though literally this means 'withdrawal of affection') from Mecca to Medina, where Islam first took root, is the event from which the Islamic calendar begins.

Though Islam spread throughout the Middle East and across North Africa by conquest, it usually treated other religions with tolerance, and this has been particularly true in Egypt. The population is 80 to 90 percent Moslem, adherents of the Sunni sect (for discussion of the Sunni and Shi'a sects, see the *Bab Zuwayla to Khan el Khalili* chapter for Cairo).

The remainder of the population includes resident foreigners of various Christian denominations, Egyptian Jews and, primarily, Christians of the Egyptian Church, called Copts, who represent anything from five to 17 percent of the population (sources vary remarkably; some Copts have told me they constitute 20 percent of the population). Copts are particularly numerous in Upper Egypt and in the larger Delta towns.

The Coptic Church

For an outline of the Coptic Church, see the *Alexandria: Capital of Memory* chapter. Suffice to say that until the Arab invasion, Egypt was a Coptic country and it remains today the only North African country in which Christianity has survived. It is not unusual when walking around Cairo, or elsewhere in Egypt, to come upon Christian celebrations, the streets festooned with decorations and lights, pictures and ikons of Christ and Mary and the various saints. Because the Copts have intermarried least with the Arab invaders, they are most truly the descendants of the ancient Egyptians, their language, now confined to liturgical use, the repository of the demotic tongue of pharaonic times.

Copts may have a small cross tattooed on their wrist, but otherwise it is impossible for an Egyptian to say whether a person is a Moslem or a Copt. Copts enjoy all civil, political and religious rights and occupy high posts in government, the military and in business. Where there is discontent amongst Copts, it derives most often from their achievement and ambition being frustrated by state inefficiency and restrictions. But then Copts are not the only ones to complain.

Time and Egyptian Calendars

Egypt is two hours ahead of Greenwich Mean Time. Noon GMT is 2pm in Egypt.

Egypt uses three calendars: the Islamic, the Coptic and the Western. Both the Western and Coptic calendars are solar; the Islamic calendar is based on 12 lunar months and therefore rotates in relation to the other two, each Islamic year beginning 11 days sooner than the last. The Western calendar of course dates from the birth of Christ; the Coptic dates from the persecutions under Diocletian (see the *Alexandria: Capital of Memory* chapter); while the Islamic calendar dates from the flight of Mohammed from Mecca in AD 622. (Because the Islamic year is shorter than the Western, you cannot simply subtract 622 from our year to determine the current AH year. In fact, 8 November 1980 saw the beginning of AH 1401 — you can work it out from there).

Another point worth noting is that a day in the Islamic calendar begins at sundown (so that technically AH 1401 began at sundown on 7 November 1980). A consequence of this is that Islamic festivals start on the evening before you would expect if going by the Western calendar, that evening assuming as sacred a character as the following waking daylight period (compare Christmas Eve and Christmas Day in Western usage).

The official calendar

You will be relieved to learn, however, that in all official transactions in Egypt the Western calendar and method of reckoning the day are used. The Islamic and Coptic calendars only really come into their own at festivals.

The **Islamic months** are as follows:

First month:	*Moharram* (30 days)
Second month:	*Safar* (29 days)
Third month:	*Rabei el Awal* (30 days)
Fourth month:	*Rabei el Tani* (29 days)
Fifth month:	*Gamad el Awal* (30 days)
Sixth month:	*Gamad el Tani* (29 days)
Seventh month:	*Ragab* (30 days)
Eighth month:	*Shaaban* (29 days)
Ninth month:	*Ramadan* (30 days)
Tenth month:	*Shawal* (29 days)
Eleventh month:	*Zoul Qidah* (30 days)
Twelfth month:	*Zoul Hagga* (29 days, or 30 in leap years)

Important **Moslem festivals** include:

Ras el Sana el Hegira, the Islamic New Year, beginning on the first day of Moharram.

Moulid el Nabi, the Prophet's birthday, on the twelfth day of Rabei el Awal, marked in Cairo by a spectacular procession.

Ramadan

Ramadan, a month of fasting from dawn to sunset. As the last full meal is taken just before dawn, working hours are usually cut short to reduce afternoon effort to a minimum. Nothing is permitted to pass the lips during fasting hours, and so while visitors are permitted to eat, drink and smoke, you should not do so in the presence of fasting Moslems out of common courtesy. Interestingly, more food is consumed during Ramadan than at any other time of year, everyone making up at night for what they gave up during the day. Every Ramadan night, therefore, has the character of a festival.

Qurban Bairam, 10-13 Zoul Higga, the month of the Pilgrimage. For days preceding the 10th, sheep, goats, cows and buffaloes fill the streets waiting to be slaughtered; on the 10th they are killed and skinned throughout the residential areas of town — not for the squeamish.

Coptic festivals centring around Easter do not follow the Western (Gregorian) calendar. Other festivals fall on fixed dates: Christmas, 7 January; Epiphany, 19 January; the Annunciation, 21 March. A national holiday that is an important Coptic-pharaonic inheritance is *Sham el Nessim*, which falls on the first Monday after the Coptic Easter and during which the entire population of whatever religion takes a day off. This is a celebration of the advent of spring; families go out into their fields or gardens, or into the country, early in the morning and eat salted fish, onions and coloured eggs. The fish and onions are said to prevent disease, while the eggs symbolise life.

Weights and Measures

Egypt officially employs the metric system, though sometimes traditional weights and measures will be encountered.

Temperature

Fahrenheit	=	Centigrade/Celsius
122		50
113		45
110		43.3
107.6		42
104		40
102.2		39
100		37.8
98.6		37
96.8		36
95		35
93.2		34
91.4		33
90		32
87.8		31
86		30
84.2		29
80		26.7
75		23.9
70		21
65		18.3
60		15.6
55		12.8
50		10
45		7.2
40		4
32		0
23		– 5
14		–10
0		–17.8

Fahrenheit into Centigrade/ Celsius: subtract 32 from Fahrenheit temperature, then multiply by 5, then divide by 9. *Centigrade/Celsius into Fahrenheit:* multiply Centigrade/ Celsius by 9, then divide by 5 then add 32.

Linear Measure

0.39 inches	1 centimetre
1 inch	2.54 centimetres
1 foot (12 in)	0.30 metres
1 yard (3 ft)	0.91 metres
29.37 inches	1 metre
0.62 miles	1 kilometre
1 mile (5280 ft)	1.61 kilometres
3 miles	4.8 kilometres
10 miles	16 kilometres
60 miles	98.6 kilometres
100 miles	160.9 kilometres

Square Measure

1 sq foot	0.09 sq metres
1 sq yard	0.84 sq metres
1.20 sq yards	1 sq metre
1 acre	0.96 feddans
1.04 acres	1 feddan
4201 sq metres	1 feddan

Weight

0.04 ounces	1 gram
1 ounce	28.35 grams
1 pound	453.59 grams
2.20 pounds	1 kilogram
1 ton (2000 lbs)	907.18 kilograms
0.99 pounds	1 rotel
0.45 kilograms	1 rotel
100 rotels	1 qantar

Liquid Measure

0.22 imperial gallons	1 litre
0.26 US gallons	1 litre
1 US gallon	3.79 litres
1 imperial gallon	4.55 litres

Chronology of Egyptian History

Pharaonic dynasties

The following is a list of the royal dynasties ruling Egypt successively or, where dates overlap, simultaneously and so indicating periods of disunity. The priests drew up long lists of monarchs, attaching to the years of a pharoah's reign the events they wished to record. An example is the list of Seti I's predecessors in his mortuary temple at Abydos. Working from such lists, Manetho, an Egyptian priest under the early Ptolemies, arranged all the rulers of Egypt from Menes to Alexander into 31 dynasties. Egyptologists have relied on Manetho's list, and have been able to confirm its essential correctness while sometimes improving upon it. The dates, however, are approximate, those around 3000 BC having a margin or error of 100 years, those around 2500 BC of 75 years, those following 2000 BC of 10 years, those around 1500–1000 BC of 10–15 years, while fairly precise dates are possible around 500 BC. This dynastic arrangement has historical validity, for Egypt's fortunes were closely linked to the rise and fall of the various royal houses. Throughout this Guide the dynasty of each pharaoh is mentioned after his name so that his place in the scheme of things can readily be ascertained. Only the most important pharaohs have been mentioned below within their dynasties; where their reigns overlap, this indicates joint rule.

First Dynastic Period (3100–2700 BC)
First Dynasty
Menes (Narmer) — unification of Egypt; capital at Memphis.
Second Dynasty
Old Kingdom (2700–2200 BC) — period of stability.
Third Dynasty (2700–2650 BC)
Zoser (2700 BC) — start of the Pyramid Age.
Fourth Dynasty (2650–2500 BC)
Snofru (2650 BC)
Cheops (2600 BC)
Chephren (2560 BC)
Mycerinus (2525 BC) — end of the Pyramid Age.
Fifth Dynasty (2500–2350 BC)
Unas (2375 BC) — Pyramid Texts.
Sixth Dynasty (2350–2200 BC) — period of decline.
Pepi I (2325 BC)
First Intermediate Period (2200–2050 BC) — collapse of central authority.
Seventh and Eighth Dynasties (2180–2155)
Ninth and Tenth Dynasties (2155–2055 BC)
Eleventh Dynasty (2135–2000 BC)
Mentuhotep II (2060–2010 BC) — reunites Egypt; capital at Thebes.
Middle Kingdom (2050–1800 BC) — conquest of Nubia.
Twelfth Dynasty (1990–1780 BC) — royal residence moved to Memphis.
Sesostris I (1972–1927 BC)
Second Intermediate Period (1800–1550 BC) — collapse of central authority.
Thirteenth through Seventeenth Dynasties (1780–1570 BC)
Hyksos rule in Lower Egypt (1730–1570 BC) — introduction of the chariot.
New Kingdom (1570–1090) BC — period of power, luxury and cosmopolitanism.
Eighteenth Dynasty (1570–1305 BC) — period of greatest contribution to the splendour of Thebes and Karnak.
Ahmosis I (1570–1545 BC) — expels Hyksos; establishes royal residence, and religious and political capital at Thebes.
Amenophis I (1545–1525 BC)
Tuthmosis I (1525–1495 BC) — burials begin at Valley of the Kings.
Tuthmosis II (1495–1490 BC)
Tuthmosis III (1490–1436 BC) — struggle with Hatshepsut; after her passing, he lays foundation of Asian and African empire.
Hatshepsut (1486–1468 BC)
Amenophis II (1439–1406 BC)
Tuthmosis IV (1406–1398 BC)
Amenophis III (1398–1361 BC) — apogee of New Kingdom opulence.
Amenophis IV (Akhenaton) (1369–1353 BC) — assault on priesthood of Amun; establishes worship of the Aton.

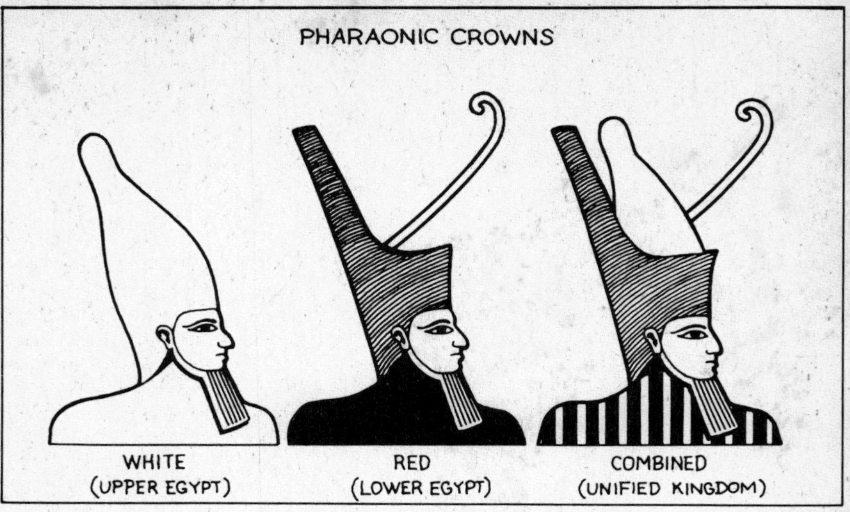

Smenkhkere (1355–1352 BC)
Tutankhaton (Tutankhamun) (1352–1344 BC) — return to orthodoxy.
Ay (1344–1342 BC)
Horemheb (1342–1303 BC) — military dictatorship.
Nineteenth Dynasty (1303–1200 BC) — restoration of royal power.
Ramses I (1303–1302 BC)
Seti I (1302–1290 BC) — new building work in Old Kingdom style.
Ramses II (1290–1224 BC) — prodigious builder, eg Rammesseum and Abu Simbel.
Merneptah (1224–1214 BC) — Pharaoh of the Exodus.
Syrian interregnum (1202–1197 BC)
Twentieth Dynasty (1200–1090 BC) — dislocations as Egypt enters Iron Age.
Ramses III (1195–1164 BC) — defeats Sea Peoples; succeeded by incompetent rulers.
Ramses VI (1153–1149 BC)
Herihor (1098–1090 BC) — Priest-Pharaoh at Thebes; rival ruler at Tanis.
Late Dynastic Period (1090–332 BC) — period of decline; often foreign rule.
Twenty-first Dynasty (1090–945 BC)
Twenty-second Dynasty (945–745 BC) — warriors of Libyan origin.
Sheshonk I (945 BC) loots Jerusalem (I *Kings* 14, 25–26).
Twenty-third Dynasty (745–718 BC) — Ethiopian kings control Upper Egypt.
Twenty-fourth Dynasty (718–712 BC) — Ethiopian kings control all Egypt.
Twenty-fifth Dynasty (712–663 BC)
Taharka (695–671 BC) — Ethiopian king defeated by Assyrians who sack Thebes.
Twenty-sixth Dynasty (663–525 BC) — Delta rulers; Assyrians ejected with Greek help.
Psammetichus I (663–610 BC)
Necho (610–595 BC) — attempts to link Red Sea and Mediterranean by a canal; circumnavigation of Africa.
Twenty-seventh Dynasty (525–404 BC)
Cambyses (525–522 BC)
Darius I (522–486 BC)

Xerxes the Great (486–466 BC) — Persian rule.
Twenty-eighth Dynasty (404–399 BC) — Persians ejected with Greek help.
Twenty-ninth Dynasty (399–380 BC) — Delta remains the vital centre of power.
Thirtieth Dynasty (380–343 BC)
Nectanebos I (380–343 BC) — great builder, eg at Philae.
Thirty-first Dynasty (343–322 BC) — Persian rule.
Alexander enters Egypt in 332 BC.

The Ptolemies

When Alexander died, his empire was divided between three of his Macedonian generals, Ptolemy taking Egypt. He established a dynasty which ruled the country for 300 years in the guise of pharaohs, albeit Greek-speaking ones, respecting the customs and religion of the Egyptians. The first three Ptolemies ruled ably, their greatest achievement Alexandria, which they adorned with Greek architecture and scholarship. In Upper Egypt the Ptolemies built archaic temples to please the priests, but otherwise they tied Egypt to the Mediterranean. Inevitably they encountered Rome, and through incompetence abroad and strife at home the later Ptolemies relied on the Romans for their very thrones. The last in the line was the great Cleopatra, who with Mark Antony attempted to create a new Hellenistic empire in the east.

323 BC: The death of *Alexander.*
323–282 BC: *Ptolemy I Soter* (Saviour). He added Cyrene, Palestine, Cyprus and parts of the Asia Minor coast to his realm, and at Alexandria, its geographical centre, he founded the Museion and Library.
282–46 BC: *Ptolemy II Philadelphus* (Lover of his Sister). To the shock of the Greeks, though with Egyptian precedent, he married his sister. He was a patron of poets, first invited the Jews to settle in Alexandria, and constructed the Pharos.
246–21 BC: *Ptolemy III Euergetes* (Benefactor). A soldier with a taste for science, during his rule Alexandria reached its height of splendour. In Upper Egypt he began the temple at Edfu. Abroad, he nearly reached India, and earned the title Conqueror of the World.
221–05 BC: *Ptolemy IV Philopator* (Lover of his Father). Setback in Syria, revolt at Thebes; he began construction of the temples at Esna and Kom Ombo.
205–181 BC: *Ptolemy V Epiphanes* (God Manifest). Child-king. Revolt at Alexandria, the interior in a state of anarchy, Epiphanes was placed under the protection of the Roman Senate, but by the time he came of age, Egypt had lost most of her overseas possessions.
181–45 BC: *Ptolemy VI Philometor* (Lover of his Mother). Seleucid invasion, Memphis captured, Egypt saved by Roman intervention.
145–4 BC: *Ptolemy VII Neos Philopator.*
145–16 BC: *Ptolemy VIII Euergetes II.* Also known as Physcon (Fatty): when he came puffing along the quay to greet Scipio Africanus the younger, the Roman sniggered, 'At least the Alexandrians have seen their King walk'. This Roman contempt applied to Egypt's sovereignty as well.
116–07, 88–80 BC: *Ptolemy IX Soter II.* Competed with his brother, Ptolemy X Alexander I, for the throne, both borrowing money from the Romans to raise arms.
107–88 BC: *Ptolemy X Alexander I.* To cover his debts he bequeathed Egypt to the Roman people, but as he had by then lost the throne his offer could not be accepted. But it was remembered.

ROYAL CARTOUCHES

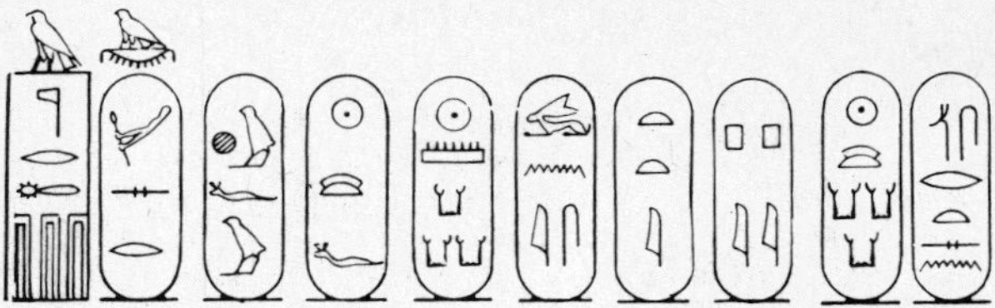

Zoser Cheops Chephren Mycerinus Unas Teti Pepi Sesostris III

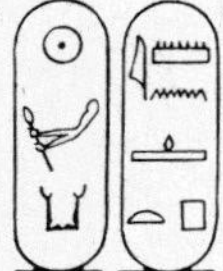

Amenophis I Hatshepsut Tothmosis III Amenophis III Akhenaton

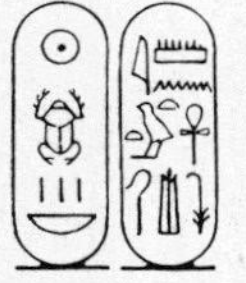

Tutankhamun Seti I Ramses II Ramses III Sheshonk Taharka

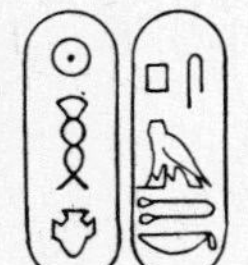

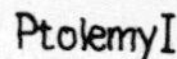

Psammetichus I Nectanebo I Alexander Ptolemy I Cleopatra Caesar

80 BC: *Ptolemy XI Alexander II.* Forced by Sulla to marry his (Ptolemy's) elderly stepmother, he then killed her and was killed in turn by an Alexandrian mob.
80–58, 55–51 BC: *Ptolemy XII Neos Dionysos.* Also known as Nothos (Bastard), he rushed back from Syria so that the vacant throne should not attract Roman annexation, and bolstered his pedigree by adding Philopator to his official names. He was the son of Ptolemy IX and father of Cleopatra VII. He built at Dendera, completed the temple at Edfu and left his mark on Philae. His reign was briefly interrupted by internal disruption.
51–49, 48–30 BC: *Cleopatra VII.* Ruled jointly with her younger brother Ptolemy XIII who banished her (**48 BC**), but in the same year she received the support of Julius Caesar and Ptolemy was drowned in the Nile. Another brother, Ptolemy XIV, succeeded to the co-regency (**47 BC**), was assassinated (**45 BC**) at Cleopatra's instigation. Bore Caesar a son (**47 BC**), but named Caesarion. He never ruled. Caesar assassinated (**44 BC**). Met Antony (**41 BC**). The battle of Actium (**31 BC**). Suicide of Antony and Cleopatra; Octavian (Augustus) makes Egypt a province of the Roman Empire (**30 BC**).

Roman and Byzantine periods

30 BC: *Octavian* (Augustus) incorporates Egypt into the Roman Empire. The Roman Emperors followed the example of the Ptolemies in representing themselves to the Egyptian people as successors of the Pharaohs and in maintaining the appearance of a national Egyptian state.
c. AD 30: Crucifixion of *Jesus of Nazareth* at Jerusalem.
AD 45: *St Mark* makes his first convert to Christianity in Egypt, a Jewish shoemaker of Alexandria.
AD 98–117: Reign of *Trajan.* The canal connecting the Nile with the Red Sea reopened (**AD 115**).
AD 117–38: Reign of *Hadrian.* Visits Egypt.
AD 204: Edict prohibiting Roman subjects from embracing Christianity. The Delta is studded with Christian communities.
c. AD 251–356: *St Anthony;* becomes the first hermit.
AD 284–305: Reign of *Diocletian.* His accession marks the beginning of the 'Era of Martyrs' from which the Copts date their calendar. Persecution of the Christians (**AD 330**).
AD 324–37: Reign of *Constantine the Great.* Converts to Christianity. Founds Constantinople (**AD 330**).
c. AD 330: Founding of the first monasteries at Wadi Natrun.
AD 379–95: Reign of *Theodosius I.* Declares Christianity to be the religion of the Roman Empire.
AD 395: Partition of the Roman Empire into East (Constantinople) and West (Rome). Notional date for the beginning of the Byzantine Empire.
AD 451: Council of Chalcedon declares monophysism a heresy, effectively expelling the Egyptian (Coptic) Church from the main body of Christianity.
AD 476: Fall of the Roman Empire in the West.
AD 622: *Mohammed's* flight from Mecca, the *hegira,* from which the Moslem calendar is reckoned. His death (**AD 632**).
AD 636: Arabs defeat Byzantine army and take Damascus.
AD 637: Arabs destroy the Sassanian (Persian) Empire.
AD 638: Arabs take Jerusalem.
AD 640: An Arab force under *Amr* enters Egypt. Fortress of Babylon taken (**AD 641**). Fustat founded; Alexandria surrenders and welcomes Arabs as liberators from Byzantine persecution (**AD 642**).

Arab and Turkish periods

All dates are according to the Western calendar (AD).
661: Murder of *Ali,* son-in-law of the Prophet; the Caliphate passes to the Umayyads.
661–750: The *Umayyad Caliphate,* with its capital at Damascus, rules over a

united Arab empire stretching from the borders of China to the shores of the Atlantic, and up into France.
750–935: *Abbassids and Tulunids.* The Abbassids put a bloody end to the Umayyads in Syria and succeed to the Caliphate, ruling the Arab world from Baghdad. *Ibn Tulun,* an Abbassid governor of Egypt, makes himself independent of Baghdad and establishes a dynasty (**870–935**).
c. 820: The Copts, resentful of their Arab conquerors, rise in revolt several times during the 8th and 9th C. After their defeat, the majority of Copts convert to Islam.
909: Establishment of Fatimid Caliphate in North Africa.
935–69: A Turkish dynasty, the *Ikhshidids,* seizes power through the governorship.
969–1171: The *Fatimid Caliphate* in Egypt, which now follows Shi'a rather than Sunni Islam. Cairo, its capital, founded (**969**). Al-Azhar founded (**971**). The Fatimid empire reaches its peak under *Caliph Abu Mansur al-Aziz* (**975–96**). He introduces the practice of importing slave troops, the forerunners of the Mamelukes. His successor, *al-Hakim* (**996–1021**), is an all-powerful psychotic; the decline of the Fatimid empire begins with his death.
1055: The Seljuq Turks take Baghdad, leading to a resurgence of Sunni Islam in Iraq, Syria and Iran.
1099: The Crusaders take Jerusalem.
1171–1250: The *Ayyubids;* the dynasty of *Saladin,* a Kurd from Syria. He converts Egypt back to Sunni Islam. Drives the Crusaders from Jerusalem (**1187**). The Mamelukes rise to power during the rule of *Shagarat al-Durr* (**1249–59**).
1250–1382: The *Bahri Mamelukes.* The most celebrated of these Mameluke Sultans are *Baybars* (**1260–77**); *Qalaun* (**1279–90**); *al-Nasr* (**1309–40**) — the beautiful mausolea of these last two are on Sharia Muizz in Cairo; and *al-Hassan* (**1347–51, 1354–61**), builder of the great madrasa bearing his name.
1382–1517: The *Burgi Mamelukes.* The most celebrated of these Mameluke Sultans are *Barquq* (**1382–89, 1390–98**), whose mosque is on Sharia Muizz, his mausoleum in the City of the Dead in Cairo; *Baybars* (**1422–38**), whose mausoleum is in the City of the Dead; *Qaytbay* (**1468–95**), known for his fortress on the site of the Pharos in Alexandria, and his mausoleum in the City of the Dead; and *al-Ghuri* (**1500–16**) whose monuments stand near Al-Azhar. *Tumanbay* (**1515–17**) was the last of the Burgi Sultans; he was hanged three times by the Turks outside Bab Zuwayla in Cairo.
1517: The Rule of the *Ottoman Turks* begins in Egypt and continues, if only nominally, until 1914.

The modern period

1798–1801: *French occupation* of Egypt. *Napoleon* lands at Alexandria; Battle of the Pyramids; Battle of the Nile (**1798**). *Napoleon* departs from Egypt (**1799**). A British army compels the French to evacuate the country (**1801**).
1805: *Mohammed Ali* becomes Viceroy of Egypt and after massacring the Mamelukes (**1811**) becomes, effectively, the independent ruler of Egypt, establishing a dynasty that was to end with *Farouk.*
1869: Opening of the Suez Canal during the reign of *Ismail.*
1882: Nationalist uprising led by *Arabi. British occupation* of Egypt begins.
1883–1907: *Evelyn Baring (Lord Cromer)* is British Consul in Egypt and effective ruler of the country.
1902: British complete construction of dam at Aswan.
1914: Britain declares Egypt to be a *British Protectorate.*
1918: *Saad Zaghloul,* nationalist leader, demands British withdrawal.
1922: British recognise Egypt as a sovereign state, but maintain an army in Egypt.
1936: Anglo-Egyptian Treaty, formally ending British occupation. British

army withdraws, except from the Canal Zone.
1939–45: Egypt nominally neutral during the Second World War, but British Army invited to return to fight the encroaching Germans. Battle of el Alamein (**1942**); *Rommel* repulsed.
1948: End of British Mandate for Palestine. Establishment of the state of Israel. Arab-Israeli war; Arab debacle. Resentful of political corruption, *Gamal Abdel Nasser* (**1918–70**) gathers round him a group of dissident army officers.
1952: 25 January, British soldiers kill several Egyptian police in the Canal Zone. 26 January, rioting in Cairo at British action and Egyptian government's inaction. 23 July, *Nasser's* group stages a coup. 26 July, *King Farouk* abdicates and leaves the country.
1953: Egypt declared a *republic*.
1954: *Nasser* becomes head of state.
1954–56: British evacuate the Canal Zone.
1956: United States cancels loan to Egypt for construction of the High Dam at Aswan. *Nasser* nationalises the Suez Canal to use its revenues to pay for High Dam's construction. Israel invades Sinai in collusion with a British and French troop landing in the Canal Zone. Britain, France and Israel withdraw after international protest.
1958–61: Egypt and Syria combine to form the short-lived United Arab Republic (name retained until **1971**).
1961: *Nasser* introduces sweeping socialist measures, limiting incomes, nationalising banks and the cotton industry, further redistributing land.
1967: The June 'Six Day War'. Israel attacks and defeats Egypt, occupies all of Sinai. The Suez Canal is blocked.
1970: *Nasser* dies. *Anwar Sadat* becomes President.
1971: Egypt's official name becomes the Arab Republic of Egypt (ARE).
1973: October, Egyptian forces cross the Canal and drive back the Israeli army. Israeli forces continue to occupy the Gaza Strip and most of Sinai.
1975: Suez Canal reopened.
1977: *Sadat* visits Jerusalem in a dramatic peace bid.
1980: Egypt and Israel exchange ambassadors.
1981: 6 October, *Sadat* assassinated. *Hosni Mubarak* becomes President later that month.
1982: Israel evacuates Sinai.
1984: Egypt's first free elections since 1952.

Glossary of religious, architectural and other names and terms

Abu: The Arabic for saint, whether Moslem or Christian. Holy man.
Amun: God of Thebes; he was made a sun god under the name *Amun-Re* and became the national god during the New Kingdom. His sacred animal was the ram. Along with his wife, *Mut*, and their son, *Khonsu*, Amun was one of the Theban triad.
Ankh: The hieroglyphic sign for 'life', resembling a cross with a loop in place of the upper arm.
Anubis: God of the dead, associated with interment. His sacred animal was the dog or jackal.
Apis: The sacred bull of Memphis, buried in the Serapeum at Saqqara.
Apse: A semi-circular domed recess, most frequently at the east end of a church.
Aton: The sun's disc; the life force. Worshipped by Akhenaton, who attacked the priesthood of Amun.
Atum: The creator god of Heliopolis, represented as a man.
Azan: The Moslem call to prayer (see *muezzin*).
Ba: A spirit that inhabits the body during life but is not attached to it; at death it leaves the body and joins the divine spirit. (See *ka*).

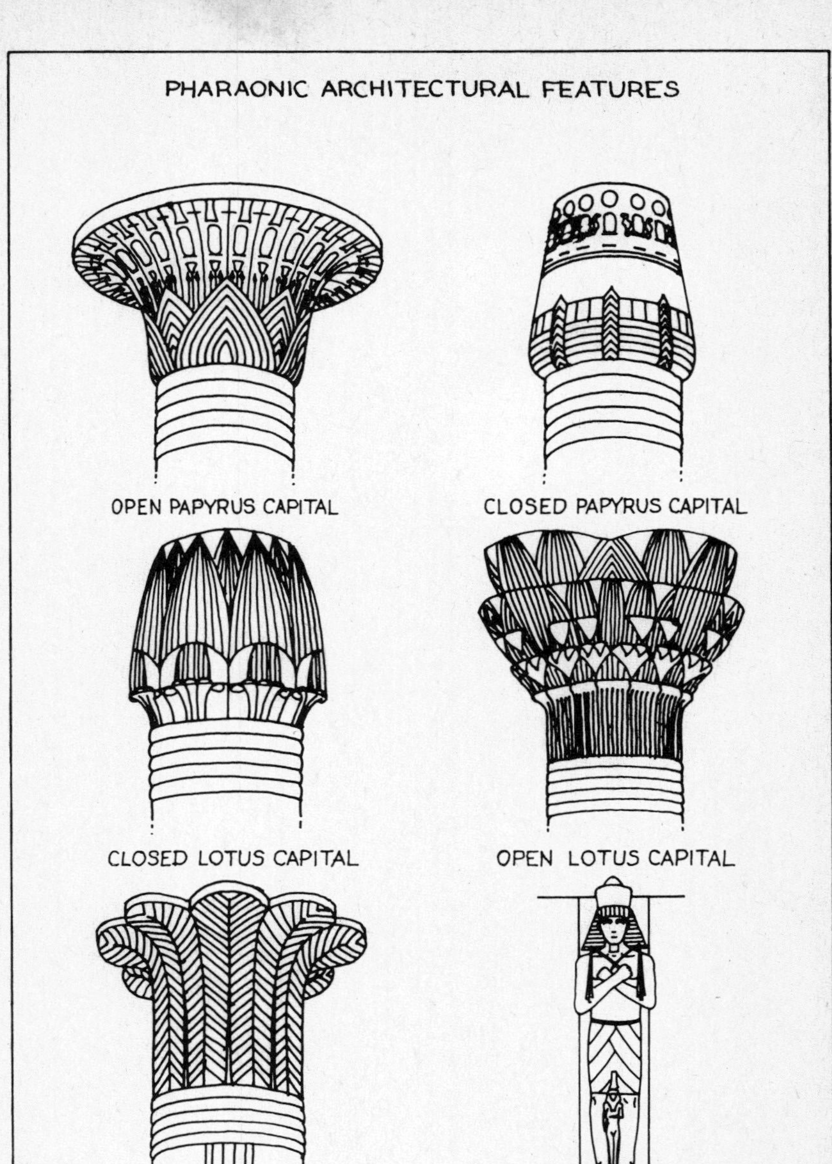
PHARAONIC ARCHITECTURAL FEATURES
OPEN PAPYRUS CAPITAL
CLOSED PAPYRUS CAPITAL
CLOSED LOTUS CAPITAL
OPEN LOTUS CAPITAL
PALM CAPITAL
OSIRID.
PILLAR

Bab: A gate, as Bab Zuwayla.
Basilica: A building, eg a church, in the form of a long colonnaded hall, usually with one or more apses at the east end, and a narthex at the west end.
Bastet: The goddess of Bubastis, a goddess of joy. Her sacred animal was the lioness or cat.
Bayt: A house, or the self-contained apartments into which Ummayad mansions and Abbasid palaces were divided.
Canopic jars: Containers placed within ancient tombs to preserve those organs and viscera thought essential for the dead man's continued existence in the afterlife.
Capitals: Pharaonic and Ptolemaic temples employed capitals decorated either with plant forms (*palmiform, papyriform, lotiform*) or other motifs (*Hathoric*, ie with the human face and cow's ears of Hathor; forms deriving from timber construction eg *tent poles*). (See illustration.)
Cartouche: In hieroglyphs, the oval band enclosing the god's or Pharaoh's name and symbolising unchanging continuity.
Cavetto cornice: One of the most characteristic decorative features in ancient Egyptian architecture, a concave moulding decorated with palmettes. It was used along the tops of walls and *pylons*, projecting at front and sides. Below it would be a *torus* moulding.
Colours: Primary colours usually had particular applications and significance in ancient Egyptian painting. *Black* represented death: mummies, also Osiris as king of the dead, were commonly depicted in black. *Blue* was for sky and water, the sky gods painted this colour. *Green* was the colour of rebirth: Osiris, who overcame death and was reborn, often had his face and limbs painted green; also the solar disc was commonly painted light green on sarcophagi, instead of its usual red. *Red* was for blood and fire; men's bodies were depicted as reddish brown or brown; it also had a maleficent connotation: Seth was painted reddish brown. *White* represented silver and was the colour of the moon; it was also the colour of the garments of the gods and the crown of Upper Egypt. *Yellow* represented gold and was also used as the colour for women's bodies until the mid-XVIII Dynasty; thereafter the only women painted this colour were goddesses.
Columns: Like capitals, ancient columns followed certain decorative motifs, eg papyrus columns modelled after either a single stem and therefore smooth, or after a bundle of stems and therefore ribbed.
Crowns: The red crown of Lower Egypt was joined with the white crown of Upper Egypt to represent unification of the country (see *colours*). No matter what headdress the Pharaoh wore, he was always shown with the *uraeus* on his forehead.
Electrum: An alloy of gold and silver. The tips of obelisks were covered with electrum. In ancient Egypt, where gold was mined in abundance, both silver and electrum were more precious than gold alone.
Evil eye: The superstition that the envious glance of any passer-by, attracted by an immodest show of wealth, achievement or beauty, can harm or bewitch. Reciting certain verses of the Koran is one way of warding it off. *Uzait Horun*, the Eye of Horus, is meant to ensure safety and happiness and wards off the evil eye; it may be painted on cars, trucks and fishing boats, or worn as an amulet, particularly by children, who are especially vulnerable. Children also leave their handprints on walls to avert the evil eye. The probable value of the belief is as a social control, minimising at least the appearance of disparity in people's fortunes and so promoting solidarity.
Exonarthex: The outer vestibule of a church.
Faience: Glazed earthenware, often decorated, formed as pottery or in blocks or tiles as a wall facing.
Fellahin: Egyptian peasants. The singular is *fellah*.

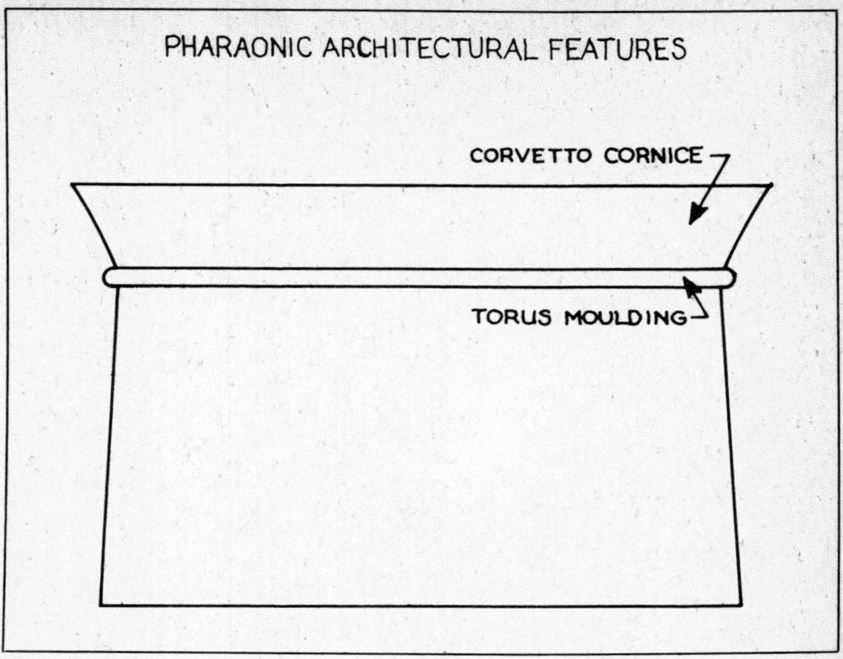

Flagellum: A flail or rattle to drive away evil spirits; it could be used only by a pharaoh and so represented the royal authority in carvings and statues. In the other hand was the *crook*, another royal symbol.
Hajj: The pilgrimage to Mecca that all Moslems should make at least once in their lifetime. When they have done so, they will often paint a scene of the event on their houses.
Hamam: A bath, public or private.
Harem: The private family (or specifically the women's) quarter in a house.
Hathor: The goddess of heaven, joy and love; the Greeks identified her with *Aphrodite*. She was the deity of Dendera and protector of the Theban necropolis. Her sacred animal was the cow.
Heb-Sed: The jubilee marking the thirtieth year of a pharoah's reign (see Saqqara).
Hegira: Mohammed's flight, or more properly his 'withdrawal of affection' from Mecca in AD 622. The Moslem calendar starts from this date.
Herakhte: A form of *Horus*, 'Horus of the horizon', often combined with the sun god as *Re-Herakhte* and so worshipped at Heliopolis. The falcon was sacred to him.
Horus: The son of *Isis* and *Osiris*, and revered as the sun god. He was represented as the sun disc or a falcon, his sacred animal.
Hypostyle: A hypostyle hall is any chamber whose ceiling is supported by columns or pillars.
Ikonostasis: The screen carrying ikons between the main part of a church and the sanctuary or choir.
Isis: Sister and wife to *Osiris*, mother of *Horus*, the patron goddess of Philae. She was highly revered at a late period. Her sacred animal was the vulture.

Ithyphallic: Denoting the erect phallus of a depicted god or pharaoh, most commonly the god *Min*. It was a sign of fertility.
Ka: A spirit that inhabits the body during life and may leave it in death, but requires the continued existence of the body (hence mummification or, by substitution, ka statues) for its survival. The ka was personal and individual, in a sense the ideal image of a man's own life. (See *ba*.)
Khan: See *wakala*.
Khnum: The patron god of Elephantine Island and the Cataracts. He fashioned man on his potter's wheel. His sacred animal was the ram.
Khonsu: Son of *Amun* and *Mut*; god of the moon. The falcon was sacred to him.
Kufic: An early style of Arabic calligraphy with angular letters.
Lily: The plant identified with Upper Egypt.
Liwan: A vaulted hall (see *mosque*).
Maat: The goddess of truth, whose symbol was the ostrich feather. Maat is actually the deification of a concept which Egyptians strove for, both personally and for the state. As well as truth, one can attempt to define it as justice, correctness, balance. The best definition is the now rare English word meet.
Madrasa: See *mosque*.
Mashrabiyya: Interlaced wooden screenwork, used for example to cover street-facing windows in a house.
Mausoleum: A domed chamber with one or more tombs inside; though simple in form, these structures, characteristic of the City of the Dead, are sometimes of considerable beauty.
Mihrab: The niche in the *qibla wall* of a mosque, indicating the direction of Mecca.
Min: The god of the harvest, frequently amalgamated with *Amun*. He was *ithyphallically* represented. The Greeks identified him with *Pan*.
Minbar: The pulpit in a mosque from which the Friday prayer is spoken.
Mont: A Theban god of war, represented with a falcon's head.
Mosque: The first mosque was the courtyard of Mohammed's house at Medina, with no architectural refinements except a shaded area at one end. Indeed, the only requirement for a mosque is that it should demarcate a space in which people may gather for saying prayers, eg an open quadrangle marked off by a ditch. From this notion developed the *congregational mosque*, of which the Ibn Tulun is the most outstanding example. Among non-congregational mosques are two special types which are of Cairene inspiration and development, the *cruciform madrasa* and the *sabil kuttab*. The *madrasa* served as a theological college, introduced by Saladin to combat Fatimid Shi'ism. Later it became more complex, a tomb appended and the madrasa formed of four *liwans*, each opening into a central court, hence *cruciform*. The outstanding example of this type is the Hassan. This pattern was subsequently modified, the court covered over, the east and west liwans reduced to vestigial proportions, a Koranic school for boys (*kuttab*) added as a floor above, a public fountain (*sabil*) below.
Muezzin: A crier who, as from a minaret, calls the faithful to prayer (see *azan*).
Mut: The wife of *Amun* and mother of *Khonsu*. Her sacred animal was the vulture.
Naos: The enclosed inner 'house of the god' (also *cella*), the central room of a temple, though sometimes referring to the entire temple. The sanctuary.
Narthex: The entrance vestibule at the west end of a church.
Nashki: A cursive form of Arabic writing, subsequent to *Kufic*.
Nut: Godess of the sky, often shown supported by *Shu*.
Okel: See *wakala*.
Osiris: Originally a vegetation god, later the god of the underworld. Murdered and dismembered by *Seth*, he was the husband of *Isis* and father of *Horus*.
Papyrus: The plant identified with Lower Egypt.

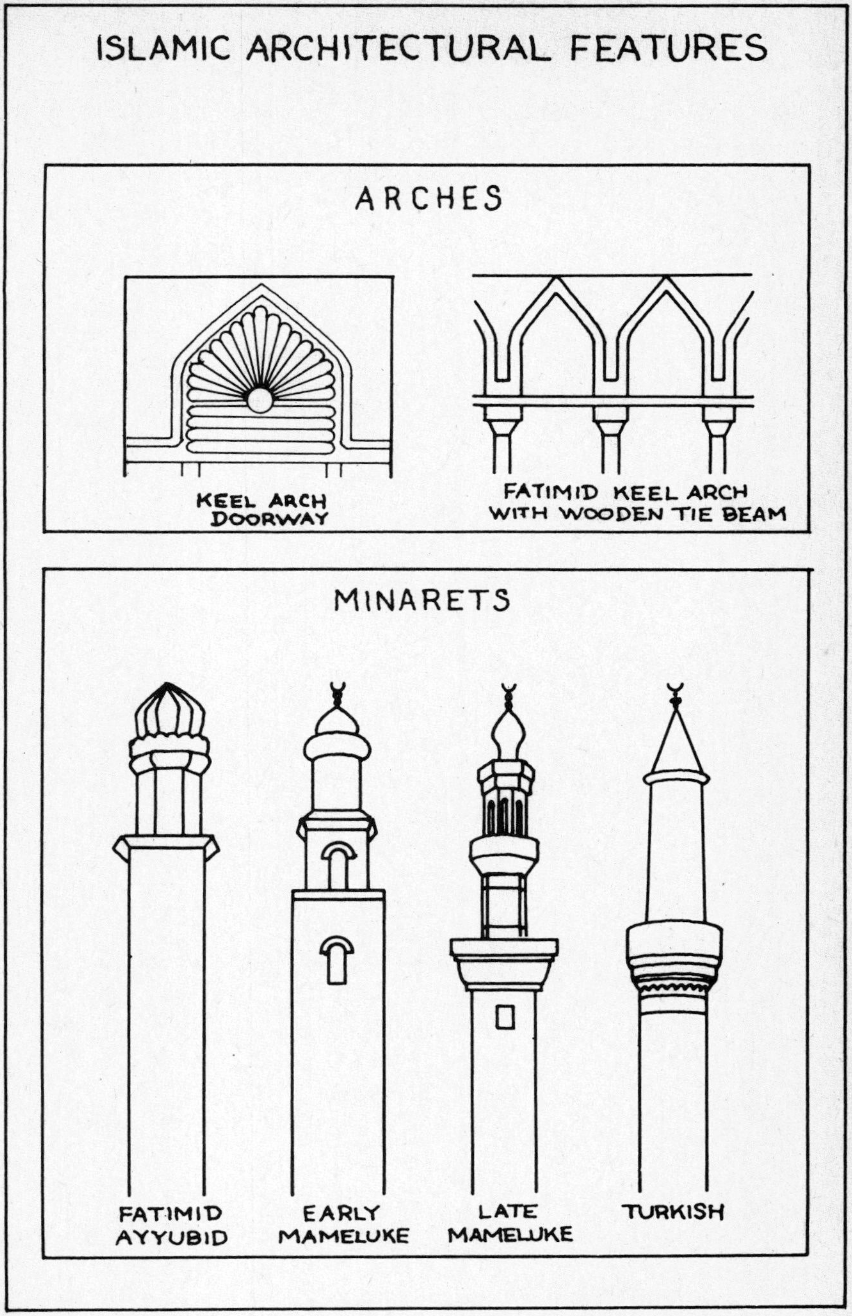
ISLAMIC ARCHITECTURAL FEATURES
ARCHES
KEEL ARCH DOORWAY
FATIMID KEEL ARCH WITH WOODEN TIE BEAM
MINARETS
FATIMID AYYUBID
EARLY MAMELUKE
LATE MAMELUKE
TURKISH

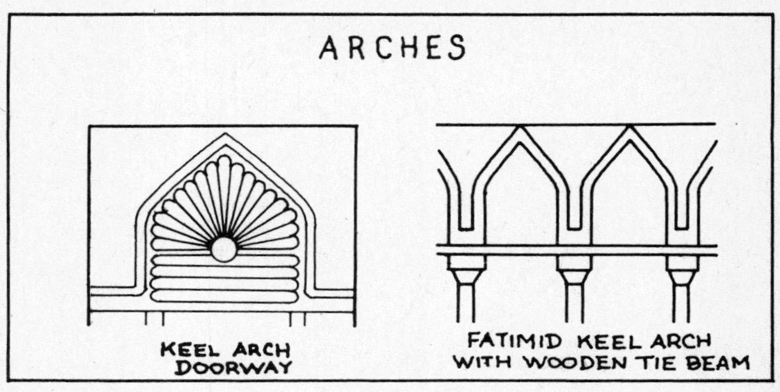

Pronaos: A columned porch, leading to the *naos*.
Ptah: The patron god of Memphis and father of the gods. His sacred animal was the bull (*Apis*).
Pylon: Arranged in pairs, forming a monumental gateway to a temple. Where there are several sets of pylons, each preceeding a court, they descend in size as the sanctuary of the god is approached, while the floor level rises, creating a focussing or tunnelling effect.
Pyramidion: The capstone of a pyramid.
Qibla wall: The wall of a mosque facing Mecca.
Re: The sun god, usually combined with another god, eg *Amun-Re* or *Re-Herakhte*. His priesthood was at Heliopolis.
Riwaq: The arcade around a *sahn*, or a student apartment within the arcade.
Sabil kuttab: See *mosque*.
Sahn: An interior court, usually in a mosque.
Sakiya: An irrigation device consisting of buckets attached to a wheel which lifts water to the fields and is driven by circling oxen.
Sekhmet: The lion goddess of war.
Serapis: A god invented by the Ptolemies, looking like *Zeus* but identified with *Osiris-Apis*.
Seth: Brother and slayer of *Osiris*, adversary of *Horus*, he became a god of war, though after the XXII Dynasty he was reduced to the god of the impure. His sacred animal was possibly the aardvark.
Shaduf: A simple lever device for lifting water to irrigate the fields. It is operated by hand.
Shu: The god of the air. He is often shown supporting Nut.
Sobek: God of the waters, patron of the Fayyum, the crocodile was sacred to him.
Squinches: Small arches or supports across the corners of a square, enabling the carriage of a dome.
Stele: An upright stone slab or pillar with an inscription or design, used as a monument or grave marker.
Thoth: A moon deity and the god of science. The ibis and baboon were sacred to him.
Torus: A convex moulding (see *cavetto cornice*).
Uraeus: The cobra worn on the forehead of a pharoah as both an emblem and an instrument of protection, breathing flames and destroying enemies.
Ushabti: A mummiform figurine, serving in the tomb as deputy for the dead man, carrying out his labour obligations.
Wakala: An inn for travelling merchants built around a courtyard, with stables

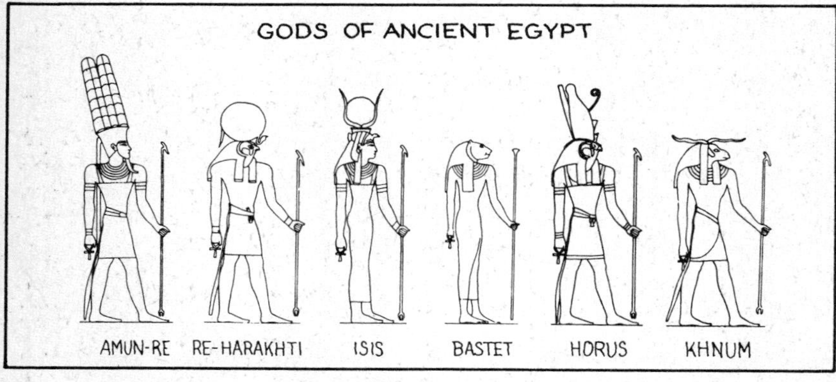

and warehouses at ground level and living accommodation above. Other names are *khan* and *okel*.

Waqf: An endowment for the upkeep of a mosque, eg a nearby apartment house, or shops built into the street level of the mosque, earning rents.

Ziyadah: The outer court of a mosque.

Some Books About Egypt

The literature on Egypt is vast, and apart from pursuing your interest in libraries and bookshops at home there are several bookshops in Cairo worth visiting (see *Practical Information* following the *Cairo: Mother of the World* chapter). Not all the following books are in print; publisher, place and most recent date of publication of those editions with which I am familiar are supplied. There may be other editions published elsewhere, and also paperback editions of those I have cited as hardcover. All quotations in the text are from books listed here.

Baedeker, Karl *Baedeker's Egypt 1929* David and Charles, Newton Abbot 1985. The most complete travel guide to Egypt ever written, this facsimile edition is still very useful, and on such subjects an 'Intercourse with Orientals' it grows more amusing with time. Hardcover.

Breasted, James Henry *A History of Egypt* Hodder and Stoughton, London 1959. First published before the discovery of Tutankhamun's tomb, this once definitive history of ancient Egypt has been superseded by later research. But it remains useful, and Breasted could write with panache. Hardcover.

Budge, E A Wallis, translation and introduction *The Book of the Dead* University Books, New Hyde Park, NY 1960. For the most part, of interest only to dead Egyptians with time on their hands. The hieroglyphs are reproduced and keyed line for line to the translation, and this can be interesting. The adamancy is sometimes startling: 'I shall live, I shall live; I shall flourish, I shall flourish, I shall flourish, I shall wake up in peace, I shall not putrefy, my intestines shall not perish, I shall not suffer injury'. And sometimes it is triumphantly beautiful: 'I have seen Osiris, my father, and I have gazed upon my mother, and I have made love. I am led into celestial regions, and I make the things of the earth to flourish; and there is joy of heart. I have tied up my boat in the celestial lakes. I have recited the prescribed words with my voice, and I have ascribed praises unto the gods'. Hardcover.

Burckhardt, John Lewis *Travels in Nubia*, London 1819. A Swiss sent out by the African Society in London to discover the source of the Niger, he started his travels in the Middle East where he perfected his disguise as an Arab merchant and apart from visiting Mecca was one of the first Europeans to travel in Nubia and the Sudan. His observations of monuments and life along the Nile and across the deserts are fascinating. He died in Cairo at the age of 34 before he was able to journey on to West Africa. Hardcover.

Cavafy, C P: the great Alexandrian poet, his work appears in several editions, eg *Collected Poems*, translated by Edmund Keeley and Philip Sherrard, Chatto and Windus, London 1975. Paperback.

Cocteau, Jean *Maalesh, A Theatrical Tour of the Middle East* Peter Owen, London 1956. Written as a journal, it is full of delightful and often penetrating observations. Hardcover.

Durrell, Lawrence *Justine, Balthazar, Mountolive* and *Clea* (*The Alexandria Quartet*) Faber, London 1963. Powerfully evocative novels set in Alexandria before the Second World War. Paperback.

Edwards, Amelia *A Thousand Miles Up the Nile* Century, London 1982. First published in 1877, Edwards was a novelist who by this account of her travels through Egypt aroused public interest in the excavation and conservation of

the antiquities, founded the Egypt Exploration Society, and established the first Chair in Egyptology in Britain. Highly readable. Paperback.
Edwards, I E S *The Pyramids of Egypt*, Penguin, Harmondsworth 1980. The established view of how and why the pyramids were built. Paperback.
Fedden, Robin *Egypt, Land of the Valley* Michael Haag, London 1985. The best general introduction to the country. Paperback.
Fowles, John *Daniel Martin* Triad/Panther, London 1978. A big fat novel to read along the Nile, where much of it is set. Some good travel writing on Egypt. Paperback.
Flaubert, Gustave: a romantic until he visited Egypt, which sharpened his eye. His travel journal has been translated and edited by Francis Steegmuller, *Flaubert in Egypt* Michael Haag, London 1983. A marvellous antidote to a surfeit of temples. Paperback.
Forster, E M *Alexandria: A History and a Guide* Annotated edition, with a preface by Lawrence Durrell. Michael Haag, London 1982. First published in 1922, this has been called the greatest guide book ever written. The whole historical perspective of the city, in all its variety, has been captured and fixed in a series of short essays brightly starred with all the virtues of this fine artist. With a marvellous economy he brings the place to life — and gives life to the great personages who inhabited it: philosophers, poets, mathematicians, courtesans. It is a work of deep affection and a noble monument raised to this most haunting of cities — Lawrence Durrell. Paperback.
Forster, E M *Pharos and Pharillon* Michael Haag, London 1983. Sketches of Alexandria past and (sometimes first person) present, first published in 1923. Paperback.
Fox, Robin Lane *Alexander the Great* Futura, London 1975. The definitive life; erudition enlivened with an imaginative insight into Alexander's mind and times. Paperback.
Frankfort, Henri and others *Before Philosphy, The Intellectual Adventure of Ancient Man* Penguin, Baltimore 1949. A stimulating analysis of Mesopotamian and Egyptian cosmogony, etc. Paperback.
Fuller, J F C *The Decisive Battles of the Western World* Abridged in two volumes. Paladin, London 1970. A highly readable and incisive view of history. The first volume touches on the Battle of Megiddo (1479 BC), the second on Alamein (AD 1942). I mention these because I have drawn on or quoted from them, but anyone interested in the detail of these battles should consult the unabridged hardcover edition or a specialised work. Also useful and authoritative, if again general, is the *History of the Second World War* by Liddell Hart. The abridged Fuller is in paperback.
Gardiner, Sir Alan *Egypt of the Pharaohs* Oxford University Press, London 1961. A scholarly introduction to Egyptology presented through a history of Egypt by an outstanding Egyptologist. Hardcover.
Giedion, S *The Eternal Present: The Beginning of Architecture* Oxford University Press, London 1964. A conceptual history of Mesopotamian and Egyptian architecture. Hardcover.
Grant, Michael *Cleopatra* Panther, London 1974. A lively reconsideration of the life and policies of the last Ptolemy. Paperback.
Herodotus *The Histories* Penguin, Harmondsworth 1972. By way of setting the scene for the great conflict between Greece and Persia, Herodotus included a lengthy digression on Egypt full of information and some misinformation acquired during his visit. The first great prose work in European literature. Paperback.
Johnson-Davies, Denys, translator *Egyptian Short Stores* Heinemann, London 1978. A must for getting into the atmosphere and mind of modern Egypt. Paperback.
Lane, E W *Manners and Customs of the Modern Egyptians* Facsimile of the 1895

edition. First published in 1836. East-West Publications, London 1978. A classic account of Egyptian, principally Cairene, life in the early 19th C. Paperback.
Mahfouz, Naguib *Midaq Alley* Heinemann, London 1975. Egypt's greatest novelist and his most popular book, set in the backstreets of the Azhar district of Cairo. Paperback.
Mahfouz, Naguib *Miramar* Heinemann, London 1978. An Egyptian response to Durrell's *Alexandria Quartet,* with an introduction by John Fowles. Paperback.
Mansfield, Peter *The British in Egypt* Weidenfeld and Nicolson, London 1971. An account of the British occupation of Egypt. Hardcover.
Mendelssohn, Kurt *The Riddle of the Pyramids* Sphere Books, London 1977. A fascinating account of the pyramid phenomenon and a radical solution to the riddle by an Oxford physicist. Paperback. See also Mendelssohn's article in the *Journal of Egyptian Archaeology* 59, August 1973, and subsequent correspondence between Mendelssohn, I E S Edwards and Christopher J Davey in *JEA* 60, 62 and 63.
Nerval, Gérard de *Journey to the Orient* Michael Haag, London 1984. An early surrealist (19th C) finds stimulation in Egypt. Written in the style of a travel journal, he soon soars on hashish wings. Paperback.
Russell, Dorothea *Medieval Cairo and the Monasteries of the Wadi Natrun,* Weidenfeld and Nicolson, London 1962. A fascinating account of the Fatimid and Mameluke periods, as well as an excellent guidebook written with love. Hardcover.
Twain, Mark *The Innocents Abroad* The New English Library, London 1966. Twain led a part of American tourists through Europe and the Middle East and wrote this absurdly funny and iconoclastic account. The part on Egypt is fairly brief. Paperback.
Wellard, James *Desert Pilgrimage, A Journey into Christian Egypt* Hutchinson, London 1970. A personal exploration of this important but neglected aspect of Egypt. Hardcover.
Wilson, John A *The Culture of Ancient Egypt* (originally titled *The Burden of Egypt*) The University of Chicago Press, Chicago 1956. An excellent and readable cultural history of dynastic and pre-dynastic Egypt. Paperback.

CAIRO: MOTHER OF THE WORLD

From the air Cairo is a city of circles and radiating avenues at the head of the Nile Delta, its houses and buildings dull brown as though camouflaged to blend with the impinging desert. The colour is of the local stone, but also the residue of sandstorms which sometimes dust the city. At sundown you can see a thin layer of sand clinging to the polished dome of the Mohammed Ali Mosque atop the Citadel, and as you walk along the cracked pavements the desert wells up from below.

Like a great lung the Nile breathes through the city, but away from the river westernised Cairo can have a heavy, airless feeling, an architectural jumble of fake pharaonic, blocklike modern, unnoticed art-deco and stolid Victorian. Yet further east against the Moqattam Hills minarets like blades of tall grass rise against the sky, marking the old Islamic city of hidden beauty and palpitating energy which lends all Cairo its excitement.

In spirit Cairo remains as it began, an Arab encampment on the edge of the desert: hot, dry, the smell of dung, glowing coals and musk, lively with throngs of people. To this sprawling caravanserai come visitors from all over the Arab, African and Asian world, fantastically varied in colour, dress, characteristics, yet easily talking, mingling, bargaining like distant villagers meeting again in their market town.

For Cairo is the largest city in Africa and the political and cultural fulcrum of the Arab world. Its population has been officially estimated at eight million, and that itself represents a doubling over the past two decades, but as many as 14 million people could be living here. It has always attracted people from the villages of the Valley and the Delta, but owes its recent staggering growth to the damage inflicted on the Suez Canal towns during the wars with Israel. At rush hours the buses threaten to burst or collapse with the pressure of Cairenes scrambling through doors and windows or clinging on outside.

But as the sun sets over the Nile the present slips away into timelessness, and from a high window over the river you can see the Pyramids at Giza glow gold against the Western Desert as they have done for one million, seven hundred thousand evenings past.

History of the City

Your orientation about the city is aided by a knowledge of its history, and its history, as with so much else in Egypt, is linked to the Nile.

Antiquity

In the Old Kingdom the capital of Egypt was at **Memphis**, 20 kms to the south of present-day Cairo — but at that time the Delta had not pushed as far north as it has today and Memphis stood closer then to the conjunction of the Delta and the Valley, controlling Egypt to north and south. In this strategic sense Cairo is heir to Memphis, for the Nile divides just to the north of the capital.

Ancient **Heliopolis**, its scant ruins near a modern suburb bearing the same name at the northeast of the city enroute to the airport, was once the religious centre of Egypt; and in pharaonic times there was a settlement, perhaps even a town, on the east bank of the Nile opposite the island of Roda, but Cairo cannot be said to have developed out of these, and even its connection with what is now called Old Cairo is tenuous. In Roman and Byzantine times when there was a fortress here, Old Cairo was called **Babylon in Egypt**, probably a Greek corruption of the ancient name of Roda, *Per-Hapi-en-Yun*, House of the Nile of Heliopolis. Fortress rather than administrative centre was sufficient role for the settlement, and Babylon never amounted to much. In the last centuries before Christ, Egypt was ruled by Alexander's successors, the Ptolemies, from their Mediterranean capital, Alexandria.

The Arab conquest

It was the Arabs, for whom the desert and not the sea provided familiar lines of communication, who developed the logic of the site. In AD 641, Amr arrived in Eypt at the head of a small army and both Alexandria and Babylon opened their gates to him. Amr was enchanted with Alexandria and wrote back to the Caliph at Medina that this should be the Moslem capital of the conquered country, but Omar replied, 'Will there be water between me and the Moslem army?' Amr returned to Babylon where only sand separated him from Arabia; the tent (*fustat*) he had pitched there before marching on Alexandria was still standing and a dove had nested in it with her young. On this spot Amr built his mosque, the first in Egypt and **Fustat**, the City of the Tent, grew up around.

Fustat was the first of several planned developments which over the centuries contributed to the growth of the medieval city. The Nile in those days lay further to the east along what is now Sharia el Gumhuriya which runs up into Midan Ramses where the railway station is. All of what is now modern Cairo lay then on the west bank of the river, if not beneath it. And an ancient canal, once joining the Nile with the Red Sea, lay still further to the east, along the line of Sharia Port Said, built when the canal, called the Khalig by the Arabs, was filled in during the 19th C. So the city developed along the narrow corridor of land between the canal to the west and the Moqattam Hills to the east, and extended northwards as successive rulers were intent on catching the cool summer breezes blowing in from the Mediterranean.

The Tulunid city

When Ibn Tulun, Abbasid Governor of Egypt, made himself virtually independent of the Baghdad Caliph in 870, he built his palace, government buildings, a hippodrome and the famous mosque bearing his name to the north of Fustat. The **Mosque of Ibn Tulun** apart, little survives of his city, and still less of Fustat. The heart of what grew into the Cairo of today was established by the Fatimids.

Cairo founded by the Fatimids

On 5 August 969, with Mars in the ascendant, the first stone of the Fatimid capital was laid to the north of the Tulunid city. The city took its name, *al-Qahira*, The Triumphant, from the warrior planet. The Fatimids, of the persistent though minority Shi'ite sect of Islam, invaded Egypt from Tunisia where their Caliphate declared its legitimacy through descent from Ali, husband of the Prophet's daughter Fatima. They imposed their Shi'ite doctrines (those same followed today in Iran) on Egypt which, apart from the Fatimid interlude, has kept within the orthodox Sunni fold. The **al-Azhar Mosque** dates from this period and is still the centre of Koranic studies for the whole Moslem world.

(Our name for the city, Cairo, derives from this al-Qahira found on maps, though as often as not Egyptians call it *Misr*. Of vague and haunting meaning, far antedating Islam, Misr is emotionally the more important name of the two and refers to both city and the country as a whole. An Egyptian abroad who says, 'I am going to Misr', means he is returning to Egypt. If he says the same thing in Luxor, he means he is returning to Cairo. In either case, 'going to Misr' carries the sense of going home. For the fellahin, Cairo is *Misr um al-dunya*: Misr, Mother of the World.)

Saladin extends the medieval city

This walled city, centred on the popular market area known as **Khan el Khalili** and extending from the gate known as **Bab Zuwayla** in the south to **Bab al-Futuh** in the north, remains astonishingly intact both in structure and in atmosphere, the medieval city nonpareil in all the world. Its walls and area were extended by Saladin, a Kurdish general in the service of the Abbasid Caliph in Baghdad. Foreign failures and the failure of the Nile itself led to the weakening of the Fatimid dynasty which trembled in confusion before the onslaught of the First Crusade. In triumphing over the armies of the West, Saladin established his own empire in Egypt and Syria and his own Ayyubid dynasty which ruled from 1171 to 1250. Orthodoxy was re-established and the Citadel begun, the redoubt of power and the centre of government throughout the troubled centuries of Mameluke and Ottoman rule.

Mameluke magnificence

Saladin's Ayyubid successors, however, relied increasingly on their slave militia, the Bahri Mamlukes. (*Mameluke* means white slave, while *bahri* means riverine and refers to their barracks on the island of Roda; these were mostly Turks and Mongols. The later Burgi Mamelukes, mostly Circassian, were quartered in the Citadel, hence *burg*.) The Mamelukes soon became an indispensible elite and successive sultans rose from their number, legitimising their authority more by the blood on their hands than the blood in their veins. The Mamelukes ruled Egypt until the Ottoman domination in 1517. In spite of the violent and repressive character of Mameluke rule, they enriched the city with their architecture, their most outstanding monuments the **Mosque of Sultan Hassan** and the **Mausoleum of Qaytbay**.

The Ottomans

Around 1300 the island of Gezira was formed as the Nile shifted westwards but the city remained largely within its old boundaries right through the Ottoman period, its architecture following traditional styles with only a few baroque exceptions inspired by the mosques of Istanbul. As a province of the Ottoman Empire, Egypt was ruled by a Turkish governor housed in the Citadel who delegated most of his authority. Though no longer providing sultans, the Mamelukes perpetuated their slave aristocracy by levees of Christian youths from the Caucasus. But their power now was chaotic and rapacious. What the Turks did not take, the Mamelukes did, and Egypt suffered from famine and disease, its population falling to two million compared to eight million in Roman times.

The brief French occupation of Egypt, from 1798 to 1801,

Napoleon and the Westernisation of Cairo

was to have a profound effect on Cairo. Napoleon stayed in what was still then a country district, on the site where the old Shepheard's Hotel was later built, overlooking the Ezbekieh lake, subsequently the Ezbekieh Gardens, only recently ruined by having a main street cut through the middle and flyover amputate one side. While reorganising the government, introducing the first printing press, launching a balloon and installing windmills on the Moqattam Hills, Napoleon also planned Parisian boulevards.

When Mohammed Ali finally massacred the Mamelukes in 1811, founding a dynasty which ended only with the abdication of Farouk in 1952, he proceeded with the Westernisation of Cairo which saw the canal filled in and the great swaths of Sharia el Muski and Sharia el Qalaa (formerly Sharia Mohammed Ali) mow down long rows of the medieval city. Fortunately, however, most of the modernising of Cairo — those circles and radiating avenues you see from the air — took place on the virgin land that the Nile provided when it settled in its present bed.

Orientation

It is in this newer, Westernised part of Cairo that we can start our orientation.

What now passes for the centre of town — for foreigners, anyway — is **Midan el Tahrir**, or Liberation Square, bounded by the Egyptian Museum to the north and the Nile Hilton to the west, with a madhouse of a bus terminus slap in the middle and a new metro station dug beneath. Hot, noisy, characterless and thick with exhaust fumes, Midan el Tahrir is among the more recent schemes to bring Cairo up to date. It was created after the 1952 revolution on the site of a British barracks, the Qasr el Nil, and at the same time powers of compulsory purchase were used to cut the **Corniche el Nil** through the many embassy and villa gardens to the south, the new roadway extending clear down to Maadi and Helwan.

South along the corniche to Garden city

A short walk along the corniche are the Semiramis Intercontinental and Shepheards — though the famous Shepheard's Hotel of the past, whose guest list included General Gordon and Sir Richard Burton and where anyone who was anyone was seen on the terrace drinking four o'clock tea, was located near the Ezbekieh Gardens and was burnt down by demonstrators in 1952. Further south along the river is the convoluted pattern of **Garden City**, a pleasant residential district of treelined streets.

Immediately to the south of Midan el Tahrir is the Mugamaa, the suitably massive headquarters of the state administration, and next to it are the American University in Cairo and the National Assembly. Behind the American University, in Sharia Mansur, is the small Bab el Luq station for commuter trains to Maadi and Helwan, and convenient too for visiting Old Cairo. Going east beyond the campus and the station you come to Abdin Palace, formerly a residence of King Farouk, now partly a museum and partly the offices of the President of the Republic.

North to Midan Ramses

To the north of Midan el Tahrir, beyond the overpass leading to the new 6 October Bridge (named for the 1973 war), is the Ramses Hilton and past that the districts of Bulaq and Shubra. On the corniche here is the Television Tower Building, housing radio and television studios and the press office. Sharia Ramses runs out from the top of Midan el Tahrir and turns northeast, leading to **Midan Ramses** with more elevated walkways and a colossal statue of Ramses II brought from Memphis in 1955. Here you will find the Mahattat Ramses or Bab el Hadeed, the main Cairo railway station for trains north to Alexandria and south to Luxor and Aswan.

Northeast to downtown

Around Midan el Tahrir and along the streets radiating out from it are numerous airline offices and travel agencies, and extending into the **downtown area** to the northeast several less expensive hotels. This downtown area is bordered by Sharia Ramses to the northwest, Sharia Tahrir to the south and Sharia el Gumhuriya to the west. Parallel to Sharia Ramses is Sharia Champollion with the office of Thomas Cook on the left-hand side just after you leave Midan el Tahrir. Sharia Qasr el Nil heads more eastwards in the direction of the Ezbekieh Gardens, though not quite reaching that far; soon after leaving Midan el Tahrir you will find American Express on the right-hand side. Further on, this street intersects several others at Midan Talaat Harb. Along Sharia Talaat Harb, beginning at Midan el Tahrir and ending at Midan Orabi, are numerous shops, cinemas and eating places — also along Sharias Adli and 26 July running east-west. This is the liveliest area of modern Cairo, particularly on a Thursday night, that is preceding Friday's day of rest.

Until the creation of Midan el Tahrir, the **Ezbekieh Gardens** were the focal point for foreign visitors. The old Shepheard's Hotel stood on the corner of Sharias el Gumhuriya and Alfi at the northwest corner of the gardens; the Continental Savoy on el Gumhuriya overlooking Opera Square, which is immediately to the south of the gardens, is now a dishevelled reminder of those grand days of tourism. The Opera House mysteriously burnt down in 1971; it had been built in 1869, and the Khedive Ismail commissioned Verdi to write *Aida* to celebrate here the opening of the Suez Canal and Egypt's return to the crossroads of the world. In the event, *Aida* was late and *Rigoletto* was performed instead before a glittering international audience which included the Empress Eugénie, wife of Napoleon III. This area around Ezbekieh, though not what it used to be, is — along with the downtown area most adjacent to it — one of the best places to stay for anyone who is serious about exploring the city on foot. It enjoys the ambivalence of being on the edge of modern Cairo and within easy walking distance of the Fatimid city to the east.

Across Ezbekieh Gardens to Islamic Cairo

The development and layout of the medieval **Islamic city** has already been outlined, and the details of its sights will be provided later. Suffice to say for the purpose of orientation that if you walk through the Ezbekieh Gardens you will come to Midan Ataba with its central post office, open 24

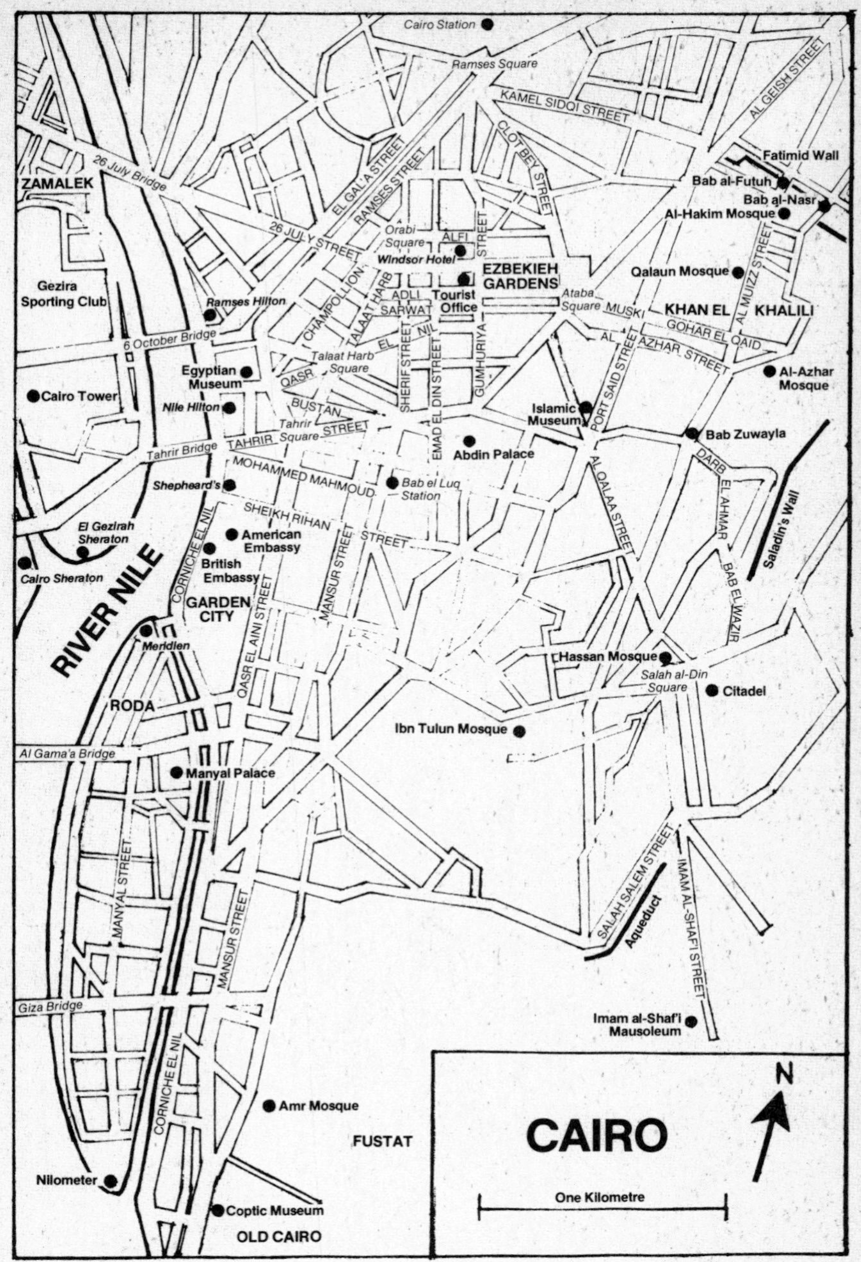

Cairo Station
Ramses Square
KAMEL SIDQI STREET
AL GEISH STREET
CLOT BEY STREET
EL GAL'A STREET
RAMSES STREET
26 July Bridge
ZAMALEK
26 JULY STREET
Orabi Square
ALFI STREET
Windsor Hotel
EZBEKIEH GARDENS
Tourist Office
ADLI
SARWAT
CHAMPOLLION
TALAAT HARB
Fatimid Wall
Bab al-Futuh
Bab al-Nasr
Al-Hakim Mosque
Qalaun Mosque
AL MUIZZ STREET
Ataba Square
MUSKI
KHAN EL KHALILI
GOHAR EL QAID
AL AZHAR STREET
Al-Azhar Mosque
Gezira Sporting Club
Ramses Hilton
6 October Bridge
EL NIL
Talaat Harb Square
QASR
SHERIF STREET
EMAD EL DIN STREET
GUMHURIYA
PORT SAID STREET
Egyptian Museum
Cairo Tower
Nile Hilton
BUSTAN
Tahrir Square
TAHRIR STREET
Islamic Museum
Bab Zuwayla
Tahrir Bridge
Abdin Palace
MOHAMMED MAHMOUD
Bab el Luq Station
Shepheard's
AL QALAA STREET
DARB EL AHMAR
Saladin's Wall
El Gezirah Sheraton
SHEIKH RIHAN STREET
American Embassy
British Embassy
Cairo Sheraton
RIVER NILE
CORNICHE EL NIL
MANSUR STREET
BAB EL WAZIR
GARDEN CITY
QASR EL AINI STREET
Meridien
Hassan Mosque
Salah al-Din Square
Citadel
RODA
Ibn Tulun Mosque
Al Gama'a Bridge
Manyal Palace
MANYAL STREET
MANSUR STREET
SALAH SALEM STREET
Aqueduct
IMAM AL-SHAFI STREET
Giza Bridge
Imam al-Shaf'i Mausoleum
CORNICHE EL NIL
Amr Mosque
FUSTAT
CAIRO
N
One Kilometre
Nilometer
Coptic Museum
OLD CAIRO

hours a day. From here you can press on into the heart of the bazaar area along Sharias el Muski or al-Azhar; or if instead you leave the square along Sharia al Qalaa (formerly Sharia Mohammed Ali and still called that by many) running south you come to the Islamic Museum at the inter section with Sharia Port Said, and still further down you reach the Sultan Hassan Mosque and the Citadel. West of the Citadel is the Mosque of Ibn Tulun.

Returning again to Midan el Tahrir for bearings, there is the Tahrir Bridge which crosses the Nile to the island of **Gezira** (*gezira* is in fact Arabic for island). The central part of Gezira is taken up with the Sporting and Racing Club, next to it rising in lotus motif the 180-metre Cairo Tower, completed in 1962. There is an open observation deck up top, and below it an enclosed coffee lounge and a restaurant of the revolving kind. There are sweeping views of the city and beyond, and this is a good place (easy too on the feet) to establish the topography of Cairo's outlying areas in your mind.

Gezira and the view from the Cairo Tower

The north part of the island is called **Zamalek**, a residential area with the occasional fine old home amidst leafy streets, though more often modern apartments. This part of Gezira can be reached directly from Midan Orabi along Sharia 26 July and across an old metal bridge. Following 26 July (named for the date on which King Farouk abdicated in 1952) across to the west bank of the Nile you see the suburb of **Embaba**, the site where Napoleon fought the so-called Battle of the Pyramids. Far to the north you can see the dark fan of the **Delta**. The suburb of **Heliopolis** is nearer, to the northeast, though the ancient site of Heliopolis is a bit to the north of it. There is nothing to see at the site but an Obelisk of Sesostris I (XII Dyn), and nearby at Matariya a sycamore called the Virgin's Tree, much visited by medieval pilgrims in the belief that under its branches the Holy Family paused for shade before the last leg of their journey to Babylon.

View north towards the Delta

Below you, barges, feluccas and small motor craft pass up and down stream, the prevailing north wind giving the impression by the ripples it causes on the surface of the river that the Nile flows south — you get the same impression from the corniche — though of course it is flowing north, one of the few rivers in the world to do so. The island to the south is **Roda** with the Meridien Hotel magnificently perched like a figurehead upon its northern prow. At its southern tip is a nilometer constructed by the Ummayads in 716. About as far down but on the east bank of the Nile is **Old Cairo** with its Coptic Museum, Coptic churches and a synagogue. Much further south is **Maadi** (along with Zamalek one of the residential areas favoured by Cairo's foreign community), and further on still the industrial town of **Helwan**, both on the east bank. The indiscernible remains of Egypt's ancient capital, **Memphis**, lies on the west bank opposite Helwan.

View south towards Memphis

Sweeping your gaze round to east and west you see how Cairo is bounded on either side by desert. The **Moqattam Hills** are to the east and beyond them the Arabian Plateau. On a spur of the hills is the **Citadel**, distinguished by the

View east towards the Citadel

Bab Zuwayla, by David Roberts in the 1840s

dome of the Mohammed Ali Mosque, and spread before it in dark sand-brown confusion is the old quarter of the city, as though lurking in past centuries behind the higher, more lightly dusted buildings of the new. The windows of the Nile Hilton cast a silvery cubistic pattern of setting sunlight on the river. Away to the west is the pleateau of the Western Desert. Along the west bank of the Nile, opposite Gezira and south of Embaba, are the new suburbs of **Agouza**, **Medinat el Mohandiseen** (Engineers' City) and, around the Cairo Sheraton, **Dokki**. Mrs Sadat continues to live in a villa here overlooking the Nile, just south of the hotel, once President Sadat's official residence. Sharia el Giza runs southwards from the Sheraton to the Zoological Gardens and Cairo University. This is **Giza**, here long before the suburbs began their sprawl along the west bank to the north and out towards the desert escarpment, obliterating the once extensive fields of the fellahin. From the Cairo Tower you can still make out some arable land but it is fast disappearing beneath the furious antlike progress all round you. It is best to be up in the tower at early evening as the sun sets over the Western Desert, the sharp outline of the **Pyramids** as ever marking the great divide between the distant haze of the void and the nearer ephemeral activity of the hive.

View west towards the Pyramids

Itineraries

Each of the following Cairo and Pyramid chapters offers an itinerary, though you might prefer breaking them down into shorter excursions or combining parts of one with another for variety. Cairo itself really deserves at least four full days of your time, and the great line of pyramids stretching along the verge of the Western Desert require another day or two. Therefore the traveller should allow himself a week in Cairo and its environs, but this may not always be possible and so under the **Practical Information** sections following each chapter the essential highlights for an abbreviated tour are listed.

PRACTICAL INFORMATION

ACCOMMODATION

For general information on accommodation, and for details on rates, see the *Accommodation* section in the *Background* chapter.

Sufficient information has been provided in the list below for you to reserve in advance; the telex numbers are particularly useful. You can reserve at any of the international hotel chains through one of their other hotels outside Egypt. Otherwise, at Cairo Airport you should go to the Tourist Information Office or, better yet, Misr Travel, both outside the customs hall, and see if they can help (see *Information*). A useful and free publication is *Cairo by Night and Day*, containing an extensive list of hotels, their amenities and prices. You can pick up a copy at most hotels or at the Tourist Information Offices at the airport or downtown. With this you can do your own hotel hunting, probably running no greater risk than having to visit 2 or 3 hotels before finding something suitable. Often a hotel will volunteer, or can be prevailed upon, to phone around on your behalf, saving legwork and taxi fares.

The following is a selective list of hotels in

the Cairo, Giza (near the Pyramids) and Heliopolis (near the airport) areas:
Nile Hilton (5-star), Midan el Tahrir. Tel: 740777. Telex: 92222 UN. This was the first international hotel built in Egypt (opening ceremonies in 1959 were attended by Nasser and Tito) and the first Hilton in the Middle East; it has become something of an institution. The big international hotels can be soulless, geared to accommodating the largest number of tourists in the smallest possible rooms, but the Nile Hilton was built at a time when this trend had not yet reached its nastiest expression; it can be a very pleasant place to stay and is located right next to the Egyptian Museum, but try to get a Nile-side room. The new Nile Hilton Centre, a 1981 extension, provides further rooms around a garden courtyard and includes also a concentration of travel agencies, airline offices, banks, shops and business facilities, in addition to those already established in the main building. American Express, Avis, Egyptair, Air Sinai, Alitalia, Japan Airlines and Ethiopian Airlines are all represented. The Ibis Café is open 24 hours; the Hilton Pizzeria is good; the Taverne du Champ de Mars, imported stick by stick from Belgium, is very agreeable. There is a first floor restaurant and in winter a rooftop nightclub which moves to the poolside in summer. Also there are tennis courts, a sauna, disco and casino. All rooms are air-conditioned and have colour TV.
Cairo Sheraton (5-star), Midan el Galaa, Dokki. Tel: 983000. Telex: 92041 SHERA UN. A 20-storey tower built in 1970 on the west bank of the Nile across the Tahrir Bridge, this Sheraton is a lively place with all the luxury facilities including a pool, and fine panoramas from its higher rooms. These are decorated continental style, all air-conditioned and with colour TV. The belly dancing is possibly the best at any of the hotels. Egyptair's office here operates at a marginally lower key of pandemonium than those elsewhere in town; also there is an Avis office.
El Gezirah Sheraton (5-star), at the southern tip of Gezira island, PO Box 34, Zamalek. Tel: 402593. Telex: 94242 SHSLS UN. This 27-storey round tower opened in 1984 and commands the most spectacular location in Cairo. Deluxe suites reached by a separate lift, with butler service and their own coffee lounge and registration desk occupy the top 8 floors. Along with the usual facilities, there is a large sundeck and marina on the Nile.
Meridien Le Caire (5-star), Roda island, PO Box 2288. Tel: 845444. Telex: 325 HOMER UN. Reservations can be made through Air France. This shares with the El Gezirah Sheraton the finest views along the Nile and has a French flavour: boutiques, bidets, rotisserie, good coffee and pastry in the 24-hour Fontana Café, French and Middle Eastern restaurants; also outdoor and indoor pools, a gym and solarium. Access is by private bridge from the Corniche el Nil to the north tip of Roda. All rooms air-conditioned, colour TV. Avis office here.
Shepheard's (5-star), Corniche el Nil. Tel: 33800. Telex: 379 SHEPOT UN. Built in 1956 to recapture the glory of the old Shepheard's, the new does not succeed, though it has some architectural charm and the rooms are spacious and well furnished. Those on the preferred Nile side have ceiling to floor picture windows and balconies. The 24-hour café is very comfortable; the restaurant is on the rooftop, a bar too, with good views of the river; and there are shops and a 24-hour bank. Rooms are air-conditioned. No swimming pool. This is more like a grand 4-star hotel, and the prices are 4-star.
Hyatt El Salam (5-star), 69 Sharia Abdel Hamid Badawi, Heliopolis. Tel: 692155. Telex: 92184 SHAMCO UN. If you must stay out by the airport (8 kms; to Cairo 18 kms — free shuttle bus to both), this is the most elegant choice. Plush rooms, air-conditioned, sound-proofed, with colour TV; restaurant, bar, café, disco, casino, cinema, business centre, pool, tennis, shopping arcade — almost a self-contained resort set in manicured grounds.
Green Pyramids (5-star), Sharia al-Ahram, PO Box 22, Giza. Tel: 852600. Telex: 93701 GPHOT UN. Opened in 1982 after the Swiss Nova Park group took over Egyptian actor Yussef Wahby's bizarre Swiss chalet style villa and added separate wings. This is a small (72-room) hotel set back from the main road to the Pyramids amidst peaceful gardens; the service is superb, the facilities personalised, the rooms generously proportioned, each with garden balconies, and the food is excellent. There are 2 luxury suites in the villa itself, with its original furniture and round black baths with gold taps. All rooms are air-conditioned, with colour TV. There are several restaurants including one by the poolside, a bar and disco. The one drawback is that it is neither in town nor by the Pyramids and so a journey is always required, which in rush hours can be

tedious — and so rates are a bit lower than 5-star.

Mena House Oberoi (5-star), Sharia al-Ahram, Giza. Tel: 853789. Telex: 92316 OB UN. An historic hotel, originally a khedevial hunting lodge (converted to a hotel in 1869) and the place where Churchill and Roosevelt initiated the D-Day plan. 11 kms from town, though linked by a regular free hotel bus service, the Mena House is convenient rather for the Pyramids (across the road) and as an edge of desert resort with golf course, riding stables and swimming pool — and with ready access to the nightlife along the Pyramids Road. Along with the old Shepheard's, this was one of the great hotels of Cairo, and the older section, decorated in Arab style and with superb views of the Pyramids, is *the* place to stay. A new section, Mena Gardens, has been added (1976), pleasant but without the old style and with less favoured views of the Pyramids — rates here are less than 5-star. All have air conditioning, colour TV. Budget Rent-a-Car office here.

Jolie Ville (4-star), Alexandria Desert Road, Giza. Tel: 855510. Telex: 92567 UN. The road to Alexandria via the desert turns off just before reaching the Mena House and is rapidly turning into a hotel strip. The Jolie Ville is 12 kms from central Cairo, and you must rely on fare-charging limos, taxis or public buses. Avis has a rental station here. Modern bungalows are set in beautiful gardens around a pool; there are views of the Pyramids. Also there are tennis courts, a children's pool, a bar, café and good restaurant. All rooms are air-conditioned.

Bel Air (4-star), Moqattam Hills, PO Box 996. Tel: 922685. Telex: 93457 BETEL UN. Overlooking the Citadel and Islamic Cairo from the east, 5 kms from Midan el Tahrir, free bus into town. A new complex (1983) of pavilions set in landscaped gardens; rooms air-conditioned, with TV; disco, pool, tennis courts. Car hire desk.

Atlas (4-star), 2 Sharia el Gumhuriya, near Opera Midan. Tel: 918311. Telex: 92564 UN. Located in the former centre of town, before Midan el Tahrir came into being, and convenient for downtown and Islamic Cairo. There is a rooftop restaurant and nightclub; the service is good, the rooms clean and, in winter, better heated than most older hotels. All rooms have air conditioning and TV.

President (4-star), 22 Sharia Taha Hussein, Zamalek. Tel: 816751. Telex: 93655 PRES UN. In a quiet residential area of many embassies and diplomatic residences towards the northern end of Gezira island. Rooms are simply furnished, large and clean; all have private baths and some have TV and a balcony. There is a restaurant, bar and the lively Cellar Pub in the basement. The service is good. Hertz has an office here.

Windsor (3-star), 19 Sharia Alfi. Tel: 915810. For those who enjoy genuine character and do not want to pay through the nose for a room in Cairo, this is the best. Well-situated in downtown Cairo, an old-style hotel in a good state of preservation with high-ceilinged rooms for ventilation, much old wooden furnishing, excellent service, good food and great atmosphere. Rooms with either shower or bath.

Continental Savoy (3-star), Opera Midan, near Ezbekieh Gardens. Tel: 911322. Telex: 92726 EGYPTL UN (ref Continental Savoy). Like the old Shepheard's, once nearby, this was a favourite with fashionable British travellers. Now rather frayed at the edges, but once through the lobby and up to the 3 sprawling floors of rooms some of the old atmosphere is with you: cavernous corridors, large high-ceilinged rooms and wooden floors. All rooms are air-conditioned, most have shower or bath.

Cosmopolitan (3-star), Sharia Ibn Taalab, off Sharia Qasr el Nil. Tel: 755715. Telex: 7451 COSMO UN. Tucked away in a quiet street downtown, this is an old traditional hotel nicely refurbished in 1983. There is a restaurant, bar, coffee shop and bank. All rooms are air-conditioned with bath.

Horris (3-star), 5 Sharia 26 July. Tel: 910855. A recently renovated downtown hotel with 14th floor restaurant and clean, bright rooms, bath or shower, some with air conditioning.

New Horus House (3-star), 21 Sharia Ismail Mohammed, Zamalek. Tel: 705682. In the middle of the Zamalek residential area on Gezira island, this is a small, friendly and very pleasant hotel. Restaurant, bar, café; air conditioning in all rooms.

National (2-star), 30 Sharia Talaat Harb. Tel: 46081. Until the end of the Second World War this was one of Cairo's better hotels and the bar was something of a hangout; old and worn now, you should check your room first, particularly the bathroom — these can sometimes be grotty. Conveniently located between Midans Talaat Harb and Tahrir. Rooms

with a view over the back alley cost less.
New Hotel (2-star), 21 Sharia Adli. Tel: 9780. Not far from the downtown Tourist Information Office, this hotel is a cut above the National, with large, simply furnished and clean rooms — and clean bathrooms.
El Hussein (2-star), Midan el Hussein, by the Mosque of Sayyidna al-Hussein on the edge of Khan el Khalili. Right in the heart of the Fatimid city and with Fishawi's tea house nearby, this is the best located hotel for those wanting to be amidst the sights and atmosphere of Islamic Cairo. Restaurant on roof with superb view over minarets and domes of medieval Cairo.
Happy Joe's (2-star), a riverboat tied up opposite 10 Sharia el Nil, Giza (near Giza Bridge). Tel: 721252. Telex: 94114 BATRAN UN. Air-conditioned rooms, restaurant.
Tulip (2-star), 3 Midan Talaat Harb. Tel: 766884. Adequate hotel conveniently situated downtown.
Balmoral House (2-star), 157 Sharia 26 July, Zamalek. Tel: 800543. An adequate hotel on the main thoroughfare across Gezira island. Air conditioning in some rooms: restaurant, café.

Garden City House (1-star), 23 Sharia Kamal el Din Salah. Tel: 28126. Near the new Semiramis Intercontinental, this is the best value in Cairo and one of the most popular and difficult places to get a room. It is best to write to Mme Georgetta Amato,who runs this family-style hotel, a month in advance, stating precisely your requirements and date of arrival, and specifically requesting confirmation if desired. From outside there is a small sign 3 storeys up; the rooms are there and on the floor above; you take the lift. The place is well-run, clean and friendly, and the food is excellent. Some rooms face the river, most have balconies. There are not many single rooms.
Golden Hotel (1-star), 13 Sharia Talaat Harb. Tel: 41159. Well located between Midans el Tahrir and Talaat Harb, the Golden has a good reputation amongst young travellers. Mr Fares Sarufim is a friendly and well-informed man, a great help in advising how to get everywhere cheaply. There is a storage room for leaving gear while travelling. Rather than turn anyone away, 'Mr Fares' will sometimes cope with overflows by offering dorm-style accommodation at a reduced price.

There are 2 **youth hostels** in the Cairo area:
El Manyal Youth Hostel, Sharia Abdel Aziz, on Roda island near Kobri el Gamaa (University Bridge). Tel: 840729.
Kohinoor Youth Hostel, 8 Sharia Shoukri, off Sharia al-Ahram, Giza. Tel: 852480.

Hostels charge around LE1 per night but are often full.

EATING PLACES

You can spend a fortune or a few piastres on a meal in Cairo, and choose between the world's cuisines. Not only restaurants, but coffee shops, tea rooms and snack bars are included here; though places which also provide entertainment will be found under the *Entertainment* heading further on.

Western style food is served at all the hotels, regardless of category. Only the restaurants at a few major hotels, however, are worth going out of your way to dine at. The Cairo Sheraton's **Aladin** (Tel: 983000) and the Meridien's **La Palme d'Or** (French cuisine) (Tel: 845444) are the best. The **Swissair Restaurant** (Tel: 981487), a short walk south of the Cairo Sheraton along Sharia el Nil, has an expensive formal restaurant upstairs, a less expensive informal restaurant downstairs (French cuisine, some Swiss specialities). Reservations are recommended at each of these restaurants. More moderately-priced Western-style food is found at the following:
Estoril, 12 Sharia Talaat Harb, in a passageway running to Sharia Qasr el Nil, near American Express. An older restaurant, a bit threadworn in its gentility, with an interesting clientele.
Caroll, 12 Sharia Qasr el Nil, off Midan Talaat Harb. A small and congenial place particularly favoured by foreign residents, it has consistently good food and service, and generous portions.
Arabesque, 6 Sharia Qasr el Nil. Good food and service, pleasant surroundings, includes a small bar. There is a gallery of Egyptian artists adjoining.

Specialty restaurants offer one fare, with variations, though alternatives may be available:
The Nile Pharaoh, a cruising restaurant got up like a pharaonic sailing barge. Oberoi Hotels for reservations, Tel: 855444. Expensive.
Scarabee, similar to the above, run by Wagons-Lits. Reservations to Helio Tours, Tel: 877708. Expensive.
Kasr el Rachid, Meridien Hotel, Roda. Extremely expensive but delicious Middle Eastern dishes. In the evenings there is an

oriental buffet. Reservations recommended. Tel: 845444.
The Farm, 23 Sharia Maryutia, off Sharia al-Ahram (Pyramids Road) — signposted. Rustic setting, though fashionable. The speciality is roast lamb. Food and service are excellent. Reservations recommended. Tel: 851870. Moderately priced.
Vue des Pyramides, at the southeast corner of the Pyramids Road/Alexandria Desert Road junction. Casual outdoor dining, with Cheops' Pyramid close by. The speciality is grilled and fried fish, though there are meat and non-meat dishes too. Very pleasant garden atmosphere, especially recommended towards sundown. Inexpensive to moderate.
Pizzeria, Hilton Hotel, Midan el Tahrir. The atmosphere is pleasant, the food good and not too expensive.
Taverna, 3 Sharia Alfi, near Midan Orabi. Principally Cypriot, though other dishes too. Their speciality is shrimp. Inexpensive to moderate.
Indian Tea Centre, off the passageway at 23 Sharia Talaat Harb. Primarily a place to come for tea and an afternoon snack, but also serving light meals in the early evening. Inexpensive.
Sofar, 21 Sharia Adli. Syrian and Lebanese specialities, though short on atmosphere. Inexpensive to moderate.

Egyptian-style restaurants do not usually impress from the outside, and may not be very atmospheric inside; they are to be judged by their fare, which is a mixture of native tradition and Egyptian versions of Turkish, Levantine, Greek, Italian and French cuisine. Some of the better places follow:
Abu Shakra, 69 Sharia Qasr el Aini, at the south end, about 3 kms from Midan el Tahrir, near the bridge crossing over to Roda at the Manyal Palace. The epitome of its type, in marble and alabaster — also a strict Moslem establishment, serving no alcoholic beverages and closed Fridays and during Ramadan. The specialities are kofta and kebab, though sometimes pigeon and grilled chicken are also available. Usually (though not always) the food is excellent. Inexpensive to moderate.
El Dahan, in Khan el Khalili, next door to the El Hussein Hotel. Also specialising in kofta and kebab. Not so much to be searched out, as to dine at if you are already wandering about the bazaar. Inexpensive.
El Shimy, 45 Midan Orabi. Friendly atmosphere and varied Egyptian menu. Inexpensive to moderate.
El Hatti, 8 Midan Halim, behind the Cicurel department store on Sharia 26 July, and virtually next door to the Horris Hotel. Unusually for an Egyptian restaurant, El Hatti sparkles — mirrors cover the walls and brilliant chandeliers hang from the high ceiling. The service, food and atmosphere all make this a worthwile place to search for. The speciality here is roast lamb. Inexpensive to moderate.
Fatarane el Tahrir, 166 Sharia el Tahrir, 2 blocks from Midan el Tahrir and on the right. The sole meal is *feteer*, a kind of pancake filled with your choice of meat, cheese, eggs, nuts, etc. Cost depends on size and filling. Inexpensive.
Filfila, 15 Sharia Hoda Sharawi, off Midan el Tahrir. You pass through the kitchen at the front and into the garden, taking your seat around a slice of tree trunk serving as a table. The speciality is fool, in all its varieties of preparation, though meat dishes, quail, ice cream, etc, are all served. Alas, the place is very popular with tourist groups and is sometimes overwhelmed by the busload. Inexpensive to moderate.

Coffee shops, tea rooms and drink and snack bars abound, convenient for resting, cooling off and perhaps a light meal during the day:

The cafés in the major hotels have the advantage of being open 24 hours; also, they are air-conditioned. There is a minimum charge. The **Fontana Café** at the Meridien is marvellous for its Nile views, while the **Arous el Nil** in the Cairo Sheraton does the best hamburgers and shakes. The Hilton's **Isis Coffee Shop**, though conveniently situated, will disappoint the connoisseur. On the other hand, the Hilton does get credit for its **Taverne du Champ de Mars**, a fin de siècle Brussels tavern, dismantled and reconstructed on the ground floor of the hotel. Beer, spirits and snacks are served from noon to 2am, and a reasonably-priced buffet meal at evening.

Numerous cafés line the banks of the Nile on Roda and Gezira islands. These are garden affairs, where beer, tea, sandwiches and snacks are served. Otherwise:
Cairo Tower, Gezira island. Coffee, tea, beer, a snack are all available up top, at a slight surcharge for having got it up there, but the atmosphere is pleasant, the views wonderful — though half the time, it seems, the lift does not work or the platform does not revolve, and so the tower is closed.
Brazilian Coffee Shop, 38 Sharia Talaat Harb and 12 Sharia 26 July. Open from 7am to midnight, this is where to come if

you care about coffee. The beans are freshly ground (unground beans can be taken away), the espresso, cappucino, café au lait — or almost any other way of drinking coffee — are excellent.

L'Americaine, corner of Sharias Talaat Harb and 26 July. A large stand-up restaurant, serving coffee, juices, pastries and ice cream.

The Indian Tea Centre, already mentioned under specialty restaurants — this is principally a tea room, with imported Indian teas and Indian-style pastries.

Groppi has three branches, at Midan Talaat Harb, on Sharia Adli, and in Heliopolis. It is **Garden Groppi**, as the one at the Midan el Opera end of Sharia Adli is called, that was so famous amongst British servicemen during the Second World War, and its outdoor café remains a pleasant place to sit by day or evening. There is a delicatessen here too, selling cold cuts, pastas, jams and bottles of wine.

Lappas, 17 Sharia Qasr el Nil, is a Groppi-like place of Groppi-like vintage, popular amongst those who do not want to be disturbed.

Café Riche, on Sharia Talaat Harb near the midan and next to the Brazilian Coffee Shop at No. 38, with a nondescript indoor restaurant (very cheap) and an outdoor café, frequented by Cairo's literati and where Nasser, Sadat and other officers met while planning the 1952 coup.

In wandering around the streets, either in modern or Islamic Cairo, you will encounter numerous simple establishments for having a snack, even a meal, and certainly a refreshing mint tea. There are also peripatetic street-vendors, good for drinks though perhaps less so for food which may not be particularly clean. In buying anything to eat, always be sure the place has running water — if so, a modicum of hygiene can be counted upon. Forget the Cokes and 7-Ups for a change; instead pause for fresh guava, mango, orange, sugar cane or strawberry juice (after you have drunk it you scoop the strawberries from the glass with a spoon). Or have a koshary, a mixed dish of rice, beans, macaroni, with various spices and sauces, usually hot (you can say no), sprinkled on. One koshary place, mentioned here by way of introduction to the dish and because its appearance is reassuringly clean and modern (before you get accustomed to sampling the fare in more uncompromising places) is the **Lux**, Sharia 26 July near the intersection with Sharia Sherif. You can have a meal here for well under LE1. Finally, the café to go to when wandering round Khan el Khalili is the famous **Fishawi's** in a small alley near the Sayyidna Hussein Mosque. Here you sit on cane chairs at marble-topped tables in a narrow passage lined with mirrors, and as coffees pass by on brass trays you are propositioned with a shoeshine, a device for making catcalls, a woman's song accompanied by a tambourine, and necklaces of jasmine flowers, their scent thick on the night air.

ENTERTAINMENT

Nightclubs catering to a preponderantly Arab clientele will keep to an oriental show, ie one or more belly dancers, an Egyptian singer and several variety acts. But at places which cater also, even mainly, to Western tourists (the major hotels and the nightclubs along the Pyramids Road and in the desert), a belly dancer will share the bill with Western acts. The Sheratons, Hiltons, the Meridien and the Mena House all have combined oriental/Western shows, with the Cairo Sheraton's **Aladin** nightclub usually presenting the best belly dancer in town. Shows start at around 11pm, but dinner may be served as early as 9.30. Reservations are recommended. The night will prove expensive, with cover charge, drinks and obligatory dinner. At some of the hotels, on some nights of the week, a buffet meal is offered instead, and this is cheaper.

At the Nile Hilton's **Tropicana**, by the pool, the strings of the oriental orchestra are warming to their drones and squeals and Nadia Hamda, one of the best belly dancers in Cairo, shows what the human body can do without seeming to try. But a few minutes later she is followed by the Las Vegas Extravaganza, half a dozen European and American girls with very little on twirling and leaping about, trying to be sexy. The comparison between them and Nadia is embarrassing. The Western conception of dancing, at least as expressed in this miserable programme, is to throw oneself about as though somehow velocity had any meaning other than to disguise a lack of sensuality. Nadia on the other hand knows how to stand still, to flick and ripple her body like some night plant licking up the moonlight and starlight, curling and uncurling to the faint brush of cosmic rays so that all the dark sky and Nadia pulse as one.

For more of this, in different surroundings, go to the **Bateau Omar Khayyam**, a fine old dahabeah tied up by the Sporting Club at Gezira. Cosy, with agreeable oriental decor, perfect for dining quietly on the Nile — except that some rock band is likely to shatter all tranquility between the belly dancing sets — though the dancing here can be superb. And in a desert tent beyond the Pyramids is **Sahara City**; there are many others out this way, all neon signposted and advertised (see under *Information* below).

I prefer the strictly Arab places, though the performances can be uneven, or downright bad. There is, for example, the **New Arizona** in Sharia Alfi, with millionth-rate belly dancers, fat and ugly, though often a good Egyptian singer and on one occasion a marvellously laid back and funny finger-cymbal player. Dinner is not obligatory; there is an entrance charge and you are expected to buy a drink. Quite a few notches up though moderately priced is the **Scheherazade**, also in Sharia Alfi (opposite the New Arizona):

The audience is predominantly Arab, and these are almost all men, though a few women and even children may be present. A few Europeans are there and bring their women: a great mistake since these now sit prune-faced throughout the performance. First a series of singers and bands from all over the Islamic world, oriental and African rhythms, wailing and plaintive drone of male singers, marvellous squeaky violins, tinkling harpsichords, also flutes, bass, tambourines. Belly dancer comes on, dead ringer for Rita Hayworth. Less squeaks and tinkles; now there are deep strokes of violins, pulsation of drums, the low hum of the saxophone. No bumps and grinds to detract from a performance of incredible sensuality, a slow motion of sea waves and sand dunes, the slightest flick an orgasm.

The Arab audience takes it generally with a warm, contained appreciation. The odd whistle, applause, a shout at some particular movement of the hips — or a shout sometimes when there is no movement: when almost nothing happens and she is at her most erotic. The perfectly still position: arms arabesqued, one leg extended, the hips at an angle, a continuous ripple running up and down her body and then one flank is gyrated ever so slightly, like the minimal, most controlled movement of a toreador before the horns of the bull. The music stops, the band claps in a flamenco rhythm, Arab after Arab comes up on the stage with gifts of flowers, flower necklaces, glasses of whiskey (which she knocks back in mid-movement), cigarettes and money, every one of them a desert king, but she is master of their fantasies.

Fire-breathers, circuses, puppet shows, belly dancers: this Arab patronage of the popular mysteries. And so, after this dance, with as much attention as it had accorded to the former, the audience watches a dull Lebanese riding a bicycle across a wire 2 metres above the stage.

At **discos** you skip live entertainment, Western or oriental, and twitch instead to the vibrating recorded music. Some of the best places for this are **Jackie's** at the Nile Hilton and **Regine's** (of Paris, London and New York fame) at the El Gezirah Sheraton (but both of these are open only to members or residents and their guests); also the **Saddle Room** at the Mena House Oberoi, and **After Eight**, 6 Sharia Qasr el Nil, a popular place where reservations are recommended (Tel: 43455); closed July and August.

Casinos (admission only to non-Egyptians) are found at the Meridien, the Cairo Sheraton and the Nile Hilton. Play is in US dollars, free drinks for punters, doors close at dawn.

Concerts and theatrical events with Western content are often sponsored by the Egyptian Ministry of Culture in cooperation with the cultural sections of one or other of the foreign embassies. The **Oum Khalsoum Theatre**, Sharia el Nil, at Agouza, just south of the Zamalek bridge, has nightly performances (October-March) in Arabic by local music and dance companies, mostly folkloric.

Cinemas are mostly located around Midans Talaat Harb and Orabi, and several are likely to be showing English-language films, subtitled in Arabic. The *Egyptian Gazette* carries listings. The problem is that the Egyptians, being able to read the subtitles, do not have to listen to the dialogue. Instead the audience chatters throughout the film, which often has its sound turned down anyway, so that you will be lucky to hear much of it — perhaps not so important when considering the entertainment potential of the audience. Tickets are cheap, and all seats are reserved. You should buy your tickets several hours in advance of the performance you intend seeing, as seats go very quickly.

It is the **popular mysteries** — the man staging a backstreet show with a snake and a guinea pig or a marriage procession of loud cries and ribald song strolling down the middle of a road — that are most entertaining in Cairo. Two fixtures appealing at this level are the **Egyptian National Circus**, a good one-ring affair usually found at Agouza, south of the Zamalek bridge; and the **Cairo Puppet Theatre** in Ezbekieh Gardens, its season from October to May, with nightly performances at 6.30 as well as Friday and Sunday shows at 11am. The puppet shows are in Arabic, which hardly matters as it is easy to follow the action, and which anyway adds to the enchantment of the productions, appealing to adults and children alike.

It is probably best to approach the son et lumiere at the Pyramids on this level too, therefore so much the better if you go to the Arabic programme, not an English-language one. The **Sound and Light** show (say this to a taxi driver and you will be taken straight there) starts at 7.30pm; there is no performance on Friday. Usually, English-language programmes are on Mondays, Wednesdays and Saturdays. The Arabic programme is on Thursday. There are also programmes in French and German. Seating for the Sound and Light is facing the Sphinx; if you do not go by taxi, you can take the 800 or 900 bus from Midan el Tahrir, terminating at the Mena House Oberoi, and then backtrack on foot through the village at the edge of the escarpment, a 15 minutes walk — though you can shorten the hike by getting off the bus along the Pyramids Road when you see (on your left) the sign for the Sound and Light, about 1000 metres before the Mena House Hotel.

After all that high- and low-lifing, you might like some recreation. The Gezira Sporting Club admits non-members to its clay **tennis courts** and its **swimming pool**. Or go for a sundown sail in a **felucca**; these can be hired by Shepheard's Hotel.

SHOPPING

While shopping at the bazaar stalls is a matter of haggling over prices, shops and department stores in the modern part of Cairo sell at **fixed prices**. Except in shops found in the arcades of major hotels, prices are usually marked in Arabic numerals, and are often stated in piastres (100PT = LE1). So an item priced at 1000 is likely to be 1000PT or LE10. Usually, common sense will tell whether piastres or pounds is intended.

Opening hours for most shops are from 9.30 or 10am to 1 or 1.30pm, and from 4.30 or 5pm to 7.30 or 8pm, though some may remain open continuously throughout the day, particularly in Khan el Khalili. Most are closed Saturday evenings and Sundays, while some may close on Fridays. During Ramadan, shops hours are likely to be from 9.30am to 3.30pm and from 8 to 10pm or even later.

In the bazaars, price is usually what you agree on after a bout of **bargaining**. A stallkeeper will always ask more than he expects to get; the traditional response is to offer half as much. After several minutes, perhaps half an hour, a price midway between the extremes is agreed. That is the traditional way, but the visitor's impatience or foolishness can spoil the market, traders asking for and getting far more than their goods are worth. This is particularly true of hawkers at places like the Pyramids, and every now and again it is worth making a ridiculous counter-offer, perhaps only one-tenth of the asking price ... and finding it immediately accepted.

Hawkers at tourist sights are taking advantage of their isolation and yours in demanding exorbitant amounts. The virtue of a bazaar is that there is plenty of competition. In Khan el Khalili you will find all the copperware, all the spices, all the wood and ivory inlay, etc, in the same area, and you should browse around, examining the goods, asking the prices, getting a feel for the market. Try to be dispassionate; the more you want something the more you are likely to pay for it. A good technique is to bargain first over something you do *not* want and then casually to start bargaining over what you do want — almost as though you did not want anything and just bargained for the sport. It *is* a sport, and there are rules as well as tricks of the game. Your first extreme counter-offer will be laughed at and you may feel silly; do not worry, that is part of the game. After a few offers and counter-offers, walk out. If the shop or stall owner stops you, it means he thinks there is still a deal to be made; if he does not you may have learnt you are aiming at too low a price — go back later, or go to another shop, with an adjusted view of the item's worth. The essence of a bargain, of course, is not to arrive at some formula fraction of the original asking price, but to feel that you have paid the right price, a price you could not have bettered elsewhere, a price that makes the item worth it to you.

Clothing will be found in the hotel shops, shops in the downtown area (Sharias Talaat Harb and 26 July, for example), boutiques in Zamalek, Heliopolis and downtown, and in the big department stores: **Chemla**, 11 Sharia 26 July, where low prices are more important than quality; **Cicurel**, 3 Sharia 26 July, for quality and higher prices; **Omar Effendi**, a good department store with several branches — on Sharia Talaat Harb just off Midan el Tahrir, on Sharia Adli near Sharia Talaat Harb, and also at Heliopolis and Dokki. Sizes are continental.

Shoes are found in the plethora of shoeshops along Sharias Qasr el Nil, Talaat Harb and 26 July.

The **galabiyya**, the full-length traditional garment of Egyptian men, is popular with both male and female visitors as comfortable casual wear. Fancier versions can also serve as evening wear for women. There are three basic styles: the *baladi* or peasant style, with wide sleeves and a low rounded neckline; the *saudi* style, more form-fitting, with a high-buttoned neck and cuffed sleeves; and the *efrangi* or foreign style, looking like a shirt with collar and cuffs but reaching all the way down to the floor. Several shops sell galabiyyas along Sharia Talaat Harb between Midan Talaat Harb and Sharia 26 July, and also the department stores. Fancier ones are at **Ammar**, 26 Sharia Qasr el Nil, and at **Atlas** in Khan el Khalili. Both are fixed price. Atlas is on Sharia Badestan which is reached by walking north along the main Fatimid street (Sharia Muizz which goes from Bab Zuwayla to Bab al-Futuh), passing across Sharia al-Azhar and across Sharia el Muski (properly known here as Sharia Gohar el Qaid), until you see a narrow alley on your right, marked by two upright metal poles rising about a metre out of the ground: turn into it, and when it ends turn right and then left. You are now on Sharia Badestan, a main street of the bazaar, but dark and so narrow it is closed to cars. Along the left is Atlas. Mrs Sadat is known to buy her evening wear here; for all the difficulty of reaching it deep in the bazaar, the place has an international reputation.

Fabric, either for galabiyyas (Atlas and other good stores will tailor-make them for you, either from their own or your fabric) or to take home, is found in variety and quality at **Omar Effendi** (see *Clothing* above); **Salon Vert**, Sharia Qasr el Nil; or **Ouf** in el Mashhad el Hussein — heading south along Sharia Muizz and approaching Sharia al-Azhar, take the first right after Sharia el Muski/Sharia Gohar el Qaid and the first left; Ouf is on the right down this alley. Each of these stores also sell off-the-peg galabiyyas.

Weavings, carpets, tents and tapestries require further adventures if you want the best. In fact, Egypt is not particularly well-known for carpets, and if you are going to Aswan you should look around there first for small rugs and weavings. Old rugs are from time to time auctioned off, and you should look in the *Egyptian Gazette* for announcements. Carpets and rugs are found in Khan el Khalili and al **El Fatarani** and **Kazarouni**, both on Sharia Qasr el Nil.

Tent-making, on the other hand, is a Cairene speciality, and you should go to the **Street of the Tentmakers** immediately south of Bab Zuwayla. There are 6 or 7 workshops along this covered section of medieval Cairo's major north-south street, creating beautiful applique tents used at mosques or street festivals (and funerals). Some are decorated with scenes of pharaonic or Islamic themes, but the best have abstract arabesque designs or intricate calligraphy. Not that you have to buy a tent; they are made in sections and you can buy a piece about big enough to serve as a pillow cover.

Two villages outside Cairo are centres of the best tapestry-weaving in Egypt. **Harraniyya**, about 3 kms along the canal road from Giza to Saqqara, was developed by the late Ramses Wissa Wassef; he taught the children how to card, dye and spin their own wool, and weave it into tapestries of their own design, usually village scenes, primitive and boldly coloured. Harraniyya's tapestries are now world-famous, and the workshop, on the right of the road, continues to be run by Wassef's wife. Tapestries cannot actually be bought here, however; for that you must go to **Senouhi**, 54 Sharia Abdel Khalek Sarwat, 5th floor, in downtown Cairo. This is also one of the best places to buy jewellery and (genuine) antiques. The other village is **Kardassa**, about 3 kms off Sharia al-Ahram (turn right several hundred metres before the Mena House at the Pyramids, at the sign for Andrea's Restaurant). Here you can buy tapestries, and also bedspreads, rugs, shirts, dresses and black Bedouin dresses with bright cross-stitching — usually old, with a patchwork look after repairs, and becoming quite expensive and rare.

There are numerous **jewellery** shops in Sharia Abdel Khalek Sarwat (near Garden Groppi) and in the small street leading off it, Sikket el Manakh. And of course, there are numerous jewellers in Mouski and Khan el Khalili. By and large, Egyptian jewellery is disappointing, much of it mimicking the more obvious pharaonic motifs (cartouche, ankh, Eye of Horus), and those of Islamic motif showing little popular imagination — hands and eyes for warding off evil, or as pieces inscribed with 'Allah'. It may seem at first exotic but is limited and grows tiresome, while anything outside these two motifs is usually conceived in bad taste. **Senouhi**, 54 Sharia Abdel Khalek Sarwat, 5th floor, will have the finest selection.

For **contemporary art, sculpture and ceramics**, try Atelier 7 at the Meridien Hotel.

Brass and copper work has long been a Cairo tradition, the standards still high today. The best place for it is in Khan el Khalili along or just off Sharia Muizz, south of the Madrasa of Qalaun. Small plates intended as ornaments and candlesticks, gongs, lamps, mugs and pitchers are the easiest to carry off — though be sure that anything you intend to drink out of is coated on the inside with another metal, like silver, as brass or copper in contact with some substances can be highly poisonous. The finest items, however, are the big brass trays which can serve as table tops (wooden stands are available).

Inlay of **wood and ivory**, and also **leatherwork**, are also plentiful in the bazaar. Egyptian leather is not the best, however. The most common items are handbags, suitcases and hassocks. Also, more interesting than useful or comfortable, are camel saddles (for buying a camel, see below). Wooden trays, boards (including backgammon and chess boards) and boxes inlaid with ivory, mother of pearl and coloured bits of wood are not quite as good as those made in Syria, but are intricate and beautiful enough. Mashrabiyyas, those intricate screens found in old Cairene houses, made from bits of wood fitted together without nails or glue, occasionally come on sale in the bazaars; you may find something at the **Wakala** (or **Okel**) **of el Ghouri** near al-Azhar which is also a craft centre.

Muski **glass**, usually turquoise or dark brown and recognisable by its numerous air bubbles, has been hand-blown in Cairo since the Middle Ages, and is now turned out as ash trays, candlesticks and glasses. It is inexpensive, but also very fragile. The best **nargilehs** (hubbly-bubblies) will have glass, rather than brass, bottoms. For these, try around the Street of the Coppersmiths, south of the Madrasa of Qalaun, and for glass visit the Wakala of el Ghouri.

Alabaster statuettes, also vases and scarabs, are produced and are cheapest in Luxor; **baskets** made of palm fronds are best bought in the Fayyum, though platter-shaped basketry, woven in brilliant colours, should be sought in Luxor or Aswan. **Aswan** also is excellent for woven fabrics, for ivory, ebony and spices, and indeed it has the best bazaar outside Cairo.

Antiquities offered to you on the street are bound to be fake. Which is not to say there are not any genuine pharaonic, Coptic and Islamic artefacts around, but they will cost a lot of money and your only guarantee of their authenticity is to buy them from a shop displaying a **licence from the Department of Antiquities**. The shop will also give you a certificate of authenticity. There are several such shops in modern Cairo and in Khan el Khalili; the best is the already-mentioned **Senouhi**, 54 Sharia Abdel Khalek Sarwat, downtown. There are more shops in **Luxor**, with prices lower than in Cairo.

One of the most enjoyable excursions, whether you intend to buy or not, is to wander through the **spice market** which lies off Sharia Muizz between Sharia el Muski (Sharia Gohar el Qaid) and Sharia al-Azhar. There are bottles of perfume essences, boxes of incense and bags of herbs and spices. Also there is kohl, a black eye cosmetic. The fragrances, and the quality of the light in awninged alleyways, awaken sensation.

A similarly enjoyable excursion (though the fragrance is not the same) is to the **camel bazaar**, northwest of the city just beyond Embaba. In Arabic it is the *Souk el Gimaal*, where camel herders from the Sudan bring their animals for sale, and farmers bring their horses, donkeys, goats and other livestock. The market is every Friday and starts very early: get there by 7 or 8am. You cross over to the west bank of the Nile and head north along the corniche (Sharia el Nil), going past the 26 July Bridge until you come to a square. Here you turn left, away from the river, following Sharia Sudan for several kilometres. After a housing estate on your left (built for felaheen pouring into Cairo), a road goes off to the right across railway tracks. Take this, and immediately after crossing the tracks turn left. You will parallel a walled-in area on your right and soon meet up with people and animals heading for the market. Eventually, a road to your left crosses railway tracks again; take this and then immediately turn right. The market entrance will be on your left.

Books on Egypt and Egyptology, but also light holiday reading in paperback, are found in the major hotel bookshops, which also sell magazines and newspapers. There is also the shop in the **Egyptian Museum**. Other bookshops around town are: **Reader's Corner**, 33 Sharia Abdel Khalek Sarwat, downtown (with branches at the Nile Hilton and the Holiday Inn out by the Pyramids), has English, French and some German books, as well as old and reproduction prints (eg by David Roberts). **Lehnert and Landrock**, 44 Sharia Sherif, near Sharia Adli — English though principally German books on Egypt, while magazines and paperbacks are almost all German. They also sell (under their own imprint) the excellent Kuemmerly & Frey map of Egypt. And they do a map of Cairo, somewhat better than the one issued free by the Tourist Office, and with the virtue of a street index. **Madbouly**, Midan Talaat Harb, with English, French and some German books downstairs. Also in Midan Talaat Harb is **Hachette** for French books. In Zamalek is the **Shady Bookstore**, Sharia 26 July near Sharia Hassan Sabri. Unless shoved aside by the new flyover, bookshops line the south side of the **Ezbekieh Gardens**, selling mostly Arabic books but sometimes second-hand foreign language books, with the possibility of an occasional 'find'. Bargaining is necessary.

INFORMATION

There are **Tourist Information Offices** at the airport (Tel: 966475), downtown (head office) at 5 Shari Adli (Tel: 923000) and at the Pyramids on Sharia al-Ahram (Tel: 850259). They can provide brochures, a good free map of Cairo (with practical information on the reverse) and copies of *Cairo by Night and Day*, filled with listings of hotels, restaurants, entertainments, travel agents, embassies, etc.

The people working at their offices are charming and helpful (most helpful is the head office), but they are used to tourists going to the obvious places by the slickest means, and so have to be pressed for alternative information. If you do not want a tour, do not want to take taxis everywhere, then make it clear that you do not mind taking the local bus or train to Memphis, Saqqara, Meidum, etc, and they will come up with the information you require.

The Tourist Information Office at the **airport**, and Misr Travel, both have desks outside the customs hall.

The **Tourist Police** are found browsing about ports of entry, in the bazaars and at tourist sights, and are recognised by a small blue strip on their left chest and a green armband with 'Tourist Police' written in Arabic and English. Otherwise they wear the normal police uniform, which is black in winter and white in summer. They usually speak at least 2 foreign languages and are helpful with information while doing their best to ensure that tourists are not fleeced. They are based at the airport (Tel: 965239), at the Midan Ramses railway station (Tel: 753555), at the Pyramids (Tel: 58458), in Khan el Khalili (Tel: 904827) and on Sharia Adli (Tel: 912644).

A useful source of information, as well as a brief up to date review of the news, is the *Egyptian Gazette* (published as the *Egyptian Mail* on Saturdays), Cairo's daily English-language **newspaper**. (In French there are 2 dailies, *Le Progres Egyptien* and *Journal d'Egypte*). The *Gazette's* 'What's On' columns will tell you of current and forthcoming concerts, gallery shows, films, etc, while its 'Round and About' columns list opening times at museums and tourist sights and may also tell you that barbers are normally closed on Mondays, while butchers do not sell meat on Mondays, Tuesdays and Wednesdays. There are also cinema, restaurant, nightclub and travel advertisements; television and radio listings; temperatures up and down the country; foreign community church services; and horoscopes — 'A romantic interlude adds interest and excitement to an otherwise mundane day. Be ready with answers at evening' (Aquarius).

Your own **hotel desk** or those at the major hotels, as well as such **travel agents** as Thomas Cook and American Express, and your own **embassy** can all be useful sources of varied information.

TRAVEL

The general information here on Cairo travel is supplemented by further details in subsequent chapters.

There are 3 ways of getting from the **airport into Cairo**. The first is to take the **public bus** (No. 400 — in Arabic numerals); the stop is about 70 metres directly across from the arrivals building and the fare is about 20PT to Midan Ramses or Midan el Tahrir, with a few stops along the way. From 7am to midnight departures are every half hour on the hour and half hour; from midnight to 7am it departs only on the hour. When travelling *to* the airport, catch the bus in Midan el Tahrir (same departure times and frequencies) at the furthest bus shelter from the Hilton. You should allow $1\frac{1}{2}$ hours for the journey to be on the safe side. At rush hours (morning, evening and from 2 to 4pm) you may not get a seat. The second way is to take an airport **limousine** from immediately outside the arrivals building; to central Cairo the fare will be about LE4.50 and a bit more if to Dokki or Giza. These limos are comfortable Mercedes. The third way is to take a **taxi**. The driver will almost certainly try to avoid using his meter, and though the fare should be no greater than for the limo, he will probably demand more. Do not give it to him. (For how to deal with taxi drivers, see below.)

The cheapest way of getting about **within and around Cairo** is by **public bus**. Fares are rarely more than 6PT, usually less. They are usually very crowded, and Cairenes are adept at boarding and exiting through the windows as often as through the doors. They are fun to watch at Midan el Tahrir (where nearly all buses originate and terminate), and quite an experience to ride. From near the Nile Hilton you can catch the No. 66 to Kahn el Khalili and the No. 72 to Midan Salah al-Din (for the Sultan Hassan Mosque and the Citadel). From the far south end of Midan el Tahrir by the Mugamaa you can catch the No. 800 or 900 to the Pyramids, departing every 10 minutes. The numbers are on the front of the buses in Arabic.

Also there is the surface **metro** from Bab el Luq station, a short walk from Midan el Tahrir east along Sharia Mohammed Mahmud. This will take you south to Old Cairo (Mari Girgis stop — which is the third after Bab el Luq) and on to Maadi and Helwan. First class to Old Cairo is about 10PT at the station, a couple of piastres more on the train. There is also an underground metro abuilding, with its hub at Midan el Tahrir.

In theory, **taxis** are a very cheap way of getting around Cairo. Unfortunately, Cairo taxi drivers hold to an opposite theory when giving rides to tourists. Occasionally you will get into a metered taxi and the driver will actually turn the meter on, in which case pay accordingly. But more often than not the driver will 'forget' to turn his meter on, or say it is broken, or simply refuse to do so. There is no point in arguing about this as you start off, or even drawing it to the driver's attention. Take your ride and then pay him according to the following scale: from Midan el Tahrir to Zamalek, Khan el Khalili or Midan Ramses (2 to 2.5 kms) 75PT; from Midan el Tahrir to Old Cairo (4 to 4.5 kms) LE1.50; from Midan el Tahrir to the Pyramids (11 kms), LE3. You can feel generous in knowing you are paying about double the proper fare. Your driver, of course, will have a fit. You then make noises about calling the police. Your driver will calm down, but even if he does not, ignore him. There is another rule of thumb, a costlier one, but which might reduce the ructions, and that is to pay a flat LE2 for any ride within Cairo. LE2 is the magic sum that taxi drivers expect from tourists, and sometimes, as when the taxi has queued at Ramses Station and taken you with all your baggage to your hotel (however near), it seems fair enough.

Limousine Misr operates from the airport and the major hotels; its cars are unmetered but stick to a fixed tariff which you can find posted in the major hotel lobbies or sometimes in the limousines themselves. By way of example, if you take a limousine from the Nile Hilton the one-way fares unless otherwise noted will be as follows (add 50% for roundtrip journeys):
Anywhere in Cairo: LE2.50
Heliopolis: LE3.50
Pyramids and nearby hotels, the airport, Maadi: LE4.50
Helwan: LE9
Sound and Light at the Pyramids (includes return trip and waiting): LE11.
Saqqara: LE16 (includes return journey, 4-hour excursion) or LE32 (8-hour excursion).
Memphis: as Saqqara, but LE1 extra.
Cairo half-day: LE11 (4 hours, 50 kms)
Cairo full-day: LE19 (8 hours, 100 kms)
Cairo day and night: LE58 (24 hours, 300 kms)

If travelling extensively in and around Cairo and further afield, it could be worthwhile **hiring a car**. Remember that you will need an International Driver's Licence and a sense of adventure: Cairenes especially have little road-sense, meandering from side to side as the fancy takes them, and the only way to survive is to meander with them. For a few pounds more you can hire a car with driver.

Avis is the internationally-known company most in evidence, while **Bita** is a reliable and less expensive local outfit. They both rent Fiats as economy models, Peugeots in the medium range and Mercedes at the top. Rates are around LE9 per day and 9PT per km for a Fiat 128, LE13 per day and 13PT per km for a Peugeot 504, and LE17 per day and 17PT per km for a Mercedes 230. Insurance and waiver charges plus a 10% tax are on top of that; a chauffeur will cost about LE8 per 10-hour day extra. You will probably have to reserve at least a day in advance. **Avis** has offices at the Meridien, Nile Hilton, Cairo Sheraton, Concord, Jolie Ville and the Sheraton Heliopolis hotels, and at Cairo airport. **Hertz** is at the Sonesta, Hyatt Salam, Holiday Inn and President hotels, and at the airport. **Budget** is at the Mena House, Marriott and Novotel Airport hotels, and at the airport, while **Bita's** office is at 15 Sharia Mahmoud Bassiouni, off Midan Talaat Harb, with also an airport branch.

The alternative to public transport or car hire are **tours by car or bus with guide**. There are morning, afternoon and evening tours to the Antiquities Museum, the Pyramids and Sphinx, Memphis and Saqqara, Islamic Cairo, Old Cairo, Cairo by night with nightclub, etc. **Thomas Cook**, 4 Sharia Champollion, just off Midan el Tahrir (Tel: 743698), has a comprehensive list of tours by car with driver/guide. The more passengers, the less expensive per person. **American Express**, 15 Sharia Qasr el Nil, a short walk from Midan el Tahrir (Tel: 753142), and with branches at the Nile Hilton, Meridien and Sheraton hotels, does coach tours which for 1 or 2 people will work out about 40% cheaper than Cook's tours. These companies also offer **tours throughout Egypt by rail or air**.

Possibly cheaper and more comprehensive is Egypt's own tourist company, **Misr Tours**, 1 Sharia Talaat Harb (Tel: 750010; telex 92035 MRSHIP UN), with an office also at 43 Sharia Kasr el Nil, and branches in Garden City, Zamalek and Maadi. They are very good, and can arrange accommodation, cruises, tours, and air, sea, road and rail travel.

Long-distance buses for destinations all over Egypt depart from Midan el Tahrir and Midan Ramses, and from Cairo Airport. **Share (service) taxis**, whether to the Pyramids or Alexandria or elsewhere are found in Midan el Tahrir near the Mugamaa.

The main Cairo **train station**, Mahattat Ramses, is at Midan Ramses, northeast of Midan el Tahrir. From here there are trains north into the Delta and to Alexandria, east to the Canal towns and south into Upper Egypt — Minya, Assiut, Luxor and Aswan. New **Wagons-Lits** carriages now operate overnight to Luxor and Aswan and tickets can be bought at Ramses Station; otherwise the reservations office for Compagnie Internationale des Wagons-Lits is at 48 Sharia Giza. Tel: 985764. Telex: 93005 WALIT UN. It is always advisable to book in advance for sleepers or any first class train. **Students** and **youth hostellers** can obtain a 50% discount (see *Background* chapter).

Overland travel between Egypt and Israel is by daily luxury coach; contact Travco, 3 Sharia Ishak Yacoub, Zamalek (off Sharia 26 July beside the Marriott Hotel). Tel: 803448. Fares are about LE30 one-way, LE50 roundtrip.

Most **airline offices** are in the vicinity of Midan el Tahrir, eg:
Air France, Midan Talaat Harb (Tel: 743494).
Air Sinai, Nile Hilton Centre (Tel: 760948).
British Airways, 1 Sharia Abdel Salam Aref, on the corner of Midan el Tahrir (Tel: 759914).
Egyptair, 12 Sharia Qasr el Nil (Tel: 59915); also at 6 Sharia Adli.
El Al, 5 Sharia al Maqrizi, Zamalek (Tel: 651912).
KLM, 11 Sharia Qasr el Nil (Tel: 740717).
Lufthansa, 9 Sharia Talaat Harb (Tel: 750366).
MEA, 12 Sharia Qasr el Nil (Tel: 743151).
Olympic, 23 Sharia Qasr el Nil (Tel: 751277).
Pan American, 2 Sharia Talaat Harb (Tel: 747399).
PIA, 22 Sharia Qasr el Nil (Tel: 744213).
SAS, 2 Sharia Champollion (Tel: 753546).
Sudan Airways, 1 Sharia el Boustan (Tel: 979198).
Swissair, 22 Sharia Qasr el Nil (Tel: 744299).
TWA, 1 Sharia Qasr el Nil, on the corner of Midan el Tahrir (Tel: 749900).

Additionally, **Air France** has a branch at the Meridien; **Egyptair** has branches at the Nile Hilton and the Cairo Sheraton; while the main offices of **Alitalia**, **Ethiopian** and **Japan Airlines** are at the Nile Hilton.

Egyptair operates both internationally and within Egypt, but it does not fly to Sinai or Israel. Instead, **Air Sinai** serves El Arish, Sharm el Sheikh, St Catherine's Monastery and Tel Aviv. And of course **El Al** links Cairo with Tel Aviv.

The time-honoured way of making a progress through Egypt is to **cruise along the Nile**. **Hilton**, **Sheraton**, **Oberoi** and **Marriott** all offer year-round sailings between Luxor and Aswan, some of these taking in Dendera and Abydos too, and usually lasting 4 nights, 5 days. The smaller the ship the more enjoyable the experience, and on this count as well as for the general excellence of their service, **Hilton's** *Isis* and *Osiris* are particularly recommended. Hilton's high season (October-May) rates are LE600 per person in a double cabin and include meals, sightseeing ashore, taxes and service charges. Singles and triples are also possible. Bookings can be made at the relevant hotels in Cairo or abroad. Cheaper by about LE100 per person are **Presidential Nile Cruises**, bookable at the President Hotel, 22 Sharia Taha Hussein, Zamalek, or at the company's office, 13 Sharia Maraashli, Zamalek (Tel: 800517; Telex: 7475 PNC UN).

More companies are offering cruises each year, building new ships or fitting up older ones. Nor do all cruises confine themselves to Upper Egypt; some will come down as far as Minya, others will start at Cairo. For information on new offerings, contact your nearest Egyptian Tourist Office, a competent travel agent at home or in Egypt, or look through the *Cairo by Night and Day* booklet.

OTHER THINGS

The **Central Post Office** is at Midan el Ataba, near the Ezbekieh Gardens, and is open 24 hours daily. Other post offices are open from 8.30am to 3pm daily except Fridays. Most hotels can supply you with stamps for cards and letters. There is a good chance that post cards sent home will arrive after you do: air mail *can* take 10 days to Europe, more to the US. Mail is faster if posted at one of the luxe hotels.

To send a parcel out of Egypt requires an export licence. You must obtain this at the Central Post Office, Midan el Ataba. Go there with your parcel unwrapped; go to the third building on the left in the rear of the complex; here it will be inspected and for a small fee sewn into a cloth cover; for a further small fee you will be guided through the remaining formalities and paperwork. Your parcel must not weigh more than 20 kilos nor exceed 1.5 metres in any direction. If sending home fabrics or souvenirs you have bought, ask first at the shop whether they will do it for you. Most shops catering to tourists have export licences and are reliable.

You can **receive mail** at your hotel or care of American Express (if you have their travellers cheques or card) or care of your embassy (the envelope should be marked 'Visitors' Mail'). American Express will forward any mail arriving for you after your departure for LE3 or so.

Telegrams in English or French can be sent from the PTT offices on the north side of Midan el Tahrir (open 24 hours daily), or in Sharia Alfi or Sharia Adli — or from major hotels. Night letters (no service to London) cost about half as much as full rate telegrams.

Most 3- and 4-star hotels and all 5-star hotels have **telex** services available to guests.

Local telephone calls can be made from some cigarette kiosks or from shops and restaurants — or from your hotel. Do not expect too much: 'Telephones of Cairo are not well'. **Long-distance calls** can be made (at any rate attempted) from major hotels or from the Midan el Tahrir (north side), Sharia Alfi or Sharia Adli PTT offices. The one at Midan el Tahrir is open 24 hours daily. You must usually reserve your call some hours in advance. If reserving at a PTT office, you will also have to pay in advance for 3 minutes minimum (if you think you will speak longer, pay for more time in advance, otherwise you will be cut off). You will be given a slip of paper with your reservation number on it; this is also your receipt. Hold onto it for when you return to complete your call, or for when you want a refund. Sometimes the PTT can refer your reserved call to your hotel.

To exchange money, go to Thomas Cook, American Express, or to the banks in the major hotels — all the 5-star hotels have 24-hour banks. You can sometimes change money at your embassy; the American Embassy gives a preferred rate to US citizens. Also there is a thriving black market on the streets. For a full-scale commercial banking service, there is Barclays Bank International, 12 Midan el Sheikh Youssef (PO Box 2335), Garden City, Cairo (Tel: 22195, 27950, 29415. Telex: 2343 CABAR UN).

If you have Egyptian pounds which you want to convert back into foreign currency before your departure, you can go to any bank (eg the one at the airport) and show them a receipt indicating that you had previously converted at least such an amount from foreign currency into Egyptian pounds. You should, therefore, always hold onto your receipts (the American Embassy does not give receipts when changing money at the preferential rate).

For **medical care**, ask at your hotel. Most will be able to refer you to a doctor or dentist, while some of the major hotels will have a doctor on call. Most Egyptian doctors have been trained in Europe or the US and speak English. Your embassy can also recommend doctors and dentists. In an emergency, the following private hospitals are recommended: the **Anglo-American Hospital**, Gezira (Tel: 806165) and the **Italian Hospital**, Abbasiyya, in northeast Cairo (Tel: 821497). A recommended government hospital is **Dar el Shifa**, 373 Sharia Ramses, just past the Coptic Patriarchate to the northeast of Midan Ramses (Tel: 829910). For **first aid** service, you can try ringing 743499.

There are several **pharmacists** around Midan el Tahrir and downtown with a wide range of medications not requiring prescriptions — describe your symptoms and, if the ailment is minor, the pharmacist will prescribe on the spot. Cosmetics, perfumes and toilet articles are also stocked.

Your **embassy** can assist you by acting as a mail drop, advising on emergency financial and medical problems, effecting emergency communications home, etc. Embassies also encourage visitors, especially those not travelling in large groups, to register with them. It should be noted, however, that embassies cannot lend money to **stranded travellers** — though they can find ways of helping you. If stranded, you can go to Thomas Cook, American Express, Barclays International or the Nile Hilton and have them send a telegram or telex requesting your bank or persons at home to arrange the transfer of money to you in Egypt. This can be accomplished in 2-3 days. Or you can go to an airline office and ask for a pre-paid ticket, the airline cabling whomever you suggest to pay for the ticket home. Authorisation to issue you with a ticket can be received back in Cairo within 2 days.

A full list of **embassies** can be found in *Cairo Night and Day*; a few are listed below.
Australia, 1097 Corniche el Nil, Garden City (Tel: 28197).
Canada, 6 Sharia Mohammed Fahmiel Sayed, Garden City (Tel: 23110).
Ireland, 2 Sharia Maarouf (Tel: 745967).
Israel, 6 Sharia Ibn Malek, Giza (Tel: 982000).
Sudan, 1 Sharia Mohammed Fahmi el Sayed, Garden City (Tel: 25043).
United Kingdom, 2 Sharia Ahmed Raghab, Garden City (Tel: 20850).
United States, 5 Sharia Latin America, Garden City (Tel: 28219).

When **leaving Egypt** from Cairo Airport, remember that there is an LE5 **departure tax**. Once that is paid, the rest of your money should be converted back to foreign currency. The **duty-free shop** sells cigarettes, tobacco, liquor, perfume, etc, but will not accept Egyptian money.

If you want a **view of the Pyramids**, sit on the right-hand side of the plane.

RODA, OLD CAIRO AND FUSTAT

For Old Cairo and Fustat, you can take the train from Bab el Luq station, east of Midan el Tahrir, getting off at the third stop, Mari Girgis. If you take a taxi, ask for Old Cairo in Arabic — *Misr* (or *Masr*) *el Qadima*. The distance is about 4 kms, though there are a few places enroute worth noting for those with flexible transport. In any case, Garden City and the northern part of Roda can form a separate excursion, enjoyed on foot.

Roda Island and the Corniche

A river walk

The Meridien Hotel at Roda's northern tip can be reached across its own bridge from Garden City, and here you can stop for a drink and a commanding view of the Nile. Gardens run along the western bank of the island to El Gama'a Bridge which crosses over the Nile to the Zoological Gardens. From there you can walk back along the west bank of the river through Dokki, visiting the Papyrus Institute on the way, coming up to the Cairo Sheraton and so back to Midan el Tahrir via Gezira.

But a quarter of the way down Roda, its grounds overlooking the smaller eastern branch of the Nile, its entrance however facing the approach road to El Gama'a Bridge, is the **Manyal Palace**, built by Mohammed Ali. It is now partly a museum, partly a Club Méditerranée hotel. On view is a reception palace, the palace proper, a private mosque and Mohammed Ali's private hunting museum, which includes a table made of elephants' ears and a hermaphrodite goat. That pretty much sets the tone of the place, which is bizarre kitsch. There is also a garden of banyan trees.

Coming down the corniche from Midan el Tahrir towards Old Cairo, at a point two or three blocks south of your view across to the Manyal Palace on Roda is a traffic roundabout called **Fumm el Khalig**. This is where the canal, now covered by Sharia Port Said and its southern extension, left the river. There is a large octagonal tower of stone here, once housing great waterwheels which lifted water from the Nile to the level of the Mameluke **aqueduct** which can still be followed almost all the way to the Citadel. At this end, the aqueduct dates only from 1505 and was an extension made necessary by the westward-shifting Nile; the main part of the aqueduct, further east, was built by al-Nasr around 1311.

To the Nilometer

A further few blocks south is the Malek al-Salih bridge crossing over to the southern end of Roda. At the lower tip of the island is the **Nilometer**, dating from the 9th C, though the superstructure with its Turkish-style conical roof dates from Mohammed Ali's time. The stone-lined pit goes down well below the level of the Nile, though the water entry tunnels have been blocked up and you can descend by steps. At the centre of the pit is a graduated column for determining whether the river would rise enough, not enough, or too much, so announcing the expected fertility of all Egypt over the coming year. A reading of 16 *ells* (8.6 metres) ensured the complete irrigation of the Valley. When it reached this level, the Nile crier, attended by boys carrying flags, would broadcast the *Wafa el Nil* or superfluity of the Nile and the dam to the Khalig would be cut amidst great festivity. The Nile used to reach its flood in mid-August, but the High Dam at Aswan now regulates its flow and it keeps a steady level year-round.

The Nilometer is usually locked but the keeper lives in a small house nearby. If you do not see him, ask one of his children to fetch him; but if he has gone off somewhere, you will have to try your luck another time.

Old Cairo

Babylon in Egypt

You arrive at Old Cairo outside a section of wall and two towers that formed part of the Roman **fortress of Babylon**, first built around AD 30 in the time of Augustus, added to by Trajan and remodelled by the Byzantines. The technique of dressed stone alternating with courses of brick is typically Roman. The portal between the towers was a water gate and excavation has revealed the original quay 6 metres below present street level, but the Nile has since shifted 400 metres to the west.

The Coptic Museum. Now the towers mark the entrance to the Coptic Museum, pleasantly set in gardens. It is a charming building, decorated with wooden mashrabiyyas from old Coptic houses, embracing green courtyards, airy and light within, its spirit in keeping with its collection. The exhibits cover Egypt's Christian era, from AD 300 to 1000, and are both religious and secular, linking the art of the pharaonic and Graeco-Roman periods with that of Islam. The museum is arranged in sections, covering stonework, manuscripts, textiles, ikons and paintings as well as decorated ivories, woodwork, metalwork, and pottery and glass. Often, as in stone carving and painting, the work is crude, though agreeably naive. High artistic achievement, however, is found in the textiles, and there are many fine chemises, tapis and cloths here embroidered with motifs of St George, or graceful women and gazelles.

The arrangement of the museum, and some highlights:

Ground floor:

Room 1: Pre-Christian reliefs and architectural fragments, 3rd and 4th C. The themes are pagan gods, eg Pan and Dionysos.

Room 2: Again reliefs and fragments, but of the 4th to 6th C and so early Christian. The cross is incorporated at every opportunity, often surrounded by flowers or backed by a shell forming the half-dome of a niche — see 7065, a shell with dolphins on either side. Technically the work is similar to the pre-Christian, but there is a sense of excitement at working with the new imagery — Pan and other pagan motifs had become so hackneyed.

Room 3: Reliefs and frescoes, 6th C. See 7118 showing Christ ascending to heaven in a flaming chariot. *Rooms 4 through 8* contain more of the same, including work from Abu Jeremias Monastery at Saqqara.

Room 9: Reliefs and frescoes from the 6th through the 10th C, including, on the stairs, a humorous cartoon of rats making an offering to a cat (8441).

Note throughout the museum the beautifully carved wood ceilings and beams.

First floor:

Rooms 10, 11 and 12 all contain textiles. Note in *Room 11*, exhibit 7948, the tapestry showing a musician and dancers (3rd-4th C), beautifully observed, fluid, rhythmic, happy. The Copts were at their best in textiles which they developed from ancient Egyptian tradition, adding to it Graeco-Roman and Sassanid influences. Plants, animals, birds and human beings blend in sumptuous decorative patterns that have a liveliness that Byzantium itself could not rival.

Room 13 contains ikons and ivories; *Room 14*, woodwork; and *Room 15*, metalwork.

Courtyard:

To the right (south) of the museum is a courtyard like that of a grand Cairo house, planted and with mashrabiyyas round the walls. Across the court is part of the Roman wall and a gate of Babylon: for a bit of baksheesh you can descend to the level of the seeping Nile and teeter across planks beneath great arches and vaults.

Coptic churches. The oldest Coptic churches sought security within the fortress walls, and usually they avoid facing onto the street and so are indistinguishable from neighbouring houses. Their main entrances were long ago walled up against attack, entry being through a small side door. Their plan is basilical, with a narthex or porch admitting to an aisled nave with an ikonostasis placed across the sanctuary. In seeking out the five churches within the fortress precincts, and also the synagogue, there is interest too in the winding little streets, glimpses within windows and doors, the decorations of the houses, the domes of some as in Upper Egypt, and the atmosphere of remove, of an almost rural village.

Alexandria was the Coptic Rome. This was never a city, never a place of monuments, and it is not a ghetto. Copts live throughout Cairo and all over Egypt, especially in Upper Egypt. But this is an old and holy place, to Jews as well as Copts, and among the 135,000 Moslems living in Old Cairo, within and without the fortress, there are 30,000 Copts and 42 Jewish families, worshipping at 29 mosques, 20 churches and one synagogue.

The Hanging Church

The **Church of el Muallaqa**, the Hanging Church, is so named because it rests on the bastions of the southwest gate into the fortress, its nave suspended above the passage. It is reached by going out from the museum grounds between the two great towers and turning left. Though the church claims origins in the 4th C, it is unlikely that the present structure, which in any case has been rebuilt, would have been built on the walls until the Arab conquest made them redundant. Certainly, it is known to have become the seat of the Patriarchate when it was moved from Alexandria to Cairo in the 11th C. The interior of El Muallaqa, with pointed arches, cedar panelling and translucent ivory screens, is intricately decorated and can be satisfying in detail — the carved white *marble pulpit* inlaid with marble of red and black is the finest in Egypt — but the overall effect is glum. Services are held in the dead Coptic language sprinkled with some Arabic. On the right, as you come in, is a 10th C ikon of the Virgin and Child, Egyptian faces, Byzantine crowns. On the same wall is an ancient ikon of St Mark, founder of the Coptic Church. El Muallaqa is dedicated to the Virgin and is properly called Sitt Mariam, St Mary. Its central sanctuary is dedicated to Christ, its left sanctuary to St George, its right sanctuary to St John the Baptist, scenes from the saints' lives decorating their ikonostases.

Now walk back out to the street and turn right so that you pass by the towers and entrance to the museum. Along the Roman wall on your right are some steps leading down to the level of the early settlement. A narrow street runs southwest and on the left is the Monastery of St George. Further on, you are obliged to turn either left or right: if you turn left and go straight on, you will come to **El Adra**, the Church of the Virgin, first built in the 9th C but destroyed and rebuilt in the 18th C. It is known also as Kasriyat er-Rihan, meaning pot of basil, a favoured herb of the Greek Orthodox Church. Al-Hakim's mother had been of that faith and for the duration of his reign it was transferred to Orthodox use. Returning back down the street from El Adra, the **Church of Mari Girgis** or St George is on your left. The original was built in the 7th C but burnt down in the 19th, only a later 14th C hall surviving. The modern church is of no interest.

Associations with the Holy Family

Returning to where you had the choice between left and right, you carry straight on, that is as though you had first turned right. You are now at **Abu Sarga**, the Church of St Sergius, reconstructed during the Fatimid period but with a crypt of much earlier date and reputed to be the halting place of the Holy Family when they fled Herod and came into Egypt. It is entered through a small door at the southwest corner. Inside it is simple stone and plaster, with a high timbered roof supported by marble columns painted with faded saints. Follow some steps to the right of the altar down to the *crypt* which in the past would fill knee-high with the Nile.

Turning right out of the church and then right at the corner, at the end of the street you see **Sitt Barbara** (St Barbara's) to the left, the synagogue to the right. Sitt Barbara is very similar to Abu Sarga and like it was restored in Fatimid times. Barbara had tried converting her father to Christianity; he responded by beating her to death. Her relics are in a velvet-covered case in a chapel to the right of the nave. In another case, so some Copts claim, are relics of St Catherine, the Alexandrian martyr broken on the wheel. E M Forster in his *Alexandria: A History and a Guide* says she supposedly died under Diocletian, but it is improbable that she ever lived; she and her wheel were creations of Western Catholicism, and the land of her supposed sufferings has only recognised her out of politeness to the French. The famous monastery in Sinai was named for her and did enjoy close relations with medieval monasteries in France to which it exported a prized oil which exuded from her bones.

Synagogue of Ben Ezra. I said that Old Cairo was no ghetto, but at the Synagogue of Ben Ezra the mood is uncertain. It is the neighbourhood temple whose neighbourhood has gone away

Synagogue of Ben Ezra, Old Cairo

— left the country or gone to other parts of Cairo. It is a forlorn place, a forgotten outpost, and can be moving.

The synagogue is the oldest in Egypt and resembles in its basilical arrangement an early Christian church. A church did stand here from the 4th to 9th C, but the Copts had to sell it to the Jews to pay Ibn Tulun's tax towards the erection of his mosque. Sources differ as to whether the original church cum temple was subsequently destroyed and rebuilt or whether the early fabric remains in what the Rabbi of Jerusalem, Abraham Ben Ezra, at least renewed in the 12th C. The Jews argue, however, that the synagogue has a longer history than that. On this site, they say, stood the temple of the prophet Jeremiah and it was here that Joseph came to worship with his wife and child. Certainly there was a Jewish community here at that time, explaining why Joseph should have come this way at all; and he was followed, after later political and religious disturbances in Jerusalem, by the apostles Mark and Peter. It makes sense that it was from this Babylon that Peter sent his First Epistle General to Christian communities throughout the East, though many scholars argue that Babylon was no more than a metaphor for Rome. But at Rome there were very few Jews and little reason for Peter to go there; and there is the suspicion that the Western Church appropriated him to that city in order there to crown him pope and martyr. At any rate, the early Christian church eventually sold to the Jews was, it is said, built where the Romans had destroyed Jeremiah's temple.

Ben Ezra's synagogue sits in a small shady garden, its exterior plain, a Star of David in wrought iron over the gate. Rabbi Cohen lives opposite. Inside there is an arch of ablaq masonry, a small stained-glass window towards the far end and where the ikonstasis would be a Star of David in light-bulbs. Pointed out to you (if Rabbi Cohen is in the mood) will be the Miracle Rock beneath which Jeremiah is supposed to be buried and the spring where (again depending on Rabbi Cohen's mood) either Joseph and Mary drew water to wash the infant Jesus or Pharoah's daughter plucked Moses from the bullrushes. The synagogue once possessed a library of 100,000 books, all gone; and discovered hidden in the walls at the end of the 19th C was an ancient Torah, now dispersed throughout the great libraries o f the Western world, though you may be shown a fragment.

Moses in the bullrushes

When I first came to this synagogue in 1967, Rabbi Cohen was already doing a modest trade in black and white post cards of himself. Now with the change in the political climate there is no stopping him. There are piles of post cards inside, in colour yet, most of them still depicting himself; and offer him anything less than $1 or £1 (no coins) and you are lucky he does not throw you out the door. On my way out, his assistant meaningfully tapped the side of his head; small consolation for leaving without a colour post card of Rabbi Cohen.

Fustat

Emerging from Old Cairo and turning right (that is walking two or three blocks north of the fortress with the railway line on your left) you come to the **Mosque of Amr**, so restored and expanded that nothing remains of the original built here in 642,

The first mosque in Egypt

the first mosque in Egypt and the point from which the country's conversion to Islam began. Except for its associations, the present mosque is without interest. Its dimensions date to 827 when it was doubled in size, and it has several times since been restored, and is being restored again now in the nastiest way. It is a shabby reminder of a cheaply won victory, and you pause to wonder what it would take to reverse the effect of Amr's 3500 men.

Behind the mosque extends what appears to be a vast and smoking rubbish dump. The curious should wander into its midst — and be amazed and rewarded with one of the most fascinating sights in Cairo. No smouldering heaps at all, but a **community of earthenware manufacturers** whose seemingly rubbish houses (you should be careful not to fall through their ceilings as you walk over them) stand, or settle, amidst a complete and complex process for the making of fine clay and the fashioning of narghile stems, drums, small pots, large amphoras and road-sized drainage pipes — indeed these people could equip a band, a kitchen or a city, and do probably meet the earthenware needs of a large part of Cairo.

There are vats dug into the ground for mixing and refining clay, subterranean workshops where potters draw from shapeless lumps beautifully curved vessels with all the mastery and mystery of a fakir charming a thick brown snake, and there are enormous beehive kilns like Mycenaean tombs fired from below with mounds of wood shavings shovelled in by Beelzebub children.

At evening these mud-covered people wash themselves off, the women appear from out of their hovels in bright dresses, flowers are arranged in soft-drink bottles, a television — wired up to a car battery — is switched on, tea is made, chairs set out, and if you are there then you will be invited to join them in watching the setting sun.

The true beginnings of Cairo

Beyond this potters community — or, more easily, by returning towards the fortress of Babylon but turning left up the road running alongside the cemetery wall (the cemetery, by the way, which is Greek Orthodox, is worth visiting) — lie the dismal **remains of Fustat**, that is the foundations and lower walls of the first Arab city in Egypt, the true beginnings of Cairo. Once famous for its glassware and ceramics, with water supply and sanitation facilities far more advanced than in Europe until the 18th C, the city was destroyed and abandoned in 1168 rather than let it fall into the hands of the Christian King of Jerusalem. It is not at Amr's mosque but here amidst this wreckage that you feel something of the spirit of Arab Egypt: a people brave and confident enough to destroy their finest creations to deny succour to their enemy, to fight another day and win and rebuild, filling their new city of Cairo which you can see rising to the north with some of the greatest monuments of medieval civilisation.

PRACTICAL INFORMATION

If taking a **taxi to Old Cairo**, ask in Arabic for *Misr* (or *Masr*) *el Qadima*. Or take the **metro** from Bab el Luq station (on Sharia Mansur), a couple of blocks east of Midan el Tahrir, asking for Mari Girgis.

The churches and synagogue close at 4pm; there are no entrance fees, but all are anxious for donations. The Coptic Museum is open in winter (November-April) from 9am to 4pm daily, closed Fridays from 11am to 1pm; in summer from 8.30am to 1pm; closing at 11.15am on Fridays. Entrance fee. Bags and cameras must be checked (no fee).

There are some other museums, exhibits and sights worth visiting in the areas covered by this chapter:

The Cairo Tower on the island of Gezira rises 187 metres and offers marvellous panoramas from its 14th level restaurant, 15th level cafeteria and 16th level observation platform. Fee for the ascent.

The Ethnological Museum, Sharia Qasr el Aini, a few blocks south of Midan el Tahrir. Open 9am to 1pm daily, closed Friday. Small fee. A small museum with displays of traditional village handicrafts and costumes from all over Egypt.

The Manyal Palace on the island of Roda is open daily from 9am to 1pm. Small fee.

The Papyrus Institute, on a houseboat tied up along Sharia el Nil, is just south of the Cairo Sheraton in Giza. Open from 9am to 7pm daily, free. Founded by Prof. Hassan Ragab, this is a workshop, research centre and small museum demonstrating the manufacture and use of this first flexible writing material. Only *cyperus papyrus*, the same plant used by the ancients, is used here (the institute has several commercial imitators, but they use the modern *cyperus alopecuròides* of inferior quality). The institute grows at least some of its own papyrus, and exhibits copies of ancient papyri and sells others. (As you go down the quayside steps, notice on your left the plaque marking the highest level of the Nile during the flood of September 1887.)

The Agricultural Museum and the **Cotton Museum**, next to each other off Sharia Abdel Aziz Radwan, near the exit of the 6 October Bridge in Dokki. Open from 9am to 4pm except winter Fridays when they close from 11am to 1pm, and summer Fridays when they close at noon. Small fee. The Agricultural Museum displays all aspects of present Egyptian rural life, while the Cotton Museum concentrates on the country's single most important crop.

An **abbreviated tour** should at least take in the Coptic Museum.

TOURING ISLAMIC CAIRO

Islam in Egypt began at Fustat (previous chapter) and flowered into a great civilisation, many of whose most beautiful monuments survive throughout the medieval quarters of Cairo. The following six chapters tour this Islamic Cairo, progressing generally from south to north.

The method

The Islamic monuments of Cairo, and there are hundreds of them, are each marked with a small green enamelled plaque bearing an Arabic number. These numbers are given after the name of each monument covered in the itineraries of the following chapters to ensure identification. Although these are historical monuments, they are often places of current worship and when touring this most conservative part of the city you should dress and act with decorum. Women should not wear short dresses or too-revealing blouses. Inside mosques you must remove your shoes, or shoe coverings will be provided. For this, and if you accept the services of a guide, or sometimes if you ask to be shown the way up a minaret, baksheesh will be expected. And there is also an entry fee to some of the monuments. In short, it is a good idea to carry around a lot of small change.

You may sometimes find yourself in a mosque at prayer time, and then, though visitors are otherwise welcome, you might be asked to retreat into an alcove or out onto the street. Normally though the atmosphere is relaxed, even to the point where many of Mohammed's precepts on mosque conduct are ignored. Egypt in this as in many other ways is more liberal than most other Moslem countries.

Comfortable walking shoes are recommended. Though you might rely on a taxi or other transport to get you to the beginning of an itinerary or to some of the major monuments along the route, walking is otherwise preferable for a sense of leisure and atmosphere, and also because some places are difficult to get at or to discover even once you are in the vicinity. There are numerous *kahwehs* along the way, that is places to sit — often just a few chairs beneath the shade of a tree or awning — for a coffee or more likely a refreshing cup of mint tea. Then there is immediate tranquility; you give your feet a rest and let the city parade by before you.

The grandeur of Islam

In the 14th C the great Arab historian Ibn Khaldun wrote that 'he who has not seen Cairo cannot know the grandeur of Islam. It is the metropolis of the universe, the garden of the world, the nest of the human species, the gateway to Islam, the throne of royalty: it is a city embellished with castles and palaces and adorned with monasteries of dervishes and with colleges lit by the moons and the stars of erudition'. Along with Cordoba and Baghdad, it was one of the great centres of the Arab world, but while Cordoba fell to the *Reconquista* and Baghdad was destroyed by the Mongols, medieval Cairo survives. The erudition Ibn Khaldun refers to was more the Moslem version of how many angels could dance upon the head of a pin, but otherwise many of the marvels he describes still wait for you, often so unobtrusively that you could pass a

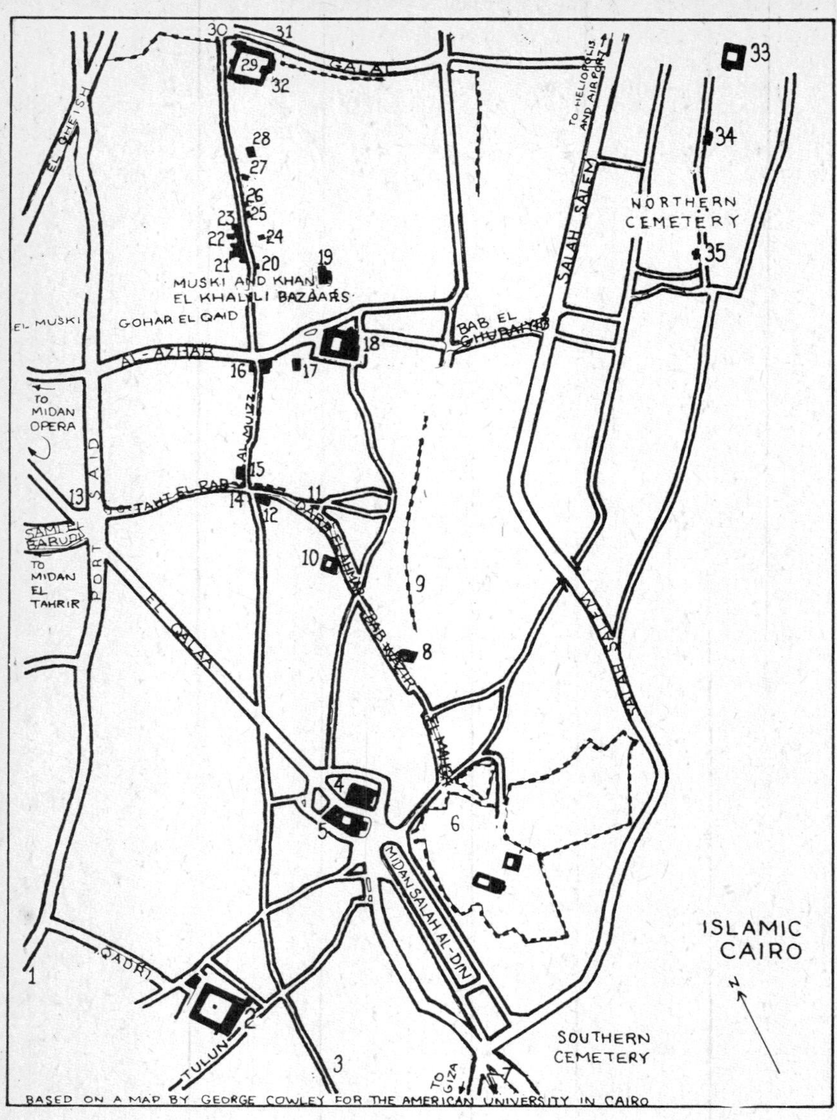

1. Mosque of Sayyida Zeinab
2. Mosque of Ibn Tulun and the Gayer-Anderson House
3. Tomb of Shagarat al-Durr
4. Rifa'i Mosque
5. Mosque of Sultan Hassan
6. The Citadel
7. Mausoleum of Imam al-Shaf'i
8. Aqsunqur (Blue) Mosque
9. Saladin's walls
10. Maridani Mosque
11. Qijmas al-Ishaqi Mosque
12. Mosque of Salih Talai
13. Islamic Museum and Egyptian Library
14. Bab Zuwayla

facade a hundred times and never guess at the grandeur within. Some of the monuments remain neglected, others have been restored over the past century or are only being restored now. The streets may be ancient, narrow and dusty, full of strange colour and smell. People may be curious, children occasionally a nuisance and merchants in the tourist bazaars importunate, but generally the inhabitants of these quarters, like Egyptians throughout the country, will be friendly and helpful. This is the heart of Cairo, a heart that anyone with the least sense of adventure will come to love.

AROUND THE CITADEL

If you have time to visit only one Islamic monument, the **Mosque of Ibn Tulun** (220) should be your choice. The mosque can be reached by going east from Midan al-Sayyida Zeinab at the bottom of Sharia Port Said or west from Midan Salah al-Din below the Citadel. The area, though not ancient, is poor and rundown, but behind its outer courtyard or *ziyadah* the mosque achieves an isolation which heightens the dramatic effect of the inner courtyard's bold simplicty.

Congregational plan

Ibn Tulun was sent to govern Cairo by the Abbassid Caliph at Baghdad and the mosque, built in 876-9, displays strong Mesopotamian influences. A congregational mosque with an inner courtyard or *sahn* of parade ground proportions, it strives to fulfill the ideal of accommodating all the troops and subjects of the fortress capital for Friday prayers. Arcades run round the sahn on four sides, deeper along the qibla wall facing Mecca. Brick piers support the pointed horseshoe arches which have a slight return, that is they continue their curve inwards at the bottom, and the arches are decorated with carved stucco (restored on the outer arches but original on the others within the arcades), a technique Ibn Tulun introduced to Cairo. The windows along the qibla wall (to your left as you enter the mosque) have stucco grilles (the fifth and sixth from the left are orginal), permitting a faint light into this deeper arcade with its prayer niche or *mihrab* and beautifully carved pulpit or *minbar*, 13th C restorations. The roof, like the repaired stucco work, is owed to the efforts of 20th C restorers. Original, however, is the Koranic inscription in Kufic style carved in sycamore running at a height round the interior of the four arcades.

The effect as you enter the sahn is of severe simplicity, yet these details of carved stucco and sycamore and returning arches offer subtle relief. You should walk round the sahn under the arcades to appreciate the play that is made with light and shadows, the rhythm of the arches, the harmony of the ensemble.

At the centre of the sahn is a 13th C fountain. All these 13th C restorations and additions were undertaken by Sultan Lajin who had assassinated the incumbent Sultan and hid in the then decrepit mosque. He vowed that if he survived to be raised to the Sultanate he would restore his hideaway, and to him belongs an explanation also for the striking *minaret* opposite the qibla wall. The original was Tulun's, in the form of a spiral, and there is a story of Tulun, normally of grave demeanor, absentmindedly twiddling a strip of paper round his finger to the consternation of his audience, excusing himself with the explanation that it was the model for his new minaret. In fact its prototype, still standing, was the minaret of the Great Mosque of Samarra in Iraq. But Lajin had to rebuild it and out of taste or for stability gave it a squared base. It succeeds in being extraordinary and along with the merlons along the parapets of the arcades, like a paperchain of cut-out men, it has the alertness of the surreal. You can climb the

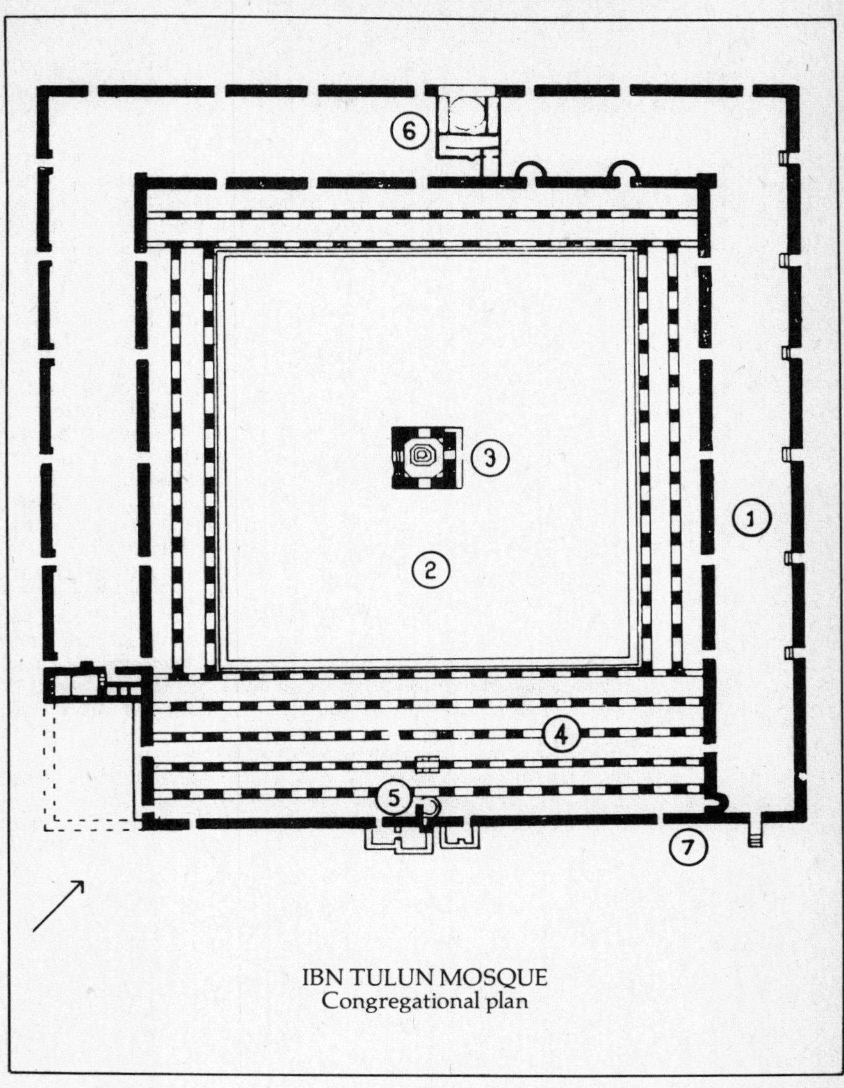

IBN TULUN MOSQUE
Congregational plan

IBN TULUN MOSQUE
1. Entry
2. Sahn
3. Fountain
4. Sanctuary liwan
5. Mihrab
6. Minaret
7. Gayer-Anderson House

minaret right to the top, though as you round the spiral there is nothing to steady you and a high breeze adds to the vertigo. There is nothing much close by but tenements with views into bedroom windows, though to the west you can see the Pyramids, to the north pick out the major landmarks of the Fatimid city, and below you again the forthright plan of mosque.

At the northeast corner of the Ibn Tulun Mosque is the Bayt al-Kritliyya, the House of the Cretan Woman, though in fact it is two 17th C houses knocked together. It is better known as the **Gayer-Anderson House**, named for the British major who restored and occupied it earlier this century, filling it with his eclectic collection of English, French and oriental furniture and bric-a-brac which can be disconcertingly anachronistic, but does give the place a lived-in feeling. Its tourist reputation must be founded on this, and its proximity to the Ibn Tulun, for otherwise it is not half as fine as the Bayt al-Suhaymi mentioned in a later chapter.

The harem

Overlooking its large reception room is a balcony enclosed in a wooden mashrabiyya screen from which the women of the harem could discreetly observe male visitors and their entertainments. Lane in his *Manners and Customs of the Modern Egyptians*, which describes Cairo in the 1830s, says the women 'have the character of being the most licentious in their feelings of all females who lay any claim to be considered as members of a civilised nation ... What liberty they have, many of them, it is said, abuse; and most of them are not considered safe unless under lock and key, to which restraint few are subjected. It is believed that they possess a degree of cunning in the management of their intrigues that the most prudent and careful husband cannot guard against'. Indeed, Lane believed that Egyptian women were under less restraint than those in any other country of the Turkish Empire, with those 'of the lower orders flirting and jesting with men in public, and men laying their hands upon them very freely'. As for those of the upper classes: 'They generally look upon restraint with a degree of pride, as evincing the husband's care for them and value themselves upon their being hidden as treasures'. The only man allowed into the harem, that is the female domestic quarters, was the husband — and so the strictures worked against men, too, the only unveiled women they could see being their wives or female slaves.

Shagarat al-Durr

The only Moslem Queen

Those interested in making a romantic pilgrimage to the **Tomb of Shagarat al-Durr** should walk southwards along the medieval city's main street, here called Sharia al-Ashraf, which passes just to the east of Ibn Tulun's mosque. The tomb (169) is at the edge of the Southern Cemetery in one of Cairo's poorest areas. Built in 1250, it is small and simple, with fine glass Byzantine mosaics in the prayer niche, an original Kufic frieze and fragments of Naskhi inscription round the cenotaph — not entirely empty, for some of her body was saved from the dogs. The only female Moslem sovereign in history, indeed the only woman to have ruled over Moslems until Queen Victoria, she played fast and loose and came to a sticky end. Her story is told later, in connection with the Mausoleum and Madrasa of al-Salih Ayyub.

Midan Salah al-Din

Walk to Midan Salah al-Din; to your left (north) are two large mosques pressed against each other like the walls of a canyon, Sharia el Qalaa cutting between them. The mosque on the right is the **Rifa'i**, a modern imitation of Bahri Mameluke style, where members of the late royal family, including King Farouk, are buried — and now also the ex-Shah of Iran. The best thing about the Rifa'i is its near-abutment with the Mosque of Sultan Hassan on the left, the canyon enhancing the massiveness of the latter. Both mosques are lit by orange lights at night, as though the light itself was old, not bright and white, and had been lingering on the facades for some long time until it darkened with age. But then in the darkness is the booming call to evening prayer, not mysterious but electrically amplified, saving the muezzin not only his voice but the long trudge up to the top of the minaret. This is one liberalisation in Islamic practice, prevalent now throughout the Middle East, which is to be regretted.

The Mosque-madrasa of Sultan Hassan (133) is genuinely of the Bahri Mameluke period and was built — of stone (reputedly from the Great Pyramid), unlike the brick of Tulunid and some Fatimid mosques — in 1356-63. Its short distance from the Mosque of Ibn Tulun allows a ready comparison between these exemplars of the two principal forms of Cairo mosque. The purpose of the congregational is to gather in and architecturally the emphasis is on the rectangular and the horizontal. But the Sultan Hassan served as a theological school, a *madrasa*. The madrasa was first introduced to Egypt by Saladin as part of his effort to combat and suppress the Fatimid Shi'ites. Class and dormitory space required a vertical structure, most functionally a cube. The central courtyard remains a feature, but opening onto each of its sides are four enormous vaulted halls or *liwans*, creating a cruciform plan. The doctrinal justification for four liwans was that each served as a place for teaching one of the four Sunni, that is orthodox, Moslem rites (Shafite, Malikite, Hanefite and Hanbalite), though the origins of the liwan are found at Hatra in Iraq, an Arab city flourishing at least 400 years before Mohammed. But it was the Mamelukes who arranged them with magnificent effect in cruciform plan and who also added to their mosque-madrasas domed mausolea. Hassan's mausoleum is appended to the south end of his mosque but his tomb is empty; he was executed two years before its completion and his body disappeared.

Cruciform plan

There are many who regard the Sultan Hassan as the outstanding Islamic monument in Egypt, and certainly it vies with the Ibn Tulun. Though entirely different in type, the two mosques share a boldness of conception and clarity of execution, gathering still more strength in restraining decoration to the minimum necessary solely to underline architectural form. There is self-confidence, and at the Sultan Hassan even architectural insolence, but rarely indulgence.

The Sultan Hassan already impresses from the outside. Though it stands beneath the glare of the Citadel it holds its own, its great cornice and the strong verticals of its facade rising to the challenge. Notice how the broad surfaces along the east and west sides are relieved by blind recesses into which the paired arch windows of the dormitories are set. Height is especially emphasised as you enter on Sharia el Qalaa the towering *portal with its stalactite decorations* — a favourite Mameluke motif. The portal is at an angle to the main east flank of the mosque and the west flank too is bent, though at first sight the building had seemed more regular. Earlier periods had enjoyed more space, but as Cairo grew and became more dense the Mamelukes had to squeeze their buildings in where they could, though they had a fetish for achieving a cubistic effect no matter how irregular the plot. The liwans had also to be cruciform regardless of the exterior and in the Sultan Hassan this has been neatly done, all hint inside of the irregularity of the outer walls suppressed except for the slight angle of the door in the west liwan.

Characteristics of Mameluke architecture

The portal leads to a domed cruciform vestibule and you turn left into a dark angled passage. It empties suddenly into the north end of the brilliantly sun-filled sahn, certainly a deliberate effect and a preparation for the play of light and shadow, concrete and void, intended for the courtyard and its liwans. It is important that you do not come too late in the day, indeed it is best that you visit the Sultan Hassan in the morning when the sun lights up the mausoleum and west liwan and begins its long and rarely accomplished reach into the full depth of the sahn. Its depth is considerable, for the liwans lift about as high as the sahn is long. The sun soon passes, illuminating hardly more than the merlons by late afternoon, and much of the architectural effect of direct sunlight and strong shadows is lost so that the mosque can then seem a disappointment. The stucco anyway is pasty brown with sand and dirt, and other details need cleaning.

The gazebo at the centre of the sahn has been rebuilt in Ottoman style and is used now for ablutions. The original fountain is met later on in this Guide at the Maridani Mosque. Hundreds of chains hang down from the liwans, the glow of their oil lamps at night a delight reserved for the imagination as they are all gone, though some can be seen in the Islamic Museum. The *sanctuary liwan* is opposite the entrance passage, a Kufic band running within it and an unfortunately fussy marble decoration on its qibla wall. The columns on either side of the mihrab are from some Christian edifice, possibly Crusader — they do not seem Byzantine. Further to either side of the mihrab are doors leading into the *mausoleum*. The right-hand door is panelled with original bronze inlaid with gold and dazzles when polished. The mausoleum dome collapsed in the 17th C and was rebuilt in the 18th C in the lofty imperial style of Istanbul, though it rests on the original stalactite squinches. Rich though the restored decorations are, the atmosphere is sombre and Hassan's cenotaph, surrounded by a wooden screen where women pray for the Sultan's intercession, is very simple. From the grilled windows there are views of the Citadel.

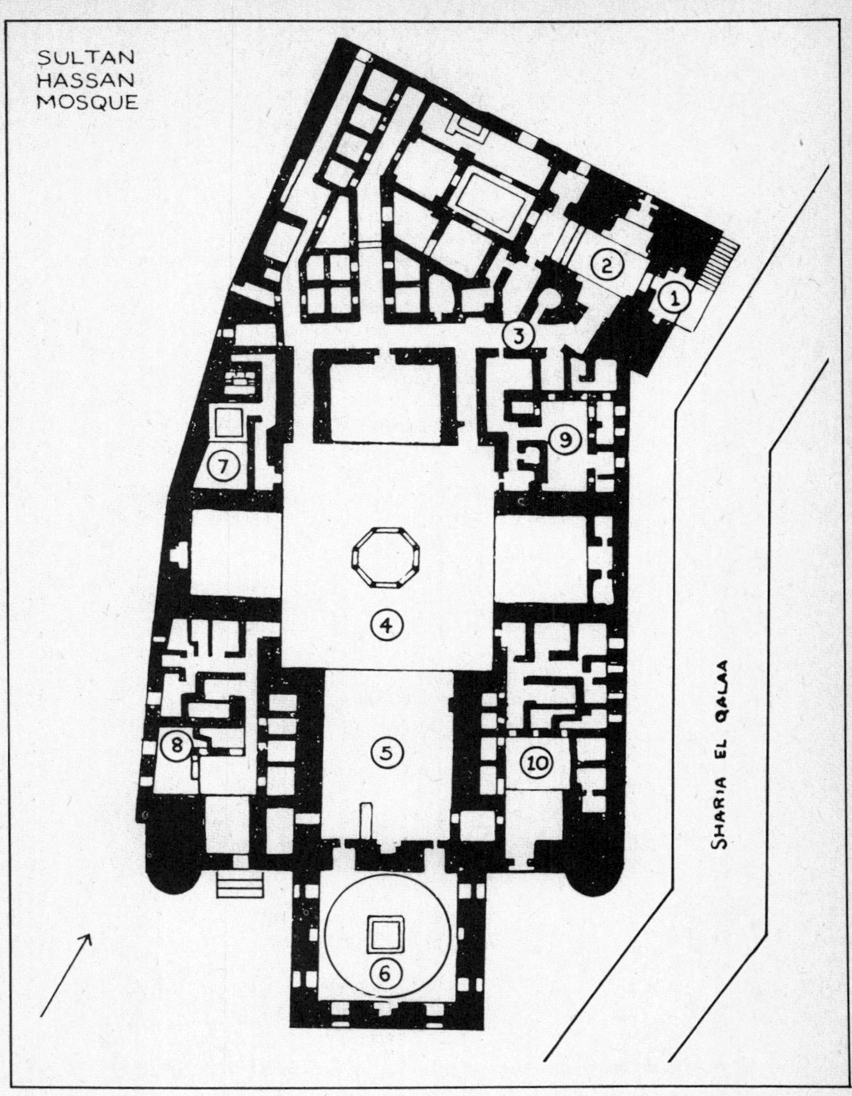

SULTAN HASSAN MOSQUE (cruciform plan)

1. Entrance
2. Vestibule
3. Corridor
4. Sahn
5. Sanctuary liwan
6. Mausoleum
7. Hanbalite school
8. Hanefite school
9. Malikite school
10. Shafite school

Visiting the Citadel

Returning towards the Citadel you once more enter Midan Salah al-Din, extended by clearances at the instruction of General Kitchener. It was here that the annual pilgrimage to Mecca gathered before winding through streets lined with thousands of spectators and leaving the city at the northern Fatimid gates of Bab al-Futuh and Bab al-Nasr. The long park to its south was a parade ground and polo field for the Mamelukes. Up a ramp at the front of the Citadel is a gate, closed to the public, **Bab al-Azab**. The crooked lane behind the gate, enclosed by high walls, was the scene of the massacre of the Mamelukes by Mohammed Ali in 1811. Only one escaped, leaping on horseback through a gap in the wall into a moat. During the Ottoman occupation and even under Napoleon the Mamelukes had survived and were a power to be reckoned with. Mohammed Ali invited them to dinner at the Citadel, bidding them homewards via this cul-de-sac and cutting them down with their bellies full.

Massacre of the Mamelukes

The entry to the Citadel is round to the left, that is clockwise round its base. There is another entrance round the rear, off the Heliopolis and airport road. Much of the Citadel is off-limits, reserved for the military, an echo of its role as stronghold of the city from the time Saladin in 1176 built his fortress here to the reign of Mohammed Ali. For nearly 700 years nearly all Egypt's rulers lived in the Citadel, held court, dispensed justice and received ambassadors. A succession of palaces and elaborate buildings thrown up during the Mameluke period were mostly levelled by Mohammed Ali when he built his mosque and **Bijou Palace** in their place. The palace, to the south of the mosque, is now a museum housing objects of its era and makes a pleasant visit if you have the time.

Turkish delight

The Mosque of Mohammed Ali, a Turkish delight on the Cairo skyline, proves disappointing close up — though perhaps not for those who have never visited an imperial Ottoman mosque in Turkey. Half domes rise as buttresses for the high central dome and the two thin minarets add an ethereal touch, more in tune perhaps with our oriental dreams than the robust Arab minarets of Cairo. But the alabaster cladding, a gesture of baroque luxe, has cheapened with time, while the pretty courtyard with its gingerbread *clock* (given by Louis Philippe in exchange for the obelisk in the Place de la Concorde), suggests a folly rigged up for fashion and amusement. That could explain why the mosque is so popular with tourists, for also the interior is vast and agreeably cool, the dome huge and the decorations in opulent bad taste. Principally, though, the architecture is routine; there is no feeling of lift or weightlessness to the dome that you find in the better Istanbul mosques, nor an appeal to spiritual contemplation. Mohammed Ali, whose *tomb* is on the right as you enter, meant this more as a symbol of the Ottoman power he had snatched.

From the parapet to the southwest there is a good view of the mosques of Hassan and Tulun and a panorama of the city which will be more or less impressive depending on the

Mosque of Sultan Hassan: soaring liwans

cinereous haze that heat and Helwan together smother Cairo with.

Across from the entrance to the courtyard of the Mohammed Ali Mosque is the **Mosque of al-Nasr Mohammed** (143), not much visited, dating from 1318-35. Once the principal mosque of the Citadel, it was built in the congregational style with an arcaded courtyard, many of the columns re-used from pharaonic, Roman and Byzantine buildings. Plain though it is outside, it is beautiful inside, all the more so as Turkish vandals stripped it of its marble panels, revealing its simple elegance. The two minarets are unique for the pincushion shape of their tops and their Mongol-inspired faience decoration, of which only traces remain.

On leaving the Mosque of al-Nasr, turn right and go round it, then take the first road to the right on the east side of the mosque. This brings you to a tower which stands over **Yusuf's (or Joseph's) Well** (305), also known as Salah al-Din's Well or Dir al-Halazun, the Well of the Snail for the spiral staircase leading 88 metres down the great central shaft to the level of the Nile. (The descent can be dangerous.) Yusuf was one of Saladin's names and the well was dug during his time by Crusader prisoners, providing a secure source of water in case of siege. The water reaches the well by natural rather than artificial channels, and was brought up by donkeys, the rock steps covered with earth to provide them with a foothold.

The Southern Cemetery

At this point you can interrupt your progress north with a visit to the Southern Cemetery, a vast, confusing and dilapidated Moslem necropolis stretching as far as Maadi. The Northern Cemetery generally offers the more impressive monuments and will be covered in a later chapter. But if you avail yourself of transport (or make the long walk there and back), the **Mausoleum of Imam al-Shaf'i** (281) in the Southern Cemetery would more than repay an excursion.

A visit to the Southern Cemetery

The mausoleum is most easily reached by heading south from the Citadel along the street bearing the Imam's name, a distance of about 2 kms from Midan Salah al-Din. A descendant of an uncle to the Prophet, al-Shaf'i was the founder of one of the four rites of Sunni Islam and died in 820. The cenotaph was put here by Saladin and the mausoleum built by his brother-successor's wife who is also buried here. The mausoleum is covered by a large wooden dome sheathed in lead and is the largest Islamic mortuary chamber in Egypt. Inside, a couple of cats, some birds chirping, men lying about or reading the Koran, and above this the magnificent dome painted red and blue and gold, a pattern of flowers rising to the highest sound of birdsong. The original lighting system of lamps suspended from carved beams is intact — the only such in Cairo.

The spot itself is of significance: it was here that Saladin founded the first madrasa in Egypt to counter the Fatimid heresy, and it became a centre of Shafite missionary work, the rite predominant even today in southern Arabia, Bahrain, Malaysia and East Africa. The majority of Cairenes, too, are Shafites, and as the Imam is revered as one of the great Moslem saints (achieved by popular acclamation, as there is no formal notion of sainthood in Islam), the mausoleum is annually — in the eighth month of the Moslem calendar, lasting for a week from, usually, the first Wednesday — the site of a great *moulid*, an anniversary birthday festival, in honour of Shaf'i. Atop the dome, like a weathervane, is a metal boat in which there used to be placed on the occasion of the moulid about 150 kilos of wheat and a camel-load of water for the birds. The boat is said to turn sometimes when there is no wind to move it, and according to the position it takes to foretoken various events, good or evil, such as plenty or scarcity, or the death of some great man.

PRACTICAL INFORMATION

To reach the starting point of this tour you can take a **taxi** or you can ride to Midan Salah al-Din (lying between the Citadel and the Sultan Hassan Mosque) on the **No.72 bus** from Midan el Tahrir. All the monuments in this chapter are quite close together with the exception of the Mausoleum of Imam al-Shaf'i — to reach this take the **No.405 bus** south from Midan Salah al-Din along Sharia Imam al-Shaf'i; it then turns left towards the Moqattam Hills and just where it does so there is a bus stop. You then walk down Sharia Imam al-Shaf'i a few hundred metres. Or take the **tram** from Midan Salah al-Din following the same route except that instead of it turning left it continues straight on, terminating just short of the Mausoleum.

The Ibn Tulun, Gayer-Anderson, Hassan, Rifa'i and Citadel all charge a **fee** from 50PT to LE2; the Mausoleum of Imam al-Shaf'i is free. (Your entrance ticket to the Gayer-Anderson is also valid on the same day for admission to the Islamic Museum). There may be additional fees, or at least baksheesh, for shoe coverings. You should not assume that any of these places will remain open after 4pm.

For those with limited time, an **abbreviated itinerary** should include the Mosques of Ibn Tulun and Sultan Hassan.

DARB EL AHMAR

Continuing our journey northwards, let us assume we are back at the Citadel. You should leave the Citadel by the northeast entrance (the one you entered if you came up from Midan Salah al-Din), turning left as soon as you pass through the gate. Down the hill you cross over the road which issues east out of the midan and you enter Sharia el Mahga. The road plunges downhill and soon becomes Sharia Bab el Wazir, the Street of the Gate of the Vizier, and later becomes Darb el Ahmar, the Red Road, as it runs up to Bab Zuwayla. This entire district is known as **Darb el Ahmar**, a name which nowadays epitomises a poorer, broken-down section of the city. At the Citadel end which is entirely residential the street is fairly quiet and fairly filthy; it becomes livelier, and you do not notice the filth so much, as you enter the bazaar area further north. Apart from the ruins of many old houses and some fine intact monuments, you may also encounter the gaiety of a marriage procession, a great noise of motor scooters, car horns, tambourines, ululations, whistling, chanting and cries, an amazing public racket by no more than two dozen people escorting the bride and groom through the streets.

Along Sharia Bab el Wazir

Soon after setting off down Sharia Bab el Wazir you come on your right to the **Mosque of Aqsunqur** (123), better known as the **Blue Mosque** and much beloved for the wrong reasons by tour guides. It was built in 1347 but usurped in 1652 by the Turkish Governor Ibrahim Agha who slapped up the tiles that give the mosque its popular name. The best Turkish tiles were from Iznik; these were made in Ottoman factories at Damascus and are poorly decorated and often marred as well in the glazing. They are along the qibla wall and around the walls of Agha's tomb which you enter through a door on the right side of the courtyard. The worst thing about the tiles is their inappropriateness, for the mosque is otherwise charmingly simple. A stand of palms and other trees makes the courtyard an agreeable place to linger after the hot desolate sahns of other mosques. The pillars round the courtyard, and especially the octagonal ones of the sanctuary, are crude, but contribute to the rustic pleasantness of the whole. The finest work is the carved stone minbar, which is original. On the left before entering the courtyard is the tomb of Sultan Kuchuk, The Little One, a brother of Hassan who ruled for five months at the age of six, but was then deposed, imprisoned in the Citadel, and three years later strangled by another of his brothers.

A small strangling

From the street you can see behind the Aqsunqur a section of *Saladin's walls* which extended from the Fatimid city in the north to Fustat in the south, the Mamelukes using a part of its southern section to carry their aqueduct. Across the street from the mosque is a **Turkish apartment building** from 1625.

Into Darb el Ahmar

Continuing north, Sharia Bab el Wazir becomes Darb el

Ahmar and set at an angle to this street, on the left-hand side, is the **Maridani Mosque** (120). Built in 1339-40 in the early Mameluke period, it is one of the oldest buildings in the quarter which until the 14th C had been Fatimid and Ayyubid cemeteries.

Entering from the hurly-burly of the street you are soon absorbed into the restfulness of the Maridani, a monument, yes, but no museum, no entry fee, no one to ask baksheesh for shoe covers for there are none, and you leave your shoes inside the door and walk about in your socks. Not that you need worry about form, but as a matter of interest a Moslem will carry his shoes in his left hand, sole to sole (the left hand being for unclean uses), and he will put his right foot first over the threshold. If he has not already performed the ablution outside, he will at once go to the inner fountain. Before praying, he will place his shoes on the matting, a little before the spot where his head will touch the ground, and again, to avoid contaminating the mosque, he will but his shoes one upon the other, sole to sole.

Removing shoes

Isolation from the outside world is as much a matter of tranquil ambience as it is of ritual cleanliness. The atmosphere attracts many who come not only for prayer: here I have seen men sleeping, boys doing their homework leaning up against the qibla screen, a dozen women talking and their children playing at the fountain (the one removed from the Sultan Hassan). Yet all of these things are against the precepts of Mohammed, and even though Lane reported, 150 years ago, eating, sewing and spinning as well, these activities ceased during prayers, though here, too, I have seen the hum of irreligion continue while men were on their palms and knees, submitting themselves to Allah.

Prayers

Prayers are performed five times a day, though mostly at home, with better off people rarely visiting a mosque except for Friday prayers. But wherever they are performed, prayers follow the same procedure, which is quite involved. First the worshipper will stand, facing Mecca, and inaudibly propose a prayer of so many *rek'ahs*, or inclinations of the head. He then says 'Allahu Akbar', God is great, and recites the opening chapter of the Koran, followed by three or more other verses, again says 'Allahu Akbar' and makes an inclination of the head and body. Next he drops gently to his knees, places his palms upon the ground, his nose and forehead touching the ground between them, and during this prostration says 'I extol the perfection of my Lord, the Great', three times. Though still kneeling, he raises his head and body, again says 'God is great', and bends his head a second time to the ground and repeats what he has said before. This — and it is a simplification of the full litany — completes one rek'ah and will take about a minute, though several rek'ahs will be performed and there must be no wandering of the mind, no irregular movement and no interruptions, otherwise the procedure must be gone over from the beginning. Islam literally means submission and that is what the procedure achieves. The concentration required explains why mosques are often so austere: architecturally they should be conducive to prayer, but should not distract with decorations. That does not explain why, nowadays, and in some mosques, women should be chattering in the corner and children splashing in the fountain, yet it does all fit together most agreeably, and if you stand here in the open courtyard of the Maridani at evening, you may see a crescent moon hanging from the approving sky.

An easy rhythm of arches on slender columns runs round the courtyard, an inner and an outer series, a third and partial fourth (on either side of the mihrab) added to the qibla arcade. A wooden *screen* separates the qibla from the courtyard, a unique feature in Cairo, and, inside, the arcade is pleasantly dark. The mihrab and the minbar wall have had their mosaic decorations well restored. The dome above the mihrab is supported by two pink granite pharaonic columns. The merlons along the parapet of the courtyard are at intervals topped by curious pots. Try, if you can, to climb up the minaret for a more immediate view of the medieval city than you can get from the Citadel.

Another 150 metres up the street is the **Mosque of Qijmas al-Ishaqi** (114), built in 1480-1 during the Burgi Mameluke period. It has been squeezed into a triangular plot where a street joins Darb el Ahmar from the right, yet despite this the Mameluke fashion for rectangular illusion succeeds, at least at first glance. Inside, however, a sacrifice has been made in the cruciform plan: the north and south liwans are merely vestigial. So restricted was the space that the *kuttab*, the Koranic school usually part of the mosque, had to be sited across the street joining from the right; it is now derelict.

But the mosque itself has been very well restored and though around this period — only a few decades before the Turkish domination — Mameluke architecture began to deteriorate, there was a last bravado of decorative artistry with fine marble inlays and beautifully carved stone and stucco. Within this covered mosque is a feast of detail, yet all of it harmonious and restful; nothing jitters, jumps or jars. The east and west liwans are supported by arches with a slight return, the stonework in alternating red and white, the vaults very fine and the stucco windows excellent. The inlaid marble floor is covered with mats (the mosque is in daily use), but the keeper will lift these if you ask, the best section being the mosaic flooring of the east liwan. You can also ask to go up the minaret from which there is a clear view of Bab Zuwayla.

The tomb chamber by the entrance is plain and dignified beneath a lofty dome. But Qijmas, Master of the Sultan's Horse and officer in charge of the yearly pilgrimage to Mecca, died in Syria and is buried at Damascus; the chamber contains the more recent tomb of a 19th C holy man. Mamelukes and Turks of Qijmas' rank built not only for Allah or themselves, but also for the community, and a *sabil* or public watering fountain was often provided. This was in keeping with Mohammed's reply when asked what was the most meritorious act: 'To give people water to drink'. You can see its grille outside at what was a convenient height for drawing water 500 years ago, though now well below street level.

Outside the Gate of the Fatimid City

Darb el Ahmar now bends to the west, a surviving section of

Fatimid keel-arches and tie-beams: Mosque of Salih Talai

Fatimid wall concealed by the buildings on your right, and opens into a square dominated by **Bab Zuwayla** (see later chapter), the massive southern gate into the Fatimid city. The place has long had a reputation for being unlucky, perhaps because it led out to the cemeteries now built over by the Darb el Ahmar quarter, though also it was the site of public executions. Tumanbay, the last independent Mameluke Sultan, was hanged here by the Turks. Twice the rope broke, the third time his neck.

Public executions

The street running directly south from Bab Zuwayla is the continuation of the principal Fatimid street to the north and extends all the way down, past the Mosque of Ibn Tulun and through Saladin's walls to the vicinity of the Mausoleum of Imam al-Shaf'i. This was the longest thoroughfare of the medieval city and along here amidst great festivity the Mecca pilgrims would begin their arduous journey. It changes its name several times and can be worth following for its own sake a little to the south where it is first the Street of the Tentmakers, becoming less colourful as the Street of the Saddlemakers before crossing Sharia el Qalaa.

On the corner of this street and Darb el Ahmar, facing the square, is the **Mosque of Salih Talai** (116), built in 1160 towards the close of the Fatimid period. A congregational mosque, perfectly rectangular in the Fatimid pattern, it is one of the most handsome in Cairo. A lower level of shops, again once at street level, was part of Salih Talai's *waqf* or endowment, as other mosques might have had fields or adjacent apartment buildings, the rents contributing to the mosque's upkeep. The facade, therefore, would have been higher, its effect still more imposing. Its five keel-arches, supported by classical columns linked by wooden tie-beams, are flanked by sunken false arches or panels topped by stylised shell niches — the whole a perfect expression of the Fatimid style. The arches, however, form a *narthex* or porch unique in Cairo. Along its interior wall another set of panels, each one immediately behind an open keel-arch, runs in muted harmony. In its proportion and reserve the narthex is a fine composition in classical measure. The mosque interior is spacious, an agreeable rhythm of keel-arches and tie-beams running round the arcades.

PRACTICAL INFORMATION

To reach the starting point of this tour go to the Midan Salah al-Din (see the *Practical Information* section at the end of the previous chapter).

The mosques visited in this chapter are still very much places of worship rather than tourist sights and they are usually open throughout the day and into the evening. There are no entrance fees, though baksheesh should be paid for services, eg shoe coverings, being taken up a minaret.

The pleasure of this itinerary is the slow walk and the occasional pause at the mosques along the way — enjoyment of atmosphere. The person in a hurry might therefore wish to skip this chapter altogether, though the best advice is that he should not be in a hurry. An **abbreviated itinerary** should bring you to the square before the Mosque of Salih Talai and Bab Zuwayla; this could be combined with a visit to the Islamic Museum or with the walk from Bab Zuwayla to Khan el Khalili (see following chapters).

THE ISLAMIC MUSEUM

The Islamic Museum, to the west of the Bab Zuwayla, is at the intersection of Sharias el Qalaa and Port Said, its entrance on the latter through a garden to which you should return later. Of course the museum could be visited before you explore any part of Islamic Cairo, but for the neophyte, anyway, a visit at this point, halfway through the tour, might be best: you will already have seen enough to make you conversant with form and curious about detail, and you will explore the Fatimid city with greater appreciation.

A revelation, met especially here, is how much you miss human and animal representation in Islamic art and architecture. This is a museum without statues or paintings, where nearly every object is beautifully worked design. A different sort of attention is required, and perhaps you wish sometimes, more here than at other museums, that the exhibits could have remained *in situ*, admired as parts of a whole.

Preservation of Cairo's Islamic treasures

But then the collection began, in 1880, precisely because the monuments from which they mostly came had suffered a long period of neglect — it was only then, in part at European instigation, that the Egyptian government first seriously undertook preservation of Cairo's Islamic treasures.

The exhibits are well presented and lit and are arranged in 23 rooms which proceed chronologically for the most part, though some rooms specialise in examples of a single subject, eg textiles, from several periods. Though no guide book is available, the exhibits are numbered and labelled, often in English and French as well as in Arabic. A satisfying tour can be accomplished in an hour and a half. The rooms are on one floor and a brief outline follows, but note that some rooms may be closed and their contents either inaccessible or to be found in another nearby room.

Note that because the entrance used to be along the side of the building facing Sharia Port Said, the room numbers start from there; but because you now enter through the north garden (reached also from Sharia Port Said) you find yourself first in Room 7 and so should walk straight through rooms 7, 10, 4B and 2 in order to begin at Room 1.

A Tour of the Museum

Room 1 contains **recent acquisitions**, though also some permanent exhibits, including a 14th C bronze lantern and a collection of Islamic coins.

Room 2 deals with the **Ummayad** period (7th-8th C) whose art was representational and drew on Hellenistic and Sassanian (Persian) sources.

Room 3 is **Abbasid** (8th-10th C) and includes **Tulunid** (9th-10th C) works. Here there is greater stylisation, with the emphasis on decoration rather than representation, with great use of stucco, characterised by its slant cut. There are stucco panels from Samarra in Iraq, and tombstones, of which 3904, dating from 858, has fine Kufic inscriptions.

Room 4 displays works of the **Fatimid** period (10th-12th C) with examples of very fine woodwork, carved with human and animal figures and foliage. The Fatimids, who were Shi'ites, did not observe the Sunni prohibition on representation of high living forms, and were much influenced by the Persians, whose craftsmen they imported.

Room 4B, off Room 4, has fine wood, marble and stucco carving of the **Ayyubid** period (12th-13th C).

Before entering *Room 5*, note above the dividing arch the windows of openwork plaster filled with coloured glass (16th-18th C, Ottoman period). (The museum, incidentally, is not visited nearly as much as it deserves to be, so that you often receive personal attention. In this case, the attendant will turn off the main lights and illuminate the coloured windows for effect.) The room contains works of the **Mameluke** period (13th-16th C). There is a beautiful 14th C fountain sunk into the floor (the attendant will turn it on). Despite the bloody succession of Mameluke sultans, Egypt during much of this period enjoyed peace and the decorative arts flourished. A Chinese influence was felt in Mameluke ceramics and pottery. Soft woods were inlaid with ivory, bone, tin and ebony, usually in star-polygons, the Naskhi cursive supplanted the squat Kufic style of decorative inscription, and arabesque floral designs found favour. A 13th C wooden door (602) at the far end of the room shows both square Kufic and cursive Naskhi calligraphy. It is from the Mosque of al-Salih Ayyub.

Rooms 6-10 are devoted to **woodwork**, illustrating the development of the art. In *Room 6* on the far wall is a carved frieze from the Maristan of Qalaun, showing scenes of hunting, music and other personal activities rarely found in Islamic art. In *Room 7* are *mashrabiyyas*, wooden screens which preserved the privacy of the house from the gaze of the street while still admitting refreshing breezes. They were also used to screen off interior harem rooms from courtyards and reception halls. The projecting niches were for placing porous water jars for cooling. *Room 8* has examples of inlaid wood, while *Room 9* displays wood and bronze work.

In *Room 10*, off Room 9, you will be asked to sit down on a lattice-backed seat round a column fountain which will be turned on for you and illuminated. This is a restful and eye-filling place to linger: gaze up at the exquisite woodwork ceiling, carved and coffered, with three dome recesses, the centre one with windows round it for ladies of the harem to see below. The period is 17th-18th C.

Room 11 is hung with 14th C bronze chandeliers, and in the cases are various **metalwork** objects, eg a perfume brazier (15111, Case 7).

Room 12 contains armour and weapons, many of them chased and inlaid. In Case 7 are swords belonging to Mehmet II, who conquered Constantinople (4264), and Suleiman the Magnificent (4263). And another in the same case, opposite the windows on the right, which has had a remarkable history: the sword of Muradbey, commander of the Mamelukes, was taken by the French general Murat after he had chased the Mamelukes up the Nile, and was presented to Napoleon who in turn wore it when calling on the Directory shortly before seizing power on 18 Brumaire 1799. He had it with him also at Waterloo, and leaving it in his carriage which he abandoned in haste after the battle, it was presented to Wellington.

Rooms 13-16 contain **pottery** of various periods from Egypt and as far west as Spain, as far east as China.

Room 17 displays **tapestries** of various periods from Egypt, Iraq and Persia, and an assortment of damaged pottery (though this room may still be closed and its contents found in Room 16).

Leading off Room 19 is an outdoor court which is *Room 18* and is principally of Turkish headstones and tombs, but also other **stonework** objects, including a sundial and water level measures.

Room 19 is devoted to the art of the book with many illuminated **manuscripts** and, in the centre case, manuscripts of Avicenna on anatomy and botany. While Europe slept through its Dark Ages, Islam sparkled with genius. Avicenna, as he was known in Europe, Ibn Sina (980-1037) in the Moslem world, was one of the greatest physicians of his time. He is mentioned by Chaucer in *The Canterbury Tales*. The Arabs did not alter the basic medical theory of the Greeks, but they enriched it by practical observation and clinical experience, recorded in manuscripts such as these, and passed on their learning to the world.

Room 20 exhibits **Turkish** art since the 15th C including tapestries, china and jewellery.

Between Rooms 20 and 21 are enamelled glass **lamps** which the attendant will illuminate, while there are more glass lamps in cases round the walls of *Room 21* and in the centre a fine Isfahan carpet that once belonged to King Farouk. The lamps are from mosques (and include some of those now entirely missing from the liwans of the Sultan Hassan) and are arranged chronologically from left to right from the 12th through the 15th C.

Room 22 contains **Persian** objects, mostly pottery, some of which (Cases 1 and 2) has been copied from Chinese models.

Room 23 is for **temporary exhibitions**.

The garden can now be enjoyed on your way out; there are welcome refreshments for sale in a flower-planted setting with a shaded gazebo, a fountain, columns and other large stone pieces. Particularly fine are the large marble panels bearing Fatimid figurative reliefs of plants, birds, fish and animals.

Concerning the fountain, there is a story that I have from a member of the family to whom it once belonged. The fountain was in their palace on Roda. Its purpose was to run a stream of water through tiled channels decorated with creatures of the Nile, the channels encircling a large dining table, the flowing water keeping the diners cool. The palace was sequestrated by King Farouk, but when Queen Marie of Roumania announced her intention to pay the family a visit Farouk kindly let them have the use of the palace for one last dinner. By now, however, the fountain would not work; yet the water flowed, the guests were cooled — the old servants were brought back, my friend explained, and formed a human chain between the Nile and the back of the fountain into which they tipped bucket after bucket of water throughout the dinner. 'They so enjoyed it', my friend said of the servants, 'wasn't that *sweet*?' Nasser later came along and bulldozed the palace; this fountain is all that remains.

In the same building but on the upper floor is the **Egyptian Library** with its entrance on Sharia el Qalaa. Containing over 750,000 volumes and a vast collection of manuscripts of the Koran dating back to the 8th C and, most outstanding visually, a collection of Persian manuscripts adorned with miniatures of imaginative conception and frequently employing living forms as distinct from the purely ornamental art of the Korans.

PRACTICAL INFORMATION

The Islamic Museum is at Midan Ahmed Maher, where Sharia Port Said and Sharia el Qalaa intersect. A **taxi** can take you here or to nearby Bab Zuwayla (the driver may know it better as Bab al-Mitwalli), or you can take the **No. 66 bus** from Midan el Tahrir.

The museum is open daily from 9am to 4pm except Fridays when it is closed from 11am to 1.30pm. There is an entrance **fee** of LE2 (LE1 for students with card) which is also valid on the same day for the Gayer-Anderson House.

BAB ZUWAYLA TO KHAN EL KHALILI

Entering the Fatimid city

We now turn to **Bab Zuwayla**, built at the same time (11th C) and in a plan similar to Bab al-Futuh and Bab al-Nasr to the north. These three are the last surviving of the 60 gates that once encircled medieval Cairo and which, well into the 19th C, were shut at night, enclosing the city's then 240,000 population. Except that Bab Zuwayla had long since found itself outflanked by the growth of the city to the south (where it was delimited by Saladin's walls), and in fact marked the city centre. The architects of all three were probably Christian, from Syria or Anatolia, and the projecting round towers connected by a walkway and an arch repeating the curve of the gateway below show Byzantine rather than Arab inspiration. Springing from the massive towers are the elegant minarets of the Mosque of Muayyad, its serrated dome further back seeming to rise between them.

The gate was named for the al-Zawila, a Berber tribe whose Fatimid soldiery were quartered nearby. But most inhabitants know it as the al-Mitwalli after El Kutb al-Mitwalli, the holiest man alive at any one time, who would assume a humble demeanour and simple dress, and station himself inconspicuously, even invisibly, at certain favourite places. Bab Zuwayla was the most famous of these in Egypt, though he could flit to Tanta in the Delta, or to Mecca and back, in an instant. His service was to reprove the impious, expose the sanctimonious, and to distribute evils and blessings, the awards of destiny. Into the earlier part of this century, passersby would recite the opening verse of the Koran, while those with headache would drive a nail into the door, or sufferers from a recent toothache would fix their tooth to it as a charm against recurrence. Locks of hair, bits of clothing, would also be attached by the sick in search of a miracle, and, it is said, even without these entreaties, the saint still makes his presence known by a gleam of light mysteriously appearing behind the west door.

Climbing the minarets above Bab Zuwayla

Passing through the gate, you should enter the **Mosque of Muayyad** (190) on your left, less for any intrinsic interest, though it is restful and has a garden, than for access to the top of Bab Zuwayla or even up one of the minarets. This is a view of medieval Cairo from its heart and it is splendid. The last of the great open courtyard congregational mosques, the Muayyad was built in 1416-20 by the Burgi Mameluke Muayyad Shaykh who had been imprisoned on the spot before becoming Sultan.

Souks and Okels

This street running north from Bab Zuwayla is Sharia Muizz (named for the Caliph of the Fatimid conquest), though over its distance between Bab Zuwayla and Bab al-Futuh it enjoys successive traditional names, each one demarcating a souk reserved to a particular trade or the sale of a particular type of merchandise — ensuring, subject to proper bargaining, price control by competition between neighbours. Alongside Muayyad's mosque, for example, the street is Shari'es-

Sukkariya, the sugar bazaar. Competition, however, was not the only control on market prices: the Mohtesib, an officer on horseback, would regularly ride through the souks, preceded by a man carrying a pair of scales and followed by the executioner. If spot checks revealed short weights, a butcher, for example, or a baker would have his nose pierced with a hook, a piece of meat, a loaf of bread, suspended from it as the poor man was himself tied to the grilled window of a mosque and left to endure the heat of the sun, the indifference of passersby. One butcher who sold short was deprived of that much flesh from his own body, while a seller of *kunefeh*, that vermicelli pasta you still see prepared along the streets at night, was fried on his own copper tray for overcharging.

Continuing up to the intersection with the modern Sharia al-Azhar, you find yourself between two Mameluke buildings, the **Madrasa of Sultan al-Ghuri** (189) on the left and his **Mausoleum** (67) on the right. Al-Ghuri was the penultimate Mameluke Sultan and the last to reign for any duration (1500-16). A keen polo player into his seventies, a grandiose builder, an arbitrary despot, a torturer, murderer and thief, in short no less than what you would expect a Mameluke sultan to be, he inaugurated his madrasa in May 1503 with a great banquet attended by the Abbasid Caliph and all the principal civil, military and religious officials, the souks down to Bab Zuwayla magnificently illuminated and decorated. But though agreeably exotic at first impression, with strong lines and bold *ablaq*, that red and white pattern of the minaret with its curious topping of five small bulbous domes, on closer inspection there is lack of elegance in the details, and in climbing up to the roof you see that the ablaq is not contrasting stone but crudely painted on.

Mameluke sunset

Across the street, the mausoleum dome, now collapsed, had to be rebuilt three times during al-Ghuri's reign, and as though shrewdly realising that this might be an unsafe place to be buried, he got himself killed outside Aleppo in a losing battle against the Turks. His luckless successor, that same Tumanbay who was hanged three times at Bab Zuwayla, is buried here instead.

Heading east along Sharia al-Azhar you come after about 100 metres to the **Okel of al-Ghuri** (64) on you right, unmistakably Mameluke with its ablaq masonry and strong, square lines. Built in 1504-5, this is Cairo's best preserved example of a merchants' hotel, the animals quartered on the ground floor and their masters above. The courtyard would be the scene of unloading aromatic cargoes, with buyers and sellers sitting round and bargaining. This okel was built just at the time that the Portuguese were dealing a blow to Egypt's overland trade with the East by their discovery of new routes round the Cape to India. Even so, as late as 1835 there were still 200 okels serving Cairo's bazaars.

The Religious Heart of Islamic Cairo

The famous **Mosque of al-Azhar** (97), 'the most blooming', is 100 metres east of al-Ghuri's caravanserai, the first mosque of the Fatimid city (completed in 971), the oldest university in the

Prayers before emerging from the Mosque of Muayyad

world and the foremost centre of Islamic theology. Its age and importance have caused it to be rebuilt and added to many times, the result confusing and unremarkable. The court and arcades are basically Fatimid, but their interest lies in the people gathered here, students and teachers at lessons, some pacing back and forth, mumbling to themselves, memorising religious texts, others dozing.

Throughout the millenium of its existence, al-Azhar has offered free instruction and board to students from all over the Islamic world, from West Africa to the East Indies, its courses sometimes lasting 15 years. *Riwaqs* or apartments are set aside around three sides of the court for specific nationalities or provinces of Egypt, and here students have traditionally studied religious, moral, civil and criminal law, grammar, rhetoric, theology, logic, algebra and calculations on the Moslem calendar which is based on the moon, its festivals changeable but always advancing against the secular solar calendar. The Chapel of the Blind at the eastern angle of al-Azhar accommodates blind students, once notorious for their outrageous behaviour. Fanatical in their belief and easily thinking themselves persecuted, they would rush out into the streets, snatching at turbans, beating people with their staves and groping about for infidels to kill.

Oldest university in the world

Al-Azhar's religious curriculum has remained unchanged since the days of Saladin, who turned al-Azhar from a hotbed of Shi'ism to the home of orthodoxy, though Nasser obliged the university to include, too, schools of medicine, science and foreign languages, so that now in many ways it is competitive with other institutions of higher education in Egypt. The more conventional buildings of the modern university are behind the mosque proper.

You enter the mosque through the double-arched Gate of the Barbers (the only one open to visitors) where formerly students had their heads shaved, and for a bit of baksheesh can ascend the *minaret of Qaytbay*. Passing into the courtyard, on the left is the *library*, worth a visit, and to the right a 14th C *madrasa* with a fine mihrab. The *sanctuary hall* directly opposite the entry gate is very deep, though in Fatimid times it did not extend beyond the fifth row of columns (that is five rows beyond the two of the east arcade), and the original mihrab remains. These columns were taken mostly from early churches. The sanctuary was extended to eight rows in the 18th C and a new mihrab placed at its furthest, qibla, wall.

Leaving al-Azhar and walking north, you cross the busy Sharia Gohar el Qaid and enter a large square, used as a parking lot, before the **Mosque of Sayyidna al-Hussein**, a modern structure with slender Turkish-style minarets. A Fatimid mosque stood here originally but very little if any of it remains. This is now the main congregational mosque of Cairo and the President of the Republic comes here on feast days for prayers, while the open square is the centre for popular nightly celebrations throughout the month of Ramadan — well worth seeing.

The Hussein, named for a grandson of the Prophet, is not open to non-Moslems. Hussein's head, brought to Cairo in 1153 in a green silk bag, is in the mausoleum, a relic of one of the most critical events in Islamic history, the schism between the Sunni majority and the Shi'ites.

The Sunni-Shi'ite schism

Mohammed was more than a prophet, he organised the Arab tribes into an enduring political and military force that within a hundred years or so of his death in 632 advanced as far west as Morocco and Spain, as far north as Poitiers and as far east as the Indus. But Mohammed died without naming a successor. His son-in-law Ali, husband of the Prophet's daughter Fatima, advanced his claim but after some argument Abu Bakr, one of Mohammed's companions, won acceptance as *Khalifat rasul-Allah* or successor to the Apostle of God. Abu Bakr was succeeded by Omar who was succeeded on his death by Othman, an old, weak and vacillating man, but a member of the powerful Umayyad family of Mecca. Tribal tensions within the ever-expanding Arab Empire led to revolt and his murder in 656. Again Ali put himself forward as the natural inheritor of the Caliphate, for not only was he related to Mohammed through Fatima, but he was a man of considerable religious learning and sincerity, while his supporters claimed the Umayyads were no more than power-seeking opportunists. The reality is that both sides cloaked political and economic aspirations in religious arguments. Ali however was opposed by Aisha, who had been Mohammed's favourite wife, along with her Umayyad family and many of Mohammed's surviving companions. He took to arms and won his first battle, but later saw his authority dissolve when rebels advanced on his army with copies of the Koran fixed to the points of their spears and

Young girl along Sharia Muizz

his troops refused to fight. Ali was assassinated and the Umayyads were installed once again in the Caliphate.

The real wound to Islam occurred, however, when Ali's son — no mere in-law of the Prophet but of his blood — led a revolt against the by now overwhelming forces of the Umayyads and after a fanatical struggle was slain with all his men. In a sense the Prophet's own blood had been shed — excusable, said the Ummayads, for Hussein was no more than an outlaw; martyrdom, replied those who had supported Ali and Hussein. It was on this matter of succession — divine right versus might — that Islam was riven, for the partisans or *Shia* of Ali refused to accept as caliph any but Ali's descendants, while the *Sunni*, followers of the *sunna*, The Way, barred the Caliphate to the Prophet's descendants for all time.

In fact, the Shi'ites went on to win some notable victories as when the Fatimids took Egypt, and to this day one-tenth of all Moslems (Iranians, most Iraqis and significant numbers in Yemen, Syria, Lebanon and eastern Arabia) still hold to the Shi'ite conviction that with the deaths of Ali and Hussein the greater part of Islam was stained with betrayal. All the same, this division within Islam is much less important than the doctrinal rifts within Christianity, and it is remarkable that it is here in the old Fatimid city, by the mausoleum containing the very head of the Shi'ite martyr, that the President of thoroughly Sunni Egypt should come to pray.

Muski and Khan el Khalili

The bazaars

Muski and Khan el Khalili are used interchangeably by both foreigners and Egyptians alike to describe what are historically two different bazaars. **Muski** lies astride Sharia el Muski, a street of Mohammed Ali's period running east from Midan Ataba, pots, pans, plastic bowls and other prosaic wares sold at its western end but blending with the oriental atmosphere of Khan el Khalili which it joins to the east.

Khan el Khalili is the larger and older of the two, and grew round a khan or caravanserai built in 1382 by Sultan Barquq's Master of Horse, Garkas el Khalili. It became known as the Turkish bazaar during the Ottoman period and has always attracted foreign merchants — Jews, Armenians, Persians and non-Egyptian Arabs — and so it is not surprising that today, along with the Muski, it is Cairo's tourist bazaar, selling souvenirs, perfume oils, jewellery, leather goods and fabrics. Of course the sight of so many tourists invites relentless importuning, but there is adventure all the same. Escape down back alleyways where an artisan sitting in his hole in the wall may patiently be making beads one by one from rough bits of stone, turning them on a spindle by means of a bow. Or start in bargaining and then break off — an accepted, indeed the expert pattern — and instead sip a proffered glass of tea, idling for hours if you like upon a pile of carpets without there being any sense of the need for business. Or go into Fishawi's, the famous café just off Midan Sayyidna Hussein. Here you can have the chance of easy conversation and a gentle smoke of a water pipe ('Do not inhale, it is not hashish.').

The Fatimid palaces

Khan el Khalili extends in part over the site of the now vanished Fatimid palaces which covered an area of 400,000 square metres and housed 12,000 domestics. The palaces, al-Muizz on the east side of Sharia Muizz and al-Aziz on the west, loomed like mountains when seen from afar; near to, they could not be seen at all, so high were the surrounding walls.

PRACTICAL INFORMATION

Instructions for reaching the start of this itinerary are the same as for the Islamic Museum.

Only al-Azhar will require payment of an entrance **fee**. You will need, however, small change for services here and elsewhere.

The Okel (or Wakala) or al-Ghuri serves also as a permanent exhibition of fellahin and Bedouin folk crafts, and those of Nubia and the oases. Folk music and dancing troupes sometimes perform in the courtyard. Open from 8.30am to 2pm daily except Friday. Free.

An **abbreviated itinerary** should at least involve a stroll from Bab Zuwayla to Khan el Khalili for the passing flavour. This could be combined with a visit to the Islamic Museum.

TO THE NORTHERN WALLS

Street of the Coppersmiths

Sharia Muizz, as you leave the awning-covered alleyways of Khan el Khalili and walk north along it, is the Street of the Coppersmiths, some bashing of metal, much flashing of sunlight. Some reminders of the Fatimid period survive, though mostly the monuments are Mameluke. There should be a mosque on every street, it is said. Here mosques fight for every corner, their domes and minarets bunched like palms in an oasis grove. The scene is still that of the *Thousand and One Nights*, ostensibly set in Baghdad, though Baghdad by then had been razed by Tamerlane and it was the Cairo of the Mamelukes that was described. Sweet juices, cool water is sold in the street, the waterseller with a large flask slung under one arm like a bagpipe, round his waist the cups. He leans forward to pour, and for a moment you imagine this an obeisance to a passing sultan, and in the sweep of robes, the clattering of donkey carts, the bursts of reflected light from the coppersmiths' stalls, you easily imagine a triumphal entry, a parade of state, singers and poets preceding the royal appearance, celebrating the achievements of his reign. You see fluttering banners of silk and gold thread, then carried before the Sultan himself the jewelled saddlecloth, symbol of his sovereignty, and above his head a parasol of yellow silk surmounted with a golden cupola on which perches a golden bird, this held aloft by a prince of the blood, a band of flutes, of kettledrums, trumpets and hautboys passing now, their music mingling in the clamour of the street and then lost.

There is spectacle enough in Sharia Muizz, and behind its facades, to remind you that this was a city of beauty and mystery. Ruthless for power, cunning in government, brutal and barbarous often, the Mamelukes at their best were resourceful and vital, with an incomparable flair for architecture. Their grandiose designs, bold, vigorous and voluminous, were gracefully decorated with the play of arabesques, the embroidery of light through stained-glass windows.

The Story of Shagarat al-Durr

You come first, on the right, to the Mausoleum and Madrasa of al-Salih Ayyub, diagonally opposite the Maristan of Qalaun. Where the street now presses its way was once, in Fatimid times, a broad avenue, so broad it served as a parade ground, the great palaces looking down upon it from either side. Throughout the Fatimid and Mameluke periods, this was the very centre of Cairo.

The **Mausoleum and Madrasa of al-Salih Ayyub** (38) need to be searched for. You turn right off Muizz into a lane — there is a tiny teashop on the corner with some round brass tables outside (an agreeable place to sit for a while). A short distance along the lane is an arch set into a facade with a Fatimid-style minaret rising from it. This is the madrasa, and you enter what remains of it by turning left into what is now used by neighbourhood youths as a playing field, liwans to east and west. The mausoleum is reached by returning to the Street of the Coppersmiths and turning right. You will see the dome on your right, and the door will be locked, but ask (or gesture to) anyone nearby for the key: they will find the keeper.

The interest of this place is historical, for it marks a political and architectural transition. Al-Salih Ayyub was the last ruler of Saladin's dynasty. His wife, who completed his madrasa and mausoleum after he died in 1249, was Shagarat al-Durr, a beautiful Armenian slave girl who ushered in Mameluke rule. While it has Fatimid elements, the madrasa was also the first to provide for all four schools of Sunni Islam, and was the first also to link madrasa and mausoleum — in short, it was the prototype for the Mameluke mosque-madrasa-mausolea to follow. Throughout the Mameluke period it was used as Cairo's central court (the schools teaching, amongst other things, law as at al-Azhar), and the street outside, Sharia Muizz, served as the place of execution.

Tree of Pearls

Shagarat al-Durr, whose name means Tree of Pearls, shares with Hatshepsut and Cleopatra that rare distinction of having been a female ruler of Egypt. She rose to power at a critical moment, when St Louis at the head of the Sixth Crusade seized Damietta in the Delta. Ayyub, dying from cancer, was too weak to dislodge him, and St Louis was content to await the Sultan's death and what he imagined would be the collapse of government and all resistance to Christian occupation of the country.

But Shagarat al-Durr was of independent nomadic stock, a society in which women went unveiled and were the equals of their men. She hid her husband's corpse in the Mameluke barracks on Roda while pretending he was merely ailing, and for three months ruled Egypt by appearing to transmit orders from Ayyub to his generals.

Egypt played for time and offered the Crusaders Jerusalem if they would abandon Damietta. St Louis refused. But meanwhile in the heat, and fed bad fish by the Delta people, the Crusaders became sick with scurvy and plague. St Louis then accepted the offer of Jerusalem, but it was the Egyptians now who refused, and the Mameluke general Baybars fell upon the

The capture of St Louis

Crusaders, capturing St Louis, who had to buy his freedom with a vast indemnity and the renunciation of all claim to Egypt.

Shagarat al-Durr now openly proclaimed herself Sultana of Egypt and ruled for 80 days as the only female Moslem sovereign in history, but the Abbasid Caliph refused to recognise her, quoting the Prophet who had said, 'The people that make a woman their ruler are past saving'. So she married the leader of her Mameluke slave-warriors, Aybak, ruling through him, but when she heard he was considering another marriage she hired assassins to murder him in his bath. Hearing his screams, seeing his body hacked at with swords, at the last moment she tried to save his life, but the assassins went on: 'If we stop halfway through, he will kill both you and us'.

When the murder was discovered, Shagarat al-Durr offered to marry the new Mameluke chief, but she was imprisoned instead and is said to have spent her last days grinding up all her jewels so that no other woman should wear them. The

Mamelukes had discovered their power to make and unmake rulers; in future they ruled themselves. Shagarat al-Durr was turned over to the wife she had made Aybak divorce who instructed her female slaves to beat her to death with bath clogs. They tossed her naked body over the Citadel wall to be devoured by dogs. Her few remains were deposited in her tomb on the edge of the Southern Cemetery not too far from the Mosque of Ibn Tulun.

Qalaun, al-Nasr and Barquq

A splendour of domes and minarets

Looking up and across Sharia Muizz you see on its west side the splendid cluster of domes and minarets that are the Madrasa and Mausoleum of Qalaun, the Mausoleum of al-Nasr, his son and successor, and the Mosque of Barquq. Qalaun — the name means duck and has an absurd ring in Arabic — was one of the ablest, most successful and long-lived (1220-90) of the notoriously short-lived Mameluke Sultans, who moreover founded a dynasty lasting nearly 100 years. His name suggests Mongol origins, and he is known to have been brought from the lower Volga region, ruled at the time by the Golden Horde. It was al-Salih Ayyub, buried across the street, who first began importing slaves from there, employing them as bodyguards. Qalaun served the country of his purchase well: Damascus and Baghdad had fallen to the Mongols, Egypt and Arabia the sole remaining bulwarks of Islam; Baybars checked the threat, Qalaun eliminated it, and then marched against the Crusaders at Acre, their last stronghold in the Holy Land, but died enroute. An outstanding builder, his tribute to his Christian enemies was the adoption of Romanesque elements in his complex here, the **Maristan, Madrasa and Mausoleum of Qalaun** (43).

First you go through a gate and down a wide tree-shaded walk, the heat and noise of the Street of the Coppersmiths falling away behind you. At the end is a modern hospital, built within the vaster limits of Qalaun's **maristan** or hospital and insane asylum — a hospital has stood on this spot for 700 years. Three great liwans of the original remain, the windows of the east liwan still displaying their carved stucco surrounds. The north liwan, it seems, is now used as a dump for surgical dressings.

Islamic enlightenment

Islam was a wonder of enlightened medical care at a time when the ill, especially the mad, were pariahs in Christian Europe. From Spain to Persia, hospitals flourished, were divided into clinics, surgery was perfected, such delicate operations as the removal of cataracts were performed, musicians and singers entertained the sick, and upon their discharge patients were given a sum of money to enable them to live until they could again find employment.

Returning now to the street and turning left, the wall on your left-hand side is that of Qalaun's **madrasa**. At the far corner the line of the building then retreats and you come to what was the original entrance to the maristan. The entrance opens onto a corridor, blocked at the far end, which runs between the mausoleum on the right and the madrasa on the left. The madrasa is damaged and recently the opportunity was taken to excavate for clues to the Fatimids' western palace which stood here. The plan is a courtyard with a liwan at either end, the sanctuary or eastern liwan suggesting a north Syrian basilical church, with three aisles and classical columns. The stucco work further in from the arch is original.

Qalaun's **mausoleum** is off the other side of the corridor. The plan has been influenced by the Dome of the Rock at Jerusalem, well known to the Sultan: an octagon approaching the circular within a square, the arches supported by square piers and classical columns. The dome has been restored. The structure perhaps does not seem light enough, the decorations too rich, and the mashrabiyya screen obstructs a total view (the best is from the entrance) — though it also has the effect of making the relatively small interior seem endless. But there is splendour all the same, in carved stucco, the stone inlay, the wood ornamentation, slowly revealed as your eyes get used to the filtered coloured light from the stained-glass windows — those high, double round-arched windows with oculi above, framed (from both inside and out on the street) by deeply recessed pointed arches, Qalaun's borrowing of the Romanesque.

On your way out through the corridor, have a look at its beamed and coffered ceiling, which is marvellous. The street is just before you, yet in this complex all has been private, cool and quiet, birds chirping, trees and shade and shafts of sunlight. The buildings and their purpose reveal a dignity and humanity; they provide the peace by which you recognise an unexpected civilisation.

The next building along, that is continuing north on Sharia Muizz and on the left, is the **Mausoleum of al-Nasr Mohammed** (44), now ruinous except for the facade with its Gothic doorway, removed from the Crusader Church of St John when al-Nasr completed his father's work and took Acre. Al-Nasr's reign marked the zenith of Mameluke civilisation; his principal monuments are the mosque on the Citadel and the aqueduct bringing water there from the Nile. He is in fact buried next door in Qalaun's mausoleum.

The third of this group is the **Mosque of Barquq** (187), the first Burgi Mameluke Sultan. It dates from 1386, about a century later than Qalaun's buildings, and the change in style is evident; the minaret, for example, is octagonal and, compared to the square blocks of Qalaun's, slender, while here is the high monumental entrance topped with stalactite decorations, seen also at the Sultan Hassan, which became typical of Mameluke architecture. This mosque-madrasa, in cruciform plan, was in use until this century and has been well maintained and restored. The portal is of black and white marble, the doors of bronze inlaid with silver. The sanctuary liwan is flat-ceilinged, not vaulted like the others, and receives support from four pharaonic columns of porphyry quarried in the Eastern Desert. The exquisite domed tomb chamber with marbled floors and walls of varying colours, painted ceiling, latticed and stained-glass windows and ornate wooden stalactites in the corners, contains the grave of one of Barquq's daughters — he was removed to his mausoleum in the Northern Cemetery.

Some Grand Cairene Houses Along the Way

Nearby are two houses of the Bahri Mameluke period. The **House of Uthman Katkhuda** (50) is in the street running east of Sharia Muizz, opposite Qalaun's mausoleum. It is about halfway down on the left-hand side. The doorway is entirely ordinary, but knock, or go to the apartment up the stairs, and someone will appear to show you round. (When soliciting local assistance, baksheesh is expected — usually demanded; but you should avoid paying until you have seen everything you want to, otherwise the demand for baksheesh will be made again and again, at each stage.)

Katkhuda was an 18th C lieutenant governor of the city who made what in fact was a mid-14th C palace into his home. Only a part of the whole remains, but it is an impressive example of Mameluke domestic architecture. Suddenly you are in a narrow hall of enormous height, its bare stone walls rising to the support of a wooden dome, distant sunlight streaming through the windows of its octagonal drum. This was the reception room, and guests sat in the raised area at the south end. The walls were once wainscotted with marble; the woodwork remains, though the consoles within the arches date from the 16th C. Ask to go up to the roof for a view of the quarter, and look at the *malqaf* or ventilator, a rectangular scoop common to old Cairene houses and always facing north to catch the Mediterranean breeze. One of the best things about this place is that you will almost certainly be the only visitor, and its fresh bareness invites pleasing, undisturbed thoughts of moving in and where to put the furniture.

Traditional air conditioning

The other house, even more so a palace, is the **Qasr Beshtak** (34). This is back on Sharia Muizz, just to the north of Barquq's mosque and on the right-hand side. The entrance is the second door along the little street of the north facade — and again you will have to find someone, with some difficulty this time, who has the key.

The Emir Beshtak was married to the daughter of al-Nasr and was a man of great wealth. He built his palace on part of the foundations of the eastern Fatimid palace and it once rose to five storeys, with running water on all floors. You pass through a courtyard, up some stairs, and enter the harem reception room, vaster yet than Katkhuda's, with mashrabiyya screens along the galleries. From these there is a perfectly medieval view of the streets below.

Koranic school and fountain

The **Sabil Kuttab of Abdul Katkhuda** (21) was built in 1744 by Uthman Katkhuda's son and is one of the most charming structures in Cairo. It stands on a triangular plot, causing a fork in the street, the kuttab's porches overhanging the roadways on either side, the great grille of what was the fountain at its base facing south towards you as you approach. The kuttab is still used as the neighbourhood Koranic school, while the rest of the block is taken up with a renovated 14th C apartment building.

You continue along the left-hand fork and at last, on the next block, on the right-hand side, discover a rare surviving Fatimid structure in this Mameluke-dominated part of the city. The **Mosque of al-Aqmar** (33) dates from 1125 and displays a typically Fatimid keel arch portal. The niche ribbing, used here for the first time, was to become a favourite Cairene motif. The medallion set into the niche ribbing is very finely executed. The recesses on either side of the portal have stalactite decorations, also appearing here for the first time and later taken up by the Mamelukes. The interior is original, but the slapdash minaret is modern. Aqmar means moonlit, so named for the pale stone — the Fatimids, who meant to stay, building in stone rather than the earlier brick and stucco.

The finest house in Cairo

The **Bayt al-Suhaymi** (339) is not a palace and not a refuge for an English major's bric-a-brac. It is a merchant's house of the Ottoman period, built in the 16th and 17th C, and completely furnished to the age. It is the finest house in Cairo and wonderfully achieves the ambition of Islamic secular architecture — the anticipation of paradise. You reach it by taking the first right a block after the Mosque of al-Aqmar. The street is called Haret ed-Darb el Asfar and the house is at No. 19 (in case you do not notice the little green and white plaque) on the left-hand side. There is a broad wooden door. Knock.

There is nothing at the facade that prepares you for what lies within. The house consists of numerous rooms on irregular levels, mashrabiyya screen windows looking out onto the streets at one side, screened and latticed windows and arched galleries giving onto a garden courtyard on the other. You will want to wander, to enjoy the perspectives across the court from every possible angle and elevation, though you will probably be guided — by well-informed students. They will take you, for example, to the women's bedroom which faces the street but is closely latticed, to the women's chapel outside it, a malqaf 'air conditioner' above your head. You will then be deposited in the harem reception room overlooking the garden, its floors of marble, its walls covered with the most delicate green and blue plant-patterned enamel tiles, and with carved and painted wood decorations. Here you can rest and perhaps send out for tea, and begin taking it all in. For it is not the plan, not the details, but the ambience of the place that seduces you and you want time.

Though this house was built in later centuries, in ambience it cannot be different from Cairene houses of earlier times, and it becomes obvious why Crusaders crusaded — the East offered such a luxuriantly pleasurable life for those with the means, far exceeding anything back in Europe. Medieval Western architecture and certainly domestic living (with the possible exception of Provence) was crude in comparison and worst of all uncomfortable. In Europe there were the seasons of cold and wet to contend with; in Egypt the heat. But here in this house they so easily defeated heat and burning sun, creating shadows and breezes, bringing plants and birds into their home, embracing a nature they had made kinder.

The Mosque of al-Hakim and the Northern Gates

Return once again to Sharia Muizz and turn right. It becomes wonderful walking along this seemingly humble street, learning its secrets, its treasures offered in this Guide still only a sampling of the many more that would require a far longer exploration. You are heading north towards Bab al-Futuh and the walls which limit the Fatimid city. But first, on your left, is

Looking across the Mosque of al-Hakim from Bab al-Futuh

Turkish minaret

the clean, pencil-like minaret of the **Silahdar mosque**, a Turkish-style structure of Mohammed Ali's time. Though centuries out of place for this quarter, the minaret is a graceful landmark that never fails to draw your attention as you pass by.

After about two blocks, the street broadens into a market area where garlic and onions are transported into the city and sold. The trucks which rumble in and out of Bab al-Futuh are painted with eyes as talismans against the evil eye. It is an appropriate place for superstition: on your right and leading to the Fatimid wall is the **Mosque of al-Hakim** (15), completed in 1010.

Al-Hakim was the third of the Fatimid Caliphs who ruled with absolute political, military and religious authority. He was a paranoic who declared himself God and answered objections by inciting mobs to burn half the city while he lopped off the heads of the well-to-do, claiming the assistance of Adam and Solomon in angel guise. Jews he made walk about Cairo wearing clogs round their necks and Christians carry heavy crosses. He would spend his wary nights riding a donkey, in the company of only a mute slave, into the Moqattam to observe the stars for portents. Then exchanging clothes with his slave he would secretly descend into the city and mix with the people to learn their complaints, though assuming the role of a qadi to punish infractions with summary decapitations. One night, returning from the hills, he was assassinated — at the instigation, it is thought, of his sister Setalmulq, whom he had intended to marry.

Some say he survived the attack and retreated to the desert. The Copts claim that Christ appeared to him, and that he begged for and was granted pardon. Others say he withdrew to the sanctuary of Ammon at the Siwa oasis deep in the Western Desert, where more than a thousand years before Alexander had heard himself declared the son of Zeus, and there formulated his doctrine of a tolerant religion, similar to Islam, which was carried by Darazi, his disciple, to Lebanon where the Druze view the life of al-Hakim as a kind of Passion, giving him his due as their messiah.

Druze messiah

For centuries this mosque had an aura avoided by Cairenes who rarely used it for worship and let it crumble. It had been used as a prison for Crusader captives, as a stable by Saladin and as a warehouse by Napoleon. As recently as 1980 it was ruinous, its roofless arcades haunting, dominated by its massive brooding minarets in keeping with the Fatimid wall. These minarets proved unsound soon after construction and needed buttressing by great trapezoid bases that project out into the street, so that they seem like ziggurats (especially when viewed from outside the walls), with pepperpot domes, placed there by Baybars II at the beginning of the 14th C. The mosque has now been entirely restored — perhaps over-restored — by the Indian-based Bohra sect of Ismailis who claim spiritual descent from the Fatimid imams. They will tell you that al-Hakim was not mad, that these are the lies of his enemies. And here certainly they have erased the darkness: there is the bright glitter of white marble and gold leaf, and at night the once forbidding arcades are illuminated by the warm glow of suspended glass oil lamps.

The return of the Mecca pilgrimage

It was at **Bab al-Futuh**, the Gate of Conquests, that the great caravan of pilgrims returned each year from Mecca and then made its way along Sharia Muizz and Shari Bab el Wazir to the Citadel. Nowadays the journey is made by jet, but in 1844 Gérard de Nerval, in *Journey to the Orient*, witnessed it like this: 'As many as 30,000 people were about to swell the population of Cairo. I managed to make my way to Bab al-Futuh; the whole of the main street which leads there was crammed with bystanders who were kept in orderly lines by government troops. The sound of trumpets, cymbals and drums directed the advancing procession; the various nations and sects were distinguished by their trophies and flags. The long files of harnessed dromedaries, which were mounted by Bedouins armed with long rifles, followed one another, but it was only when I reached the countryside that I was able to appreciate the full impact of a spectacle which is unique in all the world.

'A whole nation on the march was merging into the huge population which adorned the knolls of the Moqattam on the right, and, on the left, the thousands of usually deserted edifices of the City of the Dead; streaked with red and yellow bands, the turreted copings of the walls and towers of Saladin were also swarming with onlookers. I had the impression that I was present at a scene during the Crusades. Further ahead, in the plain where the Qalish meanders, stood thousands of chequered tents where the pilgrims halted to refresh themselves; there was no lack of dancers and singers; all the musicians of Cairo, in fact, competed with the hornblowers and kettledrummers of the procession, an enormous orchestra whose members were perched on top of camels.

'Late in the afternoon, the booming of the Citadel cannons and a sudden blast of trumpets proclaimed that the Mahmal, a holy ark which contains Mohammed's robe of golden cloth, had arrived within sight of the city... From time to time the Mahmal came to a halt, and the entire population prostrated themselves in the dust, cupping their heads in their hands. An escort of guards struggled to drive back the Negroes who were more fanatical than the other Moslems; they aspired, in fact, to the honour of being trampled to death beneath the camels, but the only share of martyrdom bestowed upon them was a volley of baton blows. As for the Santons, who are an even more ecstatic species of saints than the Dervishes and whose orthodoxy is more questionable, several of them pierced their cheeks with long, pointed nails and walked on, showered in blood; others devoured live serpents, while a third group stuffed their mouths with burning coals.'

Nerval was a precursor of surrealism; he enjoyed going over the top. But in this case that sober chronicler Edward William Lane (*Manners and Customs of the Modern Egyptians*), who observed the arrival of the caravan ten years before, is hardly less fantastic in his description, though he says the swallowing of serpents went out with the Mamelukes. The journey from Mecca took 37 days across rocky desert, the caravan moving at night. Not everyone survived: 'Many of the women who go forth to meet their husbands or sons receive the melancholy tidings of their having fallen victim to privation and fatigue. The piercing shrieks with which they rend the air, as they retrace their steps to the city, are often heard predominant over the noise of the drum and the shrill notes of the hautboy which proclaim the joy of others.'

Lane also mentions that the Mahmal was empty; its purpose was entirely symbolic, dating back to the reign of Shagarat al-Durr. She went on the pilgrimage one year, travelling in a magnificent *hodag* or covered litter borne by a camel, and for several successive years her empty hodag was sent with the caravan merely for the sake of state. The practice was continued by Egypt's rulers till 1927, when the puritanical Saudi King, on the pretext of objecting to the soldiers accompanying it, forbade passage of this 'object of vain pomp'. These days, alas, you wait in vain for pomp at Bab al-Futuh.

Along the walls

The gate is similar to Bab Zuwayla, with projecting oval towers, though the masonry is finer and the impression greater for the space outside it has been cleared and there is a magnificent view of the ensemble of **Bab al-Futuh, Bab al-Nasr** — the Gate of Victory — (to the east), the linking **Fatimid wall** and al-Hakim's minarets. The Fatimid wall extends to the west; beyond that, where it retreats, and also to the east of Bab al-Nasr, the wall dates from Saladin. You can walk both within and along the top of the wall between the gates, and to do this you should make yourself obviously interested at either gate and eventually someone with the key will come along.

Re-entering the medieval city through Bab al-Nasr, the immediate area is noisy with metal workshops. On the right (west) against the east facade of al-Hakim's mosque is the caravanserai or **wakala of Sultan Qaytbay** (11) built in 1481. It is now inhabited by tinsmiths and their families; women scrubbing, washing strung across the courtyard, children beating a kitten and throwing it into the air.

PRACTICAL INFORMATION

To reach the starting point of this tour take a **taxi** or the **No. 66 bus** to Khan el Kahlili.

Entrance **fees** are payable at the Qalaun complex and the Bayt al-Suhaymi, and baksheesh should be paid for services elsewhere.

For those with limited time, an **abbreviated itinerary** should include a visit to the Qalaun complex, the Bayt al-Suhaymi and a walk along the walls between Bab al-Futuh and Bab al-Nasr — but above all visit the Bayt al-Suhaymi.

THE CITY OF THE DEAD

Burial ground of the Mameluke Sultans

The Northern Cemetery or City of the Dead lies to the east of the Fatimid city. The Mausoleum of Barquq is one and a half kilometres from Bab al-Nasr, for example, and Qaytbay's mausoleum is a kilometre from al-Azhar. So a walk from Bab al-Nasr, visiting these two mausolea as well as that of Ashraf Baybars' — the three most outstanding buildings — and then back to al-Azhar, will cover about 3 kms. You may prefer to make a separate journey of it, hiring a taxi.

You may already have noticed the City of the Dead as you drove in on the Heliopolis road from the airport; it did not seem inviting. It has the look of a bidonville — hot, dusty, dilapidated, with a quantity of domes. It is in fact the burial ground of the Mameluke Sultans and of others who aspired to their end, and some of its mausolea are as wonderful as anything in the city of the living. Nor is the cemetery without life. There were monasteries and schools, part of the mausolea. And the poor have always made their homes here, and the keepers, while relatives visit the family plots on feast days for a picnic. This is reminiscent of the ancient Egyptian practice of feeding the dead, though it is practiced elsewhere in the Mediterranean, as in Greece where it is more a cheerful popping of the cork and celebration of life.

The Three Most Outstanding Mausolea

Follow the road that runs east outside Bab al-Nasr and on reaching the cemetery you will see ahead of you a broad building with two domes and two minarets. This is the **Mausoleum of Barquq** (149), completed in 1411. Its plan is similar to that of a cruciform madrasa, but the liwans are not vaulted, instead entered through multi-domed arcades. You enter nowadays at the southwest corner and pass through a corridor into the sahn, its vastness once relieved by a pair of tamarisk trees, now only by the fountain. On the eastern side is the sanctuary liwan with a beautifully carved marble minbar, dedicated by Qaytbay. At either end of the liwan are domed tomb chambers, Barquq (removed here from his mausoleum in Sharia Muizz) and his two sons buried in the left chamber, women of the family in the right. These domes are the earliest of stone in Cairo; the zigzag ribbing on their exteriors was to develop into the elaborate polygons of Qaytbay's domed mausoleum. From the outside, the domes are minimised by the surrounding structure, and so inside their marvellous shape and soaring height comes as a surprise.

Go back across the courtyard to the northwest corner and up the stairs. These lead you to the *khanqah* or Dervish monastery, its four storeys a warren of rooms, cells and corridors. For some extra baksheesh the keeper will usually let you go up the northern minaret for a sweeping view of the necropolis itself and all of Cairo from Heliopolis to the Citadel.

The **Mausoleum of Sultan Ashraf Baybars** (121) — he is also known as Barsbey — is south down the paved but dusty road that passes along the front of Barquq's mausoleum. This building is less visited than the other two and finding the keeper may be more difficult; at any monument, here or in the city, apprehend the first child or lounger you see and make it known you want the key — the keeper will usually soon appear. Baksheesh is then of course expected all round.

This was originally planned solely as a khanqah and so is unusually elongated; also it is recognised by its ungainly minaret which too soon comes to a point. This Baybars, whose mausoleum dates from 1432, was a Burgi or Circassian Mameluke and is not to be confused with his namesake who held St Louis to ransom. He neither drank nor swore, though was martial enough and took Cyprus from the Franks in 1426. The appeal of the place is in its few but well-chosen elaborations — the polygonally decorated dome rising above the simple facade through which you pass by a doorway with trefoil arch. The tomb chamber is at the north end of the mosque, dimly illuminated by stained-glass windows subsequently introduced, though the mihrab of mother-of-pearl and marble mosaic is original. But really you have come for the interior view of the dome and its impression alone is sufficient: it ascends effortlessly upwards, almost losing itself to infinity.

A jewel of Mameluke architecture

It is a longer distance down this same dusty road to the **Mausoleum of Qaytbay** (99), completed in 1474 and a jewel of Mameluke architecture. First, from across the square, look at the ablaq masonry of the facade, the intricate polygonal relief on the exquisitely proportioned dome, and the slender minaret of three tiers (the Mameluke fashion), each tier ornately decorated with columned recesses or raised arabesques or stalactite clusters. Along with the Ibn Tulun and the Sultan Hassan, this rates as one of the great buildings of Cairo. Unlike them it is free with decoration, but like them it uses its decoration to the highest effect — the frequent play, for example, of filigree flowers upon star-shaped polygons which has been described as 'a song for two voices', a geometrical base with floral melody.

Along with al-Nasr, Qaytbay was the grandest of Mameluke builders, emblazoning his cartouche on buildings religious and secular throughout the Middle East, as well as in Cairo and Alexandria. He was also the last Mameluke ruler of strength. Meshullam ben Menahem, an Italian Jew, described him: 'He is an old man of about 80, but tall, handsome and as upright as a reed. Dressed in white, he was on horseback, accompanied by more than 2000 Mameluke soldiers... Whoever wishes can have access to the Sultan: there is in the town a great and splendid fortress at the entrance of which he sits publicly on Mondays and Thursdays, accompanied by the governor of the city; a guard of more than 3000 Mamelukes surrounds him. Whoever has been manhandled or robbed by one of the Mameluke princes or emirs can there complain. Thus the nobles refrain from actions that might carry condemnation.' He came up through the ranks, having been bought by Ashraf Baybars, and apart from al-Nasr ruled longer than any other Sultan. The perfection of his mausoleum, however, like the splendour of his reign, marked the final apogee of Mameluke vigour. Decadence ensued; two decades later the Turks were in

City of the Dead: dome of the Mausoleum of Barquq

the city, Bab Zuwayla ornamented by the last Mameluke Sultan, a rope round his neck.

Inside is a cruciform madrasa with vestigial liwans to east and west. The decoration of ceilings, pavings, arches, windows is breathtakingly variegated, yet overall it is measured and subdued. There is deliberate though sensitive contrast with the scale of the courtyard and sanctuary in the immense height of the tomb chamber, its walls drawn into the ascending dome.

Finally, from the sanctuary, you should climb the roof to enjoy at closer hand the tracery of stone carving, as delicate as previous periods had managed in wood and stucco, on the dome and minaret.

PRACTICAL INFORMATION

Apart from resorting to a **taxi**, **bus No. 500** from Midan el Tahrir to Midan el Barquq; the Mausoleum of Barquq lies not far to the southeast.

For those with limited time the temptation might be to leave out this long journey to the City of the Dead altogether, but even the most **abbreviated itinerary** should include a visit to the Mausoleum of Qaytbay, one of the finest enclosed interiors in the world.

THE EGYPTIAN MUSEUM

The Museum of Egyptian Antiquities, to give it its proper name, is on the north side of the Midan el Tahrir, near the Nile Hilton. It was founded at Bulaq in 1858 by Auguste Mariette, the great pioneer archaeologist who first excavated the Serapeum at Saqqara, the Temple of Amun at Karnak, Hatshepsut's mortuary temple at Deir el Bahri, and the temples at Dendera and Edfu. The collection has occupied the present classical-style building since 1902 and has long since outgrown it. There are over 100,000 exhibits which could easily fill half a dozen museums this size, a unique storehouse of one of the oldest and grandest civilisations on earth.

Allowing one minute for each exhibit, you could see everything in the museum in about nine months. The average guided tour lasts two hours. The selection offered here would take one hard-working day to cover, though it would be better to break that down into two or three half-day visits.

The exhibits are numbered and some carry background notes in English, French and Arabic. The rooms are also numbered, as shown on the plans. The collection is arranged more or less chronologically, so that starting at the entrance and walking clockwise round the ground floor you pass from Old Kingdom through Middle and New Kingdom exhibits, concluding with Ptolemaic and Roman exhibits. The first floor contains prehistoric and early dynastic exhibits and the contents of several tombs, including Tutankhamun's. *Not every room is mentioned in the tour below.*

The Ground Floor

Immediately upon entering (from the south), you walk into a rotunda that is *Room 48*. Apart from the monumental Sphinx at Giza, the colossal head to the left (6051) of Userkaf (V Dyn) is the only large sculpture surviving from the Old Kingdom. The rotunda contains other giant works (out of chronological order), including three colossi (1, 2, 4) of Ramses II (XIX Dyn) and a statue of Amenophis, son of Hapu (3), architect to Amenophis III (XVIII Dyn).

The Old Kingdom

Room 47: Contains IV, V and VI Dynasty items. The walls are lined with sarcophagi. Most interesting are the figures in the central aisle cases, including, in Case B, statuettes of the dwarf (160), the man with a deformed head (6310) and the hunchback (6311), but also, in Case D, those of people grinding corn, kneading dough, preparing food (a goose about to be gutted and plucked).

Room 41: The V Dynasty bas-relief (79) with scenes of country life is particularly worthy of close observation. Farm tasks and crafts are carried on through a series of registers. The women wear ankle-length chemises, but the men wear only a cloth or are sometimes entirely naked. They are circumcised as was the Egyptian custom. There is also one episode of a malefactor being held and brought before a court.

Room 42: The very fine statue of Chephren (138) in black diorite with white marbling was found in a shaft at his Valley

Temple at Giza where he built the second of the Great Pyramids. The falcon god Horus embraces Chephren's head with his wings, at once transferring the ka and protecting the Pharaoh. The remarkably preserved wooden statue of Ka-aper (140) is vividly executed. You feel you would recognise the face in the original, and indeed when Mariette found it at Saqqara his workmen immediately dubbed it Sheikh el Beled because of its resemblance to their village headman. The living eyes are copper inlaid with quartz. It is said of some paintings that the eyes follow you; in this case it is uncanny how they fix you with their sure and level gaze when faced head on, but as soon as you shift even a centimetre they gaze off — not inert, but reflectively, into an internal dream world of their past.

Room 31: Outstanding here are the six wooden panels of the II Dynasty priest Hesire (88). This was the brief period in ancient Egyptian history when moustaches were fashionable.

Room 32: One gets so used to the rigid frontality of Egyptian sculpture that it is a surprise to see the wooden statue in the far right corner with its slight twist. At the centre of the room are the IV Dynasty statues (223, 195) of Prince Rahotep and Princess Nafrit, her skin painted yellow, his ruddy brown. He has short back and sides and sports a natty moustache. In his white waist cloth he looks all the world like an advertising executive taking a sauna. The group representing the dwarf Seneb, Chief of the Wardrobe, with his wife and two children (6055), deserves close attention. It is delightful, but also a puzzle. Despite his small size, Seneb is a man of importance; he looks pleased with himself, sure of his position, his family, his wife's proud affection. Notice his legs: they are too short to hang over the edge of the chair; instead his children stand where his legs would be — is this a mere compositional nicety or has it a symbolic intention? And look at the children, their right index fingers to their lips as though they were keeping a secret. The III/IV Dynasty 'Geese of Meidum' (136) are vividly coloured. The copper statues (230, 231) of Pepi I and his son are the first metal statues known, and that of Pepi the largest of its kind. He is a great striding figure, reminiscent of an archaic Greek kouros.

The Middle Kingdom

With *Room 26* you pass into the Middle Kingdon.

Room 22: Generally sculpture and stone monuments of the Middle Kingdom. At the centre is the burial chamber of Horhotep (300). The walls are painted with oil jars and offerings are closely listed. The decorated doors, like patchwork curtains, were for the ka to flit in and out at will. Around the chamber are ten statues of Sesostris I (301). On the sides of each throne are reliefs of the gods of Upper and Lower Egypt entwining the lotus and papyrus, symbolising the unity of the country.

The New Kingdom

With *Room 11* you pass into the New Kingdom. 400: a fine statue of Tuthmosis III (XVII Dynasty) in grey schist.

Room 12: XVIII Dynasty sculpture. The brightly decorated chapel built for Amenophis II or his predecessor Tuthmosis III once contained Hathor as cow (445, 446) — she now stands before it in a glass case. To the right is a pink granite statue (952) of Hatshepsut. Look also for the case containing a small statuette (6257), delicately carved out of Sudanese ebony, of

Thay, a royal equerry.

Room 8: It is unusual for mud brick houses, even palaces, to survive, and so our impression of ancient Egypt is largely determined, often distorted, by rock tombs and stone mortuary temples. But the Egyptians did concern themselves with this world and at the centre of this room is a model of a typical house as excavated at Amarna, Akhenaton's brief capital on the Nile near Minya.

The Akhenaton Room

Room 3 contains perhaps the most astonishing works in the museum, from the reign of Akhenaton. Some find the Amarna

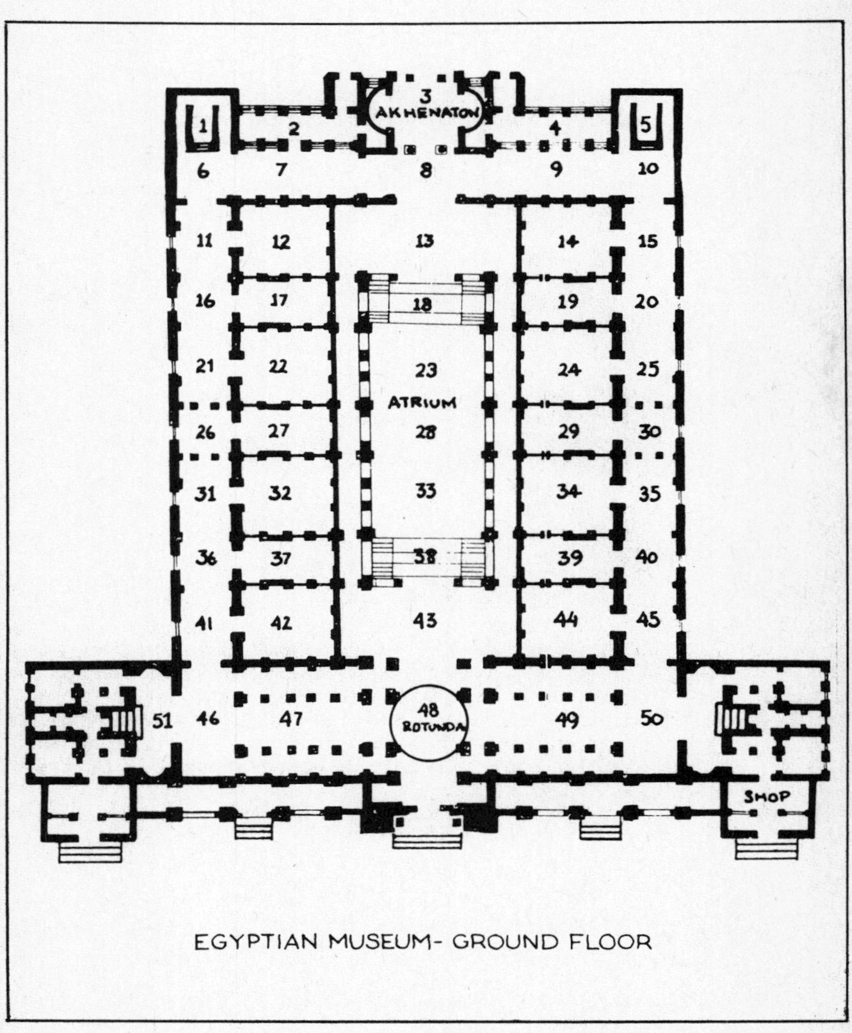

EGYPTIAN MUSEUM- GROUND FLOOR

style — particularly when applied in its most exaggerated form to Akhenaton himself — grotesque. I think it powerful and often beautiful. Staring down at you are four colossi of the Pharaoh: the glare of revolution. Elongated face, narrow eyes, long thin nose with flaring nostrils and full, perhaps sardonic lips. The belly and thighs protrude like some primitive female figure. These are from the temple he built, at Karnak, later destroyed, its blocks serving as foundations and pylon filler for others' works. In its own glass case there is a magnificent head, probably of Nefertiti, and this is not distorted at all — though examples of Amarnan distortion applied to Nefertiti are seen on the stele in Case F, and the centre stele in Case H. This distortion is sometimes called realism; there is a theory that Akhenaton was indeed deformed and that some of his family may have been also — and that the Amarna style was a mass acquiesence to this misfortune. But you might prefer to think that this style was deliberately experimental, calculated for effect, indeed to illustrate opposition, and as readily dispensed with (as with the bust of Nefertiti, above) when sheer beauty rather than shock value was desired. There *is* a note of realism, at least intimacy, in the centre stele in Case F. Instead of showing the royal family in formal adoration of the sun disc Aton, Akhenaton is seen playing with his eldest daughter Meritaten, while Nefertiti holds their other two daughters on her lap. This expression of family joy, or any personal feelings whatsoever, was seen never before and never again in depictions of the pharaohs. Note also the cuneiform tablets, the famous 'Amarna Letters', in Case A, and the representational masks, either models or perhaps death masks, eg 478 in Case D.

Coins

Room 4 contains a collection of Greek, Roman, Byzantine and Arab coins. Quite a few bear the head of Alexander, and on the left side of the first case on the right are several coins bearing the head of Cleopatra VII.

The Ramessids

Room 15: Items from the reign of Ramses II, including a painted limestone statue of a XIX Dynasty queen from the Ramesseum (Case A).

Room 14: On the right is a statue (743) of Ramses VI (XX Dyn), unusual for its attempt at movement, dragging a doubled up Libyan by the hair. A painted sunk relief (769) in the left near corner shows Ramses II similarly apprehending three prisoners, one black, one red, one brown. At the centre (unnumbered, but catalogued as 765) is a unique freestanding coronation group sculpture, Ramses III at the centre, Horus on the left, Seth on the right. Though greatly restored, enough was found to determine that the figures stood on their own legs without supports.

The Late Period

The New Kingdom, in any case tottering since the end of the XX Dynasty, ended with the XXI Dynasty. Objects from the Late Period begin with *Room 25*. One ruler of the XXV Dynasty, Taharka, left his mark at several sites in Upper Egypt, eg the remains of his kiosk in the Great Court at Karnak. In *Room 24* is his sculpted head (1185, to the right) with curled hair — he was from the Sudan (which the Greeks called Ethiopia). He enjoys the distinction of being mentioned in the Bible (II *Kings* 19, 9). Also on the left is a green schist statue of the goddess Tweri (791) — finely finished, though an utterly ridiculous image of a

Akhenaton: the glare of revolution

pregnant anthropomorphic hippopotamus. Otherwise, the most interesting items are the Osiris, Isis and Hathor group (855, 856, 857) at the centre, and to the left 1184, an attempt at portraiture of the Mayor of Thebes.

Room 30: At Medinet Habu are the mortuary chapels of the Divine Adorers of Amun. Amenardis, in white stone (930), was one of these princesses, of the XXV Dynasty.

The Graeco-Roman Period

Room 34: Note the colossal bust (1003) of Serapis. This god was an invention of Ptolemy Soter and combined Osiris with Apis, the bull god of Memphis, but with Greek features and dress.

Room 44: The contents of royal tombs of a Nubian people, the Blemmyes, who lived just south of Abu Simbel during the Byzantine period and were under the dominion of Meroë in the Sudan. Their aristocracy was strongly negroid. Long after Christianity came to Egypt, they worshipped Isis, Horus and Bes. The burial of kings and queens was accompanied by strangled slaves and servants, and gaily caparisoned horses which were led into the tombs and axed to death. Crowns, the skeleton of a horse, the caparisoned models of two others, along with spearheads, jewellery, pottery and other artefacts form this new and fascinating exhibit. The artefacts of the Blemmyes have a strong, handsome look, similar to Celtic work — a fine brutality.

Room 49: An exceptional piece is the coffin of Petosiris (6036), a high priest of Thoth at Hermopolis (c.300BC). The hieroglyphs are beautifully inlaid with stone and enamel. From Saqqara during the Persian Period is the stone sarcophagus (on the right, near the rotunda) of a dwarf dancer at the Serapeam Apis ceremony. He has been well rewarded: his true to life figure is cut on the outside of the adjacent lid, while on the inside of the lid and at the bottom of the sarcophagus is carved a sex-bomb Nut for him to lie on and stare up at for eternity.

The Atrium: large objects of various periods

On the ground floor there now remains only the atrium to visit.

At the centre of *Room 43* is the Palette of Narmer (3055), possibly the oldest record of a political event, the unification of Egypt, c.3100 BC. Narmer was probably one of the names of Menes, the founder of the I Dynasty, from which Egypt's historical period is dated. Writing was not yet able to convey complex sentences and this slate palette tells its story by means of pictures which are easily translated into words. On the obverse, Narmer is shown braining an enemy, and to the right is a complex symbol relating the significance of this action. The falcon is Narmer, holding a rope attached to the head of a bearded man. The head protrudes from a bed of papyri, representing Lower Egypt. Therefore the symbol reads, 'The falcon god Horus (Narmer) leads captive the inhabitants of the papyrus country'. Narmer came from Upper Egypt, as the crown he wears on this side shows. On the reverse, Narmer wears the crown of Lower Egypt as he reviews the spoils of his victory, which include the decapitated bodies of his foes. The centre panel shows two fantastic beasts, their necks entwined but restrained from fighting by bearded men on either side: Upper and Lower Egypt joined, if not yet altogether at ease. On either side of the room are two large wooden boats for solar sailing from the pyramid of Sesostris III at Dahshur.

Room 38 is really a stairway leading down into the well of the atrium and contains the rectangular stone sarcophagus (624) of Ay, at first an advisor to Akhenaton and later his successor. Four goddesses at each corner extend their wings protectively: Isis, Nephthys, Neith and Selket.

Room 33 displays various pyramidions from Dahshur, the capstones to pyramids. Under 6175 you can see the stone peg which slotted into the pyramid top. The sarcophagus (6337A) of Psusennas I, a XXI Dynasty pharaoh ruling from Tanis in the Deltas after Egypt had split in two, has its lid (6337B) raised over a mirror so that you can see the lovely raised relief of Nut suspended from its underside. To the left, from the XVIII Dynasty, are the stone sarcophagi of Tuthmosis I (619), that of his daughter Hatshepsut made before she came to the throne (6024) and her final sarcophagus (620).

At the centre of the atrium (*Room 28*) is a painted floor with a river scene (627) from the palace of Akhenaton at Amarna.

In *Room 23* there are two interesting lintels, the one on the left (6189) showing the Heb-Set of Senusret III (XII Dyn) very finely cut in sunk relief, while the one on the right is a tenth-rate copy by a later pharaoh.

Room 18 (the stairway leading out of the atrium well) has the colossal group (610) of Amenophis III and his wife Tiy with three of their daughters (XVII Dyn). They are serene, almost a portrait of Victorian contentment but for the play of a smile on their lips and the physicalness of their bodies. Despite the formality of the work and its size, there is a great sensuality to it. The reign of Amenophis was marked by luxury and a sudden eruption (or at least recording) of fashion consciousness: note particularly Tiy's full wig, the hair falling down to her breasts, a style associated almost exclusively with this reign.

Room 13: On the right is a fascinating document, a stele (599) inscribed on the reverse during the reign of Amenophis III with all that the Pharaoh had done for Amun, but later inscribed on the obverse by Merneptah, Pharaoh of the Exodus, with the sole known reference in Egyptian texts to the Israelites: 'Israel is crushed, it has no more seed'!

The *corridors* on either side of the atrium (allowing communication between Rooms 43 and 8 but not with the atrium itself) are lined with pottery, wall paintings and inscription fragments.

The First Floor

To see the first floor rooms in approximate chronological order you should start at Room 43 overlooking the atrium from the south and follow the corridors in a clockwise direction.

Old and Middle Kingdom tomb contents

Outside *Room 42* is a panel (6278) inlaid with blue faience, from Zoser's Step Pyramid at Saqqara. Inside the room you should spend time with the alabaster vase (3054) on the right, beautifully round and smooth and yet criss-crossed in raised stone with ropes from which it would have been suspended. In Case Q is the black Palermo Stone which bears a list of pharaohs from the I to mid-V Dynasties along with important events during the period and annual measurements of the Nile flood, thus adding to our knowledge of the Old Kingdom.

Room 37 is full of wooden coffins and sarcophagi of the Middle Kingdom. The coffin of Sepi (3101 in Case C), a XII Dynasty general, is particularly well-painted. This is the oldest anthropoid coffin in the museum. See also the dismantled panels of his sarcophagus (3104 in Cases A and L), finely painted and extensively inscribed. Artefacts from the tomb of General Mesah at Assiut are displayed in several cases and include his sandals, mirror and neck pillow, and models of Egyptian soldiers (3345), black soldiers (3346) and a pleasure barge (3347).

In the corridor facing *Room 32* is a rare and astonishing wooden ka statue (280) of the Pharaoh Hor (XII Dyn) stepping out from its naos. It actually stands on a sliding base to demonstrate the wanderings of Hor's double — and that it is his ka is clear from the ka hieroglyph of upraised arms on his head, and his nakedness. Inside the room are models (Case E: 3246, 4347) of solar boats. The solar boats are unmanned, operating on autopilot. They are the abstraction of the other boats displayed: funerary boats for carrying the dead man on a canopied bier, or for transport of the living. There is a delightful model of a boat (3244 in Case F) with its mast down, its rowers pulling at full strength, one rower taking a quick sidelong glance at you as the boat shoots by.

Room 27 contains marvellous models (6077-86) from the XI Dynasty tomb of Meketre at Thebes, including a plantation owner reviewing a parade of his cattle and workers (6080); a carpenters' workshop (6083); a pleasure garden with pool, lined with sycamore-figs, at one end a columned verandah (6084); and two boats dragging a net between them, taking fish from the Nile (6085).

New Kingdom tomb contents

Room 22 contains many interesting small figures, including XII-XXX Dynasty ushabtis (Cases I and J: 6062-72), and women, perhaps concubines of the dead man, lying on beds (Case C: 9435, 9437). Cases O, P and R contain New Kingdom funerary gear, painted linen or woven cloth for covering the chest, body and feet, beautifully designed and all the more fine for being highly perishable materials that have survived.

Room 17 is particularly interesting for the papyri on its walls from the Book of the Dead.

Room 12 contains artefacts from royal tombs: a chariot of Tuthmosis IV (3000); the mummies of a child and a gazelle (Case I: 3776, 3780); a collection of priestly wigs and wig boxes (Case L: 3779).

Room 13 at the north end of the atrium displays furnishings from the intact Theban tomb of Yuya and Tuyu, parents-in-law of Amenophis III, with beds, chairs, whippet-like chariots, mummified food and time-serving ushabtis.

The north end of the first floor and all the outer rooms along its east side are devoted to Tutankhamun's treasures, but it is not easy to include their profusion in the middle of this tour. Come back to it later. In any case, more affecting are the

Roman burials

exhibits in *Room 14* from Roman burials. These people, mostly from the Fayyum, continued the Egyptian practice of mummification, yet from their portraits, so lifelike and modern, you cannot imagine they would have accepted the ancient belief. The encaustic portraits (colours mixed into molten wax) were bound onto the mummies — there are shelves of these. A collection of panels is against the south wall (4310): the technique is superb, with shading, highlighting and perspective, two or three of them qualifying as masterpieces in their own right. Those garbage bodies, yet these living faces in which you can read whole lives. All are marked by a seriousness, rarely pompous, occasionally sad, a faint smile on one man's lips. They have faced the passing millenia with Roman steadfastness, they look at you as you look at them as though suddenly we might recognise one another.

In *Room 19* are the gods of the Egyptian pantheon.

Sketches, papyri and decorations

Room 24 is full of painted ostraka, limestone fragments. Case 18 contains interesting representations of animals: a monkey eating, a man leading a bull, a lion devouring a prisoner, etc.

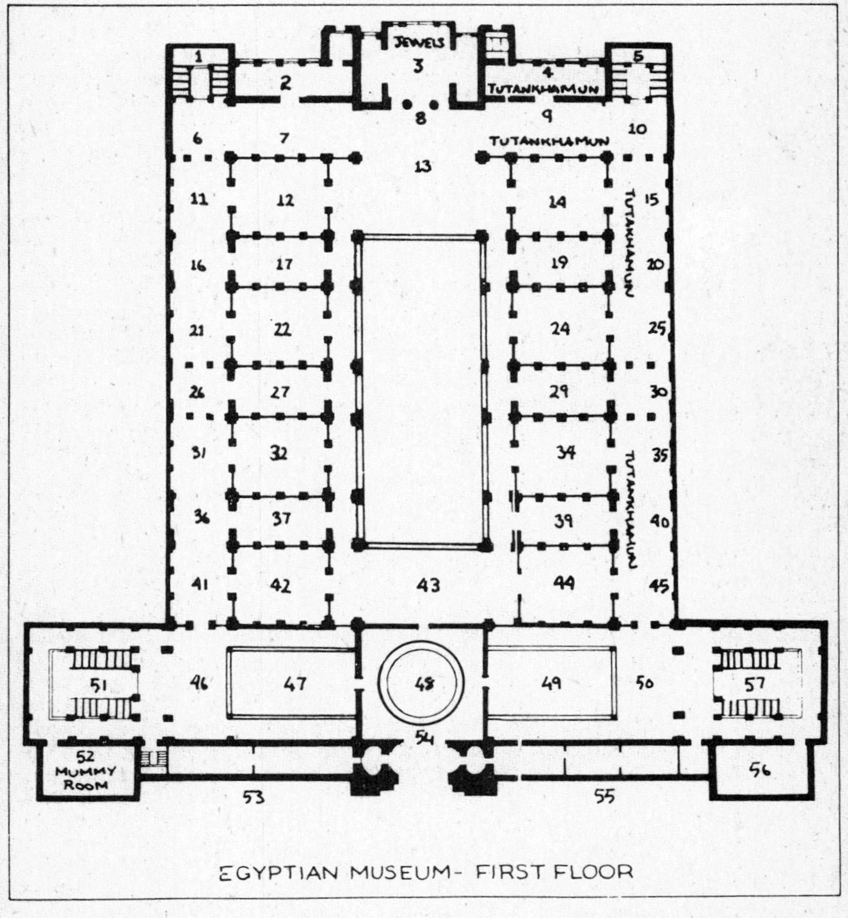

EGYPTIAN MUSEUM- FIRST FLOOR

People too: an intriguing picture of a woman relaxing and playing a stringed instrument. There is also, in the east doorway, a plan of a Theban tomb (4371), with what appear to be doorways shown in elevation.

In *Room 29* are further ostraka, but written on, and papyri — 6335 especially worthwhile: a Ptolemaic Book of the Dead in finest detail, showing the 'Weighing of the Heart' ceremony.

In the corridor outside *Room 34* is an Amarna toilet seat. Is this the loo on which Akhenaton sat?

Room 44 displays decorative details, most interesting the faience from palaces of Ramses II and III.

Room 57 is around the southeast staircase. The square red and green leather tent (3848) belonged to a XXI Dynasty queen and was used at her funeral.

At the centre of the south wings is *Room 48* with a model of a funerary complex, showing how a river temple linked with the pyramid on the desert's edge. There is also a cross-sectioned pyramid showing the internal buttressing. A case to the north contains beautifully worked statuettes from various periods.

Prehistoric and predynastic periods

Rooms 54, 55 and 53 are devoted to prehistoric and predynastic artefacts, eg pottery and tools, and are generally dull, except that in *Room 53* are mummified baboons, a dog, a crocodile and the skeleton of a mare — and these are disgusting. You can understand that the Egyptians, having convinced themselves of the efficacy of preservation, would wrap each other up. But to impose it on animals (look at their little linen-wrapped legs) seems perverse. This is perhaps an unfair view, for human beings are at the centre of our cosmology, animals only soulless lookers-on, while Egyptian religion grew out of animal worship, totemism, an admiration of their qualities (strength, swiftness, beauty), or a desire to appease; wild dogs, the 'Egyptian wolf', prowled the cemeteries by night in search of bones and bodies that the Egyptians hoped would remain unmolested, and so this predator of their eternal life was transformed into their funerary deity, Anubis. Animal cults proliferated towards the end of the pagan period and were extremely popular, religious societies collecting the sacred animals (from shrew mice to hippopotami) which died in the district, mummifying them and burying them in special cemeteries.

The Mummy Room

Room 52 is the Mummy Room where many of the mightiest men in ancient history lie naked and bird-boned in glass cases. Alas, since early 1981 visitors have been forbidden entry. The royal bodies of Amenophis III, Seti I, Ramses II and others are to be reburied either in their original tombs or in a chamber built for the purpose. This is meant as a gesture to Islam, though only the most fundamentalist Moslems can have been offended. I am inclined to agree with Jean Cocteau that the pharaohs did not intend to hide away: 'The more I walk along, the more I listen, the more I move around the columns, the more do I experience the feeling of a dark world which fastens on to ours and which will not loosen the suckers through which it takes its life. Whatever it may cost, they find it necessary to confirm their existence, to perpetuate themselves, to incarnate, to reincarnate, to hypnotise nothingness and to vanquish it... They did not hide themselves in order to disappear, but in order to await the cue for their entry on the stage. They have not been dragged from the tomb. They have been brought from the limbo of the wings with masks and gloves of gold... Seti the First! How beautiful he is, with his little nose, his pointed teeth showing, his little face which belongs to death, reduced to one requirement alone — not to die. "I! I! I!" This is the word which the rafters throw back.'

Returning to the New Kingdom

You can now walk back to the north end of the first floor for the Tutankhamun exhibition which begins at *Room 7*. You pass through *Room 6* with a collection of scarabs. This black dung beetle, running everywhere about the desert sands, pushing a ball of dung before it, symbolised the self-creator, the morning sun.

Rooms 2 and 3, though leading off from the Tutankhamun exhibition area, are not properly a part of it. In *Room 2* is a falcon-style coffin, very impressive in black with gold leaf design and gold bird's face (Case 4).

The Jewellery Room

Room 3 closes a quarter of an hour before the rest of the museum and is specially guarded: it contains jewellery from the I Dynasty through to the Byzantine period: necklaces, pectorals, diadems, daggers and much else in gold, silver and precious stones. The best workmanship is found in the jewellery of the XII Dynasty, and the stones are real (carnelian for red and orange, amethyst for purple and violet, lapis lazuli for blue, feldspar for green) — in Tutankhamun's time, as you will see in the following rooms, paste and glass were used instead and though the settings are gold it is mere costume jewellery. If I could walk out with any of it, you would find the VI Dynasty gold falcon head (Case 3: 4010) missing, and Mary Astor, Peter Lorre and Sidney Greenstreet hot on my trail.

The Tutankhamun Exhibition

Walking round the Tutankhamun exhibition, you occasionally notice a dust-free silhouette where a piece has been removed to join one of the Tut Tours around America, Britain, France, etc, and yet these absences hardly relieve the overwhelming impression of the whole. There is just so much, yet Tutankhamun was a minor figure who died young and was stuffed into a small tomb; imagine the impedimenta that Seti I tried taking with him. I have seen three Tutankhamun roadshows and have in each case preferred their careful choice and presentation to the jumble sale effect at the Cairo Museum. *Rooms 7, 8, 9, 10, 15, 25, 30, 35, 40 and 45*, and also *Room 4* (off Room 9) and part of *Room 13*, contain 1700 items in all. The eyes jadedly search for the highlights of the highlights, or otherwise fix on curiosities.

Tutankhamun's mummy, his outermost coffin of gilded wood and his granite sarcophagus are all in his tomb in the Valley of the Kings, but the second coffin of gilded wood and

The gold mask

the third of solid gold are in *Room 4*, along with the gold mask. Each of these, placed one within the other like Russian dolls, in turn were placed within a gilded wood shrine — which again fitted within three more (*Rooms 7 and 8*). These shrines remind me of Wilhelm Reich's orgone boxes, a crackpot device for concentrating orgone energy around the human body: 'Quite unexpectedly the knowledge of the biological function of tension and charge led me to the discovery of hitherto unknown energy processes in bions, in the human organism and in the radiation of the sun... This energy, which is capable of charging non-conducting substances, I termed *orgone*... The orgone energy has a parasympatheticotonic effect and charges living tissues... The human organism is surrounded by an orgonotic field which varies according to the individual's vegetative motility' (Reich, *The Function of the Orgasm*). The ancient Egyptians, however, were born and died too soon to benefit from Reich's teachings, and employed these gold casings in part because gold was thought to be the flesh of the gods, and also because it warded off all outside contamination, presumably including, alas, orgone.

A vegetating Osiris

In *Room 5* is a curiosity other examples of which you may have noticed elsewhere in the museum: a vegetating Osiris (Case 93, 1064). It is a wooden silhouette of the god, his image again carved out within this and the depression once filled with earth from which grass would sprout with symbolic effect.

Among the finer or more curious items in the east gallery (*Rooms 15 to 45*) are a jewellery casket of gilded wood (*Room 45*, Case 54, 447) in the form of a naos with the figure of Anubis on top; a chest (*Room 35*, Case 20, 324) for the Pharaoh's clothes decorated on the lid with a desert hunt, on the large panels with Tutankhamun waging war, and on the small panels with the royal sphinx trampling on his enemies; two life-size statues of Tutankhamun (96 and 181, at the entrance to Room 45 near the stairway) which guarded the entrance to the burial chamber; and the famous small throne (1), its back richly decorated with a scene of Tutankhamun's Queen placing her right hand on his left shoulder, often interpreted as a relaxed domestic scene, though probably a gesture confirming his position, as she was after all the daughter — and possibly a widow — of Akhenaton, and there was an early tradition of matrilineal succession (explaining the frequent sister and daughter marriages of pharaohs). The armrests too are beautiful, the lovely shape of falcons' wings extending in protection, the birds' heads wearing the crown of Upper and Lower Egypt. Finally, there are a pair of objects (435, 436 in *Room 15*) which are meant to be emblems of Anubis, the skin of a decapitated animal suspended from a papyrus stem. Except it looks more particularly like a fertility symbol: from an alabaster bucket base rises a gold stem with a bud at the top. Around the stem is entwined a tendril which leads down to a kind of sack on two legs (or two distended testicles) with a short broad penis pendant. Maybe that is not what it is, but that is what it looks like.

Tutankhamun's throne

PRACTICAL INFORMATION

The Museum of Egyptian Antiquities is open daily from 9am to 4pm except Fridays when it is closed from noon to 2pm. Entrance is LE3, or LE1 for students with a student card.

For sale at the ticket kiosk is *A Guide to the Egyptian Museum* (1982), LE1.50. This is the official publication and is reasonably comprehensive though descriptions are perfunctory and it is arranged by catalogue number rather than by room which makes it a nuisance to use. It is probably of little value to the passer-through.

No **bags or cameras** may be taken into the museum. These may be checked free of charge (which does not stop the attendant, *sotto voce*, asking for 50PT — ignore him) and to my knowledge will be entirely secure, but I can imagine a mistake, eg someone else being given your expensive camera, so perhaps such things should not be brought at all.

The main entrance and the entrance to its right have several **shops** selling books, cards, reproductions and junk. There is also a **post office** branch, a **bank** and a **cafeteria**. They keep the same hours as the museum.

THE PYRAMID AGE

Before taking the Giza road out to that desert escarpment where the famous Pyramids of Cheops, Chephren and Mycerinus stand, it is worth knowing something of the period in which they were built, and to know too something of that entire line of Old Kingdom pyramids which extends from Abu Roash to the north of Giza to Meidum near the Fayyum, a line that is 70 kms long and numbers over 80 pyramids. This chapter will refer to the main pyramid clusters, and will explain why and how, at the very beginning of recorded history, these most prodigious and enduring monuments in stone were built. 'Everything fears time', wrote an Arab physician in the 12th C, 'but time fears the Pyramids'.

The First Pyramid

The struggle for unity

Around 3100 BC, Upper and Lower Egypt were united under Menes and the I Dynasty established. It is not certain that Menes was an individual; he may represent a conflation of early warrior-princes, and the conquest of the Delta may not have been a single campaign but a struggle lasting over generations. There is evidence of fighting and rebellion during the I and II Dynasties, and the energies of this period would have been devoted to consolidation. Building was in

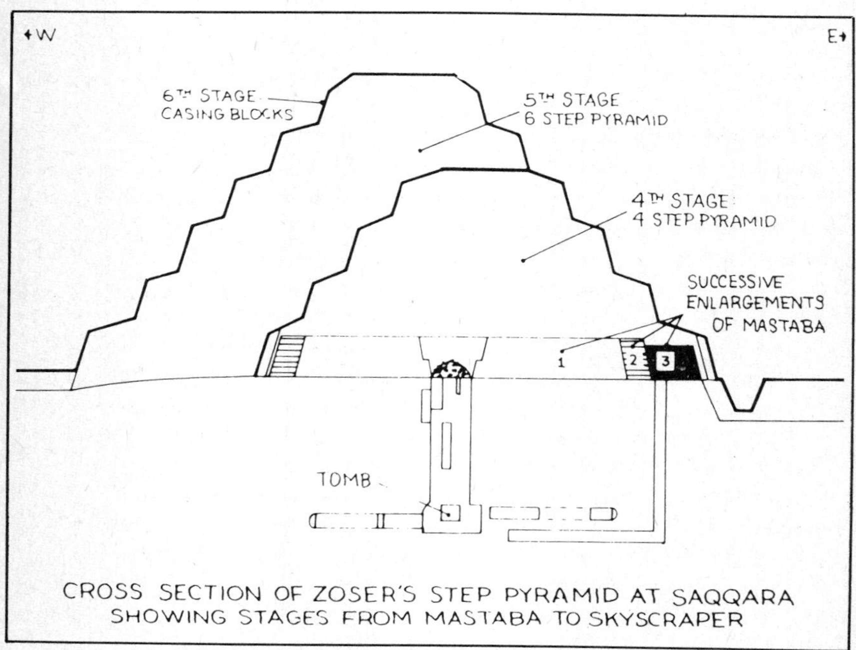

CROSS SECTION OF ZOSER'S STEP PYRAMID AT SAQQARA SHOWING STAGES FROM MASTABA TO SKYSCRAPER

mud brick and reed, though during the II Dynasty some stone was used underground in tombs.

Mastabas

Below ground these tombs were built like houses: rectangular and divided into chambers. Above ground they had a low, flat-topped form with sloping walls. This mud brick superstructure was sometimes faced with mud plaster and covered with white gypsum stucco. Mariette called them *mastabas,* the Arabic for those stone benches outside the shops and coffee houses of medieval Cairo.

The Old Kingdom

About 400 years after unification, that is c.2700 BC, Egypt entered into a long period of security and order known to us as the Old Kingdom and beginning with the III Dynasty. Awareness of the two Egypts, Upper and Lower, remained acute, as can be read from the ritual of Zoser's Heb-Sed festival at Saqqara, and the village and tribal units up and down the Nile continued to worship their local gods, that prolific pantheon that never disappeared but which eventually was overlayed by a few powerful national cults.

The III Dynasty: building in stone

During the reign of Zoser (III Dyn) there was a sudden use and mastery of stone at Saqqara. His mortuary complex of courts and chapels, 544 metres long and 277 metres wide and surrounded by a wall 10 metres high, was all of stone, beautifully detailed and architectured. And dominating the whole was the first pyramid, over 62 metres high, built in steps. Stone had risen from the darkness of the tomb into the confident light of the sun.

The explanation is not found in technology; stone was not new and tools and construction methods remained as simple as they had been in the past — the lever was used but the wheel and pulley were unknown. Rather there was peace and stability; there was a developing theocratic doctrine that invited the use of stone; and there was a man of genius who knew how to build with it.

The genius of Imhotep

That man was Imhotep, Zoser's grand vizier, chief judge, minister of agriculture and supervisor of building works. He was also high priest at Heliopolis. His range of accomplishment typified the opportunities and needs of a new civilisation, where everything was still to be invented and then organised. He was revered throughout pharaonic history, though recalled as a healer rather than as an organiser, statesman or architect, and he became a mythic figure, a demi-god, and was eventually raised to unqualified divinity — but his contemporary existence is certain from inscriptions found at Zoser's complex.

The doctrine that begged the use of stone was that of the Pharaoh's sole possession of the *ka,* the vital force emanating from the god to his son, the king, who could then dispense it to his subjects. The ka was eternal so long as it was linked to the Pharaoh, and so it was essential that ka and king be given an indestructible container of stone.

Building the first pyramid

Zoser was built a stone mastaba and this was twice enlarged. Then in three further stages, Imhotep made a qualitative leap, a sudden vertical thrust, and created the world's first skyscraper, the Step Pyramid. Political and cultural revolution in Egypt has always swept down through the Valley, nomadic in inspiration. The mastaba belonged to the earthbound world of the Delta farmers; the pyramid and generally Egyptian architecture thereafter eschewed the enclosure of space and instead posed itself against the sun and the stars. Stone permitted it; Imhotep mastered the physics required; and yearning for the vast and timeless cosmos was its inspiration.

It is interesting and important, though, that Zoser's complex remains human in feeling. Zoser was the son of the god, and even if he was the god himself, he at least relished the life of man, for in the house-like arrangement of chambers beneath his pyramid, with their faience decorations imitating domestic reeding, there is the desire to project his present life into the hereafter. This sense never again appears inside a pyramid, and rarely at any mortuary structure of a pharaoh throughout Egypt's history. Instead the savouring of the every day was excluded, divinity insisted upon, and ritual became obsessive.

The pyramid revolution

So there was a first revolution, an eruption, in stone. But the second revolution was an adventure even more astonishing and led to the perfection of the pyramid form at Giza. We think of the vastness of Egyptian history and how slowly it must have unfolded, yet from Zoser's complex to Cheops' Pyramid no more time passed than our fast-moving age took to travel from the beginnings of iron construction to the Eiffel Tower — around 75 years in fact. What is more, the age of the great pyramids was over in 200 years. What explains its sudden coming and going, and the intensity, the phenomenal labour, with which it was pursued?

You see that in rushing out to Giza you confront the apogee, but you do not meet the answer. That is found to the south of Saqqara, at Dahshur and at Meidum.

The Pyramid Production Line

The collapse of the Meidum pyramid

The pyramid at Meidum is about 90 kms by road south of Cairo and even without visiting it you can see it, if you are alert, from the left side of the overnight train back from Luxor soon after it passes El Wasta in the morning. Like all the pyramids, it stands beyond the belt of cultivation on the edge of the desert. It is an amazing sight: a steeply inclined tower rising from a low hill — and that is exactly what it was thought to be by early travellers. In fact it is a pyramid that collapsed. It did not disintegrate over time; near the moment of its completion it collapsed in one instantaneous catastrophe, only a part of the core remaining clear of the mound of debris all around.

This was the first pyramid after Zoser's and it was conceived at first as a step pyramid. A second, larger stepped structure was soon superimposed and finally a true pyramidal shell was added, its smooth sides rising at an angle of about 52°. But there were serious design faults, including the badly squared stones of the outer casing which stood on horizontal limestone blocks embedded in compacted sand instead of on a bedrock foundation given an inward slope. The weight of the pyramid, instead of being directed downwards and inwards, was directed outwards; its lateral forces simply blew it apart.

The collapsed pyramid at Meidum

The mystery of Snofru's pyramids at Dahshur

This disaster leads to an explanation of the pyramid craze that marks the succeeding dynasty to Zoser's. An inscription at Meidum says it was built by Snofru (IV Dyn). But this has disturbed Egyptologists because Snofru was known to have built two pyramids at Dahshur. If the purpose of a pyramid was to provide an indestructable container for the Pharaoh and his ka, why did Snofru need three? Snofru's inscription was explained away as a usurpation of his predecessor's pyramid: 'It cannot but seem extraordinary that one and the same king should have built for himself two pyramids of vast dimensions at no great distance from one another... and since it is hard to imagine that he erected three pyramids, the one at Meidum is now tentatively ascribed to Huny', wrote Sir Alan Gardiner, the noted Egyptologist, in *Egypt of the Pharaohs*. But that left the Bent and Red Pyramids at Dahshur. The Bent Pyramid was disposed of with the argument that it had been deemed unsafe and so Snofru decided to build another. One pharaoh, one ka and one pyramid to suit.

The Bent Pyramid rises for 70 percent of its bulk at an angle of 52°, the same as at Meidum. It then abruptly alters angle to 43.5°. The Red Pyramid rises at a constant angle of 43.5°. The lower angle of the Red would clearly be safer than the steeper initial angle of the Bent, but it fails to explain why the angle of the Bent should have been changed in mid-construction. If the steep initial angle of the Bent was thought to be unsafe, why not at once abandon the project? But if changing the angle was thought to make it safe, why build the Red

Pyramid? Of course, one could argue that it was thought the change of angle would make the Bent Pyramid safe and that unhappily this proved not to be true — though the pyramid has stood safe and sound for nearly 5000 years.

Eminent Egyptologists have said that the builders of the Bent Pyramid suddenly tired of their task and decided to reduce the pyramid's volume, and hence their labour, by reducing its angle. It has also been said that the bend in the pyramid was predetermined and meant to express a 'double pyramid', that is two pyramids of different angles superimposed, and that this symbolised some unexplained duality. And it has been said that the architect lost his nerve, but one reason for this tantalising possibility — the collapse of the Meidum pyramid at a point when the Bent Pyramid was 70 percent of the way towards completion — has not been countenanced by Egyptologists because it would reintroduce the 'unpalatable conclusion that Snofru did possess three pyramids' (Gardiner). The key word there is possess, for it signals the insistence that pyramids were built for the sole reason of providing a container for the Pharaoh's ka, and that Snofru had no business, therefore, building what he believed at that point to be two perfectly good pyramids.

The Egyptologists' evasions could have gone on indefinitely as long as they could have believed that the pyramid at Meidum had belonged to Snofru's predecessor and had merely crumbled with time. But in *The Riddle of the Pyramids*, and in articles published in the *Journal of Egyptian Archaeology*, Kurt Mendelssohn, professor of physics at Oxford, has presented a good case for believing that Meidum, while nearing completion, came down with a bang as Snofru was already well advanced on his second pyramid — which only then, and for that reason, was continued at a bent angle.

Overlap in pyramid construction

So why should several pyramids be built in overlapping succession during the reign of a single pharaoh? It is a fact that more large pyramids were built during the IV Dynasty than there were pharaohs to fill them. The answer is in the scale of the task. Herodotus says it took 20 years to build Cheops' Pyramid and 10 years to build the causeway and the earth ramps that served as a kind of scaffolding, with 100,000 men working a three month shift. Modern calculation of the workforce required does not vary substantially from Herodotus' figure, though it is likely that several thousand men, highly skilled as stone-cutters, masons, surveyors, etc, would have been employed year-round, while the larger requirement for unskilled labour would have been drawn from the fields between July and November, the period of the inundation. All of these people needed training and organisation, as well as feeding, clothing and housing, and the logistics of the operation must have been formidable. It is not the sort of operation that is easily or efficiently mounted at the uncertain occasion of a pharaoh's accession, nor is the size of a pyramid and so the time it will take to build readily geared to the uncertain duration of a pharaoh's reign. The suggestion is rather that pyramid construction was continuous and independent of whether or not there would be enough pharaohs to fill them. And this is what the evidence of

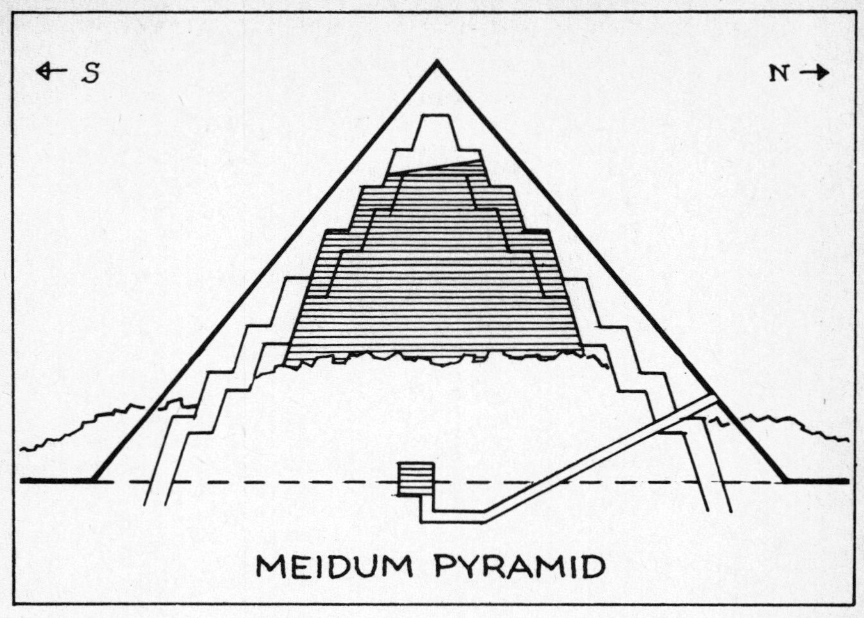

Meidum and the Bent Pyramid suggests did happen, the overlap accounted for by the fact that as the first pyramid tapered towards completion, the surplus workforce was immediately engaged on starting a second pyramid.

Pyramids and the state

Whether by intention or as a consequence, this pyramid production line must have had two important effects. The first was that the vast levy of men required would have cut across the division of Upper and Lower Egypt and the parochialism of villages and tribes throughout the length of the Valley, the breadth of the Delta. Pyramid building would complete, down to the fibres of society, the unification of the country begun by Menes by force of arms.

The second effect was that whoever was responsible for pyramid building would see their power enhanced. But production of pyramids surplus to the requirements of any one pharaoh, surplus even to the requirements of an entire dynasty, demanded a transcending organising authority. Imhotep's own career suggests the composition of that authority: in part the power of the Pharaoh, but also that of the bureaucracy and the priesthood. Pyramids created the apparatus of the state.

Symbolism of the Pyramids

There is then the pyramidal form. One can see how constructionally the pyramids began with the mastaba, Zoser's pyramid in fact a stepped mastaba. The achievement in architecture of the pure abstract pyramidal form came, briefly, at Meidum, when before it collapsed its steps were being sheathed in planes. If anything, the disaster was a spur to the technical perfection of the pyramidal symbol. That symbol preceded construction rather than technology dictated symbol seems likely. In Egyptian creation myths there is a primal hill which rises above the waters, and from it ascends the sun. And until the High Dam at Aswan finally put an end to the annual inundation, that was very much the scene in Egypt: villages huddled on mounds to avoid the flood, then its subsidence and the sun drawing from the mud the harvest. This myth is referred to at Medinet Habu and Hermopolis; Heliopolis also claimed a primal hill, the *benben*, a tapering megalith, a word whose root, *bn*, is bound up with the notion of shining, brilliant, ascending. It is depicted in II Dynasty inscriptions, that is before the pyramid age.

The primal hill

Variations on the pyramidal form continued to be popular throughout Egyptian history, as for example the obelisks whose points or pyramidions were sheathed in electrum, a mixture of silver and gold. Pliny the Elder described obelisks as petrified rays of sunlight, and more than one modern writer has remarked on the pyramid-like form of a burst of sunlight through the clouds after a rare Egyptian rain.

The building of pyramids then would have been no mere drudgery inflicted on the population by some megalomaniac pharaoh. The symbolism would have been appreciated throughout all levels of society, and it is quite likely that far from being built by slave-labour, as Herodotus claims, they were built willingly and with a shared sense of exalted purpose which at the time would have seemed far more important, and certainly would have been more conscious, than creating new political forms.

The end of the pyramid age

But here the gods died sooner than the works of men. And those works included not only the pyramids, but the creation for the first time in human history of an organisational principle, the state, that was to serve Egypt until her absorption into the Roman Empire, and is the basis of human organisation to this day. Once the pyramid production line had achieved this, their symbolism could be carried on in lesser forms, such as obelisks; in any case, it was no longer necessary to build pyramids, and apart from some inferior examples in later dynasties, by 2500 BC the age of the pyramids was over.

THE GREAT PYRAMIDS OF GIZA

Approaching the Pyramids

Half a day should be allowed for the visit to the Giza Pyramids, though you should return again at night. They are approached along a broad straight road, originally built for that same Empress Eugénie who attended the opening night at the Opera House, so that she could cover the 11 kms from Cairo in her carriage. This Sharia al-Ahram or Road of the Pyramids once passed across fellahin's fields which would flood with the rising of the Nile, but nowadays most of the route has been built up. There is therefore, at first, something ordinary about the approach, as though you were off to a funfair on the edge of town, expecting at any moment the distant screams of roller coaster passengers as they plunged down papier-maché mountains.

But even the Pyramids themselves initially conspire to deflate anticipation. One of the savants accompanying Napoleon described his approach: 'Seen from a distance they produce the same kind of effect as do high mountain peaks. The nearer one approaches, the more this effect decreases. Only when at last you are within a short distance of these regular masses is a wholly different impression produced; you are struck by surprise, and as soon as you have reached the top of the slope, your ideas change in a flash. Finally, when you have reached the foot of the Great Pyramid, you are seized with a vivid and powerful emotion, tempered by a sort of stupefaction, almost overwhelming in its effects'.

Even so, you might just as easily be overwhelmed by touts urging you to ride their donkey, horse or camel, and by

Chephren's Pyramid: the original casing – the sublime power of the plane – remains intact towards the top

numberless 'guides' and 'watchmen' who gather about you like mosquitos, endlessly trying to lure you into ruined little temples with the promise of an undiscovered mummy or reliefs of pharaonic pornography. In the old days, visitors would come with a dragoman who wielded a big stick for which you are bound to develop the greatest nostalgia. Mark Twain, who led a party of tourists here in the 1860s, attempted escape by climbing to the top of Cheops' Pyramid but was pursued by an Arab whom he offered $1 if he could race to the top of Chephren's Pyramid and back to the top of Cheops' within nine minutes, in the hope that the man would break his neck. Three dollars later an exasperated Twain, now joined by the man's mother, offered them each $100 if they would jump off the Pyramid head first.

The best times to visit the Pyramids are at dawn, at sunset and at night when they form as much a part of the natural order as the sun, the moon and the stars. Flaubert recalled the view from the top of Cheops' Pyramid: 'The sun was rising just opposite; the whole valley of the Nile, bathed in mist, seemed to be a still white sea; and the desert behind us, with its hillocks of sand, another ocean, deep purple, its waves all petrified'. My first visit was at night. I had gone to the son et lumiere, the Arabic programme, so that I would not have to listen to any of the usual tourist drivel, but could instead enjoy the play of lights to the eerie accompaniment of this booming, gutteral but poetic language. The programme over but some floodlights on, I walked up past the Sphinx and stood between the Pyramids of Cheops and Chephren. And then suddenly the lights went out. Black night. The great stones rising on either side, picked out by the moon and stars. The feeling, as Napoleon said here to his army, of 'forty centuries of history looking down upon us', feeling it in the most awesome way.

Statistics

The road arrives at the Mena House Hotel and then curves sharply to the left, mounting a gentle slope and finishing at the north end of the plateau, almost directly opposite the Great Pyramid, that of Cheops. This is the oldest of the group and the largest, and the others, Chephren and Mycerinus, stand in descending order of age and size along a southwest axis, each identically oriented 8.5° west of magnetic north; when built they were probably aligned precisely with the North Star, their entrance corridors aiming straight at it. At first the second pyramid, that of Chephren, seems largest, but that is because it stands on higher ground and retains its casing towards its peak. Its present height is 136.4 metres (originally 143 metres) and its volume is 2,200,000 cubic metres; this compares with a height of 137.2 metres (originally 146.6 metres) for the Great Pyramid of Cheops, which has a volume of 2,550,000 cubic metres. This pyramid was built of over 2,500,000 enormous blocks of limestone cut from the Moqattam and locally, though about 170,000 have been removed by Arabs and Turks since the founding of Cairo. Mycerinus is much smaller, rising only to a height of 65.5 metres, though it is still imposing, and it contributes to the satisfying arrangement of the group. Napoleon astonished his officers with the calculation that the stones from these three pyramids would be sufficient to build a wall

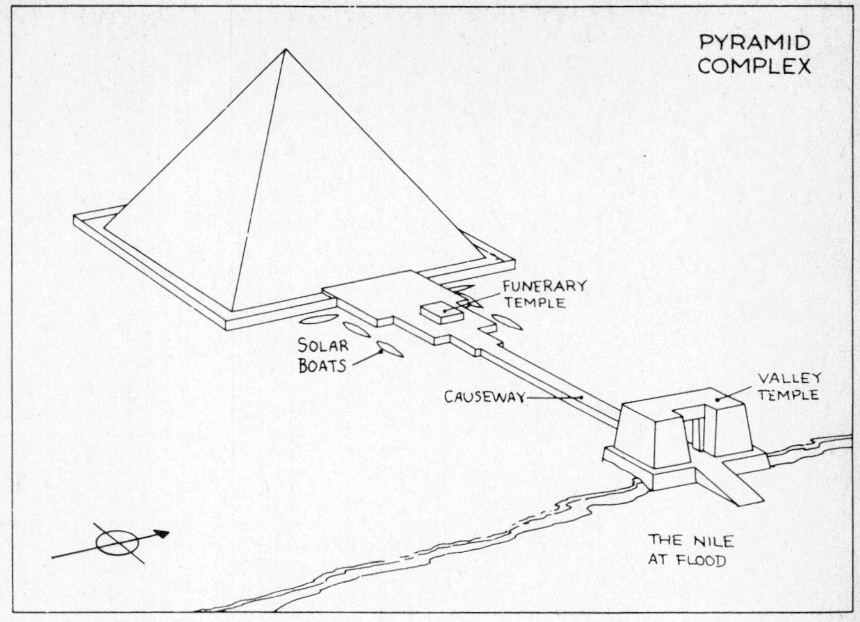

3 metres high and 0.3 metres thick around the whole of France.

But the Pyramids do not have this rocky ledge entirely to themselves. There are smaller attendant pyramids, some at least for royal wives, and suburban rows of mastabas for nobles and princes of the blood. There are the remains of temples and causeways; there are solar boat pits; and there is the Sphinx. A pyramid was never merely a self-sufficient geometrically shaped tumulus of masonry raised above a royal burial; it was the culminating point of a vast funerary area comprising, apart from the pyramid itself, three parts. First, near the desert edge and overlooking the cultivation so as to be accessible by boat in the inundation season was a modest *valley chapel*. From it led a walled-in *causeway*, as long as 500 metres, upwards to the *funerary temple* proper, this abutting on to the east side of the pyramid, where a false door permitted the deceased Pharaoh to emerge in order to partake of the offered feasts. Also, on several sides of a pyramid, set in pits, *wooden boats* have been found. Whether these were only symbolic or actually used is not known; some have supposed they enabled the Pharaoh to follow the sun god across the skies, but as they have been found facing all four points of the compass they could as easily have been intended to enable the Pharaoh to go wherever he desired. For convenience, however, they will be referred to here as solar boats.

A pyramid complex

The Pyramid of Cheops

The polished casing to the **Pyramid of Cheops** (Khufu) is

Climbing the Great Pyramid

entirely gone and so you are presented with the tiered courses of limestone blocks, an invitation to climb to the platform at the top, 10 metres square. This used to be a fairly easy and entirely safe thing to do, as guides would simply haul you up, one at each arm, a third shoving from below. Climbing the Pyramids is now technically forbidden, however, which leaves the field open to the more adventurous or the more foolhardy to make the attempt unassisted, though a Beduin will often miraculously appear when you get into trouble. The ascent is best made at the northeast corner, each 'step' in fact a metre-high block, and will take 15-20 minutes. If anything, it is more difficult on the way down. At 7 am one morning I saw the body of a man who had fallen and bashed himself against the blocks all the way down, his brain spilled out, his face gone.

Going inside

The squeamish might content themselves with going inside. Here the only thing to fear is fear itself, in the form of claustrophobia and difficulty for some in breathing due to inadequate oxygen, and also the possibility that you might get locked in, which in fact happened one night to my brother (more on the very real dangers of being sealed up, temporarily and even permanently, in ancient tombs when you read about Saqqara and Thebes).

You *enter at the north face* (1) through an opening made by Caliph al-Mamun in his search for treasure (though it is probable that this pyramid had been robbed as early as the First Intermediate Period), and soon come to the *original corridor* which descends for 100 metres to a depth of 30 metres beneath the surface of the bedrock. It reaches an *unfinished chamber* (2) of no interest, and as this corridor is constricted (1.3 metres high, one metre wide) and slippery, it is not usually open to the public. Why this lowest chamber was never finished is not known; Herodotus said it was subject to flooding by the Nile.

Instead, about 20 metres from the entrance along the descending corridor you come to a block of granite designed to prevent access to the *ascending corridor* (3), though al-Mamun merely hollowed out the rock to the left and you soon find yourself crouching your way upwards (height again 1.3 metres, width one metre) for 40 metres. The gradient is 1 in 2, and so can be quite tiring, but arrival at the Great Gallery at least permits a stretch. Here there is a *shaft* (right) which winds down to the descending corridor — purpose unknown. There is also a *horizontal corridor*, again only 1.3 metres high for most of its length, which leads to the so-called *Queen's Chamber* (4), nearly square with a pointed roof of gigantic blocks. But best by far is the ascending *Great Gallery* (5), 8.5 metres high, 47 metres long, a marvel of precision masonry, of which it has been said that neither a needle nor a hair can be inserted into the joints of the stones.

The King's Chamber

This gives on to the principal tomb chamber, commonly called the *King's Chamber* (6), 42.5 metres above the surface of the bedrock, 5.22 metres wide and 10.44 metres long, that is a double square, aligned east-west. On the north and south walls, a metre above the floor, are the rectangular mouths of the two *ventilation shafts* which extend to the surfaces of the pyramid. The chamber is built entirely in pink Aswan granite

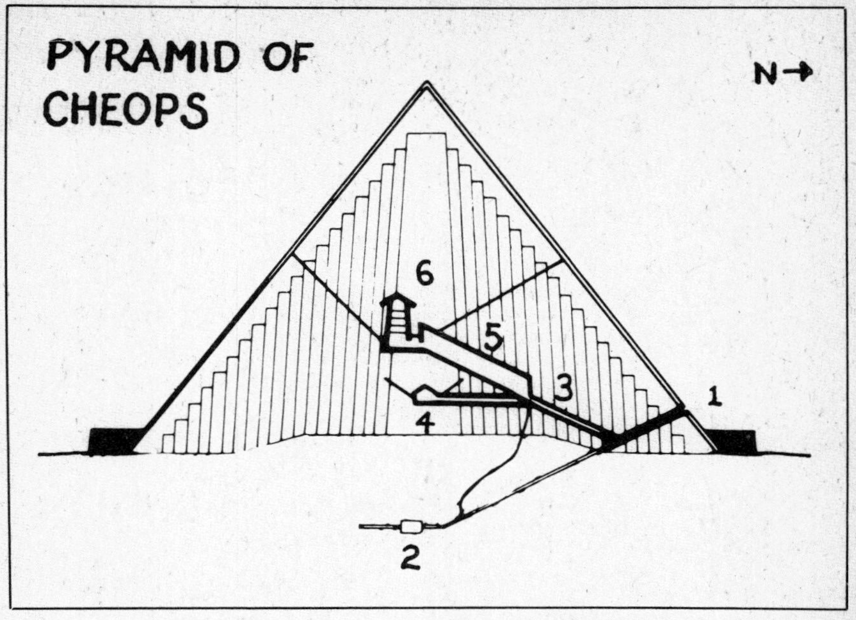

and roofed over with nine huge granite slabs laid horizontally, and above these (seen by means of a ladder leading to a passage in the upper south wall of the Great Gallery) are four more granite layers, each separated by a *relieving chamber*, possibly meant to distribute the full weight of the pyramid away from the King's Chamber, though in fact this job is accomplished by the topmost pointed roof of limestone blocks. It was in these relieving chambers that the only inscriptions in any of the Giza Pyramids were found — the cartouche, traced several times in red, of Khufu, Cheops. His mummy, if it found its way to this pyramid at all, would have been placed in this King's Chamber; the sarcophagus is empty.

It is here that you might think about the great weight upon you. Over your head is 95 metres of solid pyramid, more than enough to squash you very thin for a very long time. Unlike the Meidum pyramid, however, the Pyramid of Cheops has been shown by Swiss engineer H. Roessler (1952) to be exceptionally stable. The building blocks are far larger than those used for earlier pyramids and they are precisely fitted together, while the casing blocks overlaying the basic step structure rest upon foundations slotted into the bedrock. The weight of the pyramid itself contributes to its stability, but not simply its dead weight; the stepped inclined buttresses throw much of this weight towards the centre. At every level the pyramid's horizontal thrusts are directed towards the central core, while 35 percent of the vertical thrusts are transmitted to the inner core (that is the line running from the top of the pyramid *through you* to the base), only the remaining thrusts being carried down into the bedrock. In fact the bigger the pyramid the more stable it becomes.

Around Cheops' Pyramid

Coming out of the pyramid you can see on the north side, also on the east, the remains of the original *enclosure wall*, about 10 metres from the base. Backing against this wall on the east side is the basalt paving of **Cheops' funerary temple**, about all that remains of it, and only occasional traces too of the *causeway* that would have come up from the valley temple. The **three small pyramids**, from 15 to 20 metres high, probably belonged to Cheops' queens or sisters: the southernmost is certainly Henutsen's, daughter of Snofru, sister and perhaps wife of Cheops. She became identified during the XXI Dynasty with Isis and her mortuary temple, to the east of her pyramid, was enlarged as the shrine of the 'Mistress of the Pyramids'. Also in the vicinity of the smaller pyramids and the funerary temple are *boat pits*. A **solar boat** has been pieced back together on the south side of the Pyramid, within a glass and concrete structure.

The Sphinx

An outcrop of hard grey and soft yellow limestone, useless as building material, was left standing in the quarry from which Cheops cut many of the blocks for his pyramid. His son Chephren had the happy idea of shaping it into a figure — lion's body, god's face, though perhaps Chephren's own, and wearing the royal headdress with uraeus. The Egyptians would have regarded it as a symbol of strength and wisdom combined, but the Greeks applied their word sphinx to it, recalling a lion's body but the breasts and head of a woman given to putting riddles to passers-by, and so this most famous **Sphinx** has acquired an air of mystery quite foreign to its intention.

Nevertheless, some mysteries are associated with it. Neither Herodotus nor any other classical writer until Pliny the Elder mentioned the Sphinx, presumably because it was buried in sand. Prints and photographs of recent times show its features looming from an engulfing sea of sand, but this is all too assiduously cleared today, some mystery swept away with it. The future Tuthmosis IV (XVIII Dyn) dreamt here that if he was to become Pharaoh he must clear away the sands: his stelae between the Sphinx' paws commemorate this first known restoration. During the Turkish domination the Sphinx was used for target practice and its nose, which originally had been cemented on, fell off; 18th C drawings show that it was missing long before Napoleon was supposed to have done the damage. The uraeus has also gone, but the beard is being pieced together and should soon be stuck back on. In the son et lumiere programmes, the Sphinx is given the role of narrator which it performs, as I have said, much better in Arabic when you cannot understand a word. This is in fact one of the best times for viewing it or, after the programme, having a drink on the terrace of the Pavilion of Cheops, for then it gains in perspective against the more distant Pyramids. It may not otherwise seem as large as you have imagined: it is

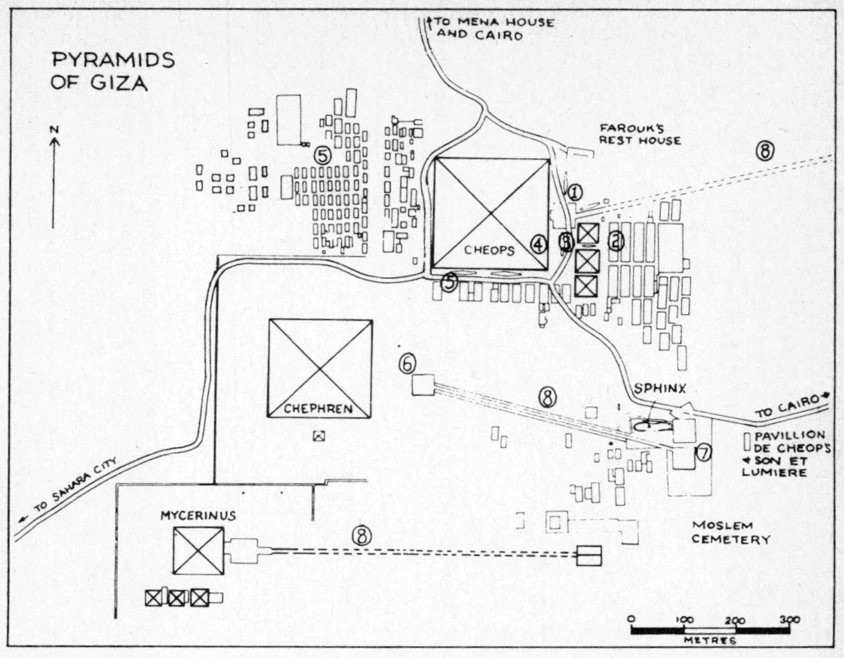

1. Cheops' mortuary temple
2. Pyramids of Cheops' Queens
3. Boat pits
4. Solar boat
5. Mastabas of IV and V Dynasties
6. Chephren's mortuary temple
7. Chephren's valley temple
8. Causeways

20 metres high and 48.5 metres long, much of its bulk crouched within the quarry so that only its head overtops the horizon.

Chephren's Pyramid Complex

Immediately in front of the Sphinx and associated with it is a IV Dynasty temple, one reason for believing the face on the Sphinx is a god's and not Chephren's, for the Egyptians did not build temples to their kings. Adjacent and to the south is **Chephren's Valley Temple**, facing east. This is the only IV Dynasty sanctuary to retain its grandeur, its exceptional state of preservation owing to having been buried in the sands and not discovered until 1853 by Mariette. The material is pink Aswan granite, majestically and simply assembled in strong verticals and horizontals, square monolithic pillars supporting massive granite architraves. It was here that Mariette discovered the magnificent diorite statue of Chephren (Room 42, Ground Floor, Egyptian Museum). The purpose of this temple is uncertain, or rather certain for some and contradicted by others. One view is that valley temples were used for mummification; others think the site too exposed and that embalming would have been done either at the Pharaoh's Memphis palace or at the base of the pyramid, in the funerary temple. There is at least more general agreement that here was performed the 'Opening of the Mouth' ceremony at which the ka entered the deceased's body. The ka always required a secure residence, hence pyramids and immutable bodies, though it would also inhabit the mortuary statue of the Pharaoh, such as that one in the Egyptian Museum, one of 23 that sat round the main T-shaped chamber.

'Opening of the Mouth' ceremony

You should now follow if you can the traces of Chephren's *causeway* up to his **Funerary Temple** at the base of his pyramid. More of this temple survives than of Cheops', the walls formed of possibly the largest blocks ever used in building, one of them 13.4 metres long and weighing 163,000 kilos. To the south of the pyramid is a ruined small pyramid, probably of a queen.

The **Pyramid of Chephren** (Khafre) compares to Cheops' in size, seemingly exceeds it in height and is also capped with its original casing. But its interior is less interesting, while the ascent is much more difficult, requiring an hour to get to the casing, progress being very dangerous thence upwards because the smooth surface offers no hold. One of the earlier explorers and snatchers of antiquities was Belzoni, born in Italy but first achieving fame for his 'human pyramid' act on the stage of the Sadlers Wells in London. He was the first European to enter this pyramid (1818) and promptly emblazoned his name on the south wall of the burial chamber. When Flaubert entered the chamber 33 years later he recorded: 'Under Belzoni's name, and no less large, is that of a M Just de Chasseloup-Laubat. One is irritated by the number of imbeciles' names written everywhere: on the top of the Great Pyramid there is a certain Buffard, 79 Rue Saint-Martin, wallpaper manufacturer, in black letters; an English fan of Jenny Lind's has written her name; there is also a pear, representing Louis-Phillippe'.

When the Egyptians built their pyramids it was with a feeling for the sublime power of the plane, without reliefs, inscriptions or any detailing whatsoever. Once the polished limestone casings were set in place, the pyramids both literally and symbolically repulsed the touch of mortals — well, that was the idea, anyway. One of the high points of a visit to the Pyramids in Roman times was the spectacle of men from a nearby village shinning up from the ground to their very tips; while one Roman woman scribbled on a casing stone, 'I saw the Pyramids without you; sadly I shed tears here', a lament copied down by a 15th C pilgrim, when the casing was more extensive than now.

Antique tourists

Last of the Great Pyramids

The **Pyramid of Mycerinus** (Menkaure) has only one-tenth of the volume of the other two pyramids and effectively marks the end of the pyramid age. The last Pharaoh of the IV Dynasty built a quite different sort of tomb at Saqqara, while the pyramids of the next dynasty were small and shoddy.

Though last of the great pyramids, Mycerinus' was built well, with granite used for the lower courses and a casing that remained intact until the 16th C. An attempt was made by the Caliph in 1215 to destroy all the Pyramids and his workmen started with Mycerinus'. After eight months they gave up. 'Considering the vast masses that have been taken away, it might be supposed that the building would have been completely destroyed, but so immense is the pile that the stones are scarcely missed. Only on one of its sides can be noticed any trace of the impression which it was attempted to be made', wrote the historian Abd el Latif. Though you can enter, the interior is not interesting. Opposite the south face are three small pyramids, while against the east are the remains of Mycerinus' funerary temple.

Mons Venus

Herodotus recorded a belief in Greece that this pyramid was in fact built by Rhodopis, a beautiful courtesan from Thrace who flourished in Egypt, charging a building stone for her services. The Pyramid of Mycerinus is built of at least 200,000 granite and limestone blocks. But it is not only for that reason that the story is untrue.

PRACTICAL INFORMATION

The *Practical Information* section at the end of the *Cairo: Mother of the World* chapter contains information on accommodation and eating places by the Pyramids, travel to them, and the Sound and Light show. Additional information is supplied here.

Although you can have a general view of the Pyramids and Sphinx at any time of day or night, **access** to the Sphinx, tombs and valley temples, and **entry** into the chambers of the Pyramids is from 8am to 4.30pm daily. The only fees are for seeing the solar boat in its glass-enclosed chamber (LE5) and for entering the Pyramids (LE3); tickets for the Pyramids should be bought at the kiosk at the top of the road coming up from the Mena House Hotel towards the north side of the Pyramid of Cheops. Con men may attempt to extort money from you for simply staring at the monuments, while others will press their services upon you as guides or try to sell you fake antiquities and other rubbish. All are to be ignored, and if necessary the Tourist Police invoked. You should accept assistance and agree a price only if you want help in climbing the Pyramids.

You can **ride on horseback or camelback** across the desert from the Pyramids to **Saqqara**. The journey will take at least 3 hours in each direction, and spending just a little time at Saqqara means an 8-hour expedition in all. For this reason you should resist offers of hire by the hour and negotiate a price for the entire day. Camels will cost about LE8, horses a bit more. There is some dispute as to which animal is better; most people prefer horses over longer distances. Either way, all but the most hardened rider can expect to end the day feeling pretty sore.

The **Sound and Light** show starts nightly (except Fridays) at 7.30 and lasts 1 hour. The English-language programmes are on Mondays, Wednesdays and Saturdays; the French on Tuesdays and Sundays; the German on Sundays (at 8.30pm); the Arabic on Thursdays. Admission is LE4 except for the Arabic programme which is LE1. Seating is on a terrace facing the valley temple of the Pyramid of Cephren, ie by the Sphinx. Bring a sweater; it can get cool on the edge of the desert, even in summer.

Almost any taxi driver will know what you mean if you say Sound and Light; if you want him to wait for you (thus avoiding any difficulty in getting a ride back), offer LE2 to LE3 per hour. Also there are buses, but these will take you to the Mena House Hotel and you will have to walk back down the Pyramids Road till you reach the Sound and Light sign (on the right as you face Cairo) and then walk to the right, through the village on the edge of the desert escarpment. Of if you are alert you can alight at the sign (it is about 1000 metres before the Mena House Hotel), saving yourself some shoe leather. Another alternative is to take a tour, which will include admission and the ride out and back for about LE11. This works out at about as much as it would cost one person to take a taxi and keep it waiting; for 2 or more people it is better to take the taxi.

MEMPHIS AND SAQQARA

Saqqara is 32 kms by road from Cairo and 21 kms south of the Giza Pyramids. The necropolis extends about 7 kms north to south along the desert plateau and looks down over the palm groves that cover the site of Memphis, about 6 kms to the southeast in the valley of the Nile. Memphis was the capital of the Old Kingdom, its palaces and shrines of that period built of mud brick for the span of the living and now vanished; Saqqara, built of stone to endure eternity, survives.

The Saqqara road is a left turn off the Road to the Pyramids at the traffic lights immediately after a canal about 1500 metres before the Mena House Hotel. It is a pleasant country road with glimpses to the right of the Libyan Desert and the V Dynasty pyramids of Abusir. (You can also ride across the desert by camel or horse from the Giza Pyramids in about three hours). You come first to the turning, on your right, for Saqqara; or you can carry straight on for the left-hand turning to the Memphis site. Alternatively, you can take the bus from the Giza Pyramids to Badrashein and can ask to be let off at Memphis. It is best to visit Saqqara early in the morning to avoid the heat, and so to call on Memphis afterwards. But for context, Memphis will be mentioned first.

Old Kingdom Capital

History of Memphis

Memphis probably began as a fortress by which Menes controlled the land and water routes between Upper and Lower Egypt and kept the conquered inhabitants of the Delta in subjection. By the III Dynasty it must have become a sizeable capital, as the Saqqara necropolis suggests, but it may not have been fixed. The IV Dynasty Pharaohs built their pyramids to the north at Giza and might well have had their palaces near there too. One can imagine Memphis developing in stages like Arab Fustat and its successors, decamping northwards. Whether it was the Mediterranean breezes that attracted, or the growing dominance of the sun cult at Heliopolis, so closely associated with pyramid development, is not known. By the VI Dynasty, however, the old site of Memphis had been reoccupied, its attraction the venerable sanctuary of Ptah. From the court of Pepi and its associated monuments came the name *Men-nefru-Mire*, The Beauty of King Mire (Pepi), later abbreviated to Menfe, in Greek Memphis.

Although no longer capital, in the New Kingdom Memphis rivalled Thebes in grandeur, embellished in particular by Ramses II's mania for building. During the 5th C BC when the Persians ruled Egypt from here and Herodotus visited the city, it was a great cosmopolitan centre, a foreshadowing of Alexandria, with many Greeks and Jews, Phoenicians and Libyans among its population, as full of oriental spectacle as Cairo is today. Herodotus, in his hydrology of Egypt, which fascinated him, wrote that 'when the Nile overflows, the whole country is converted into a sea, and the towns, which alone remain above water, look like islands in the Aegean. At these times water transport is used all over the country, instead of merely along the course of the river and anyone going from Naucratis to Memphis would pass right by the Pyramids... The priests told me that it was Menes, the first king of Egypt, who raised the dam which protects Memphis from the floods... On the land which had been drained by the diversion of the river, King Menes built his city and afterwards on the north and west sides of the town excavated a lake, communicating with the river'. As late as the 12th C, Abd el Latif could write that 'the ruins still offer, to those who contemplate them, a collection of such marvellous beauty that the intelligence is confounded, and the most eloquent man would be unable to describe them adequately'. But towards the end of the Mameluke period the dikes around Memphis fell into disrepair and at every inundation the level of the ground was raised.

Memphis today

Today the centuries of Nile mud have swallowed Memphis entirely, so much so that it is impossible to stand here and soliloquise on how the once mighty has fallen — there is, simply, so little to stir reflection. And even had the dikes been maintained, the more ancient stratas of Memphis would have been lost. Herodotus exactly describes those conditions, persisting until the building of the High Dam at Aswan, which annually drowned the Valley and the Delta and gradually covered the past with mud, so that settlements built upon themselves, one strata upon another, to form what in Arabic are known as *tells*. The earliest mud brick houses, palaces and sanctuaries have long since disintegrated beneath the wash of the annual flood, explaining why so much is known of the Egyptian dead, who dwelt in stone on high desert ground, while so little is known of the living. At Memphis there is a friendly alabaster *sphinx* dating from the New Kingdom set up in high grass, and the faint remains of the vast *Temple of Ptah*, and alabaster *mummification beds* where the Apis bulls (see the Serapeum at Saqqara) were prepared for burial. And there is a modern building erected for the sole purpose of roofing over a supine **colossus of Ramses II**, brother to the one outside the Cairo railway station. This Ramses is the victim of monumental indifference: the Egyptian government gave him to the British Museum — which failed to collect. He lies here with his right fist clenched, like a cataleptic Gulliver, bound down by brain seizure rather than ropes. A keeper, perhaps to make sure Ramses does not collect himself and stalk away, stands guard with an old rifle, its last probable use at Omdurman.

The Egypt Exploration Society is now excavating at Memphis; perhaps in a decade or so there will be more to see.

Saqqara

Touring the necropolis

The Saqqara site has a far more desert feel than Giza; the sands wash about your feet nearly everywhere. Also it is dotted with untended holes left by excavators, some of terrific depth and rarely enclosed. It would be dangerous for children on the loose, and adults should mind their step. Many tombs, once discovered and examined, have been closed again and

The world's first building in stone: the Step Pyramid at Saqqara

some have even sanded over. The most comfortable way to explore the site is to go first to Zoser's funerary complex, visiting also the Pyramid of Unas nearby, and then to drive round to the refreshment tent (or walk across the sands to it) from where you can visit the Mastaba of Akhti-hotep and Ptah-hotep, the Mastaba of Ti and the Serapeum.

Saqqara, from Sokkar, the Memphite god of the dead, was a necropolis from the unification of Egypt through the Ptolemaic period, and it is the site also of a Coptic monastery destroyed by the Arabs c.960, so that discoveries here span 4000 years. In historical range and the quantity and value of what has been found here — monuments, works of art, texts and vases — there can be few archaeological sites in all the world, let alone Egypt, to compare with Saqqara. Even so, serious examination of the site only began in the mid-19th C and what remains to be discovered is incalculable. Considering its proximity to Cairo, it is surprising how infrequently it is visited, and how briefly, with organised tours usually allowing only one or two hours. Though the heat is best avoided by an early morning visit, a full day's stay is compensated for by the early departure of tour groups when you will have the place almost entirely to yourself.

Discovery

Except for Zoser's Step Pyramid, Saqqara was ignored, its revelations unsuspected, until 1851 when Auguste Mariette discovered the Serapeum. Even the funerary complex immediately surrounding the Step Pyramid went undiscovered until 1924, and its restoration, to which Jean-

Philippe Lauer has given a lifetime, continues to this day. Cecil M Firth's campaign of 1924-7 overturned accepted notions about the origins of Egyptian architecture in stone which, because of the gigantic blocks used at Giza, was thought to have developed from megalithic monuments. Instead, at Zoser's complex, one sees a stone architecture which replicates the use of brick in its size and courses, and which also is full of imitative references to rush matting, reed and wood forms. One of the greatest achievements of Egyptian civilisation was to sever stone from the rock and to make of it a building material unsurpassed to this day. It happened here, for the first time, at Saqqara, with some hesitancy in the new technology but astonishing artistic brilliance.

Zoser's Funerary Complex

Zoser's funerary complex, dominated by the Step Pyramid, is 544 metres from north to south, 277 metres from east to west, and entirely surrounded by a magnificent panelled and bastioned **enclosure wall** of fine limestone. It still survives to a height of 3.7 metres at some places along its south side, while on the east side, near the southeast corner, it has been rebuilt with stones found in the sand to its original height of 10.48 metres. This vast white wall in itself, once easily visible from Memphis, must have conferred enormous prestige on Zoser and his architect Imhotep. Lauer was himself at first an architect and was called in by Firth when it was realised that the complex could be accurately reconstructed using the original stones.

Though there are many *false doors* in the enclosure wall for the ka to come and go, there is only one *entrance* (1) for the living, at the southeast corner. The narrow passage is through a fortress-like tower and gives onto a vestibule where you can see on either side the leaves of a *simulated double door* thrown open, complete with hinge pins and sockets. Ahead of you is a *colonnaded corridor* (2), its columns engaged and ribbed in imitation of palm stems (the protective ceiling is modern concrete). At the far end is a broad *hypostyle hall* (3) with four pairs of engaged columns, and on your right as you enter the court a half open ka door. This is where the statue base bearing Imhotep's titles was found. Before leaving the hall, notice that the columns are comprised of drums seldom exceeding 25 cms in height, one of many details of the masonry which betray Imhotep's hesitancy in working with this new material, stone.

You now emerge into the **Great South Court** (4), and along the wall to your left is a section of rebuilt wall with a *frieze of cobras* (5). The cobra, *uraeus* in Latin, was an emblem of royalty and an instrument of protection, always appearing on the Pharaoh's headdress and able to destroy his enemies by breathing flames. The cobra was worshipped in Lower Egypt, and so here in this early dynasty it also emphasises Zoser's mastery over the conquered peoples of the Delta. Near here is a shaft leading to Zoser's *southern tomb* (6), similar in its faience decoration to that beneath the Step Pyramid. There is a relief here of Zoser running the Heb-Sed race (see below). One

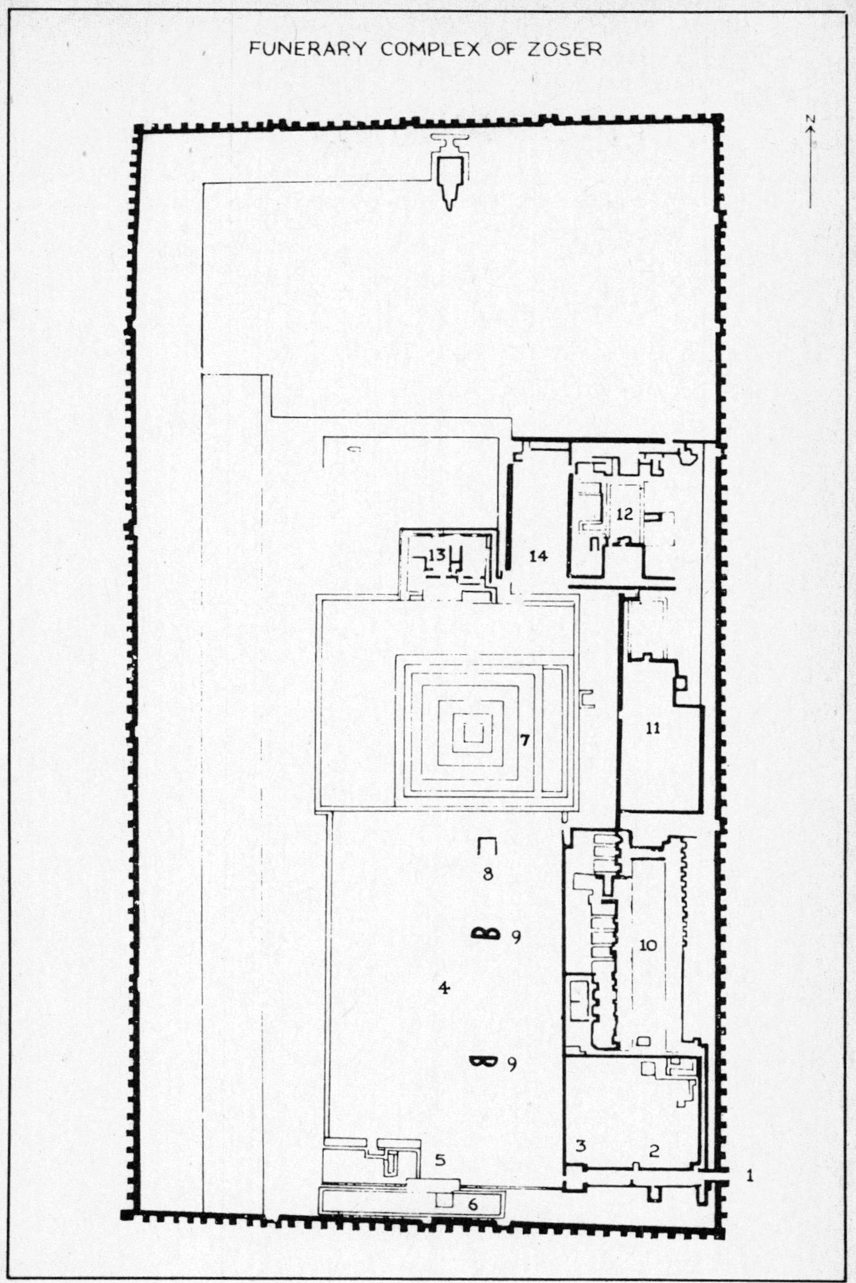
FUNERARY COMPLEX OF ZOSER
N
12
13
14
7
11
8
9
10
4
9
3
2
5
1
6

explanation for two tombs is that early Pharaohs thereby demonstrated their connection with the two Egypts, so a southern and northern tomb. Possibly the canopic jars containing Zoser's viscera were placed here, the body beneath the pyramid (where in fact a foot was found).

Zoser's Step Pyramid

The **Step Pyramid** (7) and its place in the development of pyramid building has already been referred to in an earlier chapter. Now you have a first-hand opportunity to examine its features. Despite its 62-metre height, it was built of fairly small limestone blocks, far smaller than those enormous blocks at Giza. Though working with stone, Imhotep was still thinking in terms of mud brick. But even in the enlargement of this monument from mastaba to pyramid you can detect signs of Imhotep's growing confidence in the new medium: at the southeast corner where the casing has come away you can see the smaller stonework of the *mastaba*, as you can if you walk along the east face of the pyramid. Also note how regularly the courses are laid, both of the mastaba and the pyramid as a whole, and how well shaped and fitted the stones are. In technique, Imhotep was without fault. The last enlarged mastaba measured 63 metres each way and a little over 8 metres high. Recall that the first pyramid erected over this mastaba rose four steps; the further pyramid of two additional steps increased the total volume by more than four fold. The entire monument was then sheathed in fine limestone from Tura, just to the south of modern Cairo, as were the Giza Pyramids.

Entrance to the pyramid

The original entrance to the Step Pyramid was at the north face, but in the XXVI Dynasty, known as the Saite period for its dynasty's origins at Sais in the Delta, a *gallery* (8) was dug from the Great South Court to the chambers beneath the pyramid. Permission and keys will have to be asked for at the office of the Inspector of Antiquities to the northeast of the Pyramid of Teti. The Saites admired the works of the Old Kingdom and it is quite possible they tunnelled their way into the pyramid out of sheer archaeological curiosity. After 60 metres you come to the main central shaft from where there are impressive views up into the pyramid and down towards the *burial chamber* which is sealed with a huge granite plug.

Emerging once again into the Great South Court, you see two *B-shaped constructions* (9) near the centre. These marked the limits of Upper and Lower Egypt, the gap between them symbolically spanned by Zoser in the Heb-Sed race. (A *relief* in the southern tomb shows Zoser in full stride, the two B-shaped constructions to the rear and fore.) The Heb-Sed race was one of the ceremonies during the five-day jubilee which occurred in the thirtieth year — that is at the interval of one generation — of the Pharaoh's reign. It is possible that at some earlier period, power was granted only for 30 years, the chieftain then deposed, perhaps killed, to spare the land from decline because of his failing strength. This jubilee, therefore, was a renewal of the vital forces of the Pharaoh and his ka, and so of all Egypt.

The Heb-Sed race

Also at his jubilee the Pharaoh re-enacted his coronation, sitting first on the throne of Upper Egypt, then on the throne of Lower Egypt, each time presenting gifts to the various priesthoods before they returned to their provinces. Participation in the festival obliged the priests to recognise the supremacy of the Pharaoh over their own local deities. These ceremonies, however, including the ritual race, would not have taken place here but at Memphis. The funerary complex was meant as a cosmic 'stand-in' for the actual jubilee site — it perpetuated the regenerating Heb-Sed in eternal stone. This explains the extraordinary film set quality of the Heb-Sed Court.

Significance of the Heb-Sed Court

The **Heb-Sed Court** (10) in the southeast part of the complex is rectangular and flanked to east and west by *shrines*, each one representing a province. They are hardly more than facades, as in a Hollywood Western. Access to the offering niches is by circumventing a screen wall, disguising the lack of depth, for the tall buildings are mere dummies, filled with rubble. Half open doors with hinges, imitations of the wooden originals, receive immortality in stone. In actuality, these shrines would have been tents with wooden poles and cross-supports. The chapels are not uniform; some have a curved cornice, as though the underlying frame represented flexed wood; other roofs are horizontal with the outward curve of the cavetto cornice that was to become so familiar a feature of Egyptian architecture, and torus moulding. Drawing on earlier building materials, Imhotep here invented the language of stone architecture. Cornices, torus mouldings, stone corner posts and columns and a variety of capitals appear for the first time in history at Saqqara. All the more astonishing that the effect is so delicate and beautifully proportioned.

A stone *platform* at the south end of the court is probably where the two thrones of Egypt stood for the re-enactment of the coronation, while at the north end of the court, to the left, is a *base with four pairs of feet*, most likely those of statues of Zoser, his wife and two daughters.

North of the Heb-Sed Court is another spacious court and the **House of the South** (11) with engaged proto-Doric columns. These Doric-style columns were never popular in Egypt where planes and hence smoothly-rounded columns were preferred to the Aegean play of light and shadow. There is the peculiarity of the door being placed asymmetrically, owing to the prototype facade being no more than a curtain, the door therefore needing to abut a column for support. As with the shrines in the Heb-Sed Court, the House of the South and the House of the North would actually have had wooden frames. They may have been sanctuaries, or possibly they represent government buildings of Upper and Lower Egypt.

First tourist graffiti

Inside the corridor are the first known examples of tourist graffiti, written in a cursive form of hieroglyphics and dating from the New Kingdom. The visitors, scribes from Thebes, express their admiration for Zoser's achievement, though here and elsewhere some settle for the ancient equivalent of 'Kilroy was here', while one smug crackpot, taking exception to some illiterate graffiti he must have seen, scribbled: 'The scribe of clever fingers came, a clever scribe without his equal among any men of Memphis, the scribe Amenemhet. I say:

Explain to me these words. My heart is sick when I see the work of their hands. It is like the work of a woman who has no mind'.

The **House of the North** (12) is similar to that of the South except here the columns have the form of a papyrus plant, the shaft the triangular stem, the capital the fanning head.

The **mortuary temple** (13) at the north face of the pyramid is largely in ruins. The original entrance to the burial chamber beneath the pyramid led from this temple. To the east of the temple is the **serdab** (14), as startling now as it was to Firth when he uncovered it. It is a masonry box, tilted slightly back and with two small holes drilled through its north face. A window at the side, put there by the excavators, allows you to peer in. And there is Zoser! A life-size painted *limestone statue* as you realise after the initial surprise, but for all the world like a strapped-in astronaut in his space capsule, his eyes fixed through the holes on the North Star, awaiting blast-off and immortality. The circumpolar stars and the North Star itself were 'those that know no destruction' or 'those that know no weariness', for they never set and so never died; this was the place of eternal blessedness for which Egyptians longed. And there is Zoser. It is absolutely convincing. It is this which impresses about the ancient Egyptians again and again, how they gave as well as they could mechanical effect to their illusions. They put California body-freezers to shame. Alas for poor Zoser, the unbelieving Mr Firth removed the original statue to the Antiquities Museum in Cairo; this is a copy. But then again, the substitution probably does not bother Zoser's ka, and it lives here still, and at dark of night it rockets starwards and mingles with the universe.

Pharaonic astronaut

The Pyramid of Unas

Unas was the last Pharaoh of the V Dynasty. About 350 years mark the distance between Zoser's Step Pyramid, the Great Pyramids at Giza, and this heap of rubble that is Unas' pyramid. These monuments graphically portray the rise and decline of the Old Kingdom sun cult.

The Pyramid of Unas was approached by a kilometre-long *causeway*, part of which has been reconstructed, including a very short section of its walls and roof, for it was entirely enclosed. A slit in the roof allowed the sunlight to illuminate the inscribed walls which were lively with everyday scenes. The *tombs of nobles* lie on either side, but most of these are closed or even sanded over — there are, anyway, better tombs to see elsewhere in the necropolis. On the south side of the causeway there are impressive *boat pits*. Also, about 150 metres to the south are the sanded over ruins of the **Monastery of St Jeremias**, founded in the second half of the 5th C and destroyed by the Arabs around 960. Practically all of its paintings and carvings have been removed to the Coptic Museum in Old Cairo.

The **Pyramid of Unas** looks like a pile of dirt, certainly when approached from the east. On the west side its stones are more evident, but are disarrayed. Even originally it rose only about 18.5 metres; its core was loose blocks and rubble, its casing alone of hewn limestone. Nevertheless, the pyramid has proved of immense historical importance, for when Gaston

The Pyramid Texts

Maspero entered the tomb chamber in 1881 he found the walls covered with inscriptions, the *Pyramid Texts*, which are the earliest mortuary literature of Egypt. These are hymns and rituals that preceded and accompanied the interment of the body; prayers for the release of the *ba* or soul; another section listing offerings of food, drink and clothing for use in the afterlife. Until this time, pyramids had gone unadorned. Thereafter, funerary literature underwent considerable elaboration and embroidery, culminating in that collection — or rather genre, for no such definitive compilation existed — of New Kingdom literature known to us as the Book of the Dead.

Despite its exterior, the pyramid remains internally sound and you can creep down the 1.4-metre high corridor, entered from the north face, past three enormous slabs of granite meant to block the way. Unlike the New Kingdom texts which were full of advice on how to steer a course clear of the forces of evil, which in effect emphasised the dangers that preceded safe arrival in the afterlife and were the tools of the trade of a blackmailing priesthood, the Pyramid Texts celebrate eternal life and identify the deceased Pharaoh with Osiris. Nevertheless, there is anxiety in the prayers. The confident era of the sun cult was waning; a personal god and a note of redemption marked the rising cult of Osiris. The state was weakening; the troubled times of the First Intermediate Period were approaching.

Visiting the Mastabas

Refreshments and Mariette's house

You can now trudge across the sands or drive to the refreshment tent which stands near the site of Mariette's house, where he stayed during those first serious explorations of Saqqara. The beer is cold and in the heat goes straight to your head. You can walk around the rest of the necropolis in a state of intoxication. When visiting the Serapeum, you may be grateful for that.

But first you can visit some mastabas. The double **Mastaba of Akhti-Hotep and Ptah-Hotep** is to the southeast of the tent, along your way if you are walking between Zoser's or Unas' complex and a beer. Ptah-Hotep describes himself as a priest of Maat and he may have held other positions too. At any rate, he seems to have been a very important official during the reign of Djedkare (V Dyn), predecessor of Unas. His son Akhti-Hotep was vizier, judge and chief of the granary and treasury. Their mastaba is smaller than that of Ti's, which we come to next, but is more developed and is particularly interesting for the reliefs which are in various stages of completion.

Reliefs in progress

You enter from the north and come into a *corridor*. On its left wall are preliminary drawings in red with corrections by the master artist in black. On the right wall are various stages of low relief. The background is cut away first to yield a silhouette and then the details are pencilled in and cut. In the lower registers, servants carry fowl in the arms towards Ptah-Hotep who stands at the far end of this right-hand wall. Though somewhat stylised, with his shoulders squared but with head and limbs in profile, the detailed musculature shows the artist's sound sense of anatomy.

At the top end of the corridor you turn right into a *pillared hall* and then left, passing through a *vestibule*, into *Ptah-Hotep's tomb chamber*. The ceiling imitates the trunks of palm trees while the mural reliefs, still retaining some colour, are the finest preserved of the Old Kingdom, surpassing even those in the more famous Mastaba of Ti.

Ptah-Hotep's tomb chamber: finest Old Kingdom reliefs

On the *right wall* are two door-shaped stelae, representing the entrance to the tomb. Between them is Ptah-Hotep, depicted in the panther-skin of a high priest, seated at a cornucopian table of offerings, a goblet raised to his lips. In the upper register, priests make offerings; in the lower three rows, servants bear gifts. They are lucky to get off so lightly; during the I Dynasty they were sacrificed and interred around their master's mastaba. On the *far wall* Ptah-Hotep is again at table, this time with a stylised loaf of bread before him and copper basins and ewers alongside so that he may cleanse himself before eating. In the upper register women representing various estates bring him the products of his farms, while in the second register animals are being thrown and slaughtered. The reliefs on the *left wall* are the finest and most interesting, a catalogue of events in the life of the deceased. On the right, according to the text, Ptah-Hotep is inspecting the 'gifts and tribute that are brought by the estates of the North and South'; boys are wrestling and running, caged animals (lions, gazelles, hares and hedgehogs) are drawn up, and a cow is giving birth, a peasant guiding the calf into the world. The bottom register shows domestic poultry and the text claims that Ptah-Hotep possessed '121,000 geese of one variety, 11,210 of another variety, 120,000 small geese, 111,200 goslings and 1225 swans'. On the left of this wall Ptah-Hotep 'witnesses all the pleasant activities that take place in the whole country'. In the top registers, boys and girls are playing; there is one episode of two boys seated and facing each other as their friends vault over them. This game, called *Khaza la wizza*, is still played today in Lower Nubia. The third register is devoted to aspects of viticulture; the fourth shows animal life (note the hare emerging from its hole with a cricket in its mouth); the fifth is a hunting scene, the cow tied as bait for the lion; the fifth and sixth registers show marsh and boating scenes.

Places mentioned in the text

A Zoser's funerary complex
B Causeway of Unas
C Boat pits and nobles' tombs
D Monastery of St. Jeremias
E Pyramid of Unas
F Refreshment tent
G Mastaba of Akhti-Hotep and Ptah-Hotep
H Mastaba of Ti
I Greek Statues
J Serapeum

Other sites

a Tomb of Horemheb
b Unfinished Pyramid of Sekhemkhet
c Pyramid of Userkaf
d Pyramid of Teti
e Mastaba of Mereruka
f I Dynasty tombs
g Mastaba of Hest

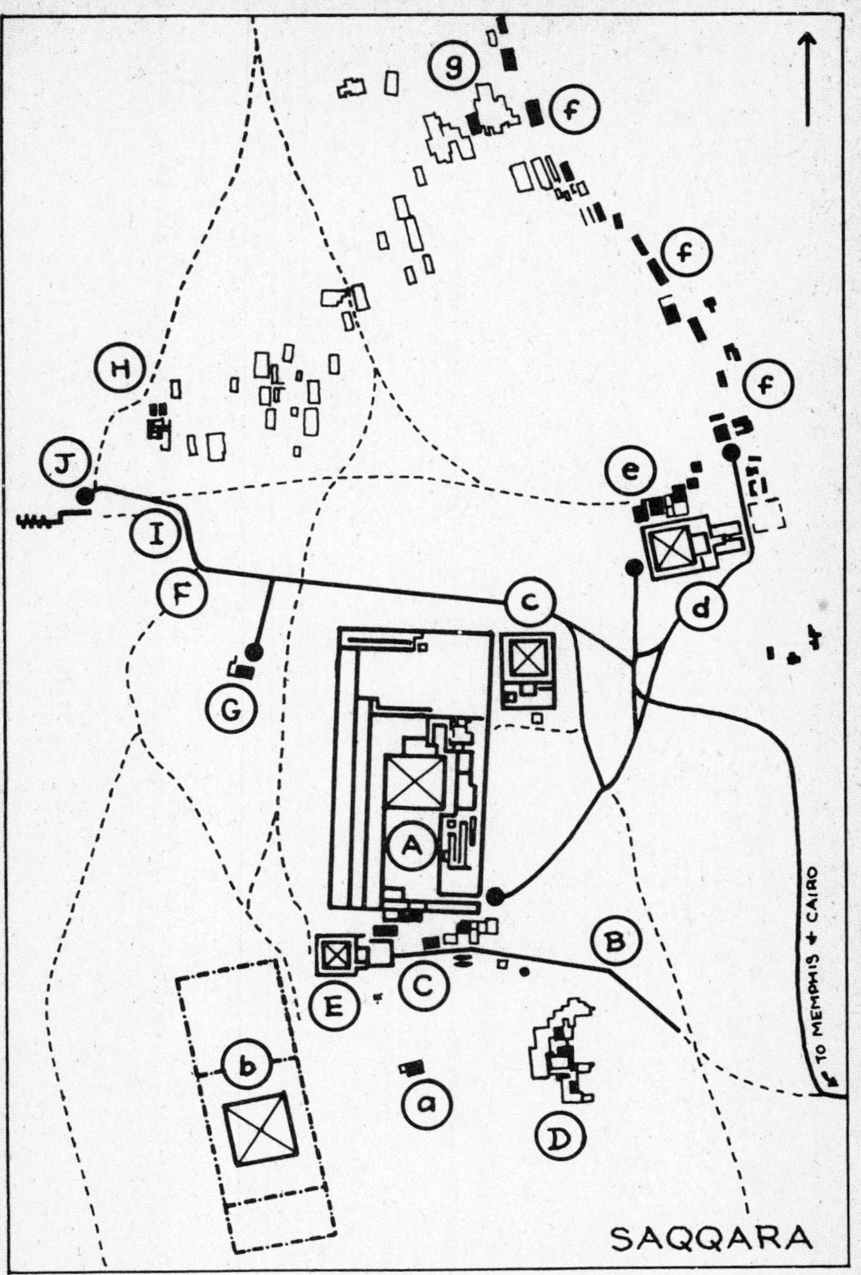
g
f
f
f
H
J
e
I
F
c
d
G
A
B
E
C
b
a
D
TO MEMPHIS + CAIRO
SAQQARA

Above the entrance is a faded mural, but you can make out Ptah-Hotep preparing for his day, a manicurist at his hands, a pedicurist at his feet, musicians entertaining him, greyhounds beneath his chair and a pet monkey held by his valet. The sophistication of this scene is all the more striking when you recall that it depicts daily Egyptian life, albeit at the very top of the social ladder, nearly 4500 years ago, that is when Europe and most of Asia were still in the Stone Age.

The purpose of tomb reliefs

The purpose of these reliefs was to provide food, indeed a complete experience of life, for the ka. They began during the IV Dynasty as it was realised that relatives and descendants did not always provide fresh offerings; the reliefs were imitative magic against default. But one can also imagine the great pleasure they must have given the tomb owner, an assurance that he was going to take it all with him, and to his relatives when they did gather in his tomb. I think of some of the more elaborate marble tombs in Greek cemeteries today; they are like small shrines with an inner chamber for the deceased and an outer chamber with seats for the living, and they are the cheeriest places, often attracting bountiful picnics. Unas a generation later was already worried about his relationship with Osiris; but here there is not a single god, no judgement, no doubt — afterlife follows on from life as assuredly as day follows day, and without even an intervening night.

Now returning to the pillared hall you turn left for the *chamber of Akhti-Hotep*, similarly though less finely decorated. A passageway leads out of the side of this and opening off it, on your left, is a chamber containing an *anonymous mummy*. The passageways leads back to the pillared hall and the entrance corridor; while negotiating it I tripped over a skeleton, perhaps belonging to a 20th C AD tourist who had got locked in.

Getting yourself entombed

I have already mentioned that my brother got himself locked into the Great Pyramid; at Saqqara a friend got himself locked into the Serapeum for half an hour with the lights off (an experience that would have turned me instantly into a skeleton); and I got locked into the Mastaba of Ti, and would have spent the night there but for a ladder left providentially in the open court. If you lack Ptah-Hotep's confidence in the coming day, make certain the keeper knows you are there and looks like the sort of fellow who would let you out.

The **Mastaba of Ti** is to the north of the refreshment tent and you can follow the road that leads to the Serapeum part of the way there. The mastaba was discovered by Mariette in 1865 and has been well restored by the Egyptian Department of Antiquities. It originally stood above ground but is now entirely sunk in the sand. Its reliefs rival those in Ptah-Hotep's tomb chamber and exceed them in variety. Ti was a parvenu and royal hairdresser during the early V Dynasty; he was also overseer of several royal mortuary temples and pyramids and controller of royal ponds, farms and stock from which he evidently enriched himself. His wife was related to the royal family and his children bore the title 'royal descendant', to which Ti himself was not entitled. Ti's wife and eldest son were also entombed here, but some later would-be arriviste made off with the goods and disposed of the bodies.

In plan, the entrance is from the north, a two-pillared

vestibule leading to a spacious open pillared court at the centre of which a flight of stairs descends to a subterranean passage ending in an antechamber and the tomb chamber. Otherwise, a corridor leads out from the rear of the open court and passes a chamber on the right, arriving at the funerary chamber and the serdab.

Once through the open court, whose reliefs have been badly damaged by exposure, the walls of corridors and rooms are finely decorated with familiar scenes. The most interesting room, with the most beautiful reliefs, is Ti's *funerary chamber*. Through the slot in the far (south) wall you can see Ti (this is a cast of the original statue now in the Cairo Museum) staring vacantly northwards from his serdab, lacking, I am afraid, Zoser's look of adventure. Needless to say his hair, or rather his wig, is well done. Most enjoyable are the *reliefs on the near (north) wall*, all concerned with life in the marshes of the Delta. Look particularly at the central relief of *Ti sailing through the marshes*. This is a classic representation of a hippopotamus hunt; the hippopotamus, to the lower right, has seized a crocodile which, meanwhile, is desperately trying to bite the hippo's leg. Ti is shown larger than his huntsmen who, from another boat, are harpooning the hippo. Below the boats are fine Nile fish of different species, identifiable as favoured catches in the river today. On the right, in a small boat with a curiously truncated stern, a fisherman is about to club a large schal fish over the head. Above Ti, among the papyrus clusters, birds are being attacked in their nests by carnivorous animals, the reeds bending with their weight. In the register below is a line of *elegant female bearers*, their transparent coloured dresses surrendered to time, their nakedness and varied poses freshly pleasing.

This relief is unusual for having two layers of meaning. Literally it is a hunt in the marshes; but symbolically it is Ti against the forces of evil and chaos. The hippopotamus was particularly feared and hated in ancient Egypt, but Ti together with a helpful crocodile is killing it. Fish and birds represented chaos, but here again man and animal are subduing them.

By way of making amends for having locked me in Ti's tomb, the keeper afterwards invited me to his little concrete hut for a glass of mint tea. It was clearly his eagerness to retreat here, out of the blistering heat, that caused my incarceration in the first place. We sat on a reed mat on the floor while he manipulated various soda cans over his burner — some of the cans for storing the water, one for boiling it, others for decanting the tea — and we smoked his hubbly-bubbly meanwhile. This he lit with bits of dried corncob he kept for the purpose and brought to a glow in the burner flame. The surrounding necropolis, my temporary entombment, the sand and heat were all forgotten in this humble private place where tea and tobacco were prepared and consumed with meticulous ritual. The keeper fussed and bubbled and tasted and grunted with the fullness of it all, and as we drank the thick sweet tea, so satisfying, and enjoyed the relaxation of the waterpipe, we looked out as from a serdab upon the desert wasteland and he called this tea and this tobacco his friends.

Tea in the desert

Tombs of the Apis Bulls

The weirdest place in Egypt

The Serapeum is the weirdest place in Egypt. A temple once stood here amidst the sands but what remains are the long underground galleries cut through the rock where the Apis bulls were buried. This was Mariette's great discovery in 1851 which began the serious excavation of Saqqara that has continued ever since. Entry is to the west of the refreshment tent; you follow the road which first bends right towards Ti's mastaba and then turns left. At this second bend was Mariette's house, and immediately by the roadside, on your left and under a protective roof, is the surprising sight of several Greek statues arranged in a semicircle. These and their unlikely connection with bull burial requires some explanation.

Apis bulls

The huge tombs of these Apis bulls were previously known only from references to them by various writers of antiquity. For instance, Herodotus wrote: 'The Apis is the calf of a cow which is never afterwards able to have another. The Egyptian belief is that a flash of light descends upon the cow from heaven, and this causes her to receive Apis. The Apis-calf has distinctive marks: it is black, with a white diamond on its forehead, the image of an eagle on its back, the hairs on its tail double, and a scarab under its tongue'. Apis thus miraculously conceived was considered to be an incarnation of Ptah, the god of Memphis. Worshipped as such during his lifetime within a special sanctuary in the Temple of Ptah, he was mummified after his death on those alabaster beds you can still see among the few surviving stones of Memphis. Then, identified with Osiris under the name Osiris-Apis, he was taken with great pomp to these underground galleries at the Serapeum and placed within a gigantic sarcophagus.

Sacred bull cults go back into the prehistory of Egypt, and during the I and II Dynasties a bull would wander across the field of the Heb-Sed race, symbolically fertilising the two lands. But animal cults enjoyed an astonishing popularity during the Late Egyptian Period as the old beliefs degenerated. Herodotus, attempting to demonstrate the madness of Cambyses, the Persian ruler of Egypt, records that 'the priests brought Apis and Cambyses, half mad as he was, drew his dagger, aimed a blow at its belly, but missed and struck its thigh. Then he laughed, and said to the priests: "Do you call that a god, you poor creatures? Are your gods flesh and blood? Do they feel the prick of steel? No doubt a god like that is good enough for the Egyptians; but you won't get away with trying to make a fool of me"', and he had the priests whipped and forbade the cult, but when finally Apis died of his wounds he was buried by the priests without the knowledge of Cambyses. In this instance, at least, Cambyses sounds quite sane, but it is understandable that the once mighty priesthood should cling to some tangible shred of belief as the old order was being attacked by foreign rulers. The Ptolemies were more shrewd and flattered the priesthood, encouraged their cults, built temples and ruled Egypt for 300 years.

The galleries of the Serapeum date from three periods, the earliest to the reign of Ramses II (XIX Dyn), enlarged by his son Khaemwas; a second to the reign of Psammetichus I (XXVI

Dyn); and the main gallery to the Ptolemies. It was the Greek Ptolemies who encouraged an identity between Osiris and Dionysos, and Plutarch comments that 'as for what the priests openly do in the burial of the Apis when they transport its carcass on a raft, this in no way falls short of Bacchic revelry, for they wear fawn-skins and carry thyrsus-rods' — a staff tipped with a pine cone, in short a phallus — 'and produce shouts and movements as do the ecstatic celebrants of the Dionysiac orgies'. (Recall the sarcophagus of the dwarf in Room 49 on the ground floor of the Cairo Museum.) It is from the Ptolemaic period that the **semicircle of Greek statues** of poets and philosophers dates. Homer is at the centre, Pindar plays the lyre at the far right, and at the far left is a base inscribed with the name of Plato. They must be turning over in their graves.

Mariette was led to the Serapeum by recalling a quotation from Strabo (24 BC): 'One finds at Memphis a temple to Serapis in such a sandy place that the wind heaps up sand dunes beneath which we saw sphinxes, some half-buried, some buried up to the head, from which one can suppose that the way to the temple could not be without danger if one were caught in a sudden wind-storm'. Mariette had found one such head at Saqqara, and removing the sand in the area found an entire avenue of sphinxes leading to the Greek statues and to the Serapeum galleries. The avenue has since sanded up again.

Mariette's description of his discovery of the Serapeum

Saqqara can seem strange enough today. When Mariette was excavating here, he described the conditions in his house: 'Snakes slithered along the floor, tarantulas or scorpions swarmed in the wall crevices, large spider webs waved from the ceiling like flags. As soon as night fell, bats, attracted by the light, entered my cell through the cracks in the door and kept me awake with their spectral flights. Before going to sleep, I tucked the edges of my mosquito net beneath my mattress and put my trust in God and all the saints, while outside jackals, hyenas and wolves howled around the house'. Of entering the Serapeum, Mariette wrote: 'When I first penetrated into the sepulchre of the Apis, I was so overcome with astonishment that, though it is now five years ago, the feeling is still vivid in my mind. By some inexplicable accident one chamber of the Apis tombs, walled up in the thirtieth year of Ramses II, had escaped the general plunder of the monuments, and I was so fortunate as to find it untouched. Three thousand seven hundred years had had no effect in altering its primitive state. The finger mark of the Egyptian who set the last stone in the wall built up to cover the door was still visible in the mortar. Bare feet had left their traces on the sand strewn in a corner of this chamber of the dead; nothing had been disturbed in this burying-place where an embalmed ox had been resting for nearly fourteen centuries'.

A terrifying moronic force

My own recollection was of Robin Fedden's words: 'One has the impression of a terrifying moronic force at work, for the tombs reveal the endemic stupidity of man'. You descend a ramp slipping under the formless desert surface and reach a *corridor* leading off to left and right. Down to the left it meets a *transverse gallery* and left into that, on the left, within a vault, is a massive *pink granite sarcophagus* with panels and across the top edge hieroglyphs — on the right an Apis bull is depicted with the characteristic black markings. The rest of this gallery is blocked off by a grate.

You now reverse direction, heading down a 150-metre gallery, lit at lengthy intervals by dim yellow lights which in the murky darkness cast a greenish glow. At some places, the lights will have gone out and you will have to walk through blackness. On either side, in alternating succession, are more vaults, in all but one of which squats a monstrous black sarcophagus — bull-size. In the silence and the dim light, this repetition of vaults and sarcophagi becomes like a bad dream you cannot wake from, and you just walk on, with literally no light at the end of the tunnel. It is macabre, and with your capillaries shot full with beer you achieve enough perspective to find it utterly incredible that the Ptolemies, whose gallery this is, could have perpetuated anything so repulsive and outlandish. The *finest sarcophagus* of all is perversely placed at the very end of this gallery, on the right, with carved decoration and polished to a glassy lustre. You can climb down into its pit and stand on a step at the back to peer inside. But it is not this sarcophagus that is worth the walk; it is the walk that is worth the walk, if only to be astonished, and for want of being able to assimilate the insanity of human belief to laugh, as finally I did in the darkness.

The finest bull sarcophagus

It was not here, but in the Rammesid gallery, now inaccessible, that Mariette found the one untouched Apis tomb, a mummified bull inside, and also in the gallery the mummy of Khaemwas, who had been appointed by his father Ramses II High Priest of Ptah. And there he found those ancient footprints. You notice footprints in the sand in this Ptolemaic gallery too, of more recent visitors, and they bring to mind, as so often encounters with Egypt's pharaonic past do, our own voyages into the cosmos, those footprints left in the dust on the surface of the windless Moon which may remain for millions of years undisturbed.

Retracing your steps from the end of the main gallery, turn to the left and then to the right. An *empty sarcophagus* almost blocks the route. A little further on is its lid. It seems to have been abandoned before the interment of the sacred bull, suggesting the cult was abruptly ended.

Other Animal Cults at Saqqara

The search for Imhotep's tomb

This account of Saqqara has covered only the most major points of interest to the layman. There is a search now going on for Imhotep's tomb which is thought to be to the northeast of the Serapeum and the Mastaba of Ti. In this area have been found the Anubieion, sacred to Anubis, with a gallery for dogs; the galleries of the Bubasteion, sacred to Bastet, filled with mummified cats; the Temple of Thoth, its galleries piled with thousands of mummified ibises, baboons and falcons; and the Isieion, the Temple of Isis, with underground galleries containing the sarcophagi of the sacred cows that had given birth to the Apis bulls. It is possible that these stacks of smaller mummified creatures were brought over hundreds of years by pilgrims as offerings to a favoured god, or as supplication by those seeking a cure. It is because of these associations with healing cults that Imhotep's shrine and tomb might be here; he was later worshipped as the god of medicine, the Egyptian equivalent of Asclepios. These cults continued into the Roman period and were only finally suppressed several centuries into our era by the victory of Christianity over paganism.

Pyramids Further South

The **necropolis of Dahshur** is a few kilometres to the south of Saqqara. Of its four pyramids, two date from the Middle Kingdom and are badly ruined — they are likely to be of interest only to the specialist. Snofru's **Bent and Red Pyramids**, already referred to in an earlier chapter, are the chief attraction. The distance between them is 2 kms and can be managed on foot; interiors of both can be visited, but a powerful light and a ladder, or at least a rope, will be necessary, and care must be exercised. But it is enough just to stand here in the desert, undisturbed by tourists or the debris left by excavations, and to see these great pyramids resting upon an endless plain confronting only the cosmos.

Much further south is the **Meidum pyramid**, or what remains of it. This was the first attempt at a true pyramid (see *The Pyramid Age* chapter) and the lessons learnt from its monumental failure, if one accepts Mendelssohn's theory, led to the successful completion of those greatest pyramids of all at Giza. For that reason, but also for the spectacle of this abrupt tower on the desert's edge, the Meidum pyramid is as much worth visiting as any.

PRACTICAL INFORMATION

You can reach **Saqqara** by horse or camel from the Giza Pyramids (see previous chapter), though you will not be left with much time to explore the site, and a visit to Memphis would probably be out of the question. There is also a bus to Badrashein, a village near Memphis; ask about it at the Mena House or the Tourist Police at the Pyramids. And there are tours or a taxi from Cairo. Refreshments and light meals are available at the Saqqara site. Site fee LE3.

Dahshur is in the midst of a military area and certain approaches are off-limits to foreigners. It would be a good idea to check in advance with the Tourist Information Office in Sharia Adli in Cairo; if necessary, permission can be obtained from the Ministry of the Interior, Midan Lazouli. There is also the problem of sand for cars attempting an approach. One way of getting to Dahshur is by donkey or camel from the refreshment tent at Saqqara; the complete journey will take from 2 to 3 hours. Camels are infinitely preferable to donkeys.

Tours do not include either Dahshur or Meidum with Memphis and Saqqara, nor with the Fayyum. But ask, eg at Thomas Cook, if they can be included at an extra cost. If driving to **Meidum**, follow the road along the west bank of the Nile south towards El Wasta; the pyramid will appear on your right but you drive past it a bit until you come to a paved road signposted for the pyramid in English and Arabic. This heads off into the desert, at first passing south of the pyramid and then coming up to its northwest corner. (See also the next chapter for combining a visit to Meidum with an excursion to the Fayyum).

THE FAYYUM

The desert road to the Fayyum

The easiest, most direct approach to the Fayyum, and also the most striking, is by the desert road from Giza. You drive out of Cairo as though to the Giza Pyramids but before reaching the Mena House Hotel you turn right onto the desert road for Alexandria. Follow this for 500 metres and then turn left; you are now on a good fast road all the way to Medinet el Fayyum. Behind you, to the east, there is a wonderful view of the Pyramids across the untrammelled sand; like a departed shore, they sink into the horizon as you commit yourself to the desert. After 76 kms you approach the edge of the depression at Kom Aushim, the ancient Karanis, on your left. From here there is a fine panorama over the whole of the Fayyum, a surprise of green cultivation and blue lakewater surrounded by rocky hills and expanses of sandy desert. An excursion to the Fayyum can be accomplished in a day, starting early in the morning. For a longer stay, it is most agreeable to overnight at Lake Qarun.

An oasis which is not an oasis

The Fayyum is a near-level basin of abundant harvests, fleshed with fields of vegetables and sugar cane, watered by hundreds of capillary canals. Groves of almonds, apricots, oranges, lemons, pomegranates, figs and olives screen the horizon, while tall acacias, tamarisks and eucalyptus trees cast dappled shadows on the grass. There are vineyards and poultry farms, water buffalo drawing the ploughs and white egrets wading in the bright crystal greenness of the rice paddies. Yet for all its fertility there is a blandness about the Fayyum — perhaps it is the lack of Nile, which gives pulse to Upper Egypt; or the absence of broad canals, which in the Delta carry the tall sails of feluccas between the fields. The lake is brackish, sometimes muddy and marshy and not suitable for swimming, though it is rich with fish and migratory birds, including the pink flamingo; its pearly surface is blackened in winter by thousands of ducks.

This lake, now filling only the northwest edge of the depression, once covered the whole and was fed by the Bahr Yusef (River of Joseph — so named by the Copts) where it left the Nile at Deirut. In the last century this life-giving waterway was extended further south to Assiut by the construction of the Ibrahimiya Canal to provide improved irrigation for the lower reaches of the Valley. Fed by the Nile, the Fayyum therefore is not a true oasis, though the Bahr Yusef frequently silts up or changes course and the Fayyum survives too on spring water while the millenial battle between man and nature to maintain and regularise the flow continues.

History of the Fayyum

The shores of Qarun were inhabited already in the prehistoric period by hunters and fishermen, but it was the Pharaohs of the XII Dynasty who turned the depression (some 45 metres below sea level at the present surface of the lake) into the garden of Egypt and a regulator of the Nile's flood by building an extensive system of canals, dikes, locks and sluices. From the XIII Dynasty on, the Fayyum became a favourite resort of pharaohs, and Amenophis III (XVIII Dyn) built a palace at El Lahun for Queen Tiy (at their palace at Thebes he built her a lake). Evaporation caused the lake to contract while the cultivable area was extended, reaching its greatest extent during the Ptolemaic period, Greek and Macedonian veterans being settled on the land. The variety of the Fayyum was sacrificed to the Roman demand that it supply Rome with corn and the harsh imperial taxes led to the irrigation system silting up. The desert slowly crept back. In modern times the trend has been reversed, though the Fayyum still does not occupy the extent it enjoyed in ancient times.

Entering the Oasis

If you have come along the desert road from Giza, your first stop will be Kom Aushim, the Ptolemaic **Karanis**, still in the desert, with a small museum and behind this the remains of two temples, the agora and some houses. It is the view of the cultivated basin below that is appealing. Entering the Fayyum proper, you can continue westwards along the southern shore of **Lake Qarun**, its far shore desert but on this side cultivated — and being developed for tourism. Excellent accommodation is now available; you can take a boat across the lake; and there is duck shooting from about November. Returning to the main road to Medinet el Fayyum, at 4 kms south of Sennouris you can turn off to the right to briefly see the site where Ammenemes III (XII Dyn) erected two **colossal seated figures** of himself to mark the northern boundary of the cultivable land. Herodotus saw these from a distance, rising above the flooded fields, and thought they must have been sitting atop pyramids. In fact they stood on either side of a lakeside harbour. One of them was seen as recently as the 17th century C by Europeans, but now only the 8-metre bases remain — the statues rose another 12 metres above these, which would have made them as high as the famous Colossi of Memnon, erected 400-odd years later.

Medinet el Fayyum, which means Town of the Fayyum, is the capital of the province and a major market centre. For centuries the water from the Bahr Yusef has been distributed here thoughout the canals of the basin, and at the centre of town four *waterwheels* still perform this task, all but embraced by an open-air restaurant (the Casino el Medina, where tour companies drop visitors); you can sit here over a meal listening to the wheels turn like air raid sirens during the London blitz. El Medina (as it is more briefly known) had earlier this century a sizable Greek population and there are a number of handsome mansions and several churches, including a large Coptic one, while its mosques include that of *Asalbay*, a concubine of Sultan Qaytbay, built after his death, in 1499. It stands on the west side of the Bahr Yusef by the Bridge of Qaytbay, south of the restaurant, and has been much restored.

Crocodile cult

A settlement stood here already in early pharaonic times and was the chief centre for worship of the crocodile god Sobek. The Greeks names it Crocodilopolis, though Ptolemy

I, in converting the town to a Hellenic centre with Greek temples and schools and even a Greek-speaking population, named it for his deified sister-wife, Arsinoë. In abandoning its crocodile cult, the town has lost what was once its greatest draw; in Ptolemaic and Roman times, tourists came from all over the Mediterranean and Europe to feed the sacred beast with specially prepared food — how much more exciting than pigeons in Trafalgar Square.

Today, to the northwest of El Medina are the rubbish dump remains of the ancient city. It requires an extraordinary imagination to conjure up any vision of its past. Not only time and treasure-hunters, but also the *sebakhin* have made a mess of it. This is an interesting example of how Egypt lives upon its past. In a land where wood is a rarity, animal dung has traditionally been used for fuel and so other fertilisers have been sought. One of these has been the debris mounds of ancient towns which yield a kind of earth, called *sebakh*, containing as much as 12 percent potassium nitrate, sodium carbonate and ammonium chloride.

The Road to the Nile

You now drive southeast towards Beni Suef, passing along the narrow corridor of cultivation which attaches like a stem the bud of the Fayyum to the Nile. At Hawarat el Makta, 7 kms from Medinet el Fayyum, a track runs northwards to the dilapidated mud brick **pyramid of Ammenemes III**. Its surrounding complex is no more than an expanse of rubble, though at the south of the pyramid was once the vast mortuary temple, now all but vanished at the hands of stone robbers, which so excited ancient travellers and which they called the Labyrinth. Herodotus, who seems to have enjoyed describing in fantastic terms sights he had never seen, said it had 3000 chambers, half below ground, half above; but Strabo, who did come here in AD 24, gives a more sober account of a still vast low building divided into sections for each nome, 'a work as important as the Pyramids' with 'long covered passages, intersecting each other and thus forming such a winding path that a stranger cannot find his way into or out of each court without a guide'. From a cemetery nearby, and also from Philadelphia to the north, came the painted wax portraits of mummified Romans which make such a striking impression now in the Cairo Museum. At the Nile end of the corridor, in the desert a short distance to the north, is the **Lahun pyramid**, that of Sesostris II (XII Dyn), a predecessor of Ammenemes III. It also was built of mud brick and cased in limestone.

The Labyrinth

If you have not already visited the **Meidum pyramid** from the north (Saqqara, etc), you can now look out for it towering in the desert to the west as you return along the main Cairo road.

The handprints are meant to avert the evil eye

PRACTICAL INFORMATION

There are numerous **tours** to the Fayyum, permitting you to see the entire area in a day. Also from Cairo there are **buses** (from Midan el Tahrir) and **trains** (change at El Wasta). These arrive at Medinet el Fayyum, at stations near the Casino el Medina where also there is a second bus station serving routes within the Fayyum.

Some tours going to the Fayyum take in the pyramid and Labyrinth at **Hawarat** and the pyramid at **Lahun**, both along the corridor of cultivation leading towards Beni Suef. I have not seen anyone advertising a pause at the **Meidum pyramid**, though someone might be induced to. If no tour and no car, take the train to El Wasta, then bus or taxi to Meidum.

If staying overnight, there are some good **hotels** on the south shore of Lake Qarun (see *Background* chapter under *Accommodation* for rates):

Panorama (3-star), Shakshouk. Tel: 21 (Shakshouk el Fayyum). Telex: 2309 KAROMA UN. A modern hotel, all rooms air-conditioned, with bath. Lake sports facilities.

Auberge el Fayyum Oberoi (opened early 1985, not yet classified, though likely to be 5- or 4-star; for information contact another Oberoi hotel, eg Mena House, Giza). This former hunting lodge of King Farouk has been turned into a small luxury hotel with swimming pools, tennis and squash courts, health club, riding school, duck shooting, a marina on the lake, disco, etc.

THE VALLEY

Lower Egypt is the Delta; Upper Egypt is the Valley where the desert and mountains encroach on either side. But the Valley only finally loses its grip on the Nile at Cairo, the Moqattam hills a last reminder, yet Upper Egypt still lies some distance to the south for it is not defined in geographical terms alone. An ancient text expresses the bewilderment of an exile finding himself in a foreign country: 'I do not know what seperated me from my place. It was like a dream, as if a man of the Delta were to see himself in Elephantine, or a man of the northern marshes in Nubia'. Culture and horizons place Upper Egypt along the thin papyrus stem of fields and river before it bifurcates, the full flower of the Delta to the north, the bud of the Fayyum to the west.

At this place, unpromisingly, is a dull-looking town, **Beni Suef** (124 kms from Cairo), celebrated for its linen manufacture in the Middle Ages and now at once crumbling and jerking into new forms as modern factories and housing blocks go up. From here two roads strike out across the Eastern Desert for the Monastery of St Anthony and the Red Sea; another Egypt, another time. You travel through it in another chapter. But following the Nile southwards you are — as nearly as geography and chronology in Egypt coincide — travelling from the Old Kingdom into the New.

Travelling up the Valley

For the traveller flying from Cairo to Luxor, the change is fairly abrupt. Less than 60 minutes intervene between the Memphite pyramids and your first glimpse of the sprawling Theban temples below. Along the way there is the amazing and beautiful sight of the long blue ribbon of the Nile snaking through the scorched desert bringing a few kilometres, sometimes only a few metres, of land to life on either side. A life fragile like the delicate green wheat which waves against vast sand plateaux, a life — if you were close enough to know it — heavy with the mass of burnt-backed fellahin whose survival has depended on the varying generosity of the river's annual flood and the constancy of their own unending field labours.

The traveller through time is isolated from the moment. From the air, this isolation seems no more than standing back from a charming tapestry to appreciate its overall effect. Travelling overland you are closer and you see the threads and knots; you long to feel for texture. You are probably travelling by train, sensibly in an air-conditioned carriage. Outside the sealed windows, sealed against the sand, sealed against the heat, sealed against fragrance and life, Egypt passes in a series of tableaux vivants.

Station signs, road signs, all are in Arabic. They might as well be in hieroglyphs. The pattern of older villages is a vestige of living 10,000 years with annual inundations: they sit on low mounds beyond the reach of a river which for two decades has ceased to rise. Their mud brick houses

Air-view of the Nile and its ribbon of cultivation: all else is desert

pack against and on top of one another, a dense metropolis in embryo. At first their roofs are flat like houses of the Delta, but as you run southwards under the sun you see the dome and barrel roofs of Upper Egypt which so admirably deflect the heavy fall of heat.

Ochre, rectangular, severe like a temple, really a landowner's country house — a former landowner anyway — embellished with a cavetto cornice, but awaiting further decoration, awaiting a new dynasty. It stands alone, enclosed by a walled garden.

Camels, carts, donkeys and women troop along the road, enduring the flame-blue sky. An old man stands up to his knees in an irrigation ditch, washing himself, naked to the passing eyes and years, no longer ithyphallic Min.

All this passes beyond touch, beyond sound. I am an air-conditioned pharaoh riding with the sun, uncontaminated, unliving, kept company through eternity by wall paintings.

The train goes slowly and stops often. At one station I am surprised by a knock at my window. Suspended from the roof of a third class train, children are knocking, laughing.

Into the Middle Kingdom and Beyond

Beni Hassan, Hermopolis and Amarna all lie near **Minya** (247 kms from Cairo) and **Mallawi** (295 kms). Though Mallawi is closer to Amarna, travellers might prefer to stay at Minya with its attractive and winding corniche along the west bank of the Nile and its better accommodation.

Middle Kingdom tombs

Beni Hassan, on the east bank of the Nile and equidistant from Minya and Mallawi, is a Middle Kingdom necropolis of 39 rock tombs belonging mostly to XI and XII Dynasty nomarchs. The excursion, taking in four of the tombs most worth visiting, will take about half a day.

The tombs are exceptional for their architecturally refined interior columns, including a fluted style designated by Champollion as 'proto-Doric', and the excellence of their paintings, done on stucco. Unfortunately, many of the paintings have been either damaged or obscured, though the Department of Antiquities is in the process of cleaning them. Agricultural, craft, hunting and sport scenes are usual, and occasionally military scenes, for the princes of this nome were powerful in their own right. *Tomb 17 of Kheti* has the best preserved paintings. *Tomb 15 of Baket*, Kheti's father, has lost its columns, but *Tomb 3 of Khnumhotep* contains proto-Doric columns and also paintings evidencing Khumhotep's wide-ranging authority. He was also governor of the Eastern Desert and is shown receiving a gift of eye-paint from a caravan of Semites, gaudily dressed and befeathered, who have crossed into Egypt with their women, their children and their goats and asses in tow. The porch of this tomb and of *Tomb 2* is extant; they were once preceded by an open court. In columns and paintings, *Tomb 2 of Amenemhat* is similar to *Tomb 3*.

On the way down from the necropolis you pass the entrance to a wadi on the left. About 500 metres along its south side is the *rock chapel of Pakhet*, the lioness goddess, assimilated by the Greeks to Artemis so that the chapel is better known as **Speos Artemidos** (Grotto of Artemis). Inside are scenes of offerings to various deities, but the chief interest of the shrine is the inscription over the entrance in which Hatshepsut (XVIII Dyn) implies that she has rid Egypt of the Hyksos invaders. That she certainly did not only heightens the belief that Hatshepsut desired to be seen as the restorer of stability and the old ways of the Middle Kingdom in her struggle against Tuthmosis III's imperial ambitions (see Deir el Bahri). As it extends deeper into the forbidding desert landscape, the wadi is cut with numerous other grottoes, once anchorite cells and early Christian tombs.

Hermopolis, near the village of El Ashmunein on the west bank of the river, lies off a secondary road between Minya and Mallawi. The remains of the Middle and New Kingdom cities here are no more than uncertain mounds of earth and rubble, though a later Ptolemaic agora has been restored and the surrounding palm grove lends a picturesque effect. An early association with Thoth, whom the Greeks identified with Hermes, accounts for its familiar name. Originally known as Khmun, meaning city of the eight primordial forces, it was said to have been built upon the primal hill from which the sun first rose above the waters to create the world out of Chaos — though the same claim was made for Medinet Habu and Heliopolis. The primal name, if not the hill or city, has tenaciously survived: from Khmun derived the Coptic Shmun, whence the Arabic Ashmunein.

Tuna el Gebel, at the end of a road running into the Libyan hills from Ashmunein, marked the western limits of Akhenaton's new city of Akhetaton. This side of the river was reserved for villages and farms. A boundary stela remains *in situ*, carved from the top of a cliff, showing the heretic Pharaoh, Nefertiti and three of their daughters with upraised arms in adoration of the solar disc. A necropolis to the south is riddled with underground passages used by the inhabitants of Hermopolis for burying mummified ibises and dog-headed baboons, sacred to Thoth. The most important building here is the Ptolemaic *tomb of Petosiris*, chief priest of Thoth at Hermopolis. It imitates the pronaos of a temple and is entered through a vestibule of four columns with floral capitals painted red, blue and turquoise though bleached where exposed to the sun. Inside, the reliefs portray traditional Egyptian themes but Petosiris and his family wear Greek clothing.

Akhetaton: Capital of the Heretic Pharoah

The Amarna revolution

The beauty of Old Kingdom art and architecture lay in its restraint, in its simplicity and its confident mastery of form. There was a moment of discovery, of harmonisation and integrity, and if the First Intermediate Period had instead marked the termination of pharaonic civilisation we might now more eagerly respond to what had been lost. But the centuries rolled on and too often carried with them only the embalmed culture of the past, integrity reduced to repetition, mastery to facility, the spirit salved with interminable formulae, authority justified and reassured with bombast. Even when using the old forms, there were brilliant exceptions as will be seen here and there further upriver. But the general impression of tedium weighs heavily on the traveller. The breathtaking impact, then, of the Amarna period is all the more powerful, the sense of something wonderful, tragic and lost all the more acute.

The sensitivity and delight, the reverence and forcefulness conveyed in the painting, reliefs, sculpture and hymns of Akhenaton's reign are probably best appreciated in museums and books, for at his capital city of Akhetaton very little of these things remain. Nevertheless, its site should be visited — in homage, perhaps; for the interest it does hold; and for its own beauty, spared the incursions of large numbers of tourists. Akhetaton, or **Amarna** as it is known, is on the east bank, 67 kms south of Minya, 11 kms south of Mallawi. Once a boat has carried you across, you must pursue your exploration of this extensive site by foot, donkey or tractor, allowing at least half a day for the visit.

Akhenaton's city

Incorrectly known as Tell el Amarna, this conflates the name of a local village, El Till, and the tribal name of the Beni Amran bedouin who live here. In wrongly supplying Tell for Till it gives the impression that a mound created of centuries of human habitation and debris (*tell*) identifies the spot. It does not, and that is what makes Amarna archaeologically so interesting. It is all one layer, the largely mud brick remains of a complete royal city begun in the fourth year of Akhenaton's reign, his residence from about his sixth year, and abandoned for all time soon after his death in the eighteenth year of his reign.

The ancient name Akhetaton means 'Horizon (or Resting Place) of the Disc', so that just as Amun dwelt at Thebes, Ptah at Memphis and other gods at their favoured places the Pharaoh Akhenaton offered this as home to Aton. On boundary stela he inscribed: 'Akhetaton belongs to Aton my Father like the mountains, the deserts, the fields, the islands, the upper lands and the lower lands, the water, the villages, the men, the animals and all those things to which Aton my Father will give life eternally. I shall not neglect the oath which I have made to Aton my Father for eternity'. From a strip of palm-spiked fields along the Nile, a plain, 12 kms from north to south, swells against a crescent ridge of the Arabian plateau. Sand fills the greater part of the arena, the remains of temples, houses and palaces trace upon it in bare outline. It is a lonely spot, of melancholy beauty, one of the most attractive in all Egypt.

Palaces and temples

From the village of El Till the ancient **Royal Road** runs southwards to the administrative centre of the city. Folk memory recalls the grandeur of this thoroughfare with the modern name Sikket-es-Sultan, Road of the Sultan. On your left (east) is a Moslem cemetery and traced in part beneath it is a vast rectangle, stretching 800 metres back towards the ridge, marking the **Great Temple of Aton**. It was deliberately desecrated and destroyed after Akhenaton's death and its foundations later quarried by Ramses II for his temples at Hermopolis. Further along on your left are the faint outlines of the temple's *magazines*. Then there are three excavated rectangles, again on the left. (Many of these features may be

The slight remains of Akhenaton's palace

difficult to distinguish owing to a shifting veil of sand and broken stone.) The first was an extension of the royal palace and was the **Residence of Akhenaton** and his queen, Nefertiti. It was divided into a *walled garden* (northwest quadrant), *private apartments* (southwest quadrant) and *storerooms* (the east half). Near the bedroom was found the celebrated picture now in the Ashmolean Museum of Akhenaton and Nefertiti seated upon an embroidered cushion, face to face, surrounded by their six daughters. The entire residence was decorated with lively scenes, and the ceilings painted with ducks and other aquatic birds flying in all directions.

The royal residence was linked by a *bridge* across the Royal Road to the **main palace complex** on your right (west), now partly erased by tillage. Set within the bridge was a Window of Appearances where the royal family showed themselves before the public, as often depicted on reliefs and tomb paintings. (Indeed it is to the detailed and realistic tomb paintings at Amarna that so much knowledge of the city's original appearance is owed.) The next rectangle to the east marks the **Sanctuary of Aton** used by the royal family, and the rectangle beyond it the *magazines* associated with it.

Along a parallel road to the east and immediately behind the royal residence stood the **Foreign Office** where the famous Amarna Letters, cuneiform tablets received from Asian princes, were found. This road continues southwards in the direction of the village of Hagg Kandil through **residential quarters**. Much of this area has been sanded over and little can be discerned; however, here lived such dignitaires as General Ramose, Vizier Nakht (neither are to be confused with their namesakes in the Theban necropolis) and Panehsi (see Tomb 6, below). Also here were the workshops of the sculptor Tuthmosis where the exquisite bust of Nefertiti, now in the Berlin Museum, was found. There is a model of an Amarnan house in Room 8 on the ground floor of the Cairo Museum. Other quarters, palaces and temples are scattered throughout the plain, their seemingly aimless distribution probably dictated by available well water, but exploration is unlikely to prove meaningful without the company of an archaeologist familiar with the site.

The Amarna necropolis

The **necropolis** at Amarna is in the eastern cliffs. Unlike at Thebes, the tomb decorations do not concern themselves with the afterlife: the Judgement of Osiris, for example, is absent, while instead there are vivid scenes of the everyday. Many of the tombs were never finished and only a few reveal signs of burial, as if the collapse of the Amarna revolution outpaced mortality. Akhenaton's body has been vainly sought both here and at Thebes; one imagines him disinterred at the restoration of Amun and left to rot like Cromwell. The **royal tomb** lies far back in the wild valley, the Darb el Malik, dividing the north and south faces of the cliff. On founding Amarna, Akhenaton proclaimed: 'My tomb will be hollowed in the Eastern Mountain, my burial will be made there in the multitude of jubilees which Aton my Father has ordained for me, and the burial of the Great Royal Wife Nefertiti will take place there in the multitude of years'. Instead, like an ominous cloud on the Amarna horizon, it was their young daughter Makitaton who first died and was entombed here. Akhenaton and Nefertiti, joyful children of the solar disc, are shown on the walls of Makitaton's sarcophagus chamber in sad mourning. The tomb is closed to the public.

There are 25 tombs along the base of the cliff face, Nos. 1 to 6 to the north of the Darb el Malik, Nos. 7 to 25 to the south. Both to see the wall carvings and to avoid tumbling down the shafts leading to the burial chambers, a flashlight should be brought. The tombs are preceded by an open court, as at Thebes, and then usually run through two or three chambers, sometimes with papyrus-bundle columns, ending at a recess in the rear wall where a statue of the deceased (if it remains) stares in surprise at its infrequent visitors. The lyrical 'Hymn to the Sun' composed by Akhenaton is frequently incorporated into the decorations. The tombs most worth visiting are *No. 1 of Huya*, superintendent of the royal harem and steward to the queen mother, Tiy; *No. 4 of Merire*, high priest of Aton; *No. 6 of Panehsi*, servant of Aton with responsibility for his granaries and herds and also vizier of Lower Egypt; *No. 9 of Mahu*, chief of police; and *No. 25 of Ay*, royal confident, Akhenaton's scribe and successor to Tutankhamun as Pharaoh of Egypt. The outstanding tombs are the last two.

Mahu's tomb (9) is one of the best preserved and is interesting for the detail it gives of his duties. He was responsible for certain desert frontier posts and is shown receiving a report of a nomadic incursion. Three offenders are brought before Mahu and the vizier for interrogation; the chief of police is true to his timeless type in accusing them of being 'agitated by some foreign power'.

Ay's tomb (25) is the finest in the necropolis. In one scene, Ay and his wife are shown receiving golden collars from Akhenaton and Nefertiti while guards and onlookers outside the palace react to the honour and excitement of it all. There are street scenes, closely observed and marvellously true to life, and peeps of palace intimacy, with a lady of the harem having her hair done, some girls playing the harp and dancing, while others prepare the food and sweep the floor. Also, on the right-hand side of the doorway is the most complete and probably the most correct version of Akhenaton's hymn. Here are some excerpts.

Akhenaton's 'Hymn to the Sun'

> At dawn you rise shining in the horizon, you shine as Aton in the sky and drive away darkness by sending forth your rays. The Two Lands awake in festivity, and men stand on their feet, for you have raised them up. They wash their bodies, they take their garments, and their arms are raised to praise your rising. The whole world does its work.
>
> The cattle are content in their pasture, the trees and plants are green, the birds fly from their nests. Their wings are raised in praise of your soul. The goats leap on their feet. All flying and fluttering things live when you shine for them. Likewise the boats race up and down the river, and every way is open, because you have appeared. The fish in the river leap before your face. Your rays go to the depths of the sea.
>
> You set the germ in women and make seed in men. You maintain the son in the womb of the mother and soothe him so that he does not weep, you nurse in the womb. You give the breath of life to all you have created. When the child comes forth from the womb on the day of his birth, you open his mouth and you supply his needs. The chick in the egg can be heard in the shell, for you give him breath inside it so that he may live. You have given him in the egg the power to break it. He comes out of the egg to chirp as loudly as he can; and when he comes out, he walks on his feet.

Like the wall reliefs, the hymn portrays in remarkable detail and variety the cumulative incidents that give wonder to life. Convention, myth and abstraction are dispensed with, replaced by the sensate reality of Aton which creates, embraces and expresses existence.

For a moment, Egypt was offered spiritual and philosophical renewal. Akhenaton broke with a past whose search for stasis was leading to sterility. The sun and soul were recovered from their long dark voyage through the underworld and set in brilliant transit across the horizons of this life. Whether it was monotheism is uncertain and probably irrelevant; the universe was alive again. More important is whether Atonism was ever anything more than a royal cult. Akhenaton's hymn, phrased in demotic, suggests his intention was to place his revelation before all mankind. Yet when he died, his religion was soon suppressed, and what is more, all mention of the heretic Pharaoh was proscribed from the king lists and he went unknown until the 19th C of our era. Can it have been just a political reaction? Dynastic infighting led Tuthmosis III to obliterate all images and cartouches of Hatshepsut, but her memory remained. It seems as if Akhenaton offered something far more than a political threat — and more than the military and administrative failures he has been accused of. Possibly Egypt had so far lost its faith in life that it could accept no substitute for its long investment in death. That may explain the empty tombs at Amarna; cold comfort, for all their paeans, to a civilisation lost to the hocus-pocus of formulae and solar boats. It is significant that with the coming of the Ramessids, tomb decorations concentrated less on the quality of this life or the next but on the rigmarole of passing from one to the other.

Like Akhenaton himself, those pharaohs who followed him and had shared at some time in their lives in the worship of Aton — Smenkhkere, Tutankhamun and Ay — were proscribed from the king lists at Saqqara and Abydos, and from that of Manetho. Akhetaton was never built on again. Horemheb's reign marked the full force of the reaction and cleared the decks for Seti I's classical renaissance. Something of Amarna art is found, straitjacketed and reduced to mannerism, in the works of Ramses II, especially in the fluid beauty accorded the female form, a touch of Nefertiti's Florentine elegance in those portraits of Nefertari, Ramses' queen, on the tomb walls at Biban el Harem at Thebes and inside the Temple of Hathor at Abu Simbel.

Nefertiti stayed on at Amarna after her husband's death. Living in exile at the north end of the plain, she had carved on the walls of her palace the names of Akhenaton and herself. And this palace she called without compromise the House of Aton.

Continuing Upriver

Manfalut, 54 kms upriver from Mallawi, is the seat of a Coptic bishop. It was the gathering point for the Egyptian army sent to the Peloponnese in 1825 under Ibrahim Pasha, Mohammed Ali's son, to suppress the Greek revolt against the Turkish Sultan — a task which the sickly but disciplined Egyptian soldiers all but accomplished, the Greeks saved only at the eleventh hour by the British destruction of the Egyptian and Turkish fleets at Navarino.

Flaubert amongst the crocodiles

On the opposite (east) side of the river, 5 kms northeast of the village of El Maabda, is the **Crocodile Grotto** contemptuously dismissed by Baedeker as 'hardly worth visiting, as practically nothing is to be seen except the charred remains of the mummies of crocodiles'. Not only crocodiles, but human mummies too, and those of snakes, fish, eggs, birds and all sorts of animals. Flaubert was enthusiastic: 'A hole, down into which we climb; we have to crawl. Sand; then very soon stones; they are large, black, slippery, sharp, hard, painful to the knees — everything oozes bitumen: we have to drag ourselves along flat on the ground — exhausting. . . Here they all are, one on top of another, packed together, undisturbed; their bones break under your feet; put down your hand and pick up an arm. How deep would you have to go to reach the earth? There are as many here as the place can hold'. Flaubert returned to France with a human foot and kept it in his study as he wrote *Madame Bovary;* one day his servant shined it up with shoe polish.

Flaubert's friend, Maxime du Camp, emerged with a head and a pair of hands and feet. Du Camp later wrote: 'When you are standing on this bed of corpses, precautions cannot be too stringent: a bit of flame falling from a candle could instantly set fire to the dry debris, full of inflammable material, and then flight would be impossible and even useless. About 20 years ago an American visited the grotto with his dragoman and a guide. Some time after he went down, a loud noise was heard, and then black smoke poured from the opening. Neither American nor dragoman nor guide was ever seen again; the fire lasted 18 months and burnt itself out; for several years no one dared venture into the dangerous cave'. Once again, dear reader, I advise you to illuminate your way by flashlight.

Shady village lane at Amarna

Largest town in Upper Egypt

Assiut (378 kms from Cairo) lies in the midst of an extensive and fertile plain on the west bank of the Nile. To the west of the railway line is the old town; to the east, running down to the tree-lined corniche, are the newer districts. It is the largest town — swelling now into a city of nearly a quarter of a million — in Upper Egypt and the effective capital of the region. Once at the head of a great caravan route to the oases of the Libyan Desert and across the Sahara, it is still a centre of trade and crafts as a walk through its bazaars will confirm. Pottery, inlaid wood and ivory carving are much overshadowed though by wheat and cotton exports, and spinning. A university has recently been established, with a strong faculty of agriculture.

Assiut's importance, like its name, goes back to pharaonic times, though it never achieved political dominance. *Tombs of the Middle Kingdom*, its period of ancient glory, are cut in the mountain, 2 kms to the southwest, and nearby is a *Moslem cemetery* with hundreds of domed mausolea. Yet higher up is the *Convent of the Virgin Mary* with a commanding view of the town and plain below.

Near the station, to the west of the railway line, is a *carpet-making school* open to visitors and in the American College the small *Museum of Pharaonic and Coptic Antiquities*.

Plotinus (AD 204–262), the great Neo-Platonist, was probably born in Assiut: 'No one could find out for certain because he was reticent about it, saying that the descent of his soul into his body had been a great misfortune, which he did not desire to discuss' (Forster, *Alexandria*).

The *barrage* at Assuit, built in 1898–1902, formed part of the British plan, which included the old dam at Aswan, for controlling the Nile. From here the amount of water entering the Ibrahimiya Canal is regulated for the irrigation of the Valley right the way down to Beni Suef. A road crosses the barrage and continues along the east bank of the river, but the main road and the railroad follow the west bank with its broader cultivation and more frequent towns and villages. One of these towns is **Sohag** (470 kms from Cairo); a few kilometres along a dusty road are the dilapidated Red and White Monasteries.

Coptic monasteries

One tradition has it that the **Red Monastery** was founded by St Helena, peripatetic mother of the great Constantine, but the Copts insist it was dedicated to a robber named Bishoi who found greater reward in prayer and fasting. Its basilical church is built of dark red Roman brick; a 10th C Pantokrator is painted on the half-dome of the central altar but is blackened by the smoke of incense and candles. The **White Monastery** once housed a colony of 2000 monks within its high limestone walls with a cavetto cornice like an Egyptian temple. Inside are more early Christian paintings going to pot. It was founded about 400 by Shenoudi, Coptic saint, father of the Eyptian Church and a ferocious disciplinarian who once flogged an erring monk to death. But by the 17th C a European visitor, Father Vansleb, found that the monks spent their time 'seeking for the philosopher's stone and in works of Chymistry — an excellent employment for such as have left the world and forsaken their riches'.

PRACTICAL INFORMATION

TRAVEL

Distances between major points in this and the following chapter are by rail and so are less than those for road or river travel. The boat journey between Cairo and Luxor follows the Nile for 740 kms; by road the journey is 730 kms; while by rail the journey is 676 kms.

To cover the distance by **boat** means joining a cruise, eg Swans or Bales (see *Background* chapter), for the complete voyage, lasting about 14 days, and visiting the most famous places — Beni Hassan, Amarna, Assiut, Abydos, Dendera and on to Luxor and Aswan. The planning is taken out of your hands, the voyage is comfortable and restful (though for the determined stone-seeker the on-shore excursions grow exhausting), and the river scenery is beautiful and ever-changing.

The overnight sleeper or day express **train** between Cairo and Luxor takes about 11 hours. The day train permits you to see the scenery enroute and is recommended in at least one direction. But rail travel is also a good way to see the Valley in stages (for train schedules, see the *Background* chapter).

The main **road** follows the railway, keeping to the west bank of the Nile between Cairo and Nag Hammadi (which lies between Abydos and Dendera) before crossing over to the east bank to continue to Luxor and Aswan. There are also alternatives, a minor road along the east bank between Assiut and Nag Hammadi, and another along the west bank between Nag Hammadi and Edfu (see also the following chapters). The main road is good along the entire length of the Valley; the drive from Cairo to Luxor will take 2 days, with an overnight stop suggested at Minya.

Road and rail travel in Egypt have not received their due. Local trains, buses and service (shared) taxis operate throughout the length of the Valley, and cars with drivers can be hired. Service taxis are particularly recommended as a quick, inexpensive and not uncomfortable way of getting from town to town. Using Minya, Assiut, Sohag and Qena as bases, you can explore out of the way places at your own pace.

There are no bridges across the Nile between El Wasta and Assiut, and so to get to sites on the east bank (eg Beni Hassan and Amarna) means taking a boat across (there are regular ferry services at all towns and many villages) and continuing on foot, by donkey or by tractor.

Before starting out on a tour of the Valley, it would be worthwhile talking with the Tourist Information Office on Sharia Adli in Cairo. They can advise on the best means of travel in each locality and provide contacts and up to date information. In some cases you should call on the Department of Antiquities in the area you are visiting. Also Misr Travel might be able to advise on local transport and accommodation.

NOTE ON VISITING BENI HASSAN

A private taxi can be hired at Minya to take you to the ferry crossing. Alternatively, take a service (shared) taxi (see below under *Notes on Visiting Amarna* for directions) to Abu Qerqaz for a trifling sum, thence a pretty country walk of about 3 kms (or a ride in a pickup truck) to the ferry.

NOTES ON VISITING AMARNA

The simplest approach is to take a train to Mallawi and a taxi from there, though if you are overnighting, Minya is the place. The penalty for starting from Minya is the longer (one hour) taxi ride and so the higher cost: Minya to the Amarna ferry and back, plus waiting 3 to 4 hours, about LE25 (regardless of the number of passengers). The money-saving alternative is to take a service (shared) taxi. These are found by turning right out of Minya train station and walking about 500 metres south, following the tracks, till you reach a flyover coming in from the right. The return crossing of the Nile by motor launch costs LE2.50, but by felucca no more than 75PT. Admission to the site, no more than 50PT; to the tombs, no more than LE2 (you discover that these fees are negotiable with the local policeman). Three hours on a donkey will cost LE1.50 to LE2; by tractor the cost is about LE4.

The Egypt Exploration Society is currently excavating at the Workmen's Village during the winter months under the direction of Barry Kemp. Much of the Amarna site described in this chapter is difficult to distinguish under the broken stone and drifting sand, the locals know next to nothing, and so a few words from an Egyptologist could prove very helpful.

To appreciate the magnificence of the site, you must go out to the cliffs and climb up to the tombs. Perhaps the most enjoyable part of the excursion is afterwards to wander along the east bank of the Nile, the path leafy and shaded, the air sweet, water buffalo tied to trees, and numerous vine trellises — these last an agreeable continuity, as it has been suggested that the square pillar bases of mudbrick noticeable in the palace area might have supported grape trellises.

ACCOMMODATION

Remember to consult the *Background* chapter, under *Accommodation*, to determine how star ratings translate into room costs.

For the less fastidious, the local no-star hotels in Minya, Assiut, Sohag and possibly elsewhere will do. Otherwise, only at **Minya** are there hotels officially recommended to tourists:

Lotus (2-star), Sharia Port Said. A modern pink building with a roof restaurant and bar, and bath, toilet, telephone and air conditioning in all rooms.

Ibn Khaseeb (1-star), Sharia Ragheb. Recently renovated.

Though in the non-star class, the **Savoy**, opposite Minya station, can be safely recommended. It is an old-style hotel, neglected, but cheap and clean.

(For more information on Minya, phone the Tourist Office: 2044 or 2155.)

In **Sohag** an acceptable non-star hotel is the **Andalos**, just behind the station, friendly, reasonably clean, with hot water, and cheap.

ABYDOS AND DENDERA

At **Nag Hammadi** (556 kms from Cairo) the Nile sweeps round in a great bend to the east and the main road and railroad go over a bridge to the other side. First **Qena** (612 kms from Cairo) on the east bank: from here a main road passes through beautiful desert and mountain landscapes to Port Safaga on the Red Sea, where you can head north along the coast to Hurghada. Flaubert journeyed by camel through the devouring heat to Quseir, to the south of Safaga, in four days; on returning to Qena he sank into a bath and then into the arms of a prostitute: 'Dark eyes, much lengthened by antimony; her face held up by velvet chinstraps; sunken mouth, jutting chin, smelling of butter, blue robe'. But the major starting point for caravans from pharaonic to more modern times was **Qift** (633 kms from Cairo), the ancient Coptos. Expeditions such as Hatshepsut's (see Deir el Bahri) would have set out for the Red Sea from around here and then continued by ship to the land of Punt, while throughout antiquity and until the Portuguese found their way around Africa Coptos thrived on trade with Arabia and India. The Eastern Desert was once a busy place, criss-crossed by the Egyptians, and later the Romans, in search of gold, emeralds, granite and porphyry. The Romans turned it into a highway and maintained staging posts a day's march from each other along the way charging a levy which rose from 5 drachmas for an able seaman or shipyard hand to 108 drachmas for luxury traffic like prostitutes. The Suez Canal, which made transhipment between the Red Sea and Alexandria no longer necessary, dealt the final blow to Qift's fortunes. There is now nothing of interest or of licence to detain you, and from here it is only another 43 kms to Luxor.

Ancient caravan routes across the Eastern Desert

Shrine of Osiris

Along the way we have missed out Abydos (reached via Baliana, 40 kms west of Nag Hammadi) and Dendera (6 kms west of Qena), both on the west bank of the Nile. The express sleepers and shuttle jets between Cairo and Luxor spoil us, make it seem hard to explore the route described from Beni Suef, and so these famous temples are usually visited as day-trips by taxi or air-conditioned tour bus from Luxor, or as part of a river cruise. They are mentioned here out of geographical integrity but will probably be footnotes to your stay at Luxor — and historically that is not altogether untrue.

Osiris and the afterlife

The local god of **Abydos** had been a patron of the dead and the identification of Osiris with him towards the end of the Old Kingdom was both natural and rapid. The crucial role Osiris played in the Egyptian conception of the afterlife soon turned Abydos into a national shrine. Rather like Mecca is to Moslems today, it became the goal of all Egyptians to visit Abydos during their lifetimes, or failing that, between death and burial. Frequently on the tomb walls at the Theban necropolis you see the mummy of some notable making the voyage by river to Abydos. Some were even buried here as

Old, Middle and New Kingdom tombs testify. The appeal was to lie for eternity at that very spot where the head of Osiris was buried after Seth had cut him to pieces and scattered his remains (see Philae).

It is a measure of Akhenaton's assault on the established religion that not only did Aton supplant Amun but that the Judgement of Osiris did not appear on the tomb walls at Amarna. After Akhenaton and his successors were proscribed and Horemheb restored the old ways, the XVIII Dynasty was replaced by the XIX Dynasty from the south (so often the source of zeal) — by the brief reign of Ramses I and by Seti I who now had to consolidate. Ironically, Seti bore the name of Osiris' mortal enemy — his sensitivity on this point is demonstrated at Abydos where his cartouche reads Menmare Osiris-Merneptah rather than Menmare Seti-Merneptah — and both to remove any doubts about his loyalty to the past, and to identify his dynasty with the national god, Seti built a temple of fine limestone at Abydos. But Seti was more than a reactionary; he declared a renaissance, and in art he ignored both Akhenaton's expressionism and the overblown style of the XVIII Dynasty empire. His bas-reliefs at Abydos are finely formed and beautifully coloured Old Kingdom revivals — though perhaps a touch effete: it is these one comes to see.

Renaissance of Old Kingdom style

The pylon of **Seti's mortuary temple** has collapsed and the walls of the first and second courts are reduced almost to foundation level. You enter the temple by the central door of seven (the three on either side were sealed by Ramses II) and pass through the first hypostyle hall, completed by Ramses and of inferior work, into the second hypostyle hall which was the last part of the temple decorated before Seti's death. The *seven doors* are explained by the unusual feature of *seven sanctuaries* lying beyond, dedicated, from right to left, to Horus, Isis, Osiris, Amun, Re-Herakhte, Ptah (with fine though bleak profiles of the god) and Seti himself. But it is in the *second hypostyle hall* that you should pause, for this contains the remarkable *reliefs*. Seti appears in distinctive profile, a stylised but close likeness as determined by comparison with his mummy at the Cairo Museum.

Also unusual is the wing built onto the temple to the left of the sanctuaries. The first passageway on the left is known as the *Gallery of the Kings* for its famous list of Seti's predecessors. Though the list is incomplete (in particular, Hatshepsut, Akhenaton, Smenkhkere and Tutankhamun are all missing, for political reasons) the 76 cartouches from Menes onwards have assisted archaeologists in determining the correct order of pharaonic succession. The list is on the right wall, upper two registers; and represented as revering their ancestors are Seti himself and his son, the future Ramses II, with youthful side-lock and holding up two papyrus prayer rolls.

Immediately behind the temple is the **Cenotaph of Seti I** or the Osireion. It stands on lower ground and was sunk within an artificial mound, an association, perhaps, with a creation myth (see Hermopolis and Medinet Habu). Funerary texts decorate the interior, and across the ceiling of the fine transverse chamber is a beautiful *relief of Nut*, goddess of the sky. Her arched body is supported by Shu, god of the air. She is

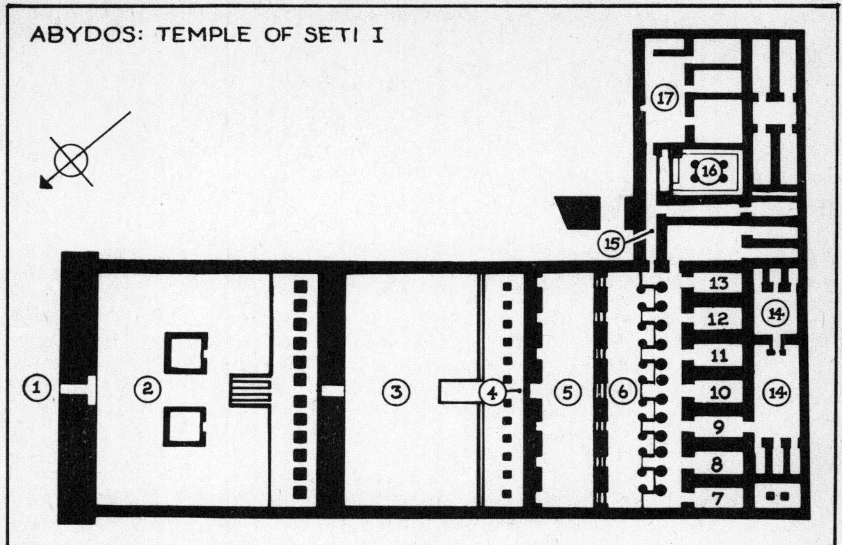

1. Pylon (destroyed)
2. First court (destroyed)
3. Second court (largely destroyed)
4. Present entrance
5. First hypostyle hall
6. Second hypostyle hall
7. Sanctuary of Horus
8. Sanctuary of Isis
9. Sanctuary of Osiris
10. Sanctuary of Amun
11. Sanctuary of Re-Herakhte
12. Sanctuary of Ptah
13. Sanctuary of Seti
14. Inner Sanctuaries of Osiris
15. Gallery of the Kings
16. Sanctuary of the Boats
17. Hall of Sacrifices

swallowing the winged disc at the end of day, but the birth of morning is already seen in the winged ball at her feet. The **temple of Ramses II** is 300 metres to the right of Seti's but is almost wholly destroyed above foundation level. The fine-grained limestone, architectural details picked out in red and black granite, and the bas-reliefs (Ramses normally employed sunk relief) suggest a standard of execution higher than was to be bothered with later in Ramses' prodigal reign.

The Worship of Hathor

The goddess of love — in the form of a cow

The primitive roots of Egyptian religion — an animal fetishism that it never quite escaped and at the end, as seen at Saqqara, retreated to — are illustrated in Hathor, the cow goddess, goddess of joy and love and identified by the Greeks with Aphrodite, despite her bovine features. One thinks of the Dinka and other Nilotic tribes of the southern Sudan, whose entire culture is based on cattle. The cow to them is the epitome of beauty; it is tended for its milk and aesthetic satisfaction, never for its meat unless it dies. The Dinka have contempt for agriculture, the nomad's disdain for those tied to the land. Perhaps it was so with the pre-dynastic Egyptians as their grasslands were swallowed by the desert and they were forced to labour for their existence along the Nile — a yearning for a stolen way of life expressed through Hathor, one of the most ancient and revered of their gods. At any rate, the worship of Hathor at **Dendera** went back to the earliest times.

Cheops built, or rather rebuilt, here, as did numerous pharaohs throughout the Old, Middle and New Kingdoms. By Ptolemaic times the ancient cosmology had become much simplified. Deities, concepts and aspects were often assimilated to the dramatis personae of the Osiris myth. Through the incestuous working of mythology the fertility goddess Hat-Hor, literally Castle of Horus, first suckled the son of Osiris and then lay with him at Edfu in culmination of a great pageant issuing each year from Dendera. As it was important that each pharaoh should trace his ancestry back to Horus (see Philae), it was especially necessary that the foreign Ptolemies should stress their links with the Osirid trinity and with the wet-nurse and bed-mate of Horus. The **Temple of Hathor** at Dendera was part of this Ptolemaic assertion, and the Romans too found it expedient to contribute stones to the story.

Ptolemaic temples

Cosmological simplification and single-mindedness of political purpose — and perhaps a Greek concern for harmony — gave unity to Ptolemaic temples in contrast to the sprawling accretions of earlier dynasties. The old motifs in architecture and decorations were retained to gratify the priesthood in exchange for their absorption into the machinery of Alexandrian rule, and perhaps to impress the populace — though not to include them, as the abstruseness of Ptolemaic inscriptions makes clear. Non-pharaonic nationalism was shut out, though it intruded in the protesting defacings of later centuries.

The temple *facade* (1) is a pylon in outline, relieved by six Hathor-headed columns rising from a screen. A winged disc hovers at the centre of the huge cavetto cornice, an inscription above it, in Greek, from the reign of Tiberius — the facade and pronaos are Roman works. A central doorway admits to the *pronaos* (2), a great hypostyle hall, again with Hathoric columns. Its ceiling decorations include the signs of the Egyptian zodiac, the various deities traversing the heavens in their sacred boats amidst bursts of stars. The columns bear reliefs of the ankh and sceptre in alternation — life and prosperity. The grooves at the column bases were made by the insistent fingers of the faithful. The divinity reliefs on the columns were once covered with gold, and it is possible that even the floor bore a veneer of gold and silver. The successive chambers become smaller, lower, darker. The *second hypostyle hall* (3) of six columns is decorated with scenes concerning the temple foundation rites: turning the first spadeful of earth, laying the first stone, etc. This was the Hall of Appearances where Hathor consorted joyfully with the gods and goddesses of her court before voyaging to Edfu. Beyond this is the temple proper, the sanctuary at its centre surrounded by a corridor lined with chapels. But first you pass through the Hall of Offerings and the Hall of the Ennead.

The *Hall of Offerings* (4) marks the scene of the daily cult

Temple at Dendera: Hathoric columns

ritual in which offerings were laid out before the sanctuary, and from where the divine images were carried in New Year processions up the staircases to the roof to a kiosk where they made contact with the rays of Re — a spiritual emergence from darkness into light. The processions are depicted ascending and descending on both the east and west stairway walls. (See below for a description of the roof.)

The *Hall of the Ennead* (5), immediately before the sanctuary, contained statues of Hathor's nine consorts, these being the primal elements or deities following on the creation (eg air, moisture, earth, sky) as opposed to the pre-creation forces (see Medinet Habu) — that is, the elements of cosmic order rather than the elements of cosmic disorder.

The *sanctuary* (6) itself would normally be bolted and in complete darkness. It was opened and illuminated by torchlight to permit the Pharaoh to adore the goddess, and for her consorts to dine in communion with her. These rituals are depicted on the inner walls: on the right, the top pictorial register shows, from right to left, the Pharaoh opening the door after repeating four times 'I am pure' (frames 1 and 2), meeting Hathor (frame 3) and offering libations (frame 4); the same sequence is on the left wall. The surrounding *chapels* each had their different ritual and ceremonial functions. Most interesting are the three chapels immediately behind the sanctuary: at the centre the Per-Ur (7), to its left the Per-Nu, and to its right the Per-Neser. The *Per-Ur chapel* was the starting point for the New Year procession and its decorations include the Pharaoh offering the goddess a drink of intoxicating liquor, as Hathor was the goddess of joy. From the *Per-Nu chapel,* Hathor embarked on her annual voyage to Edfu and congress with Horus. In the *Per-Neser chapel* the goddess is represented in her terrible aspect, for example as a lioness goddess (by Ptolemaic times Hathor had assimilated the lioness goddess Sekhmet and the cat goddess Bastet, reflecting the terrible and gentle aspects of her nature). In the corridor outside the Per-Nu chapel you can descend steps to the 32 *treasure crypts* beneath the temple.

To reach the *roof* you follow the west corridor back to the Hall of Offerings, pausing first about halfway along the length of the Sanctuary to look at the *New Year Chapel* where rituals were performed preparatory to Hathor's communion with the sun. On the ceiling is a magnificent *relief of Nut* the sky goddess giving birth to the sun whose rays illuminate Hathor. The stairway, decorated with reliefs of the New Year processions, ascends to an elegant stone kiosk which was covered by a removable awning where Hathor was exposed to the sun's revivifying force. Also on the roof, but having nothing to do with the worship of Hathor, are the twin *Chapels of Osiris* (one above the west stair, the other above the east). First there is an open court, decorated with a procession of priests; then a covered court, on its ceiling a *zodiac,* unique in Egypt (the original is in the Louvre); and innermost an entirely enclosed room, representing the tomb of Osiris and decorated with resurrection scenes.

Reliefs of Cleopatra

On the outside rear (south) wall of the temple colossal *reliefs* show Caesarion, son of Julius Caesar, with his mother, the great Cleopatra and the last of the Ptolemies, behind him, making offerings to a head of Hathor. The carvings are entirely conventional and in no way portraits. It is odd seeing Cleopatra in this anonymous form — for domestic consumption — when she is so much better known, or imagined, in flesh and blood, the centre-page fold-out who bedded the two most powerful Romans of her day.

Birth houses

The birth house is a particular feature of Ptolemaic temples and served to legitimise the dynasty through its ritual association with the birth of Horus (see Philae). At Dendera there are three **birth houses**. The *Temple of Isis* (8), to the rear (south) of the Hathor temple was built by Augustus and is in ruins; *a second monumental birth house* (9), also built by Augustus, with reliefs completed under Trajan and Hadrian, is to the front of the Hathor temple court (a *Coptic church* (10) built of stones from this birth house is squeezed between them); *a third* (11), bisected by the west wall of the court, was begun during the reign of Nectanebos I (XXX Dyn) and completed under the Ptolemies.

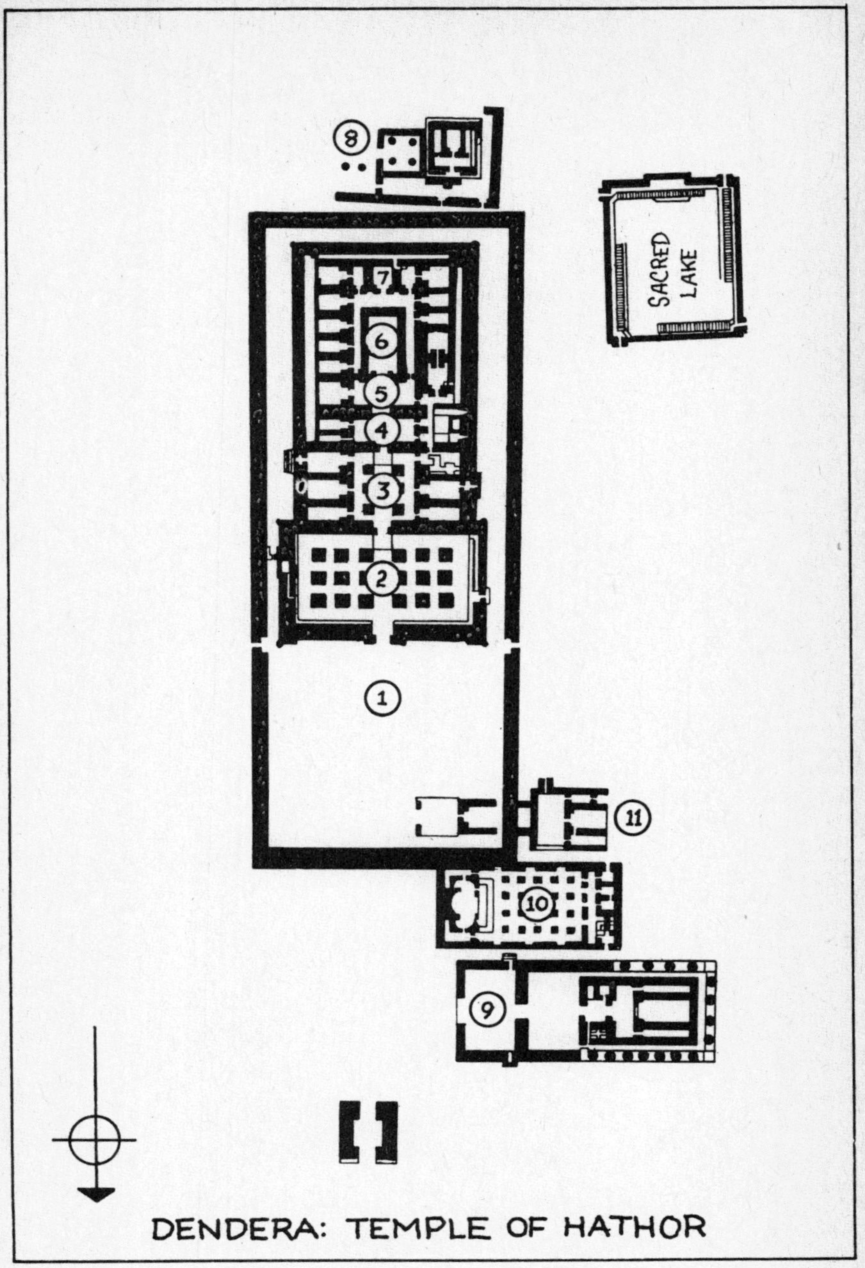

8
7
6
5
4
3
2
1
11
10
9
SACRED LAKE
DENDERA: TEMPLE OF HATHOR

PRACTICAL INFORMATION

For general information about travel in the Valley, see the *Practical Information* section at the end of the preceeding chapter.

Sohag (see previous chapter) and Qena can serve as bases for visits to Abydos and Dendera — at **Qena** the **New Palace Hotel** (1-star) in the station square should be carefully scrutinised first; otherwise try **El Farah Hotel** in the main street running away from the station: no stars, but clean and cheap. **Nag Hammadi** has no accommodation that would be acceptable even to the less fastidious. However, 7 kms outside Nag Hammadi on an industrial estate is the **Aluminium Hotel** (3-star), which needs to be telephoned on a Cairo number: 757947. Of course **Luxor** is the most comfortable base, but also quite a distance; a tour would be simplest, otherwise by private or service (share) taxi or bus. Some of the boats cruising between Luxor and Aswan also come downriver to Dendera and Abydos.

If on your own, **access to Dendera** can be from Qena (about 6 kms over the new bridge): private taxi or carriage, or an agreeable country walk; also a local bus plies along a nearby road. Entry to the site is about LE2; it opens around 7am and closes at 6 pm. **Access to Abydos** (about LE1) is more difficult and is probably best reached enroute between Sohag and Qena or vice versa.

Some **cruise boats** moor overnight near Dendera; in the morning it is best to disembark half an hour before the others, eschewing the coach and enjoying the walk to the temple. One of the most beautiful stretches of the Nile lies between Dendera and Luxor: the river spreads wide, its course lost among islands and stands of reeds. Here you see tilting figures punting their flatboats along or harbouring amongst the vegetation, fishing.

LUXOR

At Luxor the Nile flows north-northeast and the town and the temples in the area take the river as their axis, but to simplify matters it will be assumed here that the river flows north and that the temples therefore lie along one or the other of the cardinal axes of the compass. The name Luxor is loosely applied by travellers to include three distinct places: the town of **Luxor** on the east bank of the Nile (676 kms south of Cairo), the village of **Karnak** and its immense temple 4 kms north on the same bank, and on the west bank of the river opposite Luxor and Karnak the **Theban necropolis**. A chapter is devoted to each of these places in turn. Accommodation is primarily in Luxor, the base of your explorations.

The Setting

The landscape all about is placid and horizontal, with a broad cultivated plain on either side of the river. The desert to the east rises gently to the Arabian plateau, while to the west a low range of hills, the Theban Mountain, interpose themselves between the cultivation and the Libyan Desert. The Nile is majestic, at sundown an implacable lava flow. By day, feluccas seem to stride upon its surface like pond insects, and distant palms rise from the level stillness, distinct and exactly outlined in the clear air and brilliant light. 'The palm — an architectural tree. Everything in Egypt seems made for architecture — the planes of the fields, the vegetation, the human anatomy, the horizon lines' (Flaubert). For the ancient

Along the Nile between Dendera and Luxor

Egyptians, the richness and never-failing fertility of this landscape was a source of wonder. As capital of the New Kingdom it was the focus of an architectural activity so grand, and still so well preserved, that it can lay just claim to being the world's greatest outdoor museum.

Greatest outdoor museum in the world

The Historical Background

The name Luxor derives from the Arabic *el qasr,* meaning castle or military camp (hence the Alcazar, the Moorish palace in Seville). The Arabic derived in turn from the Latin *castrum,* and may have referred to the Roman base here, though possibly to the appearance of the town to the end of the 19th C when it lay largely within the remains of the Temple of Luxor. The ancient Egyptian name for the settlement was Weset, though it is best known by the Greek name Thebes, 'where the houses are full of treasures, a city with a hundred gates' (The *Iliad*). At the height of its glory during the XVIII and XIX Dynasties, Thebes covered all the ground of Luxor and Karnak, and may have had a population as high as one million. During the Old Kingdom, however, when the capital was at Memphis, Thebes was only one of four humble townships in the nome — Tod and Armant to the south, Medamud to the north — each following the cult of falcon-headed Mont, a god of war. In the retreat to regional rule during the First Intermediate Period, Thebes emerged as the power binding Upper Egypt together. After a struggle it re-united the country under its administrative and religious authority, inaugurating the Middle Kingdom. Thebes repeated the pattern when following the disintegration during the Second Intermediate Period and the Hyksos invasion of Lower Egypt, it liberated the country and now also became the permanent residence of the Pharaohs throughout the New Kingdom. It is tempting to believe that apart from its prowess in war and its strategic position between the Delta and the Cataracts, Thebes achieved ascendancy over the townships of its nome and eventually over all Egypt because of the special beauty of its situation. Certainly the great Pharaohs of the New Kingdom responded, sometimes sensitively, sometimes grandiously, to the architectural possibilities of the landscape.

Orientation

The **Temple of Luxor** is on the Nile, only the corniche road, Sharia el Nil, separating it from the river. The temple and the gardens lying along its west side are the focus of the town. All roads meet here. From the **station**, it is a short straight carriage ride (the usual means of transport) to the gardens with the Luxor Hotel on the left. A bit further and you are on the **corniche**, the New and Old Winter Palace Hotels immediately to the south, the Savoy and Etap Hotels north of the temple. The Etap and New Winter Palace are unimaginatively modern; the others were the grand hotels of the twenties and thirties and retain an atmosphere. The town proper extends on either side of the street running between the station and the gardens; the corniche with its hotels and touts is a quite separate world. Nowhere in Egypt, except at the Giza Pyramids, are the touts so much a plague as here along the corniche — insisting that you take their carriage, sail in their felucca, buy their home-made mummified ibis or at any rate give them baksheesh — and on the other side of the river where a mob of car and donkey drivers will harrass you to accept the worst deal at the most outrageous price. The irritation comes close to spoiling Luxor altogether.

Tour Schedule

The briefest possible tour of the area requires two days, one on either side of the Nile. Three or four days are required for a comprehensive impression, though still only an impression, of ancient Thebes and its necropolis. You must bear in mind that outside of winter, mid-afternoons get very hot (around 40° C) and you may want to limit your excursions to the early morning and the late afternoon. On the east bank there is the enjoyment of carriage rides; on the west bank the choice is between donkey or car, the latter being infinitely preferable. Best of all for the sound of limb, and cheap, breezy and free of constraint, is to hire a bicycle in Luxor and use it on both sides of the river. Karnak and the Temple of Luxor can be visited on the same day, the latter best seen in the late afternoon as it glows in the rays of the sinking sun, or at night when it is unsparingly and intelligently floodlit. Rising as early as possible, the whole of the second day should be devoted to the west bank, and the third day too, if you have the time. A fourth day will allow you to revisit Karnak, and perhaps one or two temples or tomb clusters on the necropolis side, and will allow you greater leisure to shop in Luxor and visit the excellent museum there.

The Temple of Luxor

Close to the hotels and landing stages for the Nile cruise boats, a visit to the Temple of Luxor can be casually arranged following a more rigorously organised morning. The temple is appealing: it is well preserved, its unity clearly stated, yet there is the intriguing irregularity of its plan. The temple was built largely under Amenophis III (XVIII Dyn) on the site of an older sanctuary. He also built the Third Pylon at Karnak and began the Hypostyle Hall there, and erected an enormous mortuary temple on the west bank of which only the Colossi of Memnon remain: he was the first Pharaoh of the New Kingdom to go in for the gigantism that broadcasts the imperial pretensions of the period. He would have been delighted with the reaction of the French army in 1799: while in pursuit of the Mameluke Muradbey it rounded a bend in the Nile and came suddenly upon the temples of Karnak and Luxor. 'Without an order being given, the men formed their ranks and presented arms, to the accompaniment of the drums and bands', wrote a lieutenant.

Imperial pretensions

Since 1885 when excavations began here, the temple has been gradually cleared of the village once within it, the rubble blocking the pylon entrance, and the kom to the north which has revealed the *forecourt* and *avenue of sphinxes* leading to Karnak. It was from Karnak that Amun came during the annual Opet festival, but by water, amidst a floating

The Opet festival

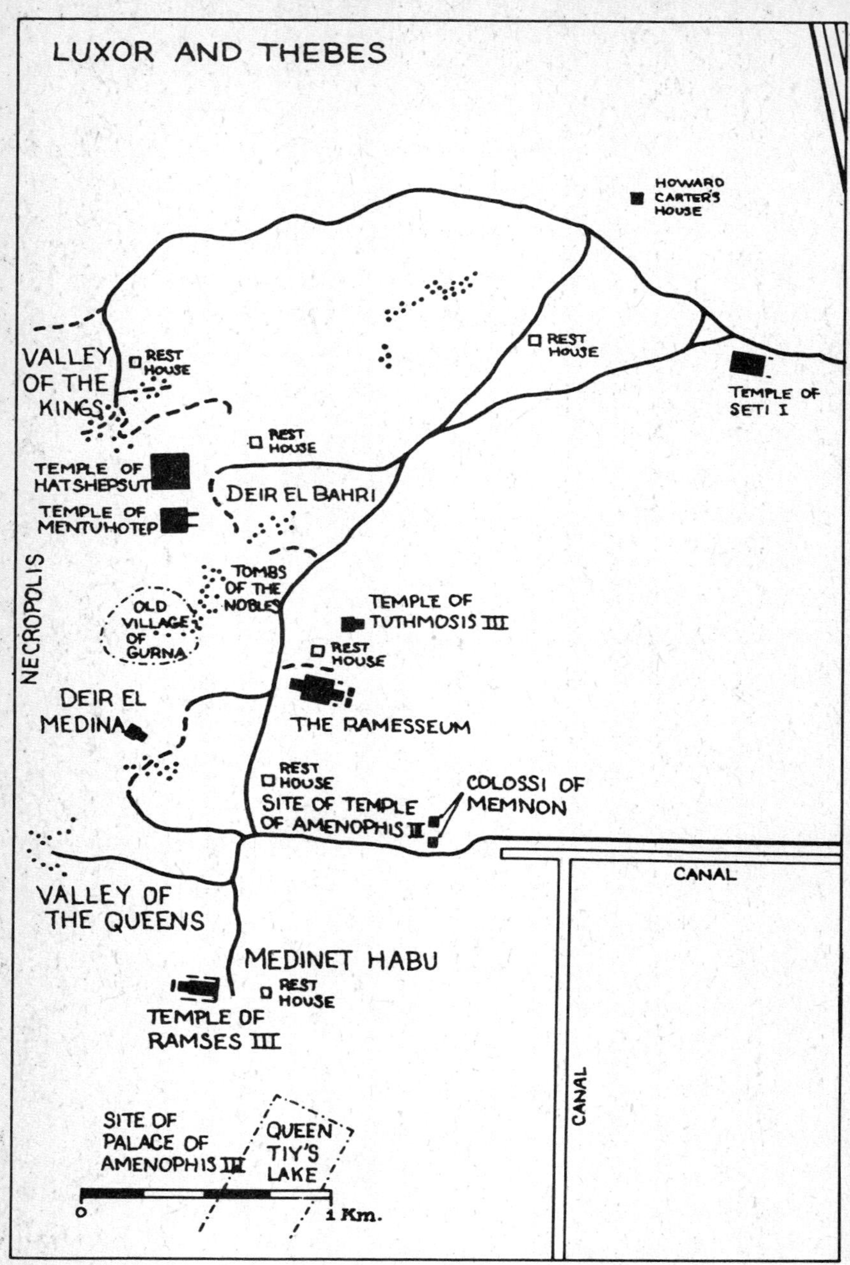
LUXOR AND THEBES
HOWARD CARTER'S HOUSE
REST HOUSE
TEMPLE OF SETI I
VALLEY OF THE KINGS
REST HOUSE
REST HOUSE
TEMPLE OF HATSHEPSUT
DEIR EL BAHRI
TEMPLE OF MENTUHOTEP
NECROPOLIS
TOMBS OF THE NOBLES
OLD VILLAGE OF GURNA
TEMPLE OF TUTHMOSIS III
REST HOUSE
DEIR EL MEDINA
THE RAMESSEUM
REST HOUSE
SITE OF TEMPLE OF AMENOPHIS III
COLOSSI OF MEMNON
CANAL
VALLEY OF THE QUEENS
MEDINET HABU
REST HOUSE
TEMPLE OF RAMSES III
CANAL
SITE OF PALACE OF AMENOPHIS III
QUEEN TIY'S LAKE
0
1 Km.

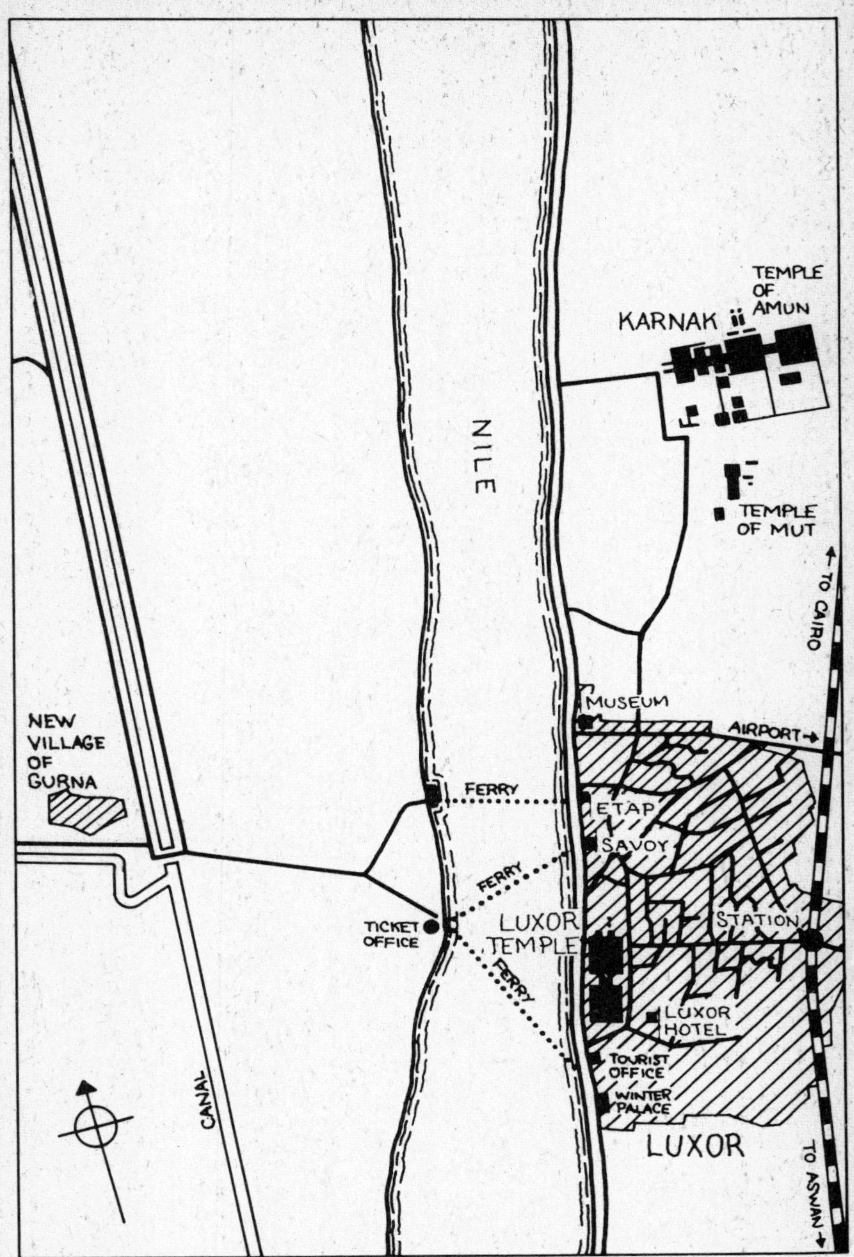
TEMPLE OF AMUN
KARNAK
NILE
TEMPLE OF MUT
TO CAIRO
MUSEUM
AIRPORT
NEW VILLAGE OF GURNA
FERRY
ETAP
SAVOY
FERRY
TICKET OFFICE
LUXOR TEMPLE
STATION
FERRY
LUXOR HOTEL
TOURIST OFFICE
WINTER PALACE
LUXOR
CANAL
TO ASWAN

procession of great splendour to this Harem of the South with his wife Mut and their son the moon god Khonsu. The forecourt wall is the work of Nectanebos I (XXX Dyn), as are the sphinxes which are set at a lower level to the excavated remains of post-pharaonic houses on either side. In the northwest corner of the forecourt is the restored *Serapeum* dedicated by the Emperor Hadrian on 24 January AD 126, his birthday.

Now turning south to look at the **pylon** (1): this and the court behind it were additions by Ramses II (XIX Dyn), the pylon a gigantic billboard advertising Ramses' dubious victory over the Hittites at Kadesh. The *west (right) tower* shows the Egyptian camp within a circle of shields and Ramses on his throne holding a council of war while beneath him two spies are being interrogated by beating. In the right light, or by floodlight, you can see that Ramses has been reversed on his throne, now facing east where he once faced west. (The floodlighting also attracts bats which enjoy fluttering to rest upside-down within the deeper incisions of the drama.) The *east (left) tower* shows Kadesh on the left, surrounded by the waters of the Orontes, while to the right an heroically proportioned Ramses in his chariot is pursuing the broken enemy. In vertical lines below these scenes on both towers is the *Poem of Pentaur* (see Abu Simbel for partial translation), comparison of which with Hittite sources, and also taking into account the contemporary situation, including the superior iron weaponry of the Hittites to the Egyptian bronze, suggests that the battle was less glorious for the Egyptians than Ramses made out. The *vertical grooves* along the pylon facade were for supporting flagstaffs, the apertures above to receive the braces securing the staffs and to admit light and air to the interior. Except at the corners above the entrance passage, the cavetto cornices are missing. Originally the pylon stood 24 metres high; its width is 65 metres.

Ramses' propaganda

In front of the pylon were six *statues of Ramses,* two sitting, four standing. Only the two seated figures on either side of the entrance and the westernmost standing figure remain, and these are all badly damaged. Also there were two *obelisks* of exceptionally fine detail standing on plinths decorated with dog-headed baboons in relief. Mohammed Ali offered the pair, plus one at Alexandria, to France. It is said that the French desire for an obelisk was first expressed by Josephine to Napoleon before he embarked for Egypt: 'Goodbye! If you go to Thebes, do send me a little obelisk'. Napoleon left Egypt under circumstances that denied Josephine the pleasure. In celebration of the Bourbon restoration, Louis XVIII renewed the idea. In the event, the task proved so difficult and lengthy that Champollion's identification of the west obelisk as the finest in Egypt left the French satisfied with it alone, and in 1836 it was erected in the Place de la Concorde. As the obelisk was lowered at Luxor, Ramses' name was found engraved on the underside of the shaft; his titles, his achievements, his piety had already been carved on the four sides of each obelisk, but being a great ursurper of other pharaohs' monuments, he knew well the value of this secret protestation of ownership. Standing before the temple in 1850, Flaubert wrote: 'The

The French desire an obelisk

obelisk that is now in Paris was against the right-hand pylon. Perched on its pedestal, how bored it must be in the Place de la Concorde! How it must miss its Nile! What does it think as it watches all the cabs drive by, instead of the chariots it saw at its feet in the old days?' One hundred years later, Cocteau was more caustic: the plinth of the obelisk removed to Paris 'was surrounded by the low reliefs of dog-faced baboons in erection. This was not thought to be proper and so the monkeys' organs have been cut off'.

The *entrance passage* through the pylon is decorated with carvings of the XXV Dynasty, a period when Egypt was ruled by Ethiopian or Cushite pharaohs, one of whom, Shabaka, is shown on the east (left) wall wearing the white crown of Upper Egypt, running a ritual race in the presence of an ithyphallic Amun-Re.

The Court of Ramses II (2), entirely surrounded by a double colonnade of bud-capital papyrus columns, lies within. Belying the seemingly universal symmetry and regularity of Egyptian architecture, it is immediately obvious that this court does not lie on the same axis as the Colonnade of Amenophis III, which in turn is out of line with the temple proper, but these are very slight divergencies while that of the court of Ramses II is striking. An explanation is found in the northwest corner of the court, a small **temple to Amun, Mut and Khonsu** (3) built by Tuthmosis III and Hatshepsut 100 years before Amenophis, 200 years before Ramses. The granite columns are original, while the carvings were redone by Ramses II who integrated the temple into his court, aligning his court to suit.

In the northeast corner of the court, surviving the clearance of the old village within the temple, is the **mosque and mausoleum of Abu Haggag** (4), a local holy man.

The interior walls of Ramses' court are adorned with reliefs. Especially interesting is the *representation of the pylon facade* at the west end of the south wall, complete with colossi, obelisks and fluttering banners. Approaching this, along the west wall, is a procession led by 17 of Ramses' sons (he fathered over 100 in his 90-odd years) and followed by priests and sacrificial oxen. The unnaturally long hooves indicate the oxen have been fattened in their stalls for the occasion, while the model of an African's head between the horns of the fifth ox and the Asiatic head with long pointed beard between the horns of the sixth symbolises the Egyptian triumph over

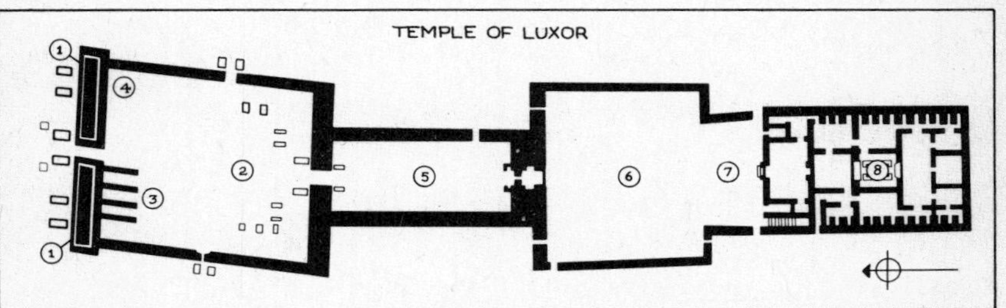

Africa and Asia. The southern half of the court is further embellished with standing *colossi of Ramses,* while the triumph motif is repeated round the bases of the black granite seated colossi on either side of the southern doorway: the shields and bound figures of vanquished Asiatics on the east base, of Africans on the west.

The works of Amenophis III

Passing between these last two guardians of Ramses' memory, you enter the imposing **Colonnade of Amenophis III** (5). The 15.8-metre high papyrus columns with calyx capitals bearing massive architraves contribute greatly to the serene profile of the temple when viewed from the river. Originally, however, this columnar rhythm would have been lost behind flanking walls, the upper three-quarters of which have collapsed. The remaining courses bear fine and fascinating *reliefs from the reign of Tutankhamun,* a celebration of the re-establishment of the Amun orthodoxy, depicting the god with Mut and Khonsu accompanied by the Pharaoh and priests on their voyae from Karnak to Luxor at the height of the inundation period. Crowds of common folk follow by land, and there are scenes of rejoicing, of musicians and dancers, and of sacrifice. The series begins at the northwest corner with Pharaoh sacrificing to the boats at Karnak, and continues with the water-borne procession and, at the southwest corner, the arrival at Luxor. Starting at the southeast corner, the procession returns 24 days later to Karnak.

The colonnade leads into the **Court of Amenophis III** (6), once enclosed on east, north and west by double rows of clustered papyrus columns with bud capitals, an ensemble that appeals through its harmony. The east and west sides are well preserved and still carry their architraves. On the south side is the **Hypostyle Hall** (7) with four rows of eight columns. On either side of its south wall are reliefs of the coronation of Amenophis by the gods. To the left of the central aisle, between the last two columns, is a Roman alter dedicated to Constantine. Cocteau noticed a more recent intrusion: 'Suddenly, in the hypostle hall, I was struck dumb. What could that be? High up, on top of the wall, Rimbaud had carved his name. He carved it, at the height of a man, and now that the temple is cleared, it shines forth like a sunflower. It blazes out, royal and sunlike, above suspicion, dreadful in its solitude'.

Now you enter the *temple proper.* A central chamber, its roof once supported by eight columns, was stuccoed over when turned into a chapel of a Roman Imperial cult, but this has now mostly been removed to reveal reliefs of Amenophis. The side chambers were dedicated to Mut (east) and Khonsu (west). Through the central chamber is the Offering Chapel with four columns, and beyond that the **Sanctuary of the Sacred Boat of Amun** (8).

The inner sanctum

The sanctuary consists of a chapel open to north and south set within a chamber. The chamber walls are decorated with reliefs of Amenophis, while the chapel was rebuilt by Alexander the Great and both its exterior and interior walls bear reliefs of him before Amun and other gods. A room to the east of the sanctuary has badly damaged scenes of Amenophis' coronation and on the north wall Pharaoh

During the heat of the day in Luxor

hunting in the marshes. Immediately to the north is the *Birth Room* with reliefs on the west wall referring to Amenophis' divine birth. At the left of the lowest register, Khnum is moulding the infant Amenophis and his ka on a potter's wheel. Moving from left to right across the middle register, Thoth foretells to Mutemuia, mother of Amenophis, the birth of her son; the pregnant Mutemuia is conducted by Isis and Khnum; her confinement; Isis presenting the infant to Amun; and Amun with the infant in his arms. The top register shows Amenophis and his ka nurtured by the gods and presented to Amun; to the far right, in the corner, Amenophis has become Pharaoh. The remaining rooms at the south end of the temple are without present interest, though the central chamber was a sanctuary once containing the intriguingly described 'divine image of millions of years'.

The temple of Luxor is experienced most intensely at night when the floodlights throw the carvings into deeper relief and the black night rests like a roof on the brightness of the stone, enclosing you. On the dome of the mosque of Abu Haggag, cursive green neon proclaims 'Allah'. Once a year the saint's boat is carried in procession as was Amun's 3500 years before.

Ramadan Celebrations

At Ramadan the mosque is the focus of the nightly festivities. Hundreds of men gather in the gardens, some off to the sides playing cards, gambling, smoking hashish, many more listening raptly or dancing wildly to the drums, tambourines, ouds and violins, and to the teasing, climaxing, repeating passages of the imam's songs. They are religious songs, but passionate, or occasionally playful: a boy and girl are walking down a street hand in hand, they enter a house, they 'go to God together'. The audience laughs and shouts, but the lyrics are always secondary, and it is the narcotic beat and wailing of the music and the imam's exquisite phrasing that draws cries from the crowd. The imam twirls and sings, his eyes closed, his head shaking violently from side to side. A policeman in baggy khakis embraces him, rushes into the crowd to collect fistfulls of paper money and presses it into the imam's hands.

Night frenzy

Two or three dozen men begin to dance, arranging themselves in facing rows. First half-whirls, to the right, to the left, then hopping up and down, now jackknifing, eyes closed, bodies sweating, shouting, whirling, hopping and jackknifing in unison, beyond exhaustion. An onlooker intervenes to ask a young boy, an old man, to rest. But they all dance until they can barely stand, can merely twitch, or until they collapse.

It was less surprising that these men were killing themselves dancing than that others could resist joining the frenzy. I asked one onlooker why he did not dance. 'I am angry.' Then he showed me a photograph of himself taken five months earlier. He was bearded then. 'Now I have no beard because I am angry.' At first I though he *was* angry, he said it with such emphasis, but he meant sad. His wife had died five months ago. 'I was happy with my wife, I loved her. I enjoyed sex with her, she washed my clothes, I gave her money to buy things.' How did she die, I asked? 'One morning I woke up and she was still in bed. I said to her, wife, you must get up and make my breakfast. But she did not get up, and I saw that she was dead.' But what did she die of? Had she been sick? 'No, she was not sick. She just died that morning.' But she must have died of something. For what reason? 'My God took her away. Maybe in two years I will look at women, but now I do not look at women. I am very angry.'

The Luxor Museum

The Museum of Ancient Egyptian Art is along the corniche to the north of the Etap Hotel; the presentation is superb, with some well chosen objects lit to best advantage. The exhibits include jewellery, furniture, pottery and stelae, but most outstanding are the stone *statues and busts.* The latter are most finely represented by granite and basalt works identified by the cartouches as Tuthmosis III, Amenophis II, Amenophis III (all XVIII Dyn) and Sesostris III (XII Dyn), any of which could stand in place of another for all they depict an individual (except for that of Sesostris with big ears). The craftsmanship is excellent, however, and the enjoyment of working with the graceful curves of crowns, necks and waists is clear. There is a marvellous alabaster statue of Sobek with crocodile's head and man's body, and one of Amenophis III, usurped by Ramses II by altering the cartouche — which shows how little the figure itself served to identify. A series of scenes in sunk relief on limestone blocks found within the Ninth Pylon at

Karnak show *Akhenaton and Nefertiti worshiping Aton*, but also the most ordinary daily palace tasks. At least when Akhenaton attacked the Theban priesthood, he obliterated images of their god Amun; the post-Amarna counter-revolutionaries reverted to the traditional method of defeating a predecessor's bid for immortality: for example, *exhibit 150* is a block showing Akhenaton worshipping Aton — so clearly understandable and evidence of his heresy — yet it is defaced only to the extent that his cartouche is gouged. Always the name, the sign, rather than the idea.

PRACTICAL INFORMATION

ACCOMMODATION

During Luxor's high season (October through May) it is not advisable to show up expecting to get a room at the hotel of your choice, so it is wise then to reserve in advance. See the *Background* chapter under *Accommodation* for general information, also for rates.

Note that there is some no-star accommodation on the West Bank, and that near Karnak a Hilton is abuilding (a pity).

Winter Palace (5-star), Sharia el Nil. Tel: 755216. Telex: 92160 WINTER UN. At the southern end of the corniche, this is now 2 hotels, the New Winter Palace connected to the Old Winter Palace. The latter dates back to the heyday of leisured travel earlier this century and has been refurbished and air-conditioned. At the rear, the rooms overlook a well-planted garden, while the Nile-side rooms offer beautiful views across the river and towards the Theban Mountain. But it has been reduced to a dormitory appendage of the New Winter Palace, a characterless modern edifice; and worse, meals must be taken at the new hotel, a voluminous mess hall with third-rate food and service. Half board is compulsory year-round. There is a swimming pool, a bar, a terrace (all at the new hotel), a bank and shops, while the arcades on either side of the drive leading up to the Old Winter Palace are lined with more shops and agencies.

Etap (4-star), Sharia el Nil. Tel: 82160. Telex: 92080 ETAPLX UN. Along the corniche to the north of the Temple of Luxor, this is a new and large air-conditioned mausoleum, though with several redeeming features. All rooms face the Nile and have small balconies; there is a good bar; half board is not compulsory, and the restaurant food and the service are better than at the Winter Palace; several nights a week there is entertainment, including belly dancing; and there is a pool. Also, in the lobby there are several shops, including an Hachette bookshop.

Savoy (4-star), Sharia el Nil, between the Temple of Luxor and the Etap. Tel: 2200. Telex: 92160 WINTER UN (specify Savoy, as this is the Winter Palace's telex — they are both part of the Egyptian Hotels Company). Also dating from the grand days of travel, the Savoy has large, high-ceilinged rooms, not all of them air-conditioned, but usually cool all the same. Those overlooking the Nile have balconies and beautiful views. Unfortunately the place is being allowed to run to seed and refurbishment is called for — it is definitely not a 4-star hotel either in appearance and facilities or in price. In the garden are a number of bungalows, newer, better-appointed, all with air conditioning, but without the Nile view and atmosphere of faded glory. Half board is compulsory year-round, but at least the restaurant is agreeable, the food good and the service too. Best of all (and you do not have to be a guest to enjoy it) is the terrrace on either side of the main entrance, a convivial gathering place for afternoon tea or drinks at night.

Luxor (4-star), in its own grounds facing the Temple of Luxor. Tel: 82400. This dates from the same period as the Savoy and Old Winter Palace, and has recently been refurbished, though the rooms seem bare and lack Nile views. It is built in Moorish style, or a '20s version of it, with ablaq arches and columns along the verandah, the lobby darkly decorated in black, green and wood, and with art deco pharaonic prints on the walls. There is a good African-style bar and a bank for changing money. Half board is compulsory year-round.

Ramoza (2-star), Sharia Saad Zaghloul

Tel: 82270. Telex: 23604 PBLXR UN RAMOZA. A modern hotel near the station. Air conditioning available. Good food, pleasant people.
Philippe (2-star), Sharia Nefertiti, off the corniche just after the Etap. Tel: 82284. A new hotel, clean and friendly, with a good reputation. There is a downstairs restaurant and bar and a rooftop garden. Rooms to the rear are air-conditoned; those to the front, with a glancing view of the Nile, have small balconies.
Horus (1-star), right off Sharia el Mahatta (the road runing down from the station) as it reaches the Temple of Luxor. Tel: 2165. Gaudy from the outside, simple and decent within, the Horus offers a range of rooms and prices, so you should ask to be shown a few first. A restaurant serves basic meals.
Radwan, second left off Midan el Mahatta, to the right of the New Karnak Hotel. Tel: 2214. A no-star place with rooms round a central garden where inexpensive meals are served beneath the minaret of a neighbouring mosque. Both private and dorm-style accommodation. Pleasant, clean and cheap — the best deal for the shoestring traveller.

There is also a **youth hostel** on Sharia el Manshia (Tel: 2139).

EATING PLACES AND ENTERTAINMENT

As many of Luxor's hotels require that you take lunch or dinner at their restaurant, independent restaurants catering to visitors are few.
The **Etap** and **Savoy** offer better meals than the rest, and the Etap's come with entertainment, including belly dancing, several nights a week. Meals at the **Winter Palace** are as mediocre as they are expensive.

Atop the Tourist Bazaar building next to the New Winter Palace is the **Marhaba Restaurant** with beautiful views, air conditioning in summer and moderate prices. The menu is Egyptian, a change from the bland Western fare at the hotels.

There are several agreeable cafés, a bar and a restaurant/bar along the riverbank by the Temple of Luxor. Recommended is the **Chez Farouk** (excellent fish); you can also stay on here into the night drinking beers and listening to the music. At the simpler places along the corniche there is sometimes very good Egyptian music and dancing. An Egyptian will come up to the musicians, give them some money, reel off a list of people to whom he dedicates his dance, and then dance — usually alone and oblivious to onlookers. The dances are regional, some Nubian, some of Luxor, occasionally one from Suez where many Nubians work on the Canal.

The **Savoy** has a terrace on either side of its entrance which is a very pleasant place to while away the late afternoon or late evening with a drink or other light refreshments.

The **swimming pools** at the Etap and Winter Palace are usually open to non-guests for a fee — which in the case of the Etap entitles you to drinks and snacks at the bar to that amount.

There is a certain earnestness about Luxor: so many antiquities lying on either side of the river, requiring early risings to see them before the day grows too hot, and so visitors go to bed early too and nightlife is limited. There is a disco at the **Etap's bar**.

SHOPPING

The principal market street in Luxor is **Sharia el Birka**, to the right off Sharia el Mahatta (the station road) as it comes to the gardens behind the Temple of Luxor. Galabiyyas, spices, etc, can be purchased here.

Along the front of the Old Winter Palace are arcades of agencies and shops selling the usual souvenirs. Here you will find **Aboudi's shop** (see *The Necropolis of Thebes* text), selling books, film, jewellery, but alas not his guide. Next to the New Winter Palace is the **Tourist Bazaar**, a soulless concrete building with nasty shops. Arcades in the Etap have brighter **boutiques**, and there is also an **Hachette bookshop** there.

Touts on both sides of the river will importune you *ad nauseum* with their phoney pharaonic relics. If you want one of these, be sure to knock the price right down, offering no more than one-tenth of what is asked. Decent replicas of **antiquities** are on sale in the arcades by the Old Winter Palace, and sometimes even the real thing — but be sure the shop has a licence from the Department of Antiquities and is prepared to offer a certificate of authenticity for what you buy. Genuine antiquities cost less in Luxor than in Cairo.

OF INTEREST

Temple of Luxor, opens 9am in winter, 7am in summer, closes 5pm; then open (floodlit) from 6 to 9pm in winter, 7 to 10pm in summer. LE2. It is very much worth seeing when floodlit.
Luxor Museum, open evenings only, 4 to 9pm in winter, 5 to 10pm in summer. LE2. Well presented.
Dr Ragab's Papyrus Museum (as in

Cairo), on a boat tied up near the museum. Open 9am to 2pm, 4 to 10pm. Free.

INFORMATION

The first thing to do is to go to the **Tourist Police/Ministry of Tourism** (Tel: 2215) at the Tourist Bazaar next to the New Winter Palace, and there determine the official rates for car, carriage and donkey hire on both sides of the Nile, the cost of taking the tourist ferry and the people's ferry, and the up to date entry fees for all temples, tombs, etc. You will then be fully armed against the touts.

Misr Travel, Thomas Cook and **American Express**, all in the arcades by the Old Winter Palace, can also provide a variety of information and assistance.

TRAVEL

The most pleasant way to get about Luxor, and to Karnak, is by **carriage** (caleche). The cost is no more than 50PT for around town, LE1.50 to Karnak.

Bicycles can be hired for about LE1.50 per day. Try along the street running down from the station.

Ferries to the West Bank are a few piastres, the people's ferry costing less than the tourist ferry (see *The Necropolis of Thebes* chapter).

A very pleasant time can be had by sailing about the Nile in a **felucca**. Bargain with any of the boatmen along the river (get advice on rates first by checking with the Ministry of Tourism; also you might be able to arrange it all through Misr Travel). You can sail all the way up the Nile to Aswan, though you will probably get a better price coming downstream from Aswan (see *Aswan*).

Another way of covering the distance between Luxor and Aswan, with the possibility of sightseeing along the way, is to take a **service (shared) taxi**. These depart from the north end of the gardens behind the Temple of Luxor. You can go from Luxor to Esna, Esna to Edfu, Edfu to Kom Ombo and Kom Ombo to Aswan, each leg costing about LE1 and usually requiring a change of taxi.

Trains and **planes** link Luxor with Cairo and Aswan. For rail schedules, see the *Background* chapter. The **Egyptair** office is in the arcade by the Old Winter Palace. Also here are **Jolley's, Eastmar, Misr Travel, American Express** and **Thomas Cook** — all of these offer tours, though these are geared mostly to groups. You can often join a group tour by going to one or the other of these agents the evening before and asking if there is space.

For a Luxor-Aswan **cruise** you should already have made arrangements in Cairo or from abroad (see *Background* chapter), though possibly one of the above agents can help you out.

KARNAK

A carriage ride

Take a carriage along the corniche to the First Pylon of the main temple at Karnak, but when leaving ask the driver to return you to Luxor by the road which passes the Gateway of Euergetes and which continues past pastel facades, offering you a glimpse of village life too easily missed in bustling from one ancient site to another. Somewhere deep beneath this present roadway of your return journey lies the old *sacred way*, lined with sphinxes that joined the temples of Karnak and Luxor, visible now only at either end, where it leaves Euergetes' gateway, and where it enters the forecourt of the Temple of Luxor.

The Karnak site covers an enormous area, sufficient to accommodate ten European cathedrals. The Hypostyle Hall alone is large enough to contain Notre Dame. At least two half-day visits are required to see the entire complex; if you can manage only one, then you will have to be content with walking through the main temple, that of Amun. A return can be made at night for the *son et lumiere*, though one could do without the *son*. The size and complexity of the site, the arrangement of its structures on both an east-west and north-south axis, the multiple extensions to several of these structures by successive pharaohs, and in some areas its ruinous state, contribute to the lack of unity and proportion at Karnak. But this has probably always been so, even in its days of completeness. Karnak astounds, but does not awaken the sensibilities. When Egypt stood at the height of empire, when Thebes ruled over Egypt, and when Amun was supreme over all, his temple here possessed 81,000 slaves and their families, 240,000 head of cattle, 83 ships, and from 65 cities and towns their vast annual tribute in gold, silver, copper and precious stones. 'Every breath that wanders down the painted aisles of Karnak seems to echo back the sighs of those who perished in the quarry, at the oar, and under the chariot wheels of the conqueror' (Amelia Edwards). It is a grandiloquent and overbearing monument to power without spirit.

Thirteen Centuries in Stone

Apart from its size, Karnak represents a vastness of historical time. The main Temple of Amun, from the foundations of the original Middle Kingdom temple to the First Pylon built (probably) during the XXV Dynasty, saw construction over 1300 years. Comprehension of the site requires a brief historical review.

Although the war god Mont, associated with Thebes during the Old Kingdom, continued to be worshipped at Karnak, Amun achieved pre-eminence by the beginning of the Middle Kingdom and was honoured during the XII Dynasty by a series of temples facing west, the principal orientation throughout subsequent periods. All that remains of these are the alabaster foundations of what was to become the most venerable part of the extended Temple of Amun, and limestone blocks belonging to the White Chapel of

The Hypostyle Hall at Karnak

Sesostris I, recovered from the foundations of the Third Pylon and re-erected in the 'open air museum' to the north of the Great Court.

With the expulsion of the Hyksos from Egypt and the elevation of Amun to victorious national god, the early Pharaohs of the XVIII Dynasty set about turning Karnak into the principal sanctuary of their kingdom. Amenophis I and his son Tuthmosis I built chapels around the Middle Kingdom temple, while in front of it (to the west) the latter built the Fourth and Fifth Pylons and erected a pair of obelisks. Hatshepsut added two further obelisks between those of her father, chambers with carved decorations in front of the original temple, and initiated the north-south axis of the complex by building south. Her nephew Tuthmosis III continued building along the north-south axis with the Seventh and Eighth Pylons, and constructed the Festival Hall behind (to the east of) the Middle Kingdom temple.

In the century that passed between the Asian conquests of Tuthmosis III and the reign of Amenophis III, artistic and architectural restraint gave way to an overblown imperial style, expressed at Karnak by the Third Pylon built by Amenophis and his start on the great Hypostyle Hall. Empire introduced foreign influences and new wealth to the country, required an enlarged bureaucracy, and upset the status quo. Amun, who had lent his sword to Pharaoh's victories, saw the coffers of his priesthood and of the old aristocracy from which it was drawn swell with tribute, and so their power grew. But another class, which owed its very existence to empire, grew up around Pharaoh. Tuthmosis IV married an Asian princess, and her son Amenophis III married Tiy, an Egyptian commoner. Tiy was given unusual artistic prominence alongside her husband, and her parents, Yuya and Tuyu, were buried in splendour in the Valley of the Kings. Pharaoh and temple no longer represented identical interests. Before decamping to Amarna with his court of parvenus, Amenophis IV (Akhenaton as he became) did some building at the east of Karnak, where several of his statues now in the Cairo Museum were found, while some blocks now in the Luxor Museum were re-used in the foundations of later pylons and the Hypostyle Hall.

Divisions between Amun and Pharaoh's court

But the Amarna revolution did not survive the death of Akhenaton, and the reign of Tutankhamun marked the beginning of the counter-revolution which proceeded with a vengeance. The power of Amun was reaffirmed, and as though to sweep away all memory of heresy, internal conflict and the diminution of empire associated with the last Pharaohs of the XVIII Dynasty, Seti I of the XIX Dynasty declared his reign the era of 'the repeating of births', literally a renaissance. Both he and his son Ramses II outdid all that had gone before, both in architecture and in military propaganda, to make good any deficiencies in this assertion. Between them they completed the Hypostyle Hall. It remained only for later dynasties to build the Great Court and the First Pylon for Karnak to assume the form it has today. The Ptolemies embellished, and the Copts cut crosses in stones.

The XIX Dynasty made its peace with Amun, but the cost in

Amun dominates Egypt

sacrificed wealth was greater than could be borne for long without Pharaoh becoming a mere creature of the priesthood. The Hypostyle Hall, the Ramesseum, Abu Simbel, may all have glorified Ramses II, but only through Amun who long survived that long-lived Pharaoh. By the time Ramses IV (XX Dyn) came to the throne, that is 200 years after Akhenaton's resistance and only 60 years after the death of Ramses II, the Temple of Amun owned at least 7 percent of the population of Egypt and 9 percent of the land, with some estimates trebling those percentages, while the family of the High Priest of Amun directly controlled the collection of Pharaoh's taxes and management of Pharaoh's lands. Pharaoh had become no more than an instrument of a ruling oligarchy, and Karnak was its juggernaut.

Touring the Temple of Amun

You approach the maw of the beast along a short **processional way** (1) lined with ram-headed sphinxes with figures of Ramses II in mummy wrappings between their forelegs. This exactly expresses the new enveloping relationship between god and Pharaoh, for the ram was identified with Amun. A now filled-in canal once linked the temple with the Nile, giving egress during the Opet festival for gods, priests and Pharoah aboard their boats. The **First Pylon**, 113 metres wide and 43 metres high, is the largest at Karnak and nearly twice the size of the entrance pylon at the Temple of Luxor. It was probably built during the XXV (Ethiopian) Dynasty, a trumpeting echo of XIX Dynasty bombast, but left unfinished, the south tower higher than the north and neither bearing any decoration. The north (left) tower can be climbed for magnificent *views* over Karnak and the surrounding countryside.

The massive outer pylons

The **Great Court** (2) was built by the rulers of the XXII Dynasty but encloses earlier structures. Columns with papyrus bud capitals line the north and south sides of the court, while a tall doorway in the southeast corner leads to the south end of the **Second Pylon** on which is cut a scene commemorating the victory of Sheshonk I (Shishak of the Bible) over Rehoboam, son of Solomon. The pylon itself was built by Horemheb, an XVIII Dynasty general who became military dictator and finally last Pharaoh of the dynasty he had served. Like the Ninth and Tenth Pylons, also built by Horemheb, the Second Pylon made use of blocks that had once formed temples to Akhenaton's god, Aton. Continuing the palimpsest of politics, Ramses I and II cut their names on the pylon over that of Horemheb, and Ramses II had two *colossal figures* of himself in pink granite stand on either side of the pylon entrance. Of the one on the left hardly anything remains; nor does that sector of the avenue of rams which once ran through the area that became the court, to continue beyond the First Pylon towards the Nile. Instead, at the centre of the court Taharka (XXV Dynasty) built a **kiosk** (3) with ten enormous columns 21 metres high with papyrus calyx capitals, only one still standing. In the northwest quadrant of the court is the **Temple of Seti II** (4), a simple arrangement of three chapels facing south, the one at the centre to hold the

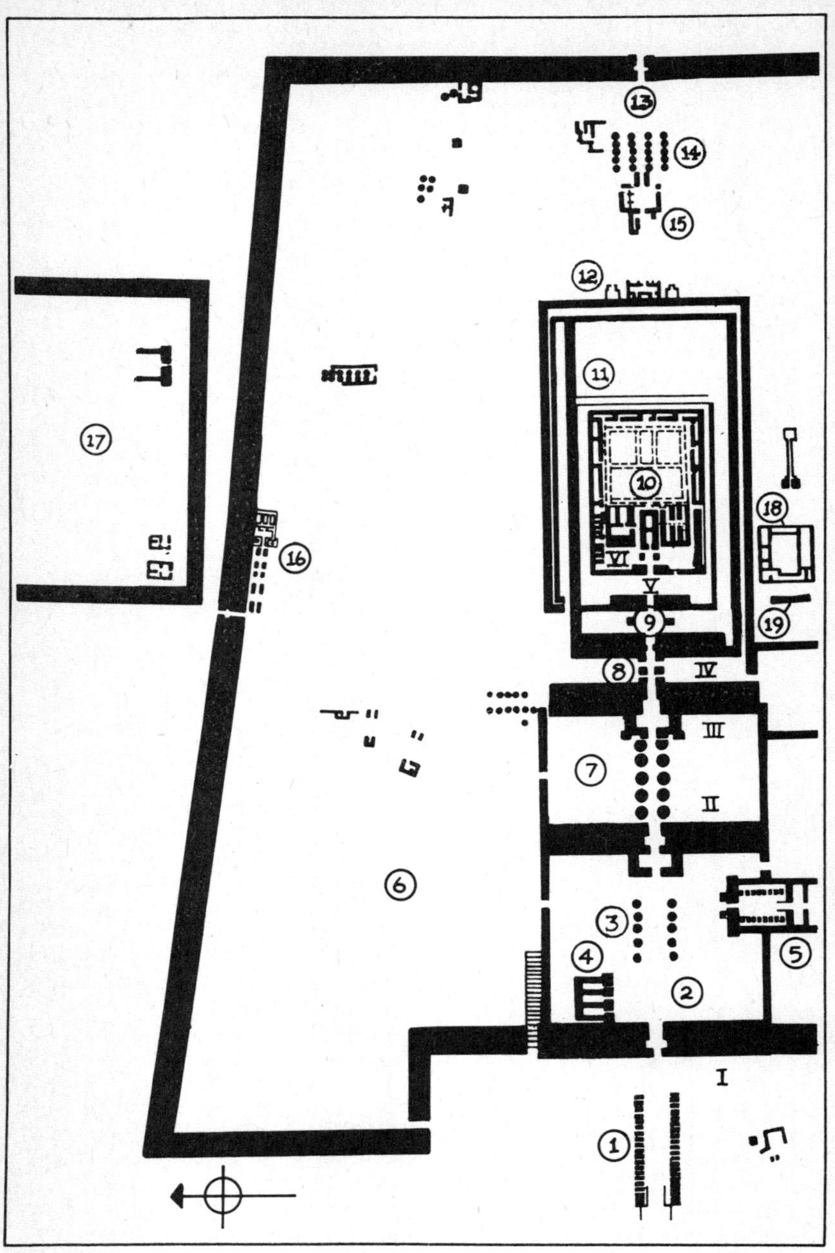

13
14
15
12
11
10
VI
V
9
8
IV
III
7
II
17
16
18
19
6
3
4
2
5
I
1

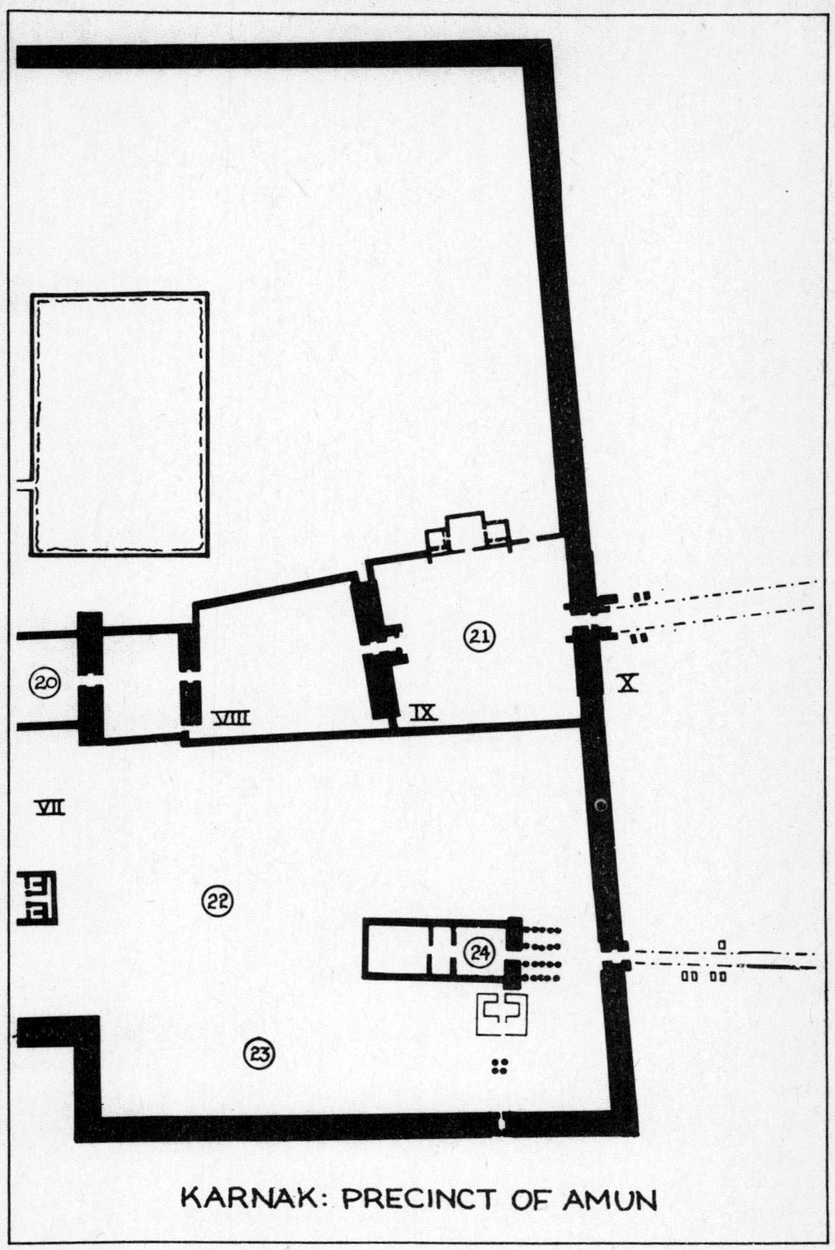

KARNAK: PRECINCT OF AMUN

sacred boat of Amun, those to the left and right to hold the boats of Mut and Khonsu, during preparations for the Opet festival. The **Temple of Ramses III** (5) intersecting the south wall of the court similarly served as a station chapel during processions and is a fine example of a simple pharaonic temple. Its pylon, facing north, is decorated with the obligatory triumphal scenes on the outside and with jubilee scenes, assuring the Pharaoh a long life, on the inside. An open court leads to a pronaos of four columns and then to a hypostyle hall of eight columns beyond which are the three boat chapels, Amun's at the centre.

A doorway on the north side of the court leads to the '**open air museum**' (6) where blocks and architectural fragments from around the site have been gathered for study. The reconstructed *White Chapel* of Sesostris I and the alabaster *Chapel of Amenophis I* are the finest 'exhibits', but entrance to the museum requires a special permit from the Director of Antiquities at Karnak. No permit is required, however, to ascend the *outside staircase* at the north end of the Firsty Pylon for views from the top.

Spectacular forest of stone

Passing through the Second Pylon, you enter the **Hypostyle Hall** (7), certainly one of the most spectacular sights in Egypt. It is the height and massiveness of the columns that is overwhelming rather than spaciousness or even rhythm or repetition of form, for on either side of the central aisle the columns are packed tightly together in overgrown forests of stone. The eye is permitted no perspective and is incapable of taking in more than a glimpse of the whole at any one moment. It is best to come early in the morning or late in the afternoon when the effect of the columns is heightened by the black diagonals of their shadows. Tourists wander round the column bases as priests and pharaohs once wandered, like ants, and the idiot in us all is enthralled. An American woman is told by a guide that the columns are fitted drums, no mortar. She pushes against a drum to observe that the column does not fall — 'Wow!' she says.

The *columns* are in fact composed of semi-drums, the 12 along the central aisle (probably originally 14) rising to 23 metres and with a girth of 15 metres. It requires six men with outstretched arms to span one of these columns. Like the papyrus columns forming the Colonnade of Amenophis III at the Temple of Luxor, these also have calyx capitals and were probably erected as a processional way. But Seti I and Ramses II elaborated on the plan by adding a further 122 columns with bud capitals, creating extensive wings on either side. The entire hall was roofed over and the 10-metre difference in height between the central and wing columns was accounted for by raising *stone lattice windows* from the architraves of the wing columns closes to the nave, providing lateral support for the higher central roof otherwise resting on the taller columns. Several of these windows, in a better of worse state of preservation, remain in place.

The central columns are richly painted and cut in sunk relief with standard temple themes, most often Pharaoh making various offerings to Amun and other Theban gods. These *cult*

Amun enjoying a high profile

scenes, with recurrent images of Amun in a state of erection (ithyphallic), are continued on the phallus-like columns of the wings, those in the north wing executed in bas-relief during the reign of Seti I, those in the south wing in the sunk relief preferred by Ramses II. The inside walls of the Hypostyle Hall are similarly decorated, but the *outside walls* proclaim the military exploits of Seti I in Palestine and Libya (north wall) and of Ramses II against the Hittites (south wall).

Of some romance in the study of ancient history is a *stele* standing upright against the west wall of the Court of the Cachette which runs into the south wall of the Hypostyle Hall: it records a treaty between Ramses II and the Hittite king. Not only is it one of the earliest codifications of international relations, but its cuneiform version (now in the Museum of the Ancient Orient, Istanbul) was found inscribed on clay tablets at the Hittite capital across the Mediterranean and when independently translated served to confirm the accuracy of the labours of philologists in the two languages.

The intimate relationship between the structure of the Temple of Amun and the development of the Egyptian state has already been outlined. It is worth noting the irony that the great columns of the Hypostyle Hall stood on bases formed of re-used blocks from the time of Akhenaton (since removed and replaced mostly by concrete) and that these in turn stood on no firmer foundation than sand. Pretension was careless of the future, though a century of archaeological engineering has made good the past. Yet though grandiosity so suited the Pharaohs of the XIX Dynasty, it is arguable that it was dictated by the temple itself. It was a canon of Egyptian temple architecture that as you approached the innermost sanctuary, perspective should narrow — that pylons and columns should get smaller, ceilings lower, and that even the temple platform should rise so that you walked upwards towards the sanctuary as walls and ceilings funnelled in around you. Once Amenophis III decided to build his Third Pylon, it had to be larger than the one before, and the Hypostyle Hall, the Second Pylon and finally the First Pylon had to grow more massive still.

Pattern of Egyptian temples

A constricted *court* lies between the **Third Pylon** of Amenophis III and the **Fourth Pylon** of Tuthmosis I, a narrow gap of space and time between traditional and imperial Egypt. When the Fourth Pylon still marked the entrance to the temple, two pairs of **obelisks** (8) were erected before it by Tuthmosis I and Tuthmosis III. Only one obelisk survives. Of the pink granite pair raised by Tuthmosis I, originally tipped with electrum (a natural alloy of gold and silver), one fell as recently as the 18th C, some of its parts lying nearby, and the other leans a little but is still stable. Beyond the Fourth Pylon the outline of the temple becomes difficult to follow. The successive pylons are closely set, and the buildings have undergone repeated alterations and suffered extensive damage. But many beautiful details reward your exploration, and the absence of both overwhelming architecture and overwhelmed tourists encourages tranquil reflection.

The numerous columns in the open space behind the Fourth Pylon suggest that this, at least in part, was a

The quarrel between Tuthmosis III and Hatshepsut

hypostyle hall. It was built by Tuthmosis III and may have been part of his extraordinary attempt to disguise the existence of Hatshepsut's two magnificent **obelisks** (9). The lower shaft of one of these remains on its base, the upper shaft lying near the northwest corner of the Sacred Lake where you can closely examine its inscriptions. The second obelisk is *in situ*, the tallest completed obelisk in Egypt and of ancient obelisks second in height only to the Lateran obelisk in Rome. It stands 29.5 metres high and was covered in electrum not only at the pyramidion but also down half its shaft, so that as its inscription tells, 'Hatshepsut made as her monument for her father Amun two great obelisks of enduring granite from the south, their upper parts, being of electrum of the best of all lands, seen on the two sides of the river. Their rays flood the two lands when the sun-disc rises between them at its appearance on the horizon of heaven'. Step-mother to Tuthmosis III and originally regent to the young Pharaoh, Hatshepsut soon proclaimed herself Pharaoh and relegated Tuthmosis to the shadows for the remainder of her life. He later showed his resentment by chopping out her name wherever he found it, and here at Karnak went to the absurd length of building a now removed sandstone structure around her obelisks to a height of 25 metres.

Symbols of Upper and Lower Egypt

The **Fifth Pylon** was also built by Tuthmosis I and leads almost immediately to the badly ruined **Sixth Pylon**, the smallest of all, built by Tuthmosis II. In the *court* beyond it he erected two tall pink granite *pillars*. Carved in high relief on their north and south sides are three lilies (south pillar) and three papyrus flower (north pillar), the heraldic plants of Upper and Lower Egypt, beautifully stylised. At the north end of the court are two colossal sandstone *statues* of Amun and his 'grammatical consort' Amonet in the likeness of Tutankhamun. Further along the main axis of the temple, on the spot where Hatshepsut's Red Chapel once stood (its quarterzite blocks engraved with scenes of the procession of the sacred boats are in the 'open air museum'), is the granite **Sanctuary of the Sacred Boats** built by the half-brother of Alexander the Great. The interior decorations in bas-relief and the exterior ones in sunk relief are finely worked and vividly coloured in yellow, red and blue. High though the standard is, however, its mock-traditional Egyptian terms were adopted by the Ptolemies for political expedience and are sadly inferior to the terms governing the greatest period of Greek art only 100 years before.

The Sanctuary

On the north side of the sanctuary, where there was much rebuilding, a *wall* erected by Hatshepsut was found concealed behind a later wall of Tuthmosis III, thus preserving the original freshness of its colouring. The wall has now been removed to a nearby room, and shows Amun, his flesh painted red and with one foot in front of the other, and also Amun in the guise of ithyphallic Min, a harvest god often amalgamated with Amun, his flesh painted black. The wall of Tuthmosis, known as the **Wall of Records**, was erected after the battle of Megiddo (Armageddon) in northern Palestine, fought in April 1479 BC. Breasted wrote of Tuthmosis that 'he was the first to build an empire in any real sense; he was

Battle of Armageddon

the first world-hero. He made, not only a world-wide impression upon his age, but an impression of a new order'. Modern political history, insofar as it tells the story of territorial imperialism, began that April day when Tuthmosis, instead of destroying his enemies, organised the vanquished into agencies of tribute and annually recorded on this wall the share that was due to Amun.

The original temple

The open space beyond the sanctuary marks the site of the original **Middle Kingdom temple** (10), its plan suggested by the remaining alabaster foundation stones.

To the east of the original temple is the **Festival Temple of Tuthmosis III** (11), and running north-south within it the Festival Hall of many columns and pillars where Tuthmosis celebrated his jubilees, those reinvigorations of temporal power and divine spirit (see Saqqara). The pillars form a rectangular cloister around a central and taller colonnade. The two rows of ten columns are unique in Egypt, affecting the form of tent poles or upturned tree trunks (as in Minoan Crete), broader above than below. The capitals, like bells or inverted calyxes, are incised and painted in patterns of overlapping leaves or of vertical stripes. The architectural suggestion is of an outdoor tent or, as echoed in stone at the Heb-Sed Court at Saqqara, of a temporary timbered building. Early in the Christian era the hall was converted into a church, and the occasional haloed saint may be discerned on its columns.

A chamber at the southwest corner of the hall contained, until taken to the Louvre, the *Table of Karnak*, a list of 57 predecessors of Tuthmosis. It is probable that statues of ancient pharaohs carried in procession were also kept here. From the northwest corner of the hall, an antechamber leads into a corridor lined with fine *reliefs* of Tuthmosis in the presence of Amun. Without the hall but in the northeast area of the Festival Temple is a small room with four papyrus bundle columns with bud capitals still supporting the architraves, though the roof is gone. This is popularly known as the *Botanic Garden* for its bas-reliefs of plants and animals seen in and perhaps brought from Syria by Tuthmosis.

Towards the East Enclosure Wall

A footbridge leads east across the remains of *enclosure walls*, and against this wall, on the axis of the main temple, is a *counter-temple* (12) facing east. Beyond this is the **east gateway** (13) to the Karnak complex, set in an outer wall of mud brick and built by Nectanebo I (XXX Dyn). From the avenue of rams before the First Pylon to this gateway, it is half a kilometre. Before exploring the breadth of the complex, have a look at the two structures standing between the counter-temple and the east gateway. The one to the east is a ruined **portico** (14) built by the same Taharka who built the kiosk in the Great Court; he placed similar structures at the north and south ends of the site, so covering the four cardinal points. Adjacent to this to the west is a small **temple** (15) built by Tuthmosis III. On the centre line of this temple is a large square base on which once stood the world's largest obelisk, the *Lateran obelisk* in Rome.

The Lateran obelisk

It was a considerable achievement for the French to get the 22.5-metre high obelisk of Ramses II from the Temple of Luxor to the Place de la Concorde in the 1830s, yet the giant 32.3-metre obelisk that stood at this small temple at Karnak was removed by order of the Emperor Constantine in the 4th C AD, consigned originally to Constantinople but having its course changed upon the Emperor's death and delivered to Rome instead where it was erected in the Circus Maximus in AD 357. It fell or more probably was toppled some centuries later, but in 1588 was re-erected in the Piazza San Giovanni in Laterano. Hieroglyphs on its shaft state that Tuthmosis III 'made as his monument for his father Amun-Re, Lord of the Thrones of the Two Lands, the setting up for him of a single obelisk in the Upper Court of the Temple in the neighbourhood of Karnak, on the very first occasion of setting up a single obelisk in Thebes'. It is stressed that the erection of a single obelisk was unusual, and it is probable that the Lateran obelisk comes from the same quarry of pink granite as that in which the great unfinished obelisk at Aswan still lies, and that the unfinished obelisk, until faults in the stone were discovered, was intended to complete the pair.

The North Complex Area

The Temple of Ptah and the Precinct of Mont at the north end of the Karnak complex are reached by a winding path that leads from the north wall of the Great Court of the Temple of Amun. The ground is overgrown and barely excavated.

Against the north enclosure wall and shaded by palms, the **Temple of Ptah** (16) is approached through an east-west series of five doorways. If the inner doorway is locked, call to what looks like a sentry tower atop the mud brick wall. Shout. The keeper is probably asleep and will have to put on his galabiyya before coming down to let you in. Each of the doorways is carved with scenes and texts of the Ptolemaic period. The fifth doorway leads into a columned vestibule; to the rear is a small pylon marking the entrance to the temple proper. Beyond the antechamber are three chapels dating from the reign of Tuthmosis III, and most unusually the *cult statue of Ptah* (with head missing) is still in the middle chapel; while in the chapel to the right is the startling apparition of *Sekhmet*, her bare-breasted body surmounted by the head of a lioness. The keeper will close the doors to enhance the eerie effect of the single shaft of sunlight from an aperture in the roof casting a greenish glow within.

Eerie cult statues

A gateway (also often locked) leads through the enclosure wall to the **Precinct of Mont** (17), god of war, its structures largely dilapidated and only of specialist interest. The main temple, totally ruined, was built by Amenophis III.

The South Complex Area

Exploration of the south end of the Karnak complex can begin at the **Sacred Lake**, restored and cemented. A grand-stand at its east end is where visitors sit for the culmination of the *son et lumiere*. Near the northwest corner is a giant *scarab* dedicated by Amenophis III to Atum, the god of the rising sun. Also here is the base with underground chambers of an **Osireion** (18) built by Taharka, and the broken-off top of Hatshepsut's other **obelisk** (19). On the pyramidion a kneeling Hatshepsut is being blessed by Amun: his figure was recut by Seti I within the gouge caused by Akhenaton's attempt to obliterate the god of his priestly opponents.

At the south ends of the Third and Fourth Pylons of the Temple of Amun begins the second (north-south) axis of the Karnak complex, a *processional way* consisting of a series of open courts bounded by walls along their east and west sides and separated from each other by pylons. The Seventh and Eighth Pylons led originally to a Middle Kingdom temple and a temple of Amenophis I which both stood in what is now the Court of the Cachette. The temples were taken down by Tuthmosis III, but not before he had erected the Seventh Pylon. A large votive pit in the **Court of the Cachette** (20) was excavated early this century and found to contain several thousand bronze statues and 800 of stone. The best are on display in the Cairo Museum.

Considerable restoration work is being carried out along the north-south axis and the pylons may be closed off to the public. Nevertheless, the keepers will not hesitate to show you around for some baksheesh, and will lead you up the inner stairways to the tops of the pylons, or encourage you to follow them as they leap like goats across deep gaps in the towers and walls.

Seven *statues of Middle Kingdom pharaohs* stand or sit before the north face of the **Seventh Pylon**, while on its south side are the remains of two *colossi of Tuthmosis III*. On the outside of the east wall between this and the Eighth Pylon is an interesting **relief of the High Priest of Amenophis**, his arms raised as though adoring Ramses IX (XX Dyn), who extends his palm in a reciprocal gesture. The very presence of the High Priest, adoring or not, is unusual, but it is revealing that the priest is as large as the Pharaoh and is even the focus of the composition. The relief is a vivid illustration of how much priestly power and arrogance had grown within a century after the reign of the great Ramses II.

Evidence of priestly power

The **Eighth Pylon** was built by Hatshepsut and, though the oldest part of the north-south axis, is well preserved. On its south side a *relief* shows Amenophis II slaughtering his enemies, while of the original six *colossi* on this side of the pylon, four remain, the figure of Amenophis I, on the left, the most complete.

The **Ninth and Tenth Pylons** were built by Horemheb in part with blocks from buildings erected by Akhenaton in honour of Aton. In front of the north side of the west tower is a *stele* erected by Horemheb proclaiming the restoration of the Amun orthodoxy. On the east side of the court between the Ninth and Tenth Pylons is a small **temple** built by Amenophis II, probably for his jubilee, with a graceful portico of square pillars. The fine bas-reliefs inside the hall, some of their colouring well preserved, show Amenophis before various deities. On the *interior wall of the court* between this temple and the Tenth Pylon, Horemheb is shown in relief leading captives from Punt bearing gifts for the Theban triad, and to the right of this he appears with fettered Syrian captives.

Both claims of foreign triumph are almost certainly false, at best mere conventions, for Horemheb is known to have spent most of his energies imposing law, order and the old religion on post-Amarna Egypt, while there is no evidence at all that he led his armies abroad.

From the Tenth Pylon an **avenue of sphinxes** (21) runs for several hundred metres to the **Precinct of Mut**, still not entirely excavated and all the more picturesque for its ruins rising from the overgrown scrub. Consort of Amun and originally a vulture goddess, Mut was depicted during the New Kingdom with the skin of a vulture on her wig. Approached through a propylaeum cut with Ptolemaic cartouches, her badly ruined temple, built by Amenophis III, consists of two courts, a hypostyle hall and sanctuary. All around it, rising from the scrub, are *figures of Sekhmet*, the lion goddess, beautifully worked and with care taken to use the pink veins in the bluish granite to highlight certain features such as the *ankh* sign or the goddess's breasts. A *sacred lake* enwraps the temple and across it, to the west, is a *temple of Ramses III*. Another *temple, of Amenophis III*, is in the northeast corner of the precinct.

Goddesses in the grass

But still within the main Karnak enclosure, in the south west corner, is the **Temple of Khonsu** (22), the moon god son of Mut and Amun. It faces south towards the Gateway of Euergetes and so towards the avenue of rams which disappears beneath village houses before emerging again before the entrance pylon of the Temple of Luxor. For the most part in a good state of preservation, its simplicity and clarity of layout make it a classic of New Kingdom architecture. It was started by Ramses III, though possibly completed and certainly almost entirely decorated by his successors down to Herihor (XXI Dyn), who like Horemheb rose from the army to seize power as Pharaoh, and went one better by making himself High Priest of Amun as well (see Gurna). The *pylon* is small but well proportioned, and decorated with a variety of religious scenes. On the *rear wall of the first court*, to the right, is a carving of the temple facade, banners flying. To the left is Herihor performing rites before the boats of the Theban triad. Beyond this is a small transverse hypostyle hall leading to the dilapidated sanctuary. Walking through its centre chapel once containing the sacred boat of Khonsu, you come to a small hall of four columns with reliefs of Ramses IV, but also, on either side of the entrance, Augustus. From the southeast corner of the sanctuary a staircase leads up to the roof, from which there are good views of the ruins.

Immediately to the west is the smaller **Temple of Opet** (23), a hippopotamus goddess and mother of Osiris. It was left unfinished by Euergetes II, though otherwise finely decorated throughout the Ptolemaic period and into the reign of Augustus.

Ptolemaic exit

You can now leave the Karnak site through the **Gateway of Euergetes I** (24), its concave cornice adorned with a winged sun disc.

PRACTICAL INFORMATION

A **carriage** to Karnak should cost around LE1.50 and a bargain can be struck for having the driver wait for your return. Go one way along the corniche, return along the back road which traces the old sacred way.

An **abbreviated tour** should cover the Temple of Amun, ie from the First Pylon to the Sixth Pylon and the Sanctuary.

The Karnak temples complex is open from 7am to 5pm (LE3). The **Son et Lumiere** (LE4) lasts 90 minutes and starts at 6pm and, when there is a second performance, again at 8pm.

The performances are in varying languages:
Sunday: French, then German.
Monday: English.
Tuesday: French, then German.
Wednesday: English, then French.
Thursday: Arabic.
Friday: English, then French.
Saturday: English, then French.

Note that the Arabic performance costs only 25PT and gives you the pleasure of the *lumiere* without the drivel of the *son*, at least none that you are likely to understand. It is a saving well worth making.

The performance starts at the Processional Way lined with rams; the spectators are led through the First Pylon, the Great Court, and into the Hypostyle Hall. They are then seated by the Sacred Lake for the final treatment.

THE NECROPOLIS OF THEBES

Visiting the West bank

Because of the intense heat of the afternoon, it is usual to cross over to the west bank of the Nile very early in the morning and to complete your explorations by about one o'clock. If you do not mind the heat, there is no reason not to stay until the tombs close at 6 o'clock. Certainly you will have fewer fellow tourists to contend with, and if pedalling your own bicycle the breeze and dry air will evaporate the heat away. The disadvantage of a bicycle is the long incline to the Valley of the Kings, and then not being able to walk over the escarpment and down to Deir el Bahri, the Temple of Hatshepsut. So that expedition is best done by car: the driver will leave you at the Valley of the Kings and collect you later at Hatshepsut's temple. All the rest of the west bank should be covered by bicycle if you are up to it; it leaves time on your hands and frees you from the impatient harrassment of your driver. Distances can be long and donkeys are recommended only for those seeking the perversely picturesque.

In the bad old days, when donkeys were the only means of getting about the west bank, there was a wonderful Cook's dragoman called Mohammed Aboudi, who later opened a shop in Luxor and published a near to useless and vastly entertaining guide. Alas, neither is extant. But for a while Aboudi was private secretary to Cole Porter both in Europe and in Egypt, and it was perhaps this connection which encouraged Aboudi to leaven his guide book with his own poetry. It deserves what further lease on life I can provide; for example:

O East is East and West is West in Luxor or in London town;
But Aboudi, our faithful Aboudi, will never let us down.
Through all the plagues of Egypt, donkey-boys, the flies, the sand,
This trusty modern Moses leads us toward the Promised Land.
Weird tales of long dead ages come tripping from his tongue,
With him through tombs and temples we pass in wondering throng.
And when foot and brain are weary with the sights we've come to see,
He calls our patient donkeys up to bear us home to tea.
Surely in future ages the tourists all will stand,
An unabridged edition of Rosetta in each hand,
And read the hieroglyphics which proclaim how Pharaoh's Cook,
By his henchman, great Aboudi, mighty hosts through Egypt took!

★ ★ ★

There's one thing more, if you can stick it:
The law of this land is very intricate.
At each temple gate is an Arab picket,
So please don't forget your little ticket;
And galloping donkeys is not allowed!

Ferries, and car and donkey hire

Before leaving the east bank, it is a good idea to ask at Thomas Cook or one of the other travel offices about the going rate for car and donkey hire on the other side to prepare yourself for the bargaining that is about to come. The 'tourist ferries' leave from the corniche opposite the main hotels and disembark you at the ticket kiosk downstream on the west bank. If you take what the locals call the 'people ferry', you will be landed near a village a bit upstream from the kiosk. Either way, you will have to decide as soon as you land what tombs and temples you want to see and purchase the appropriate tickets by the river bank: you cannot buy them at the sites. While you are doing this, you will be accosted by every car driver and donkey-boy in sight. Strike what you know to be a fair bargain, and do not pay until your visit is complete.

Outline of the tour

A tour of the necropolis involves following a north-south arc, starting at either end. If you want to follow the path from the Valley of the Kings to Deir el Bahri, you should start at the north, visiting first the Temple of Seti I, continuing thence to the Valley of the Kings, Deir el Bahri, the Tombs of the Nobles, the Ramesseum, the Valley of the Queens, Medinet Habu and back to the river via the Colossi of Memnon. This guide describes the tour in that order.

And dangers enroute

While not wishing to inhibit the curiosity of travellers, it is worth mentioning that on either side of the river here, as at Saqqara, care should be taken at excavations and you should not get off the beaten track if exploring on your own. I cite a recent newspaper report: 'The mystery of a Canadian woman's disappearance 2 years ago at Luxor was unravelled this week when police located her remains in an archaeological ditch. Before dying she had scribbled on a post card that she fell inside the labyrinth after losing her way, and she was preparing herself for death from thirst and hunger. The police located her skeleton this week, her clothes still on, in a distant area behind the pharaonic temples where archaeological digs were underway'.

The New and Old Villages of Gurna

From the west bank landing stage the road runs to the **new village of Gurna** and continues on past the Colossi of Memnon towards the Theban Mountain. At the village another road runs north towards the Temple of Seti I. Built in the late 1940s, the new village, with plumbing, theatre and recreation centre, was designed to lure the modern Thebans down from their old village of Gurna spread across the nobles' tombs. Until recently, all enticement failed, and even now only ill is spoken of new Gurna. Constructed in the traditional way out of mud brick, the houses fall down and are infested with scarabs say the villagers. Nor are they as cool in summer as the rock tombs which serve as convenient extensions to many of the older houses. It seems the familiar argument between new and old, but there is a twist. Over the past 3000 years or more, easy access to the Theban tombs has provided villagers on the west bank with an extra source of income. It was partly to check this that the new village was built, and for this same reason that new Gurna is so much resented. **Old Gurna** at the foot of the Theban Mountain has not yet been entirely abandoned, nor entirely has been tomb robbing.

Modern tomb robbing

There are at least 900 tombs built into the rock. The authorities say all have been checked and locked. But there are constant rumours of secret finds beneath the houses and even the wall paintings in known tombs are occasionally removed. The modern heydey for tomb robbers was a century ago with the explosion in Europe and America of archaeological and tourist interest in ancient Egypt. Luxor saw a roaring trade in tablets, statuettes and scarabs, both real and faked — home-made scarabs were fed to turkeys to 'acquire by the simple process of digestion a degree of venerableness that is really charming', wrote one visitor. Mummies were dragged out of their tombs and unrolled, stripped of their valuables, broken up and left to crumble in the sands. In earlier centuries, mummy cases were chopped up for firewood, and from at least the 13th C through to the 19th C 'mummy' was highly regarded in Europe for its medicinal properties, the export demand sometimes proving so great that Egyptians often substituted modern corpses. In *The Innocents Abroad*, Mark Twain wrote of the Egyptian railways: 'The fuel they use for the locomotive is composed of mummies three thousand years old, purchased by the ton or by the graveyard for that purpose. . . .Sometimes one hears the profane engineer call out pettishly, "Damn these plebeians, they don't burn worth a cent — pass out a king"'.

Not that the humble quest for loot has always been without its larger benefits, or that even the poorest Egyptians have not sometimes shown respect for the objects of their peculations. In an effort to save their royal masters from contemporary tomb robbers, priests in the XXI Dynasty removed the mummies from their tombs in the Valley of the Kings and stacked them, 30 in a shaft, in a nearby rocky cleft. In 1875, Abdel-Rasul, sheikh of Gurna, found the cache and kept it secret for six years, selling off bits and pieces as he needed money. Archaeologists traced these clues to their source, and the mummies are those until recently on display in the Mummy Room of the Cairo Museum. As these long-dead Pharaohs sailed down the Nile by steamer, fellahin lined the banks at village after village, the women ululating in lament, the men firing their rifles in homage.

A case of looting in pharaonic times

Under the powerful Pharaohs of the XVIII and XIX Dynasties local officials were closely supervised and tomb looting kept in check. But under the weaker rulers of the XX Dynasties tombs were robbed. A picture of surprising detail can be built up from surviving papyri of the necropolis workers enduring food shortages and late payments of wages, of riots, pay disputes and strikes. There are also documented accounts of bribery and collusion amongst workers, priests and officials. One papyrus describes a major Theban law case during the reign of Ramses IX (XX Dyn) in

At Gurna: this housholder has made the pilgrimage to Mecca

which the mayor of Thebes brought to the vizier's attention stories of tomb robbing at the necropolis. The matter was investigated by the chief of the necropolis police and the stories denied; the vizier then ensured that the mayor of Thebes was disgraced for making malicious and politically inspired accusations. Some years later, however, as the tomb robbings continued, the case was reopened and it became clear that both the vizier and the chief of police were up to their eyeballs in corruption. Examined by birch and screw, the stonemason Amun-pa-nefer admitted tunnelling into a royal tomb and stripping the Pharaoh and his Queen of gold, silver and precious stones. 'And we made the gold which we had found on these two gods — from their mummies, amulets, ornaments and coffins — into eight shares. And two kilos of gold fell to each of us.'

Amun-pa-nefer then described the chain of corruption: 'We then crossed over to Thebes. And after some days, the agents of Thebes heard that we had been stealing in the west, so they arrested me and imprisoned me at the mayor of Thebes' place. So I took the two kilos of gold that had fallen to me as my share, and gave them to Kha-em-Opet, the District Clerk of the harbour of Thebes. He let me go, and I joined my companions, and they made up for me another share. And I, as well as the other robbers who are with me, have continued to this day in the practice of robbing the tombs of the nobles and people of the land who rest in the west of Thebes. And a large number of the men of the land rob them also'. Presumably the bribe was shared out amongst other officials higher up the ladder, though no share falling to the mayor of Thebes who was either an honest man or complained because he was being cut out of the action.

The case has its anecedotal interest, but it throws light too on the causes underlying the enfeeblement of the New Kingdom from the XX Dynasty on. In describing Karnak it was mentioned how an ever greater proportion of the nation's wealth went to the priesthood; much gold and silver was also literally buried underground in the tombs, taken out of circulation. Yet it was precisely at this time that the world was shifting from the Bronze Age to the Iron Age, and while Egypt had copper mines, she had no iron — the essential metal for weapon superiority. Under the Empire, iron could be expropriated abroad; as the rule of the Pharaohs weakened and the Empire shrank, Egypt was forced to buy iron abroad, payment to be made in gold and silver. The value of these precious metals rose during the period 1160 to 1110 BC (Ramses V through Ramses X, approximately). Food shortages and wage delays followed; the necropolis workers struck and many of them turned to tomb robbing. The bonanza of precious metals and stones they clawed back from the tombs and put into circulation — however corrupt the channels might have been — soon relieved the situation. By that time, however, the Empire was finished, the moral authority of the administration had been sapped, and power fell to Herihor, a general who became military dictator, assumed the High Priesthood of Amun and made himself Pharaoh and founder of the XXI Dynasty. His power extended only over Upper Egypt however; Lower Egypt was ruled by merchant princes at Tanis and the country was never long united again.

Iron Age economic crisis

Rise and Fall

Even more so than Karnak, the tombs and mortuary temples of the Theban necropolis tell of the rise and fall of the New Kingdom and the Egyptian Empire.

The **Mortuary Temple of Seti I** (XIX Dyn) lies off the road to the Valley of the Kings and is usually bypassed by tourists in haste. This in itself should recommend it; also that the works of Seti's reign — most famously his temple at Abydos — are amongst the finest and most restrained of the New Kingdom. The temple was founded in honour of Amun, but also devoted to the worship of Seti's father, Ramses I. The first two pylons and courts have been destroyed; what remains is the temple proper and a tour of it is made both at ground level and, the better to see certain reliefs, by leaping goatlike after the resident guide, from architrave to broken architrave.

A colonnade facing east towards the Nile admits, through a central door, to a *hypostyle hall* with six columns decorated with reliefs of Seti and Ramses II making offerings to divinities. On either side of the hall are small *chapels* with very fine reliefs of Seti, his ka, his sacred boat, Thoth and Osiris, as he offers sacrifices and performs ceremonies enroute to the afterlife.

The *sanctuary*, once containing Amun's sacred boat, lies beyond. Reliefs show Seti offering incense before the boat. To the left (south) of the hypostyle hall is the *chapel of Ramses I*. On the side walls of the central chamber, Seti is again depicted offering incense to Amun's boat, and anoints a statue of Ramses I with his finger. The chambers on either side were given inferior reliefs by Ramses II. The right (north) side of the temple is ruinous; a larger hall, dedicated to Re-Herakhte, was built by Ramses II and decorated with crude reliefs.

Flawed renaissance

The obsessive appropriations of Ramses II and their inferior quality stand out amongst the works of Seti I who consciously sought a renaissance in taste and values. But then Seti's own reliefs suffer from the New Kingdom preoccupation with gaining access to the afterlife: they are reassuring encounters with the gods at death, but do not concern themselves with the quality of life. If not yet in empire, certainly in spirit Egypt was in retreat.

To the Valley of the Kings

The flat alluvium suddenly quits and it is utter desert to the Valley of the Kings. On a barren hill where the road from Seti's temple is joined by the road from Deir el Bahri sits a large domed boulder of a **house where Howard Carter lived** during his search for the tomb of Tutankhamun. The road climbs towards the oven of white sand and sun that is Biban el Muluk — the 'Gates of the Kings'. Unblinking tomb entrances stare vacantly from the close valley walls. Each ramp is cut and swept, each doorway numbered in order of discovery. The most exclusive suburb in the world, where the mightiest dead once lay in silent, motionless expectation of awakening. Anxious priests, covetous archaeologists, and robbers caring more for life than life after, carried them away. Anubis and Osiris remain, paintings on the walls.

Better than Beverly Hills

Burials at the **Valley of the Kings** date from the XVIII through the XX Dynasties, with Tuthmosis I being the first to select the site. Though the Pharaohs and, rarely, certain exalted but non-royal personages were entombed here, offerings to the dead were made at the mortuary temples built on the plain. The tombs therefore were entirely private receptacles for the sarcophagus, and their decoration concentrated exclusively on the formulae efficacious in transferring the deceased from this world into the next. The tombs and their decorations can be impressive, and their contents of course were staggering, but they do not speak of life, of humanity, or even of personal death and resurrection — they are monuments of state and of ideology, and less vivid, less revealing than the tombs of the lesser dead elsewhere in the Theban necropolis.

Tomb construction and decoration

A similar pattern of construction and decoration is followed in each of the tombs. Three corridors lead to an antechamber giving onto the main hall with its sunken floor for receiving the sarcophagus. The tombs were cut into the soft limestone by two teams of 25 men working alternating ten-day shifts. They normally lived at Deir el Medina, but when on shift stayed in huts within the valley. Construction of a tomb began at the beginning of a reign and never took more than six years to completion. Once the interior surfaces were prepared, the designs and inscriptions were sketched in black; the designs filled in, the hieroglyphs outlined, in red; the decorations carved and finally painted. In some tombs, notably that of Horemheb (57), these various stages of decoration are evident.

Decorative themes

The dead Pharaoh, absorbed in the sun god, sailed through the underworld at night in a boat, with enemies and dangers to be avoided along the way. This is the recurrent theme of the decorations, the inscriptions being extensive quotations from the Amduat or Book of the Underworld and the Book of the Gates which provide instructions for charting the course. Pictorially, there are three registers, the middle one showing the river of passage, the top and bottom registers depicting the shores with their inhabitants of deities and demons. The registers are divided into 12 sections for the 12 hours of the night. The Book of Day and Night is also sometimes employed: after this nocturnal voyage the naked body of the goddess Nut gives birth each morning to the sun. This is beautifully represented in the sarcophagus hall of the tomb of Ramses VI.

Visiting the Tombs of the Pharaohs

In all, 62 tombs are known in the Valley of the Kings. A few of these were known and visited by tourists in Ptolemaic times as indicated by Diodorus and Strabo and the occasional Greek and Latin graffiti. Most are of little interest except to scholars and are closed to the public. Only tombs 2, 6, 8, 9, 11, 16, 17, 34, 35, 57 and 62 have electric lighting, and most visitors will be content to see those of *Tutankhamun (62), Ramses VI (9), Seti I (17)* and *Ramses IV (2)*, and then possibly the tombs of *Amenophis II (35)* and *Horemheb (57)*. Not all of even these tombs will necessarily be open when you visit. The identity of all 62 tombs is given on the accompanying map, but only those electrically lit are described below.

1. Ramses VII
2. Ramses IV
3. Intended for Ramses III
4. Ramses XII
5. Intended for Ramses II
6. Ramses IX
7. Ramses II
8. Merneptah
9. Ramses VI
10. Amenmeses
11. Ramses III
12. No inscriptions
13. Intended for royal functionary
14. Tausert, wife of Seti II
15. Seti II
16. Ramses I
17. Seti I
18. Ramses X
19. Son of Ramses IX
20. Hatshepsut
21. Unfinished
22. Amenophis III (in the Western Valley)
23. Ay (in the Western Valley)

24 & 25. No inscriptions (in the Western Valley)

26 to 33. Unfinished

34. Tuthmosis III
35. Amenophis II
36. Maherpra, fan-bearer to Hatshepsut (contents in Cairo Museum)
37. No inscriptions
38. Tuthmosis I

39 to 41. No inscriptions

42. Possibly Tuthmosis II
43. Tuthmosis IV
44. No inscription
45. Private tomb
46. Yuya and Tuyu, parents of Queen Tiy, wife of Amenophis III (contents in Cairo Museum).
47. Siptah
48. Vizier Amenemopet

49 to 54. No inscriptions

55. Tiy or Smenkhkare
56. No inscriptions
57. Horemheb
58. Tutankhamun annex

59 to 61. No inscriptions

62. Tutankhamun

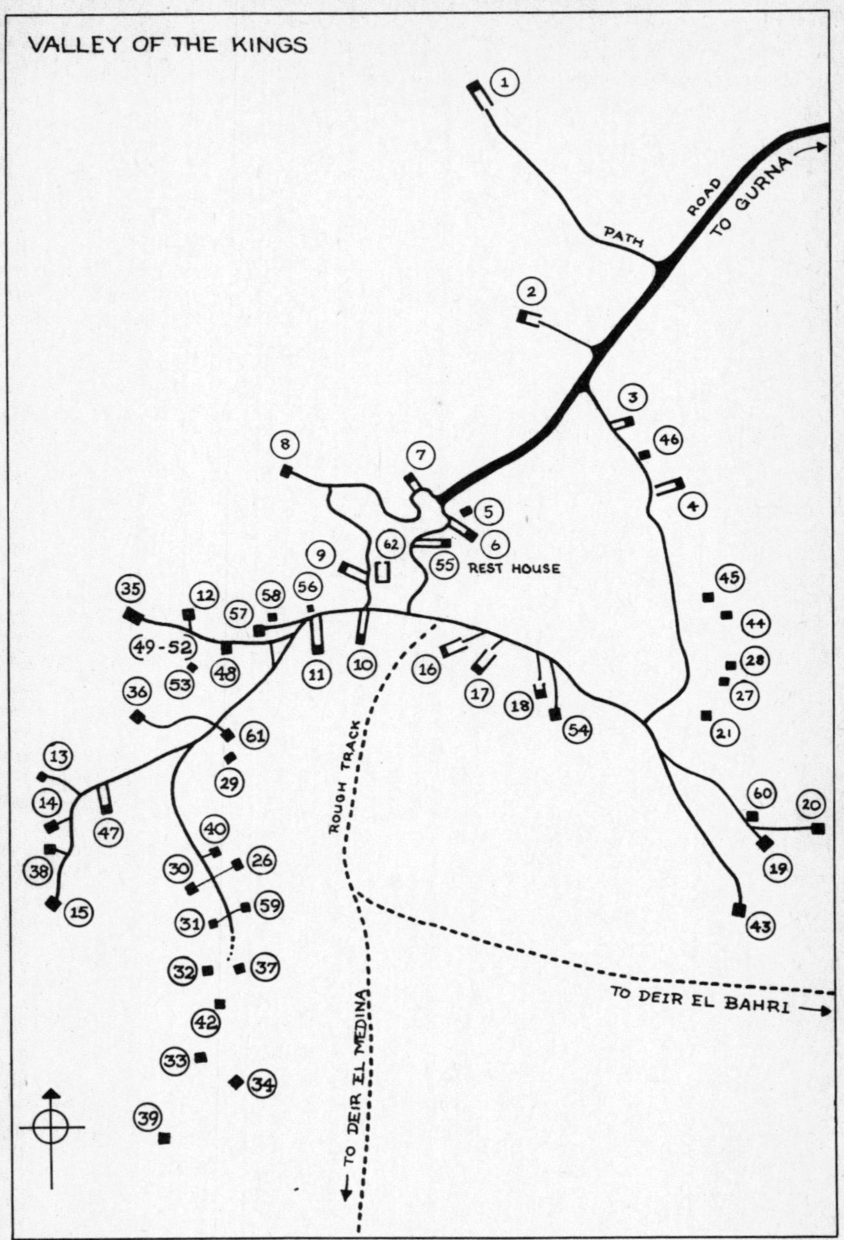

VALLEY OF THE KINGS
PATH
ROAD
TO GURNA
REST HOUSE
ROUGH TRACK
TO DEIR EL MEDINA
TO DEIR EL BAHRI
1
2
3
4
5
6
7
8
9
10
11
12
13
14
15
16
17
18
19
20
21
26
27
28
29
30
31
32
33
34
35
36
37
38
39
40
42
43
44
45
46
47
48
49-52
53
54
55
56
57
58
59
60
61
62

Ramses IV: brilliantly lit

Tomb 2: Ramses IV (XX Dyn). Only electrified and therefore made more accessible to the public in 1983, the bright and excellent lighting of this tomb contributes towards a favourable impression — for though the decorations are third rate the overall effect is entirely enjoyable. There is much Ptolemaic and Coptic graffiti throughout, though particularly by the entrance; robbed in antiquity, Ramses' body never found, the tomb remained long open to the curious. Steps and then three high white corridors descend gently in a straight line to the sarcophagus chamber. The ceiling here is decorated with the goddess Nut in duplicate. The huge sarcophagus of pink granite is covered with texts and magical scenes, while Isis and Nephthys on the lid were meant to protect the hijacked body — the empty sarcophagus has been retrieved from the tomb of Amenophis II where the priests had hidden it. Throughout the chambers and corridors of the tomb, against all the whiteness, are small patterns of red, blue, yellow and some green pastels and this is pleasing, despite the poor carving and line and the sloppy application of colour. Indeed this slapdash effect has a quality of gaieté, as though the whole affair was a French reproduction.

Tomb 6: Ramses IX (XX Dyn). A flight of steps on either side of an inclined plane leads you down to the tomb door, its lintel decorated with the solar disc, the Pharaoh worshipping it on both sides. Behind him stands Isis (left) and Nephthys (right). The tomb is of near-model design: three corridors, an antechamber, but then a pillared hall and short passage before the final sarcophagus chamber. The decorations are similar to those in Tomb 9.

Tomb 8: Merneptah (XIX Dyn). Pharaoh of the Exodus, Merneptah's tomb descends steeply through corridor steps. Such descents are typical of XVIII and XIX Dynasty tombs; those of the XX Dynasty are shallower. Over the entrance, Isis and Nephthys worship the sun disc, while the entrance corridors are decorated with scenes from the Book of the Gates and other texts. In the small antechamber is the huge granite lid of the outer sarcophagus; a further flight of steps leads down to a pillared hall with barrelled roof containing the pink granite lid of the inner sarcophagus. Carved on the lid is the recumbent figure of Merneptah as Osiris.

Ramses VI: extensive funerary texts

Tomb 9: Ramses VI (XX Dyn). Though decorated in sunk relief of workmanship inferior to that of the previous dynasty, the colouring remains fresh. The tomb was originally constructed for Ramses V and ended with *Chamber E*. On the left walls of this part of the tomb is the complete text of the Book of the Gates with a summary of the creation of the world on the left part of the rear wall of *E*. Another text, the Book of Caverns, decorates the right walls, while the ceilings of *C*, *D* and *E* are decorated with the Book of Day and Night. *Corridors F* and *G* show the hours from the Amduat on their walls. In *Chamber H* are portions of the Book of the Dead; on the left wall is chapter 125, the declaration of innocence. The pillared *Chamber I* contains fragments of the great granite sarcophagus. Its vaulted ceiling is splendidly painted with the Book of Day and Night, the sky goddess Nut appearing twice, back to back, framing the Book of Day on the entrance side, and on the far side the Book of Night.

Tomb 11: Ramses III (XX Dyn). One of the largest tombs in the valley, the second half is ruinous and not illuminated. Once again the decorations are inferior sunk relief, but they are exceptionally varied and remain freshly coloured. This is sometimes called the 'Harpers' Tomb' after the two harpers playing to divinities in the last of four small chambers opening off the left-hand side of the second corridor. This tomb is unique in having ten side-chambers off its entrance corridors; where they do occur in tombs, they were for receiving tomb furniture. Beyond these the tomb turns to the right and then to the left and the third chamber along is a sloping passage with side galleries and four pillars: the perspective through here to the rooms beyond is impressive.

Tomb 16: Ramses I (XIX Dyn). Though founder of his dynasty, Ramses I reigned for only a year or two and was interred in a simple tomb. A sloping corridor and steep flight of steps leads to a single almost square chamber containing the open sarcophagus. The decoration — painted, not carved — is brilliantly coloured on grey ground. The Pharaoh is variously shown with Maat, Ptah, Osiris, Anubis and other deities, and portions of the Book of the Gates are depicted (on the left wall, notice the 12 goddesses representing the hours of the night).

Seti I: superb decorations

Tomb 17: Seti I (XIX Dyn). At 100 metres, this is the longest tomb in the valley. Its reliefs are wonderfully preserved and so beautifully executed that they rival the famous decorations in Seti's temple at Abydos. Beneath a ceiling painted with vultures flying towards the back of the tomb, the walls of *Corridor A* are decorated on the left with Seti before the falcon-headed Re-Herakhte, god of the morning sun. The sun in other forms, as disc, scarab and ram-headed god follows, and the text of the Sun Litany continues on the right wall. This and other texts are continued in *Corridor B* with staircase. On the upper part of the recess in the left wall are represented 37 forms of the sun god. *Corridor C* is decorated with the fourth (right) and fifth (left) hours of the night from the Amduat. In *Chamber D* the Pharaoh is shown on four walls in the presence of various deities. *Chambers E and F* show the Pharaoh on each side of the square pillars with a deity. The wall decorations are various hours from the Book of the Gates. The pattern of construction and decoration of the tomb so far is now in a general sense repeated , with *G, H* and *I* coresponding to *B, C* and *D. Corridors G and H* are decorated with the Ritual of the Opening of the Mouth which ensured that the mummy's organs were functioning, particularly to permit eating and drinking. The decorations in *Chamber I* are similar to those in *D. Chamber J* is in two parts, the first a pillared hall with hours from the Book of the Gates on the walls, the second with the Amduat on the walls and astronomical figures on the vaulted ceiling. The northern constellation here was intended to permit Seti to orient himself with the sun. The sarcophagus (now in the Sir John Soane Museum, London) rested in the depression in this second part; a passage behind runs for 46 metres, apparently to nowhere. A side room, *K*, to the right, is known as the Chamber of the Cow for its representation of the sky goddess Nut in the form of a cow. The texts here recount the myth of the destruction of mankind, the Egyptian equivalent of the Mesopotamian and Biblical story of the Flood.

Tomb 34: Tuthmosis II (XVIII Dyn). At the far end of the rising valley and requiring a steep climb up wooden steps to reach the entrance, and then a steep descent within, this tomb is unusual for the rounded shape of the sarcophagus chamber. A pit that you now cross by footbridge in one of the approach corridors was probably meant to deter tomb robbers, though later the priests removed Tuthomosis' mummy to a rocky cleft (see Gurna) for safekeeping; it is now in the Cairo Museum, though the red granite sarcophagus remains *in situ*.

Tomb 35: Amenophis II (XVIII Dyn). This tomb is unadorned except for the sarcophagus chamber, approached by a long corridor and steep flights of steps. A shaft at *A* is crossed by a modern gangway leading to *Chamber B* with unfinished walls. The walls of the *Sarcophagus Chamber C* are painted yellow in imitation of papyrus and bear the complete text of the Amduat as though inscribed on a continuous scroll. The blue ceiling is painted with yellow stars. The tomb was not discovered until 1898. Amenophis' mummy was found *in situ,* a floral garland still round its neck, and was only removed to the Cairo Museum in 1934. The quartzite sarcophagus was left in the tomb. Three mummies were found in side room *D,* and nine royal mummies, hidden there by priests, were found in room *E.* These last included Tuthmosis IV, Amenophis III and Seti II, now all in the Cairo Museum. It is to the late discovery of the tomb that the survival and identification of these mummies is owed.

Tomb 57: Horemheb (XVIII Dyn). The plan is almost identical to that of Tomb 17 (Seti I) and some of the decorations are finely executed. The principal interest, however, is in the partially finished work, showing the various stages of decoration.

Tomb 62: Tutankhamun (XVIII Dyn). This most famous of Egyptian tombs is neither large nor impressively decorated. It bears all the marks of hasty burial following the early death of Tutanhkamun in about his nineteenth year. Even its fabulous contents, seen by millions of people around the world, cannot have compared to the funerary treasures of far greater pharaohs entombed in the valley. This relative lack of importance of a briefly reigning puppet pharaoh of the Amun priesthood's counterrevolution probably assisted in the long secrecy of the tomb's existence and whereabouts. Also, nearly above it, was the entrance to the grander tomb of Ramses VI (Tomb 9), the debris from which early on covered the entrance to the young Pharaoh's tomb.

Tutankhamun: treasures of a nobody

The tomb was discovered on 4 November 1922 by Howard Carter and opened by him and his patron Lord Carnarvon on 26 November in the presence of experts from New York's Metropolitan Museum of Art — or so the official story went. But in a last great irony in the history of looting at the Valley of the Kings it has recently been revealed by Thomas Hoving, ex-director of the Metropolitan Museum, in his book *Tutankhamun, the Untold Story* that between discovery and public

I
H
G
F
E
D
C
B
A
TOMB 9:
RAMSES VI

J
K
I
H
G
F
E
D
C
B
A
TOMB 17:
SETI I

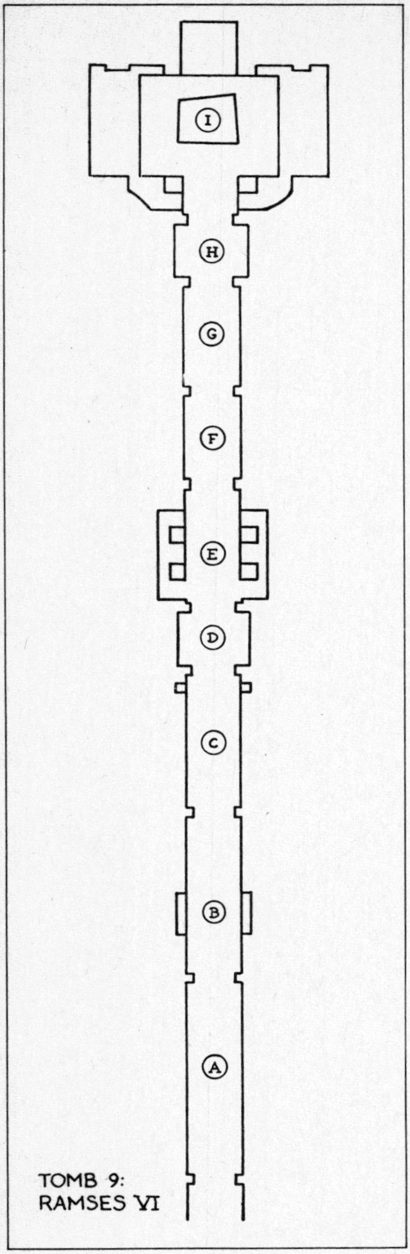

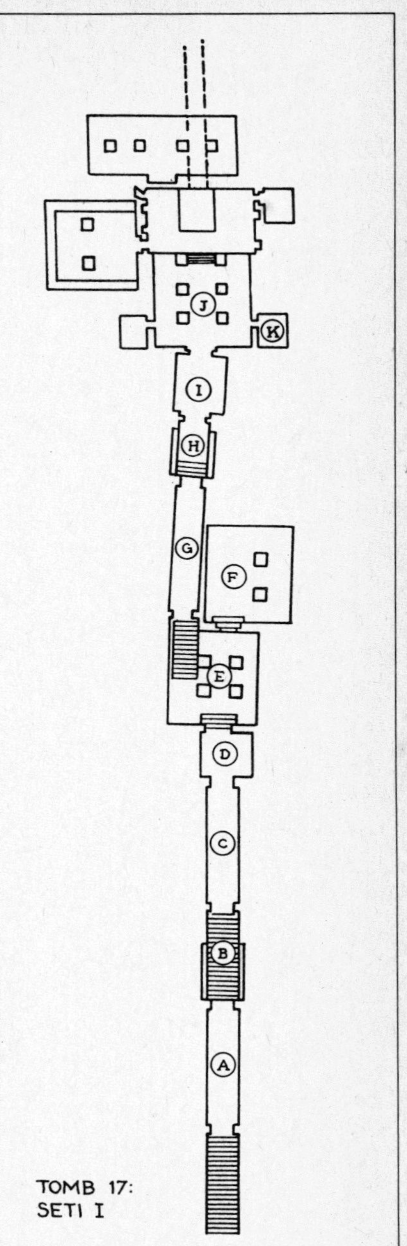

entry, Carter and Carnarvon sneaked into the tomb, stole 35 items, and then walled it up again.

The door at the bottom of the entrance stairway *A* was found walled up and sealed with the royal seal. The entrance corridor *B* was found filled with stone debris through which a tunnel had been dug soon after interment in an unsuccessful attempt to rob the tomb. The undecorated *Chambers C, D* (now walled up) *and F* contained most of the funerary objects now on display at the Cairo Museum. *Chamber E*, originally walled off from *C* and at a lower level, contained the four gilded wooden shrines, one inside the other, within which lay the rectangular stone sarcophagus, then three mummiform coffins, the innermost of solid gold, and then finally the mummy of Tutankhamun himself. The wall has now been replaced by a railing beyond which visitors cannot venture.

From here you can view what remains in the tomb: the sarcophagus, the largest of the mummiform cofins within it, and, unseen within that, the badly decayed mummy of Tutankhamun. This chamber was the only one decorated, its paintings betraying signs of haste. On the right wall, the coffin is transported on a sledge. To the rear from right to left, Ay, the young king's successor, performs the rite of the opening of the mouth (note a suggestion of the Amarna style); Tutankhamun sacrificing to Nut; again the young Pharaoh, this time with his ka, before Osiris. On the left wall is the sun god's boat, while on the all but impossible to see entrance wall. Tutankhamun, accompanied by Anubis and Isis, received life from the goddess of the West.

To Deir el Bahri

Mountain paths to Deir el Medina and Deir el Bahri

You can leave the Valley of the Kings by the road you came, that same ancient road along which the bodies of the Pharaohs were drawn here on sledges. Or you can leave on foot, climbing the *path* to the right of Tomb 16, opposite the rest house. As it gains the ridge, there is usually a donkey boy waiting but the donkeys should be declined. Almost certainly, a guide will fasten himself on you in hope of baksheesh. He can be useful for those who are not foot sure, but otherwise he is not necessary either. On the ridge, the path divides. One heads south, rising slowly over the mountain; the other runs to the left and level along the ridge. The first leads to Deir el Medina and is the same path the workmen used when returning home from their shift at the tombs. There are sweeping views of Nile valley, magnificent in the afternoon with the sun in the west. The second path soon creeps high along the edge of the amphitheatre of Deir el Bahri and offers changing angles and elevations of Hatshepsut's temple, and views towards the Nile. You continue along until you are above the old Cook's rest house at Deir el Bahri and then pick your way down, to be met by your driver after visiting the temple. Both walks are highly recommended, but the second (about 30 minutes) is a must for a full appreciation of Hatshepsut's architectural achievement.

The **mortuary temple of Hatshepsut** at Deir el Bahri is the finest building in Egypt. Elegant, revolutionary, it satisfies and provokes in whole and in detail. Along with the

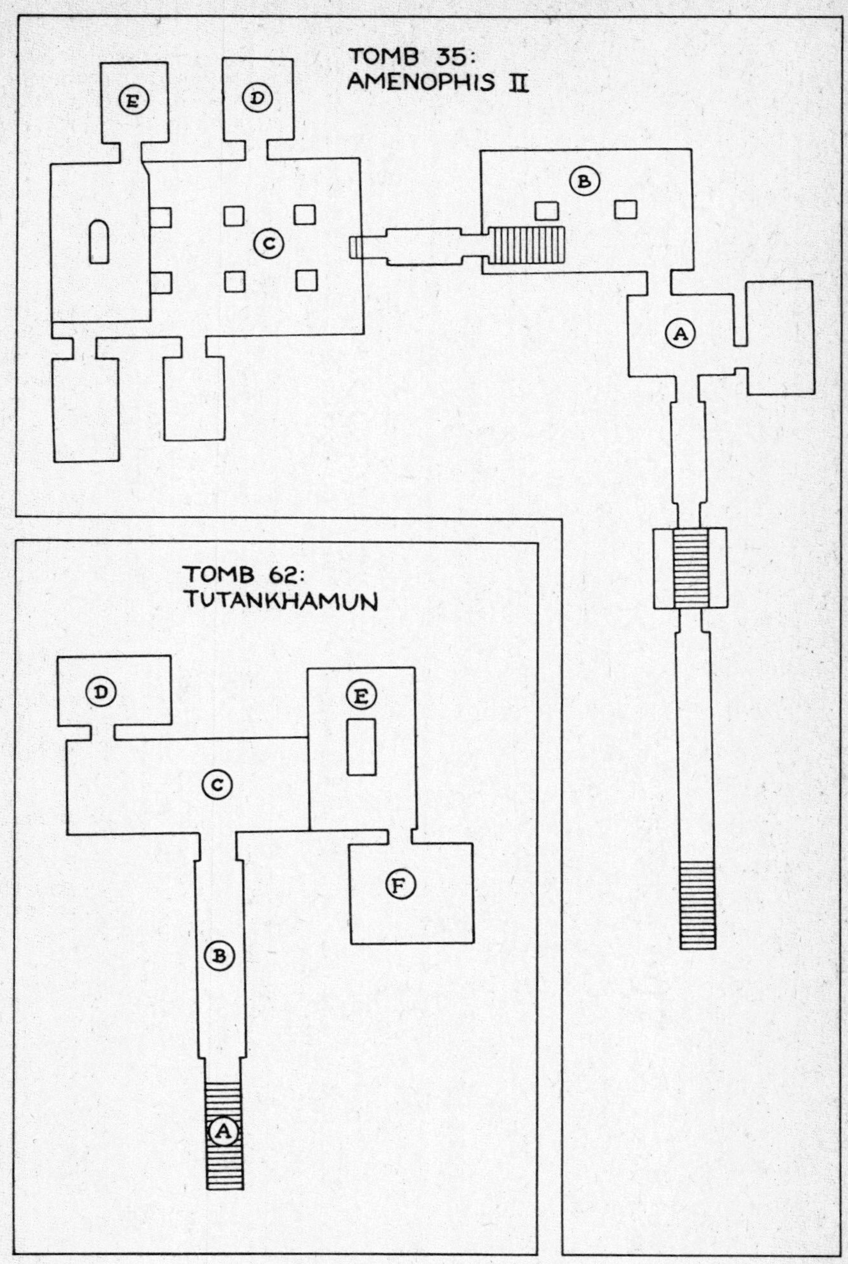

TOMB 35:
AMENOPHIS II
E
D
B
C
A
TOMB 62:
TUTANKHAMUN
D
E
C
F
B
A

Parthenon, the Taj Mahal, the interiors of Chartres and Hagia Sophia, it is one of the great buildings of the world. Not that the temple has received its fullest due: though far older than the others, it was unknown in modern times until Mariette made preliminary excavations in the third quarter of the 19th C. The temple was only entirely cleared in 1894–96 and since then has undergone sporadic restoration, still in progress today.

Hatshepsut's Reign

Interpretation of the events following the death of Tuthmosis I (XVIII Dyn) is marked by controversy amongst archaeologists which mimics, even if it does not rival, the original dynastic struggle played out between Hatshepsut, his daughter, and Tuthmosis III, his grandson. By any interpretation, Hatshepsut emerges as one of the most formidable figures in Egyptian history, only the third woman to rule as queen, the first to rule as king. In the ruthlessness and romance the story implies, and the high policy at stake, parallels between the reigns of Hatshepsut and Elizabeth I easily suggest themselves to the imagination.

Hatshepsut married her father's son and successor, Tuthmosis II, and during the lifetime of her husband her full titles were 'Pharaoh's daughter, Pharaoh's sister, god's wife and Pharaoh's great wife'. But Tuthmosis II died before Hatshepsut could bear him a child, and it was one of her husband's secondary wives who became 'Pharaoh's mother' to Tuthmosis III. But for her sex, Hatshepsut's claim to the throne through her father was at least as good as Tuthmosis III's and through her mother she was descended from the Ahmose family who had thrown the Hyksos out of Egypt. But as Tuthmosis was later to advertise, his future as Pharaoh was proclaimed by no less a god than Amun who while Tuthmosis I was sacrificing at Karnak stood the young prince in the place usually occupied by the sovereign. This conveniently has Tuthmosis III designated heir in the lifetime of his own father, but betrays the more pedestrian likelihood that the priests of Amun eventually sided with the army in its support of Tuthmosis and his imperial designs against Hatshepsut and her party in the civil service who preferred a peaceful domestic policy.

The struggle with Tuthmosis III

Tuthmosis III, when finally he became sole Pharaoh well into his manhood, launched Egypt upon her period of conquest abroad and bloated magnificence at home so often celebrated in stone at Thebes. Yet as powerful a pharaoh and warrior as he was to become, Tuthmosis was no match for Hatshepsut in her prime. In the first few years following her husband's death, Hatshepsut reigned as widow-queen, but she soon took the momentous step of assuming the title of Pharaoh, co-reigning with but entirely overshadowing her stepson. She went so far as to pose and dress as a man — at least on reliefs — and to wear the pharaonic beard. In this way she ruled for about 20 years.

Hatshepsut's favourite, Senmut

Elizabeth I had her Essex; Hatshepsut had her Senmut, a man of modest birth who rose to occupy a score of high offices, including Steward of Amun, probably giving him control over the vast wealth of the Karnak temple, and Minister of Public Works, with the suggestion that he was the architect at Deir el Bahri. As such favourites often do, Senmut overstepped the mark. He used his royal mistress's temple for his own purposes, introducing reliefs of himself in niches that would be concealed behind opening doors, and though building himself a tomb at Gurna, planned secretly to be buried within the great court at Deir el Bahri. Most of his reliefs were hacked out and his sarcophagus smashed, yet in his secret tomb the name of Hatshepsut was left untouched, suggesting the destruction was wrought not by Tuthmosis III, who in malice destroyed so much that was Hatshepsut's, but by Hatshepsut herself in rage at this attempt to extend familiarity into the eternal. The last record of Senmut comes about five years before the end of his mistress's reign. In those last years she was alone.

How Hatshepsut's reign ended is not known. Perhaps she fell victim to a coup d'etat, or merely died a natural death. In any case her inward-looking peace policy was suddenly eclipsed and Tuthmosis III, obliterating her name and her image wherever he found them, within 75 days of her death was leading his army into Palestine.

Conception of Hatshepsut's Temple at Deir el Bahri

Into the rugged eastern flank of the Theban Mountain nature has cut an immense amphitheatre facing Thebes. Its sheer

Hatshepsut's temple: at grips with the landscape

golden walls embrace the site like the wings of some mighty hovering solar disc. Just off centre, to the left and rising from the cliffline, is a pyramidal peak. A magnificent backdrop, it invites a performance, and would condemn any but the most brilliant to insignificance before it. The Middle Kingdom Pharaoh Mentuhotep II (XI Dyn) built a temple here; you can see its *ruins* to the south of Hatshepsut's. What impression it made cannot fairly be judged from its remains. Like Hatshepsut's temple, it rose in terraces but then was surmounted by a pyramid, a Memphite legacy perhaps. Mentuhotep II and III were both entombed here. But a pyramidal structure set against the pyramidal peak seems superfluous, and any structure vying with the cliffs for height can only have been overwhelmed.

Mentuhotep's earlier design

Mentuhotep's temple was already in ruins when 500 years later Hatshepsut was drawn to the holy site. (Whether out of convenience or some similar feeling of awe, Hatsehpsut's temple was taken over by early Christians as a monastery: *Deir el Bahri*, the Northern Monastery). She was obviously influenced by the earlier temple, and in all probability would have replicated it on a larger scale: the foundations suggest a pyramid was intended. One purpose of a pyramid is to protect the tomb, but her father Tuthmosis I had abandoned this idea for the greater security of descreet entombment in the Valley of the Kings. It remained necessary therefore to build only a mortuary temple at which the appropriate ceremonies would be performed. At some point Hatshepsut decided to build wide instead of high.

Taming the mountain

If it is true that circumstances dictated this decision, or suggested that the alternative was now pointless, it is no less true that the new form was seized upon with conviction and executed with genius. The terraces of Hatshepsut's temple emphasise the stratification of the cliff behind and the line between rock and sky. At the same time, the bold rhythm of the pillared colonnades, vertical shafts of light-reflecting stone framing and contrasting with the shadowed ambulatories, reflect the dark gashes of gullies and fissures in the cliff face itself. Even the peak seems brought into the conception: a pyramid offered by nature. The temple mediates between the wildness of the mountain and the cultivation of the Valley. The power and contradiction of the landscape is gripped and tamed with a confidence and elegance that is breathtaking, and then played throughout the structure so that as you walk round the temple you feel it, never too much, but to a measure that insists on the spiritual nature of a man.

Tour of Hatshepsut's Temple

The Lower Terrace. The main temple complex may originally have been preceded by a valley temple near the Nile; if so, it

1. Lower Terrace
2. Colonnades
3. Lower ramp
4. Middle Terrace
5. Birth Colonnade
6. Chapel of Anubis
7. Punt Colonnade
8. Chapel of Hathor
9. Upper ramp
10. Upper Terrace
11. Sanctuary of Amun
12. Sanctuary of Hatshepsut
13. Sanctuary of the Sun

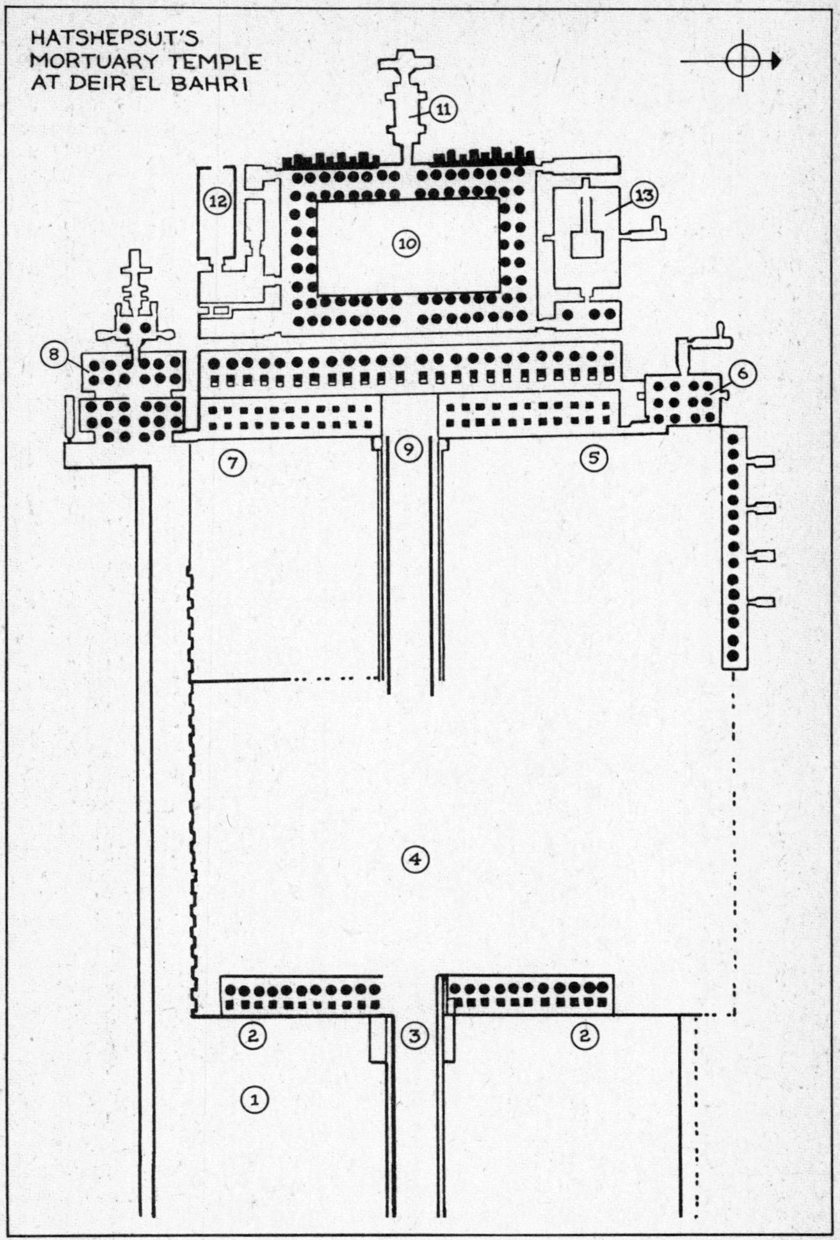
HATSHEPSUT'S
MORTUARY TEMPLE
AT DEIR EL BAHRI
1
2
3
2
4
5
6
7
8
9
10
11
12
13

has been lost beneath the tilled alluvium. From this temple ran a promenade lined with sphinxes to the Lower Terrace, a zone of transition between the profane and the sacred. This was a garden with myrrh trees and fountains, as though a foretaste of that life which endures in the desert of the other world. A pair of *lions* (the left-hand one survives) stood at the bottom of the ramp leading up to the Middle Terrace and another pair (the right-hand one survives) stood at the top. These were at once guardians of the temple and witnesses to the rising sun, proof of rebirth. **Colonnades** are on either side of the ramp, to the north and to the south. On their pillars are simple devices stating a variation of Hapshepsut's name surmounted by the solar falcon wearing the double crown. Within the colonnades, the retaining walls of the Middle Terrace are decorated with vividly coloured *reliefs*. Not all of the original courses have survived, and where they have, the decorations have suffered deliberate defacement, first by Tuthmosis III, later by Akhenaton. Representations of Amun were restored at the counter-revolution, but Hatshepsut remains obliterated; the Pharaoh seen is Tuthmosis III, who, as co-ruler, had been included in the original decorations. The carvings within the **North Colonnade** depict an idealised country life, continuing the theme established by the gardens of the Lower Terrace. Of the greatest delicacmy are the scenes (right) of water birds being caught in nets. The reliefs within the **South Colonnade** depict the transport down the Nile of two obelisks cut at Aswan at Hatshepsut's order. At the far ends of the colonnades stood large Osiris statues of Hatshepsut (the north one imperfectly restored).

From the profane to the sacred

The Middle Terrace. The lower ramp leads up to the Middle Terrace. At its centre rises a second ramp to the Upper Terrace. Again, at the rear of the Middle Terrace and on either side of the second ramp are colonnades and at their farthest ends, pressing against the rock of the cliff face, are the Chapels of Anubis (north) and Hathor (south). Along the north side of the terrace is an unfinished colonnade.

The north and south colonnades of the Middle Terrace have double rows of square pillars, simple but well-proportioned and achieving a modest grace. On the walls of the **Birth Colonnade** (north) are *reliefs depicting Hatshepsut's divine parentage:* Amun has assumed the form of her father who sits facing Ahmosis, her mother, on a couch. The couple gaze at one another, their knees touching in a scene at once conventional and reserved and yet sensitively conveying their ardour. The Queen is led to the birth chamber, accompanied by strange deities, a smile of suffering and delight playing on her lips. The child, conventionally shown as a boy, is fashioned by Khnum on his potter's wheel, and also its ka. Just as Tuthmosis III justified his claim to the throne with the story of Amun's selection of him at the Temple of Karnak, so these reliefs serve the same purpose for Hatshepsut. Not that we should think that either Pharaoh was simply cynical; overriding the political propaganda was probably a sincere belief in their divine birth, and these beliefs certainly have all the delicacy and feeling of a belief honestly integrated in

Hatshepsut asserts her divine birth

Hatshepsut's character, sustaining her in her rule. On the lateral faces of the pillars, Tuthmosis is shown with Amun; on front and back it is Hatshepsut (defaced) with Amun.

The facade of the **Chapel of Anubis** continues the line of the colonnade, but with *columns* (fluted, with simple capitals, like Doric columns). From a distance, the columns are indistinguishable from the pillars, but stand in the northwest corner of the terrace and look along the facades towards the ramp: that almost unnoticed variation creates a subtle yet entirely harmonious contrast. There is a touch of Greece here, and in the discreet widening of the distance between the central columns as if inviting the visitor into the sanctuary within. The *walls* of the hall are brilliantly coloured and show the co-rulers (Hatshepsut hacked out), Anubis, protector of the dead, and facing each other at either end, the falcon headed sun god (north wall) and his wife Hathor (south wall). Cut into the rock in a series of right angles are several **chambers** with vaulted roofs of brick, though lacking the wedge-shaped keystones of true weight-bearing vaults which do not appear in Egypt until the 8th C BC (and not universalised until taken up by the Romans).

On the south side of the ramp is the *Punt Colonnade,* named for the *decorations on its rear wall* of the expedition to the land of Punt (probably the coastal region of the modern Somali Republic) instigated by Hatshepsut. Amun had told her: 'It is a glorious region of god's land, it is indeed my place of delight; I have made it for myself in order to divert my heart'. Hatshepsut's ancestors had often sent expeditions there to procure the precious myrrh necessary for the incense in temple services, but now, as she recorded, Amun desired her 'to establish a Punt in his house'. So the purpose of the expedition was to obtain for the first time living myrrh trees; to plant the terraces of this temple dedicated to Amun with them.

Journey to the land of delight

The walls illustrate and relate the story. After presumably crossing the desert to a Red Sea port, the expedition sailed southwards in five ships. The Egyptians are shown being greeted on the shore by the chief of Punt and his extraordinarily corpulant wife — a rare instance of humourous caricature, the rolls of fat from her body reaching right down to her ankles. In exchange for gifts, the beached ships are laden 'very heavily with marvels of the country of Punt; all goodly fragrant woods of god's land, heaps of myrrh resin, of fresh myrrh trees, with ebony and pure ivory, with green gold of Emu, with cinnamon wood, with incense, eye cosmetic, with baboons, monkeys, dogs, with skins of the southern panther, with natives and their children. Never was the like of this brought for any pharaoh who has been since the beginning'. Back at Thebes, Tuthmosis III and Hatshepsut are shown offering incense to Amun's sacred boat, his offering paltry compared to hers. But later he had Hatshepsut defaced; Tuthmosis' portrait, however, is beautifully carved, his individuality realised in a way lacking in the idealised representations on the pillars.

At the far south end of the colonnade it is the **Chapel of Hathor** that continues the facade. This time there are pillars, not columns, but still, and unnoticed from any distance, they differ from the rest in having the cow-eared head of Hathor serve laterally as capitals. Beyond the first pillared chamber, and then the second, decorated with a procession of boats along the Nile, is the **Sanctuary of Hathor** with vaulted roof. After all the hacking out of Hatshepsut's figure you yearn to see one intact and here, in the furthest recess of the sanctuary, that desire is satisfied. Either because the room was sealed or because at least here in Hathor's sanctuary Tuthmosis respected Hatshepsut's right to some modest remembrance, she survives, albeit in stylised and masculine form. She meets Amun, she suckles regenerating milk from Hathor, and above a recess in the left wall she and Tuthmosis III are shown kneeling, she to the left with an offering of milk, he to the right with wine. Also within this chamber, in a little alcove on the right and towards the floor, is a figure of Senmut, Hatshepsut's favourite.

Rare portrait of Hatshepsut

The Upper Terrace. The second ramp leads to the Upper Terrace, badly ruined and currently being restored (it may be closed). A portico of Osiris pillars stood a short distance from the edge; their restoration is well underway. On what remains of the rear wall are *reliefs* of boats accompanied along the Nile banks by a festive procession of soldiers, and of the Festival of the Valley during which Amun visited the necropolis.

Passing through the last wall against the cliffs is a granite doorway leading into the **Sanctuary of Amun** hewn out of the rock. The walls are decorated as elsewhere in the temple but are blackened with smoke. In Ptolemaic times the sanctuary was cut deeper and was dedicated to the healing cults of Imhotep, counsellor to Zoser, and Amenhotep, son of Hapu, counsellor to Amenophis III.

At the left (south) end of the Upper Terrace is the **Sanctuary of Hatshepsut.** The *reliefs* are of high quality and show processions of priests and offering-bearers. At the right (north) end of the terrace is the **Sanctuary of the Sun,** an open court with an altar in the centre. A flight of steps on its west side permitted a priest to mount the *altar* gaining a magnificent view of the Valley and river below and the rugged horizon to the east, and to await the rising of the sun. The seclusion of this sanctuary and its emphasis on worship of the rising sun suggests a private royal communion above and beyond the convolutions of the evolved and traditional state religion, and may have influenced Akhenaton in his attempt to destroy mythology and present Aton to the world.

Origins of the worship of Aton?

The Noble Tombs

Over 400 private tombs are accessible in the Theban necropolis, and as many as 100 of these hold some interest for the non-specialist. But to see that many would require three to five days. This Guide concentrates on only four of the most outstanding tombs, all close to the old village of Gurna (Sheikh Abd el-Gurna) and requiring an hour or so to see: *Nakht (52), Menna (69), Ramose (55)* and *Khaemhat (57).*

Artistry of private tombs

The private tombs are interesting because they often give a vivid picture of contemporary life instead of the impersonal ritual decorations of the royal tombs. The artists have been more free to express themselves and the sensitivity of their work has been greater. The limestone on this side of the mountian is of poor quality, not suited to carving; the decorations are generally paintings on stucco walls of white, grey or yellow ground. The tombs date from the XI Dynasty through to the XXVI Dynasty, but most belong to the New Kingdom and the four described here are XVIII Dynasty. The tombs are, strictly, mortuary chapels; a filled-in shaft led to a deeper chamber containing the sarcophagus.

Tomb 52 (beside the road from Deir el Bahri to the Ramesseum): **Nakht** was a scribe and astronomer of Amun in the middle of the XVIII Dynasty. A short passage leads to a *transverse first chamber*, the only decorated part of the tomb. The paintings are brilliantly preserved and depict country life: the supervising of field labours by Nakht; the deceased and his wife banqueting and making offerings. The chamber beyond, as was the custom, contained a statue of the dead man with his wife, but this was lost while being shipped to America. A shaft here runs down to the sarcophagus chamber.

Tomb 69 (on the north side of the hill, at the bottom): **Menna** was an estate inspector under a mid-XVIII Dynasty pharaoh, and like the previous tomb the emphasis is on country life. The paintings are finely executed and excellently preserved. In the *entrance passage*, Menna, his wife and daughter are shown worshipping the sun. In the left wing of the *first chamber* are a variety of rural scenes, while the right wing depicts various ceremonies, with the dead man and his wife receiving offerings, Anubis facing Osiris, Re and Hathor. A lively hunting and fishing scene occupies the centre of the right-hand wall of the *second chamber*, though generally mourning and burial scenes are depicted.

Tomb 55 (near the mayor's house in the village): a relatively grandiose structure with wall carvings, the unfinished tomb of **Ramose** is one of the most fascinating in the necropolis. Ramose was governor of Thebes and vizier in the early years of Amenophis IV's reign and took pains to honour himself with two hypostyle chambers (only the first is open) decorated in the most exquisite classical style.

From an open court you enter the first chamber and follow the decorations from the near wall of the right wing: *classical reliefs* show Ramose and his wife in several offering ceremonies (A). These scenes are continued along the near wall of the left wing. The groups of seated figures are friends or relatives of the dead man (B). Continuing clockwise, the south wall (C) bears a painting of the procession to the tomb with bearers of offerings, mourning women and priests; to the right, the dead man and his wife worshipping Osiris; and below, four representations of the dead man before his tomb. The west wall in the left wing resumes the reliefs (D) and shows Ramose four times offering flowers to Amenophis IV seated under a canopy with the goddess Maat. At the very south (left) end of this wall you can see that prior to cutting the relief the figures were drawn in black outline over a red grid, suggesting the usual artist's concern to transfer the scene in the same detail and proportions as it appeared on the (perhaps smaller) original sketch.

Contrast between classical and Amarna styles

Now passing across the closed entrance to the second chamber you come to the north end of the west wall and suddenly the style has changed from the classical to the *Amarnan* (E). The explanation is that while Ramose was working on his tomb, Amenophis IV had become Akhenaton, introducing both Aton and a new art. Ramose never did finish his tomb here because he followed Akhenaton to Amarna. This wall shows Akhenaton and Nefertiti at their palace window under the rays of Aton, receiving homage from Ramose. In sketch form you can see Ramose receiving a decoration (a gold collar, as at Ay's tomb at Amarna) and acclaimed by courtiers and representatives from Nubia, Libya and Asia, and also Ramose receiving bouquets in the temple. It is interesting to compare these new-style portraits of Ramose to his classical portrait at the north side of the east wall. And it is significant to note that not only Akhenaton and Nefertiti are depicted with elongated heads, but now Ramose (though not quite so much) is too — in some measure countering the argument that Akhenaton and his family were portrayed in this way because they were afflicted by some deforming disease or gene.

Tomb 57 (to the south of Ramose's tomb): **Khaemhat** was a royal scribe and inspector of granaries in Upper and Lower Egypt under Amenophis III. His is another carved tomb, as fine and even firmer in style than that of Ramose. In the *entrance court*, to the right of the doorway, are reliefs showing the complete set of instruments employed in the opening of the mouth ceremony, while to the left is Khaemhat adoring Re. The *first chamber* presents scenes of country life and, particularly, aspects of Khaemhat's official life: unloading of boats, an amusing market scene, cattle herds, the harvest. The *second chamber* shows the funeral procession and ceremonies in honour of Osiris. The *chapel* beyond contains several statues with finely modelled heads; in the left wing, on the right-hand wall, the dead man in the act of worship; in the right wing, on the right-hand wall, the cast of a portrait of Khaemhat.

A coffin was traditionally carried through a banquet, giving the lie to an unending feast of life. Macabre it might seem to us; to the Egyptians it must have carried with it some promise against time: 'You live again, you live again for ever, here you are young once more for ever' — the final benediction of the priests as the dessicated mummies of these titled dead were interred in their tombs.

The Ramesseum

The Ramesseum, the **mortuary temple of Ramses II**, is part of a still larger rectangular complex enclosed by its original brick wall. The area was filled with vaulted brick storehouses, now entirely ruinous, which were once invaded, as is known from an extant papyrus, by desperate tomb workers who had not been paid for two months: 'We have reached this place because of hunger, because of thirst, without clothing,

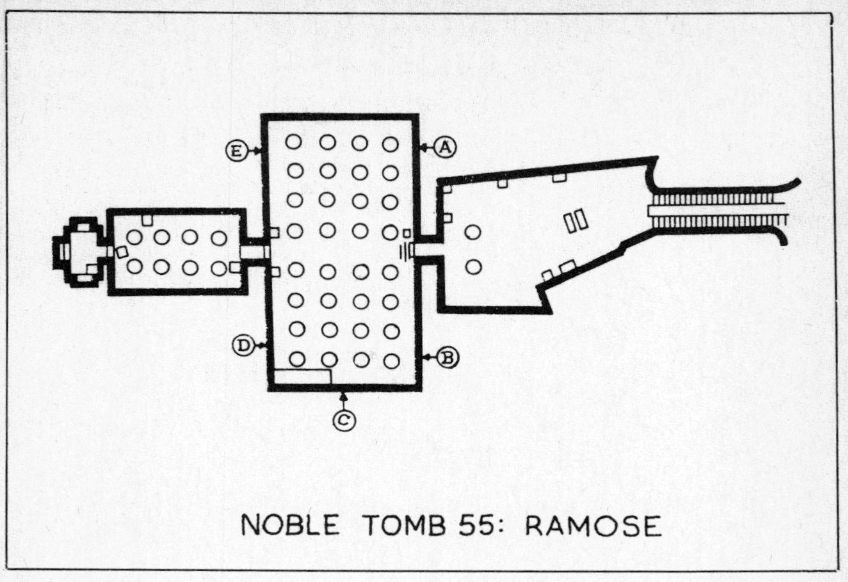

NOBLE TOMB 55: RAMOSE

without oil, without fish, without vegetables! Tell Pharaoh, our good lord, about it, and tell the vizier, our superior. Act so that we may live!' So that the great Ramses should live forever this grandiose temple was built, and enough of its stones remain piled atop one another to remind us of *his* hunger. Diodorus was impressed. Coming upon the granite colossus of Ramses he fancifully interpreted its inscription, corrupting the Pharaoh's praenomen, User-maat-Re, as he went: 'I am Ozymandias, king of kings. If any would know how great I am, and where I lie, let him excel me in any of my works'. To which Shelley offered time's reply:

Shelley's Ozymandias

I met a traveller from an antiáque land
Who said: Two vast and trunkless legs of stone
Stand in the desert ... Near them, on the sand,
Half sunk, a shattered visage lies, whose frown,
And wrinkled lip, and sneer of cold command,
Tell that its sculptor well those passions read
Which yet survive, stamped on these lifeless things,
The hand that mocked them, and the heart that fed.
On the pedestal these words appear:
'My name is Ozymandias, king of kings:
Look on my works, ye Mighty, and despair!'
Nothing beside remains. Round the decay
Of that colossal wreck, boundless and bare
The lone and level sands stretch far away.

You approach the temple at its north flank and so to reach the **First Pylon**, measuring 67 metres across, you must turn left through the ruined **First Court**. The outer wall of the pylon is as intelligible as a quarry face, but on the pylon wall facing the court there are excellently carved *reliefs*, albeit of Ramses' all too familiar exploits against the Hittites (see the Temple of Luxor). A double colonnade on the south side of the court formed the facade of the **royal palace** of which little remains. A colonnade of Osiris pillars runs along the north side of the court. At the far (west) end a flight of steps leads to the Second Court; on the left, as you ascend, is the fallen **Ozymandias**. Weighing more than 900,000 kilos and once standing at 17.5 metres this was one of the largest free-standing statues in Egypt, surpassed by the Colossi of Memnon only by virtue of their pedestals. The index finger alone is a metre long.

The inner surface of the north tower of the **Second Pylon** is decorated, again, with the battle of Kadesh, though the top register more peacefully portrays the festival of the harvest god Min. The front and back of the **Second Court** is lined with Osiris pillars, and where three stairways rise to the west portico, another *granite colossus*, not quite so large as the first, lies in fragments, the head in good condition with only the nose smashed. On a nearby throne, next to the name of Ramses, Belzoni carved his name. An Italian artist and one-time seminarian, in the early years of the 19th C Belzoni appeared on the stage of Sadler's Wells and elsewhere in England with his famous human-pyramid act, 'bearing on his colossal frame, not fewer, if we mistake not, than 20 or 22 persons'. He later turned serious explorer and succeeded in removing from the Ramesseum the giant bust of Ramses II now in the British Museum.

On the rear wall of the **portico** (reached by stairways at the rear of the Second Court) between the central and left-hand doorways, are three rows of *reliefs*: the bottom register shows 11 of Ramses' sons; the middle shows Ramses with Atum (a Heliopolitan god) and falcon-headed Mont who holds the hieroglyph for 'life' to the Pharaoh's nose, while to the right Ramses kneels before the Theban triad and Thoth inscribes the Pharaoh's name on a palm branch; the top shows Ramses sacrificing to Ptah, and to the right offering incense to an ithyphalic Min. Against the outside north wall of the portico and the Great Hypostyle Hall are the scant remains of an earlier *temple of Seti I*, its alignment probably accounting for the overall alignment of the Ramesseum which accordingly skews to the south instead of fitting squarely within the rectangular walls of the complex.

The **Great Hypostyle Hall** had 48 columns of which only 29 still stand. It was similar to the one at Karnak (to which Ramses II made a major contribution), a higher ceiling over the central aisle allowing illumination through windows set upon the architraves of the adjoining rows of shorter columns. The **First Small Hypostyle Hall** of eight papyrus bud columns still retains its ceiling, decorated with astronomical signs. Only four out of eight columns survive in the **Second Small Hypostyle Hall**, while of the *shrine* beyond nothing remains.

Here, as elsewhere beneath the glaring sun of Egypt, the

Agriculture amongst the tombs

columns, the reliefs, the sculptures are streaked with white. Ramses boasted and Shelley cut him down to size; and Flaubert dispassionately observed: 'Birdshit is Nature's protest in Egypt; she decorates monuments with it instead of with lichen or moss'.

To the Valley of the Queens

From the Valley of the Kings there was a mountain path that led down to Deir el Bahri, or if you had continued along the crest southwards it would have brought you to the village of the ancient tomb workers, **Deir el Medina**. This can also be reached by road, travelling 700 metres or so west from the Ramesseum. It is worth making this detour on your way to the Valley of the Queens for a brief glimpse of the proletarian past. There are rows of humble *houses*, 70 in all, mudbrick walls rising on stone foundations along straight and narrow alleys. They had a second storey or at least a living area on the roof, reached by stairs. Some have simple wall decorations inside. The men who worked at the Valley of the Kings (which they called The Place of Truth) were freemen whose food was delivered to the village by serfs, and whose houses were swept by slaves. They fashioned their own *tombs*, and decorated them not so much with scenes of the everyday as did the nobles but with the afterlife, borrowing from their experience in the pharaonic tombs. And over their tomb entrance they would construct a man-size pyramid. Several of

Tomb workers' tombs

these can be visited. The tombs and village date from the XVIII to XX Dynasties.

Deir el Medina means the 'monastery of the town', for the small **Ptolemaic temple** here was occupied by monks during the early years of Christianity. Dedicated to Maat and to Hathor whose head adorns the pillars between the outer court and pronaos, this elegant temple is worth a look if you have the time, though other more considerable Ptolemaic temples await you upstream at Edfu, Kom Ombo and at Philae.

Beyond, in the **Valley of the Queens**, Biban el Harem, there are over 70 tombs of queens, princes and princesses of the XVIII though mostly XIX and XX Dynasties. These dead, however, were not gods and so their tombs were not built on the same scale as those of the Pharaohs. Nor did the friable limestone at this end of the Theban Mountain permit much carved decoration; the tombs are more often only painted, though many were left unfinished and have merely the appearance of caves.

Smallpox victims

Tombs 43, 44 and 55 belong to *sons of Ramses III*, and it is the last of these, the **Tomb of Prince Amun-her-khopshef**, that is worth visiting for the freshness of its paintings. A smallpox epidemic towards the end of Ramses' reign killed several of his sons, and here in the *hall* at the bottom of the entrance steps it falls to the father to introduce his son to the gods. The *sarcophagus chamber* at the end of the corridor contains a mummiform sarcophagus and, in the far right corner, in a glass case, a six-month-old foetus. The **Tomb of Queen Titi** (52), wife of one of the Ramessid pharaohs, may also be visited, but the rooms are small and low, the painting faded. The outstanding tomb is **Nefertari's** (66), celebrated wife of Ramses II, but owing to damage caused by salt deposits it is closed except by special permission. There are several striking portraits of Nefertari; one, on the left wall of the antechamber, shows her beneath a canopy playing a board game, her wig covered with the skin of a vulture, the protective symbol of Maat. Above the door to the corridor leading to the burial chamber is Maat herself, wings extended in protection about the cartouche of the Queen.

Medinet Habu

The last great pharaonic temple

Though built by Ramses III of the XX Dynasty, the temple complex of Medinet Habu is in the great building tradition of the XIX Dynasty Pharaohs and has many points of similarity with the Ramesseum and is better preserved. Not long after the reign of Ramses III, the power of the Pharaohs declined and Egypt herself became divided once more. Medinet Habu is the last major architectural work of the pharaonic period. Though Egypt was threatened by foreign invaders early in Ramses' reign and a palace conspiracy against him and the succession of his son was uncovered, the greater part of his 30-odd years of rule seems to have passed in peace. A papyrus, probably part of the palace archives here, declares: 'I caused the woman of Egypt to walk freely wheresoever she would unmolested by others upon the road. I caused to sit idle the soldiers and the chariotry in my time, and the Sherden and the

Kehek [Sardinian and Libyan prisoners, or their children, who were recruited to the royal bodyguard] in their villages to lie at night full length without any dread'.

In nomen and praenomen, Ramses III imitated his great predecessor of the XIX Dynasty and the designers of Medinet Habu freely borrowed from the Ramesseum. They sometimes cut reliefs celebrating triumphs by Ramses III over Asian foes who had either long since perished on the field of history, or who since the reign of Ramses II lay beyond the enfeebled might by Egypt. This motif is echoed in the lofty **gatehouse**, a unique feature in Egyptian architecture, through which you enter the site. It was meant to resemble one of those Syrian fortresses which the Egyptian armies had met with so often in their Asiatic campaigns, but here the purpose was not military, the upper storeys serving as a resort where the Pharaoh could amuse himself with the women of the harem. The carved heads of captured prisoners enlivened the view from the east window above, reached now by a staircase on the south (if this is closed, offer baksheesh).

Pharaonic erotica

Scenes inside the *top apartment* shows Ramses waited on by harem girls, their bodies bared of even their transparent dresses once suggested by a light wash of paint. To the left of the west window the Pharaoh is stroking one of the girls under the chin.

To the north (right) of this gateway is an earlier **XVIII Dynasty temple** built and partly decorated by Hatshepsut. Her image and name were obliterated, as elsewhere, by Tuthmosis III; Akhenaton scratched out all reference to Amun but Horemheb and Seti I replaced them; and Ramses III then decorated the north and south walls to suit his own

The primeval hill

purposes. This temple stood on one of the most sacred spots in Egypt, the primeval hill which first rose clear of the receding waters of Chaos. An inscription identifies it as the burial place of the four primal pairs — Ocean and Matter, the Illimitable and the Boundless, Darkness and Obscurity, and the Hidden and Concealed ones — who preceded even the creator god, Re-Atum. While preserving this older temple, Ramses III levelled the ground behind to build his own mortuary temple dedicated to 'Amun united with Eternity', and a palace and other structures, set within gardens, surrounded by walls, and linked to the Nile by a canal.

Through the gateway and to the south (left) are the **mortuary chapels of the Divine Adorers**, princesses who were the chief priestesses of Amun at Thebes. The chapels are late additions, dating from the XXIII through the XXVI Dynasties.

Straight ahead (to the west) is the **First Pylon of Ramses' mortuary temple**. The pylon would have almost the same dimensions as that at the Temple of Luxor except that it has lost its cornice. A stairway at the north end leads to the top for an excellent *view* across the temple towards the Theban Mountain. The pylons, columns and chambers are smaller as you gaze westwards; the platforms at each stage of the temple are higher; an architectural funnel pointing towards the final sanctuary — as at Karnak, and with Egyptian temples generally.

The *reliefs* on the pylon towers depict campaigns against the Nubians and Syrians, campaigns never fought by Ramses III and probably copied from the Ramesseum. But in the eighth year of his reign, Ramses III was in desperate struggle with the Sea Peoples, a coalition of northerners including Sardinians, Cretans, Philistines and others, not all of whom have been identified, who by sea and by ox-carts carrying their women and children overland were bent on permanent settlement in the rich Delta pasturelands. One group, whom the Egyptians called the Danu, the Danaoi of the *Iliad*, here emerged into history for the first time. The invasion is recorded in dramatic detail along the *north outer wall* of the mortuary temple (walk round to it before passing through the pylon) and should not be missed. It is the only Egyptian relief portraying a sea battle. An inscription graphically describes the outcome: 'A net was prepared for them to ensnare them, those who entered into the river-mouths being confined and fallen within it, pinioned in their places, butchered and their corpses hacked up'. In a single sweeping picture the artist has combined the various phases of the engagement: the Egyptians stand on their decks in steady order; an opposing vessel is held fast with grappling irons, the enemy in confusion, many of them falling into the water; while from the shore Ramses standing upon the heads of captives joins with his archers in shooting volleys of arrows at the invaders. In places, deep grooves have been cut into the wall by ancient visitors seeking to obtain stone dust from this sacred place for use in magical charms.

Battle with the Sea Peoples

The **First Court** was the scene of ceremonies and entertainments which would have included sword fights and wrestling. The *east wall* celebrates Ramses' victory in his eleventh year against the Libyans: trophies of enemy hands and genitals are counted by scribes and soldiers are rewarded for their valour. The Pharaoh himself might have distributed rewards from the window in the south wall, decorated on either side with reliefs of prisoners' heads. This was the facade of the **royal palace**; its central hall surrounded by six columns was for holding audiences; the private apartments were on the south side.

The mortuary temple continued in use for only 200 years, though the smaller temple of Hatshepsut remained a place of worship right through Ptolemaic times. In the Ptolemaic and Roman periods, the First Court was filled with houses and a monastery, the **Second Court** with the principal church of what was now a town of some size. *Traces of the church* can still be seen, for example the base of an octagonal font on the south side. Osiris figures against the pillars along the east and west sides were removed in building the church, and the central pillar on the north side was removed to make way for the apse. A few of the Osiris figures remain at the north end. Along the *west colonnade*, which is also the facade of the temple proper, the colours on the reliefs are especially bright. In the central register on either side of the doorway, Ramses is shown variously with Atum and Mont entering the temple; being crowned in the presence of the Theban triad; and being purified before receiving the emblems of his rank from the

Early Christian church

gods of Heliopolis. In the lower register on either side, Ramses' name is written in alternation with figures of his sons. None of their names, however, is inscribed as there appears to have been some uncertainty over the succession. On the architrave over the doorway is a brightly painted winged solar disc.

Beyond is the **First Hypostyle Hall**, roofless now but once with a raised ceiling over the central aisle as at the Ramesseum and Karnak. To the right are a series of *sanctuaries*, the first for the cult of the living Pharaoh. To the left are *treasure chambers*, still with their original roofs. The central chamber of these shows the weighing of gold on its south wall; sacks of gold on the west wall; and precious stones on the east wall. Off to the left of the **Second Hypostyle Hall** is the *funerary chamber* of Ramses III with Thoth represented on the south wall inscribing the Pharaoh's name on the sacred tree of Heliopolis. In the **Third Hypostyle Hall**, on either side of the central aisle, are statues of Ramses with Maat and with Thoth. At the west end of this hall are three *sanctuaries*; to the right, that of Mut; to the left, Khonsu; between them, the sanctuary of Amun, once finished with electrum, its doorway of gold, the doors themselves of copper inlaid with precious stones. The granite pedestal, now to one side of the sanctuary but originally at its centre, supported Amun's sacred boat.

Sanctuaries of the Theban triad

You should now walk back through the temple to the First Pylon and turn to the right to view the reliefs along the *outer south wall*. Above, Ramses is shown hunting various desert animals; below, most vividly, he is shown impaling with his hunting spear writhing bulls in a marsh.

The Works of Amenophis III

The remaining sights on the west bank of the Nile are associated with Amenophis III (XVIII Dyn) who ruled over Egypt at the height of her prosperity. He began the penchant for the grandiose, and though it later served pharaonic bombast, in the works of Amenophis there is always a more tolerable touch of grandeur and opulence. It is unlikely that he was ever personally engaged in any military exploits, though some inscriptions make this claim by way of convention; rather he comes across as a man who enjoyed life to the full, and had the means to enjoy it more fully than any other man of his times. A smile of contentment plays upon his lips as he sits with Queen Tiy in the colossal group at the Cairo Museum; a stela found at Amarna and now at the British Museum shows him in later years, his weary frame and jaded expression suggesting that he had known pleasures beyond even this ability to enjoy them.

Though the ancient Egyptians built their temples of stone, their homes and even their royal palaces were built merely of mud brick and so have barely survived the millenia. **Amenophis' palace** lies about a kilometre south of Medinet Habu. Though badly ruined and rarely visited, it is one of the few royal residences in Egypt of which substantial portions remain. The palace contained living and state apartments for Amenophis, a separate residence for Tiy, a large festal hall built for the Pharaoh's jubilee and quarters for courtiers and for the harem. When excavated, traces of plastered walls were found, bearing lovely paintings of birds and water plants prefiguring the art of Akhenaton. These have now disappeared.

House of Joy

Though Tiy clearly enjoyed her husband's love and confidence, and was often represented as his equal in size, Amenophis did not deny himself the delights of an extensive harem. The dowry of a Hittite princess whom Amenophis married as a secondary queen included 317 damsels for most of those other nights of the year. Another text shows that having already married the sister of a Babylonian king, he was now clamouring for the king's daughter as well. And in his old age Amenophis is known to have married one of his own daughters by Tiy. Little wonder he called his palace the 'House of Joy'.

To the east of his palace Amenophis shared his bounty by digging for Tiy an enormous **lake**, 370 metres broad by 1940 metres in length, whereon the imperial couple might sail in the royal barge named 'Aton Gleams' — again suggesting that in spite of his indulgence Amenophis played some role, insensible though he might have been of the effect, in raising his son to Aton and bringing religious revolution to Egypt. Amenophis claimed, improbably, that the lake was dug in 15 days, though signs of haste are apparent in the mounds of excavated earth still lying along its western boundary.

Amenophis also built a *mortuary temple* which has now vanished beneath ploughed fields between the Ramesseum and Medinet Habu. Responsibility for its principal destruction lies with Merneptah, Pharaoh of the Exodus, who used it as a quarry for building his own temple immediately to the north. All that remains are the two famous **Colossi of Memnon** which once guarded its outer gates. The Colossi are along the road leading back to the new village of Gurna and are visible from some distance. They are in fact gigantic statues of the enthroned Amenophis himself, rising 19.5 metres from the plain. At one time they wore the royal crown and were even higher. Both are damaged and are lacking their faces; the one on the right (north) broke at the waist during an earthquake in AD 27 and was later crudely repaired, the top having been sawn into blocks. Cocteau described them as victims of rainless thunder storms: 'Crucified, sitting against great crosses; the lightning has left nothing untouched except their legs'.

If it was lightning that crucified them, it was Greek and Roman tourists who cut grafitti into the legs of the figure on the right. The inscriptions reach as high as a man can stretch and were usually cut by visiting notables, including eight Roman governors. The Colossi had early on been accorded the wonder due to the divine, perhaps because of their imposing size, perhaps because Amenophis was recognised as both Pharaoh and god. But their cult status was to elaborate: a commoner, Amenophis, son of Hapu, was architect of his Pharaoh's mortuary temple and raised the Colossi. The vast undertaking impressed both king and public, and like Imhotep at Saqqara, he was divinised. In Ptolemaic times the Colossi this son of Hapu erected and the wise sayings attributed to

The vaulted ceiling in the tomb chamber of Ramses VI in the Valley of the Kings, showing the goddess Nut

him attracted followers throughout the Graeco-Roman world. All memory of Amenophis III was forgotten, and the Greeks decided the statues were of Memnon, son of Tithonus, a legendary king of Egypt, and Eos, the Dawn, who went to fight in defence of Troy and was slain by Achilles.

The singing Colossus

But it was the north Colossus that eventually attracted so much curiosity, for after it was shattered by the earthquake it would sometimes emit a musical note as the sun rose over the eastern mountains. The Emperor Hadrian came in AD 130 with his wife and a large retinue, and camped for several nights at its feet to hear the phenomenon. He was at last rewarded with three performances on a single morning and was declared to have been exceptionally favoured by the gods. The association with Memnon was now expanded to account for the sound: fallen at Troy, he now greeted his mother Eos with a sweet and plaintive sound when she appeared at dawn, and she in turn wept tears of dew upon her beloved child. Nowadays it is thought that the rapid change in temperature as the sun rose caused splittings off of quartzite particles which resonated within the fractures. Certainly, once the Colossus was repaired in AD 199, it cried out no more.

The last time I visited the Colossi I climbed upon the pedestal of the northern one to get a closer look at the inscriptions. As I stood knee high to the diminutive figures of Amenophis' mother Mutemuia on the left and Queen Tiy on the right, a voice began to sing. Hadrian may have heard a few squeaks, but this was a beautiful and passionate love song, and I recognised the voice of Oum Khalsoum, until her death Egypt's greatest singer. The appearance from around the other side of a young Egyptian with a portable radio revealed the source of this singing Memnon. After days of wandering around the tombs and temples of the necropolis, I realised that with the possible exception of Hatshepsut's temple at Deir el Bahri, I would rather hear that marvellous voice than see all the stones of Thebes.

Envoi

At evening at a café on the Luxor embankment you watch the Nile and sky go black, infinity lost in the sensual embrace of the goddess Nut, her breasts sparkling with stars, the moon rising along her thighs. Ouds, drums and tambourines pulse through the body of her night. A dancer ties a long scarf round his waist, the knot at one side; it writhes in orgiastic rhythm but his head is high and motionless like a woman's bearing water. Time is led a dance through coils of music. A censer is swung across your table to drive away the evil that covets and holds.

PRACTICAL INFORMATION

There is some no-star **accommodation** on the west bank; **Habu**, near the entrance to Medinet Habu; **Sheikh Ali** (known also as the Mersam Hotel), opposite the Department of Antiquities at the intersection past (ie behind) the Colossi of Memnon; a place of no name across the road from the Colossi themselves, and **Wadi el Melouk**, at old Gurna on the road to Carter's house. They are all small and very simple.

Sites on the west bank are open from

5am to 6pm. **Tickets** are required for the major sites and must be purchased in advance from the ticket kiosk at the tourist landing on the west bank. Fees are:

Mortuary Temple of Set I LE1
Valley of the Kings (Biban el Muluk) LE5
Mortuary Temple of Hatshepsut (Deir el Bahri) LE2
Tombs of the Nobles (Sheikh Abdul Gourna) — there are 4 areas per area LE1
Mortuary Temple of Ramses II (Ramesseum) LE1
Deir el Medina (3 tombs) LE1
Valley of the Queens (Biban el Harem) LE1
Mortuary Temple of Ramses II (Medinet Habu) LE2

Tickets are date-stamped and good only on the day of purchase.

If you are with a tour, you will probably board the **tourist ferry** in front of the Winter Palace or Savoy and go straight to the tourist landing on the other side. However, just north of the Savoy, down an earth bank, is the more frequent **people ferry** (as the locals call it, carefully distinguishing themselves from mere tourists). The tourist ferry costs 20PT (10PT with a bicycle).

The people ferry will land you a couple of hundred metres south of the tourist landing and ticket kiosk, but smack amidst the taxi drivers and donkey boys. You negotiate a price (see *Practical Information*, under *Information*, at the end of the *Luxor* chapter), travel to the kiosk to buy your tickets, and you are off.

The number of people that can fit in a **taxi** is 5 to 7 and the fare per full 8-hour day therefore varies accordingly. Also a taxi can be hired as private, ie it sticks with you throughout the day, or not private, ie the driver zooms off in search of passing custom while you are down a tomb or whatever and catches you up when you need him. You can imagine the variations in rates all this produces. However, for a private taxi, expect to pay LE8 to LE12; for a non-private taxi, LE5 to LE7.

Also you can try your luck on odd journeys, hiring a taxi to the Valley of the Kings, walking over the ridge to Deir el Bahri, catching a taxi from there to somewhere else.

Donkeys cost about LE1.50 for the whole day, to all the sites. They are uncomfortable and unless you are possessed by some masochistic nostalgia for pre-internal combustion engine forms of transport should be avoided. In any case, donkey boys can be bastards: they have a habit of agreeing to a price, then increasing it as you trot along, and tossing you off the donkey if you do not give in. My first time at the necropolis I was de-donkeyed 3 times enroute to the Valley of the Kings, finally agreed to an extortionate price, and when I got back to the Nile leapt onto the ferry and left the donkey boy screaming on the west bank for his money. Possibly he is now the taxi driver who gives me such a hard time.

Whether by donkey or taxi, always agree clearly on the price beforehand and do not pay a single piastre until the boy or driver has fulfilled his side of the bargain.

Bicycles, hired for about LE1.50 per day in Luxor, are the best way to get around — if you are fit. As you peddle along past tombs and temples you are surprisingly cool and sweatless in the dry air (though beware of sunstroke); the instant you stop the sweat pours off you in buckets. Bring water.

The one disadvantage of a bicycle (apart from heart attacks and sunstroke) is not being able to **walk** from the Valley of the Kings to Deir el Bahri — this is highly recommended.

Refreshments are available at the Valley of the Kings (restaurant), Deir el Bahri (soft drinks), Deir el Medina (café) and elsewhere.

If you are **shopping** for souvenirs there are any number of touts at the landing stage willing to oblige, with scarabs, mummified ibises, their grandmother's big toe and God knows what else. If you really must buy this rubbish (all phoney), offer no more than one-tenth the asking price: it will be accepted with alacrity. For a more interesting selection of alabaster bowls, figurines, etc, there is a **workshop** (near the Wadi el Melouk hotel) along the road to Carter's house where you can watch these things being made (it can take 5 days to make an alabaster bowl) — the prices are, yes, one-tenth of those asked by the hawkers at the landing stage. The people here are continuing in the line of their ancient forefathers, churning out artefacts which are in a sense no less authentic. You can imagine pharaonic craftsmen working with a bit more belief, perhaps, but no less a mercenary spirit. Notice also on some of the houses of old Gurna, as elsewhere in Egypt, the paintings depicting visits to Mecca, successors to paintings in the noble tombs below.

An **abbreviated intinerary** should include, at the very least, the Valley of the Kings and Hatshepsut's mortuary temple at Deir el Bahri.

A RIVER JOURNEY

It is godly to cruise the Nile through Egypt. Before the roads and the railways there was only this river and as the pharaohs and the hoi polloi sailed upon it and watched their world unroll it cannot have helped making a special impression on them all. The echoing silence of the deserts spoke of the void beyond the grave. But here along the river was the rhythm of bright green fields perpetually tender, small brown figures absorbed in their patch, fishermen like spikey water insects poling through the reeds. A flap of egret wings as you glide by, distant, breeze-blown, upon the artery of life itself. It is like the most beautiful murals in the ancient tombs, too sweet not to carry into eternity.

Ptolemaic tentacle

Like a string of citadels extending Alexandrian power towards Nubia, the Ptolemies built temples along the Nile at Esna, Edfu and Kom Ombo. Cruise boats ply between Luxor and Aswan throughout the year and offer an agreeable way of enjoying the lush Valley scenery and visiting the temples enroute. The experience can only be improved, for the more adventurous, by hiring a felucca and entrusting yourself to the power of the current and the winds.

Esna

A short walk up from the quayside through the constricting streets of Esna (54 kms from Luxor) and beside an awning-shaded market is the temple, squatting in a pit. It had been covered over with houses; now it is partly laid bare behind railings and you descend a staircase into the excavations. Ptolemy VI rebuilt this **temple to Khnum**, the god who fashioned man on his potter's wheel, over the ruins of earlier structures, but almost all that remains to see is the later *hypostyle hall* built by the Emperor Claudius in the 1st C AD — a deliberate anachronism in a foreign style. The carvings within are of a poor standard, but the roof is intact and supported by 24 columns with 16 different capitals. It is these you come to see. It is best to stand here, slowly revolving, looking upwards at the myriad palm and composite plant capitals, arranged without order or symmetry, but with the most pleasing effect, as though you were standing amongst trees, admiring the subtle and powerful architecture of a forest.

Esna was once a terminus for caravans picking their way from oasis to oasis across the desert from the Sudan, but this trade virtually expired with the passing of the last century. It remains though a merchant town and weaving centre, and can be interesting to wander about. The barrage, too, built in 1906, is busy with trucks and carts trundling from one side of the Nile to the other, and in the morning with barges and cruise boats waiting to pass through its locks. It was for another reason that Flaubert paused here in 1850: by an edict of Mohammed Ali's in 1834 prohibiting prostitution and

The learned women of Esna

female dancing in Cairo, the *almehs* (literally 'learned women') of Egypt had concentrated in Qena, Esna and Aswan. Flaubert entertained a mystique about prostitution: 'A meeting place

Forest of columns: temple to Khnum

of so many elements — lust, bitterness, complete absence of human contact, muscular frenzy, the clink of gold — that to peer into it deeply makes one reel. One learns so many things in a brothel, and feels such sadness, and dreams so longingly of love!'

At Esna he was propositioned aboard his boat by an *almeh* followed by her pet sheep, its wool spotted with yellow henna. He went with her to the house of Kuchuk Hanem, 'a tall, splendid creature, lighter in colouring than an Arab; she comes from Damascus; her skin, particularly on her body, is slightly coffee-coloured. When she bends, her flesh ripples into bronze ridges. Her eyes are dark and enormous, her eyebrows thick, her nostrils open and wide; heavy shoulders, full, apple-shaped breasts'. She danced the Bee, which required that the musicians be blindfolded, and slowly removed her clothes. 'When it was time to leave I didn't leave. I sucked her furiously — her body was covered with sweat — she was tired after dancing — she was cold — I covered her with my pelisse, and she fell asleep with her fingers in mine. As for me, I scarcely shut my eyes. Watching that beautiful creature asleep (she snored), my night was one long, infinitely intense reverie — that was why I stayed. I thought of my nights in Paris brothels — a whole series of old memories came back — and I thought of her, of her dance, of her voice as she sang songs that for me were without meaning and even without distinguishable words. That continued all night. At three o'clock I got up to piss in the street — the stars were shining... As for the *coups*, they were good — the third especially was ferocious, and the last tender — we told each other many sweet things — towards the end there was something sad and loving in the way we embraced.'

Back in France, while he was writing *Madame Bovary*, he wrote to Louise Colet, his jealous mistress: 'You tell me that Kuchuk's bedbugs degrade her in your eyes; for me they were the most enchanting touch of all. Their nauseating odour mingled with the scent of her skin, which was dripping with sandalwood oil. I want a touch of bitterness in everything — always a jeer in the midst of our triumphs, desolation even in the midst of enthusiasm'. And he reminded Louise that 'you and I are thinking of her, but she is certainly not thinking of us. We are weaving an aesthetic around her, whereas this particular very interesting tourist who was vouchsafed the honours of her couch has vanished from her memory completely, like many others. Ah! Travelling makes one modest — you see what a tiny place you occupy in the world'.

Edfu

Equidistant from Luxor and Aswan (105 kms), Edfu is spread upon the mound of an ancient city. The **Temple of Horus** is on the western outskirts of the present town, at a spot where Horus and Seth met in titanic combat for the world. The temple is suitably monumental and the best preserved in Egypt. Construction began under Ptolemy III Euergetes and it was completed, down to its decorations, by the mid-1st C BC. It is therefore hardly a century or two older than the many technically superior imperial ruins in Rome. But you forget this and applaud the Ptolemies' phoney archaic style, for this is pure theatre. Remembering Justinian's boast that with Hagia Sophia he had surpassed Solomon's temple, at Edfu despite a mouthful of popcorn you cry out, 'Cecil B DeMille, they have outdone you!'

Hollywood spectacular

On the *pylon towers* Neos Dionysos, in New Kingdom gear, snicker-snacks amongst the Bandersnatch, while in the *colonnaded court*, against the elaborate floral columns of the pronaos, is the Jabberwock itself — one of a pair of granite falcon-Horuses which stood on either side of the entrance (the other, headless, has keeled over in the dust). You walk through a series of ever smaller, ever darker halls and chambers to the *sanctuary* of the god, weirdly illuminated through three small apertures in the ceiling by a dim green Nilotic light. The reliefs on the lower row on the right-hand wall within correspond to those at Dendera, in this case showing Philopator entering the sanctuary and worshipping Horus, Hathor and his deified parents. His pendant arms indicate an attitude of reverence.

Leaving the sanctuary and walking back towards the pronaos, you enter an antechamber, off which, to the left

1. Pylon
2. Court
3. Pronaos
4. Hypostyle hall
5. Antechamber (staircases to roof)
6. Antechamber
7. Sanctuary of Horus
8. Relief of Horus slaying Seth
9. Nilometer

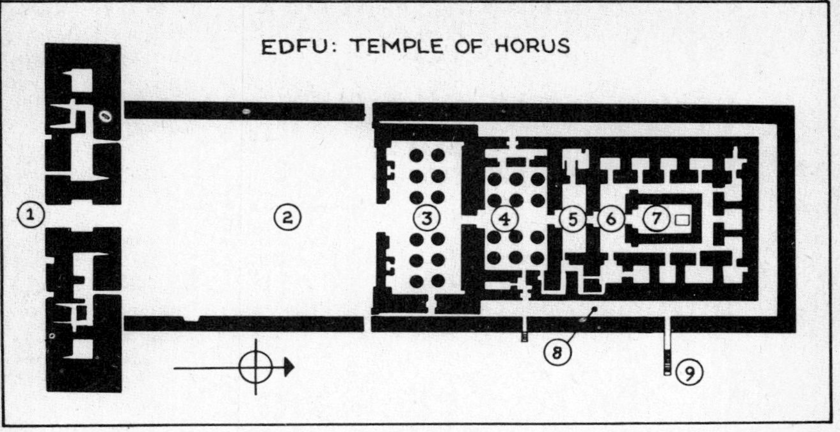

(east), is a vestibule (a fair amount of red and blue paint on the capitals) giving on to (north) an elegant little *New Year Chapel* decorated on the ceiling with the goddess Nut, pale green with a blue skirt of stars. She is beautifully shaped, with unusually fine breasts and profile, as though here there is a Greek concern for beauty and not just conventional form. Returning to the antechamber you pass (south) to a second, outer antechamber with a staircase on either side leading to the roof. As at Dendera, the residing deity required at least an annual dose of sunshine, a reimpregnation of soul from the sun. This occasioned the New Year procession up to the roof, and the decorations along the staircase walls reproduce the ceremony in full detail.

Other rites celebrated annually were the conjugal visit of Hathor (see Dendera); the triumph of Horus over Seth (see the inner face of the east enclosure wall); the coronation in the main court of a live falcon as the living symbol of Horus on earth; and the re-enactment of the divine birth of Horus and the Pharaoh at the Birth House outside the pylon (with episodes of the ceremony carved on its walls).

The Changing Landscape Towards Kom Ombo

Southwards beyond Edfu the palms and cultivation on the east bank give way to the Arabian Desert and at **Silsileh** (145 kms from Luxor) the Nile passes through a defile, now with only hills on either side but thought once to mark a cataract. The rock bed of Egypt changes here from limestone to the harder sandstone used in almost all New Kingdom and Ptolemaic temple building. During the reign of Ramses II the Silsileh quarries were worked by no fewer than 3000 men for the Ramesseum alone.

Above Silsileh the mountains again recede from the river and the desert is kept at bay by canals. Irrigation and the fellahin bring harvests of cane and corn to the fields. The reclaimed land on the east bank around **Kom Ombo** (164 kms from Luxor, 46 kms from Aswan) supports a large Nubian population displaced from their homeland by the rising waters of Lake Nasser. The village is on the Luxor-Aswan road; nearby is a sugar refinery supplied by barges landing near the temple 4 kms to the west.

A suggestion of Greece

The **temple** stands on a low promontory overlooking the Nile. Its elevation, its seclusion, the combination of sun and water flowing past as though in slow but determined search for the Mediterranean, at last suggests something of Greece. It has ruined well, and there is something in its stones of that Hellenic response to light, the uncompromising noonday glare, the soft farewell to the setting sun without fear of night.

The usual Ptolemaic (and Roman) appeasement of the fossilised Egyptian preisthood is apparent, however, as soon as you abandon mood for detail — even Marcus Aurelius must stoically appear on an outer corridor wall in pharaonic garb offering a pectoral to Sennuphis, divine wife of Haroeris. The naos was begun by Ptolemy VI Philometor; the hypostyle hall and pronaos were added by Neos Dionysos; and Augustus added the court, the outer enclosure wall and the now destroyed pylon. It is a symmetrically twin temple, the left side dedicated to falcon-headed *Horoeris* (the older Horus), the right to *Sobek*, the crocodile god. The two parts of the temple are only physically divided, however, at the two sanctuaries.

Two temples in one

The temple faces more or less west, towards the Nile. You approach from the south, past a massive ruined *gateway* built by Neos Dionysos. In front of you, between an ancient brick wall and the outer temple wall, is a small *chapel of Hathor*, the gift of a wealthy Roman woman. Through its gratings you can see sarcophagi and the piled up mummies of crocodiles — not belonging here, merely tossed in after being dug up in a nearby cemetery.

Only a few courses of the temple *pylon* remain, and the stumps of the 16 columns once surrounding the *court* — at its centre is the stone altar used in sacrifices. Except for the three centre columns framing the dual passageways leading to the twin sanctuaries, the *pronaos* facade has lost the upper parts of its columns where they rise above the screen. But there is no loss of effect. The surviving columns burst in floral capitals, and above them, across the remaining section of the cavetto cornice, are two winged discs emphasising again the duality of the divine presence here. Within the pronaos the ceiling is decorated with flying vultures and the supporting capitals proclaim the unity of Upper and Lower Egypt, some the lily, some papyrus — and one eccentrically a palm. On this side of the screen are *reliefs* of various Ptolemaic pharaohs receiving the blessings of Egypt's high gods and the double crown of Delta and Valley.

In the hypostyle hall beyond, and in the three rising ante-chambers after that, are more *reliefs*. One, between the doors into the sanctuaries, shows Ptolemy Philometor and his sister-wife before Sobek, Haroeris and Khonsu who inscribes the Pharaoh's name on a palm stalk, the equivalent of St Peter confirming entry into heaven. Philometer wears a full Macedonian cloak, a rare exception to the traditional guise.

The Jabberwock at Edfu

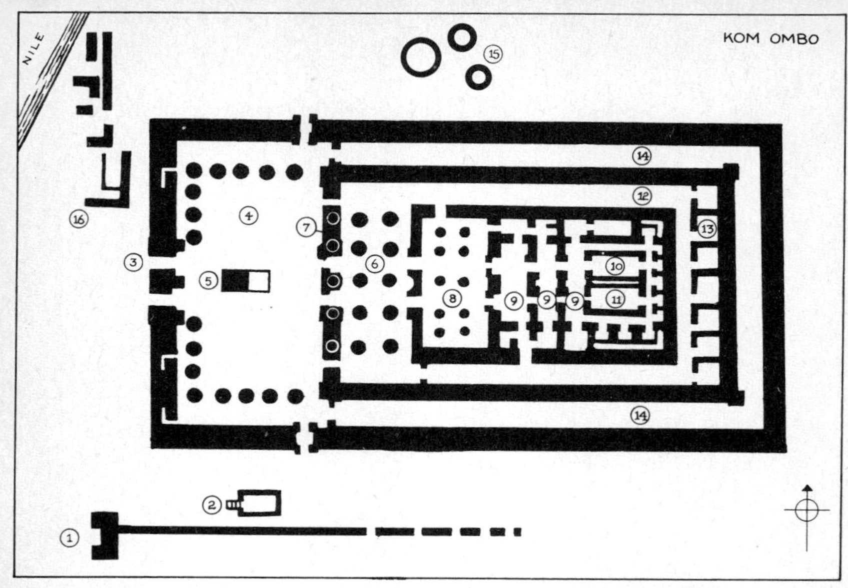

1. Gate of Neos Dionysos
2. Chapel of Hathor
3. Pylon (destroyed)
4. Court
5. Altar
6. Pronaos
7. Coronation reliefs
8. Hypostyle Hall
9. Antechambers
10. Sanctuary of Haroeris
11. Sanctuary of Sobek
12. Inner corridor
13. Stairway in centre chapel
14. Outer corridor
15. Roman wells
16. Birth House

Hocus pocus

Little is left of the *sanctuaries*, but they are all the more revealing for that. Between them, at a lower level, is a crypt which communicates with a chapel to the east. The crypt is now exposed but was once covered with a sliding slab. It is not difficult to imagine someone creeping down there from the chapel to make spectral noises at appropriate moments — the priests to fool Pharaoh, or one of Pharaoh's men to fool the priests? Probably the priests fooling each other, the Ptolemies having the last laugh.

Beyond the rear wall of the naos are seven *chapels* leading off the *inner corridor*. A stairway in the centre chapel leads upwards for a view over the temple. The chapels are at various stages of decoration. An *outer corridor*, entered from either end of the court, is decorated with Roman reliefs. It is here, just to the left of dead centre along the north section of outer wall that you will find Marcus Aurelius. To the left, in the northeast corner, is a display in relief of medical instruments: suction cups, scalpels, retractors, scales, lances, bone saws, chisels for surgery within the skull, dental tools, etc — testimony to the remarkable degree of medical sophistication in Egypt nearly 2000 years ago.

Along the north flank of the temple are two *Roman wells* in which, perhaps, the sacred crocodiles were kept. At the north-east corner of the temple is what is left of the *birth house*, much of which has fallen, along with its portion of the terrace, down to the Nile. It is Egypt reclaiming her own.

PRACTICAL INFORMATION

There is no star-category **accommodation** along this route. You should base yourself in Luxor or Aswan. See the *Practical Information* sections of the *Luxor* and *Aswan* chapters for **travel** details.

All 3 temples (LE2 fee at each) can be seen in a day if you hire a car with driver at either base, arriving at evening at the other. If relying on train, share taxi or local bus, count on seeing only two temples enroute, returning to the third from your new base — though you may find you are able to manage all 3.

It is difficult to choose between the three temples for an **abbreviated itinerary**. Certainly at Esna there is least to see; it is a cameo experience. Edfu has the most imposing temple. Kom Ombo is pleasingly situated. When I first had to choose, I went to Kom Ombo — I liked the name.

ASWAN

Aswan (210 kms from Luxor, 886 kms from Cairo) is where the Valley closes upon the river, no more buffer of cultivation on either side, instead a universe of desert sundered by the pulsing Nile flowing out of Africa. At this point the Nile is only 87 metres above sea level, so low a height for so massive a river, you would think it would disdain the 87-metre inducement to go further, but there is a continent of water behind, urging it on through the cataract above Aswan, and the current is strong. The layer of sandstone covering Upper Egypt from Edfu southwards is ruptured here by the thrust of underlying granite which the river has hewn into the rocks and islands of the First Cataract. Even before construction of the British dam at the turn of the century and the giant hydro-electric dam in the 1960s, this is where traffic on the Nile stopped. Camels transported cargoes round the rocks while lightened boats took there chances through the granite passage. The more intrepid passenger might stay aboard: 'We see the whole boat slope down bodily under our feet. We feel the leap — the dead fall — the staggering rush forward. Instantly the waves are foaming and boiling up on all sides, flooding the lower deck, and covering the upper deck with spray. The men ship their oars, leaving all to helm and current; and, despite the hoarse tumult, we distinctly hear those oars scrape the rocks on either side' (Amelia Edwards).

Racing the rapids

Frontier Outpost

Aswan is where Egypt ends. Beyond lie Nubia and the Sudan, and the traditional routes of invasion and trade. The ancient Egyptians garrisoned the 500-kilometre stretch of river to the Third Cataract, and a fleet patrolled the Nile between the First Cataract and the Second at Wadi Halfa. An uprising or an attack on a caravan, and signal fires relayed the summons for help to Aswan. Two thousand years and more later, Aswan marked the southernmost margin of the Roman world, and when Juvenal fell into disfavour at Rome for writing satirical verses against the Emperor's court, it was to Aswan that he was posted, to guard the Empire he had mocked. It is the High Dam that accounts for the modern military presence. Its breach would send a tidal wave down the whole length of the Nile Valley and inundate half of Cairo. But that presence and the object of its protection lie out of sight some kilometres south of the town, which for all of its growth and the influx of workers in recent years retains an atmosphere of remoteness and tranquillity.

Over the centuries the Tropic of Cancer has shifted slightly to the south, but in classical times it fell across Aswan, proved by a famous well into which the sun's rays plunged perpendicularly at midday during the summer solstice, leaving no shadow. Hearing of this, Eratosthenes (276–196 BC) of the Mouseion at Alexandria concluded that the earth was round and had a diameter of 12,560 kms — an error of only 80 kms. A triumph of constructive thought inspired by a place whose

Idle contentment

genius lies in the inducement to idle contentment. Following the day's fierce sun and dry desert heat, there is the beauty at evening of sand, sky and water fading impercepitably through deepening violet, a lift of breeze on the Nile, a movement of palms, a flight of ibis, and the graceful glide of swallow-tailed feluccas. The final pleasure is to know that when morning comes at Aswan there is so little to do. Those who insist on doing it can easily do it all in a couple of days. Those who want to do nothing will want to stay far longer.

Long favoured as a winter resort with daytime temperatures around 23° to 30°C, the increase and changing style of tourism in Egypt has led greater numbers of travellers to challenge the summer heat which usually ranges from 38° to 42°C during the day, though it can climb much higher. Air conditioning and a siesta during early afternoon, and the low humidity, make even the hottest July and August days bearable.

Orientation

The **station** is at the north end of town, some distance back from the river. The temperature, often 10°C higher at Aswan than in Cairo, hits you as you step off the train, and darker skins, lighter builds, introduce you to the tropics. A taxi, or better yet a carriage, will take you to your hotel and provide you with your first glimpse of the setting. As you emerge onto the corniche, you see a bare hill rising from the opposite bank and cut into its face the small dark openings of the ancient tombs of Aswan's governors and princes.

The facades at this end of the **corniche** are new and concrete, but the sweep of the Nile is impressive. The older town lies behind. A few streets back, running parallel with the corniche, is the best **bazaar** outside Cairo, alive with Arabs and Nubians and blacks trading in gum, spices, ivory, ebony and other exotic prizes out of Africa, as well as local weaves and manufactured goods. Although Aswan is not the crossroads of trade it once was, and the days of the caravans are gone, the flavour remains and the imagination recalls magnificently shawled and turbaned guards, huge scimitars dangling at their sides, accompanying a hundred camels laden with elephant tusks out of Ethiopia, driving the dust before them in clouds. The picturesque inner town deserves exploration, especially at evening. There are a few simple but good restaurants, and a large Coptic church.

African bazaar

In ancient times this area was known as Syene and famous for its nearby quarries of pink granite, but it was always secondary to the main commercial and administrative settlement of Yebu, which stood at the southern end of the long palm-covered island on your right. Yebu was Egyptian for elephant, and the island today bears the Greek translation, **Elephantine**. Perhaps in the earliest millenia of their history, before the desert had crept down to the Nile, the Egyptians first encountered elephants here, though it is more likely that Yebu owed its name and much of its importance to the ivory trade from the south. The most obvious feature at this northern end of Elephantine is the unfortunate bulk of the Aswan Oberoi Hotel, like a control tower without an international airport. On the far side of Elephantine, and largely obscured by it, is **Kitchener's Island**; it was from Aswan that Kitchener set out to conquer the Sudan in 1896–98 and the island is a botanical garden begun by him.

Continuing along the corniche, the Philae Hotel is on your left, and after it the Grand Hotel of ashen glory (it has recently burnt down), second only to the Old Cataract as the favoured place to stay between the wars. It is along this **quayside** that the Nile cruise boats tie up when visiting. Ferries leave from here to Elephantine. Further on at the roundabout with the Egyptair office, the road from the airport enters town. Ferries also leave from here to Elephantine, and to the Amun Island Hotel in mid-river, and feluccas may be hired. One arm of the Nile runs through the narrow channel between the massive embankments of ancient Elephantine town and the great doughlike outcrops of pink granite on the east bank, the road rising round the shaded public gardens that overlook the river here. Surmounting the outcrop is the Old Cataract Hotel; near it is the New Cataract, and beyond that the Kalabsha Hotel.

Murder on the Nile

Devotees of nostalgia must make a pilgrimage to the **Old Cataract Hotel**, a russet pile atop a loaf of pink granite, surrounded by gardens, with beautiful views along the Nile in either direction and across the tip of Elephantine to the **Mausoleum of the Aga Khan** and against the distant desert horizon the old **Monastery of St Simeon**. John Fowles in *Daniel Martin* describes the interior: 'Pierced screens, huge fans, tatty old colonial furniture, stone floors, silence, barefooted Nubian servants in their red fezzes; so redolent of an obsolete middle class that it was museum-like' — it has since been refurbished, though not spoilt. The exterior features in the film of Agatha Christie's *Death on the Nile*; the terrace, cocktail in hand, amidst the calm, is the perfect place to plot an elegant murder.

Elephantine

The purposeful excuse for visiting Elephantine Island is to see the scant ruins, the ramshackle museum and the ancient Nilometer. The **Nilometer** is under a sycamore tree, a few boat-lengths north of embankments bearing *inscriptions* from the reigns of Tuthmosis III and Amenophis III (XVIII Dyn) and Psammetichus II (XXVI Dyn). Its square shaft can be entered directly from the river or down steps from above. Though probably dating from an earlier period, it was rebuilt by the Romans, the scales marked in Greek. It was restored in the last century, when Arabic and French inscriptions were added. Strabo records that 'on the side of the well are marks, measuring the height sufficient for the irrigation and other water levels. These are observed and published for general information. This is of importance to the peasants for the management of the water, the embankments, the canals, etc, and to the officials on account of the taxes. For the higher the rise of water, the higher are the taxes'. The High Dam put an end to the annual inundation, and under Nasser this ancient basis of taxation was abolished. The more modest fluctuations in the level of the Nile are still measured,

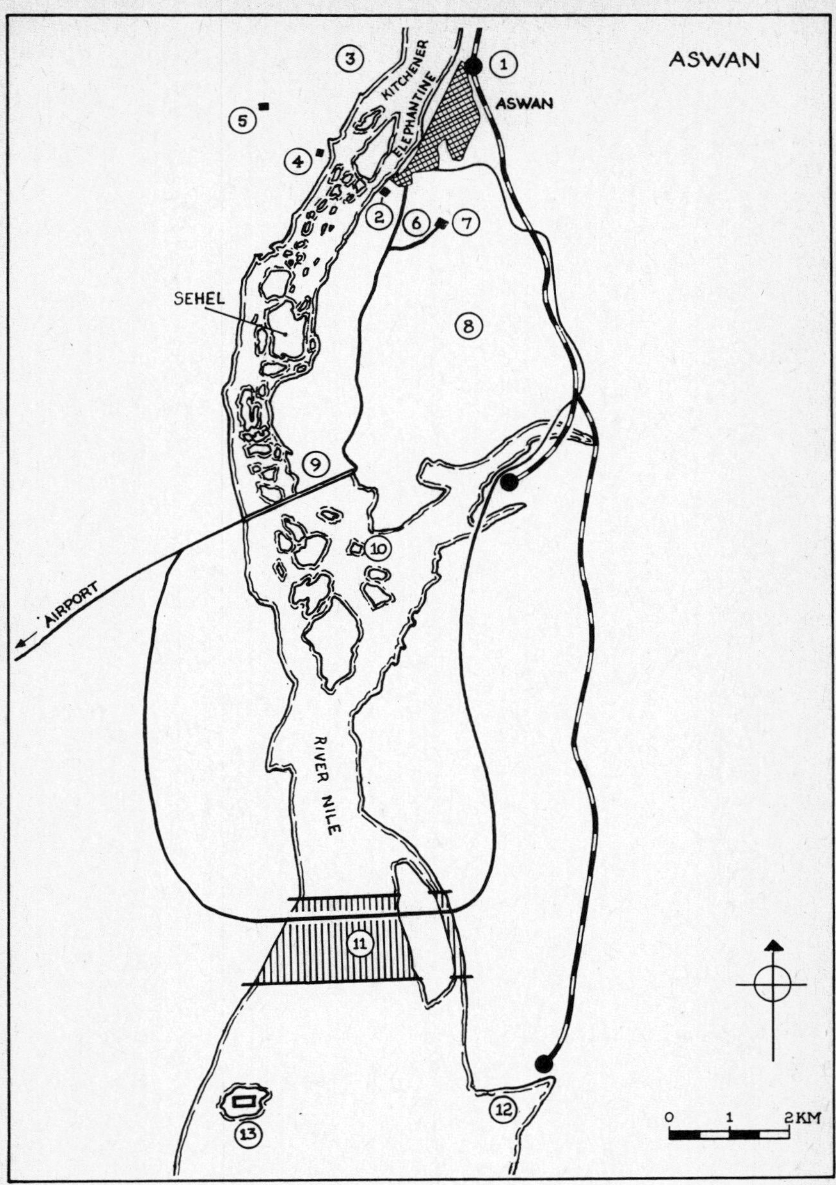

1. Station
2. Cataract Hotels
3. Nobles' tombs
4. Mausoleum of the Aga Khan
5. Monastery of St Simeon
6. Fatimid cemetery
7. Obelisk
8. Quarries
9. Aswan Dam (built by British)
10. The new Philae
11. The High Dam
12. New harbour (for Wadi Halfa)
13. Kalabsha temple

however. In 1984 the US Agency for International Development granted Egypt $4.5 million to install a satellite communcations system that will tell irrigation engineers in Cairo the level of every waterway in the country.

Nilometer in space

The **ancient town** of Yebu stood at the southern end of the island. Excavation began at the beginning of this century after evidence suggested there had been a sizeable Jewish colony here in the 6th C BC, but there is little to see that makes any impression on the amateur. Most of the remains are of mud brick and the dusty ground is littered with shards. There are the foundations of three *temples*, and the fragments of a small temple down by the water reconstructed with the aid of much yellow brick. The island was home to Khnum, a ram-headed god of the cataracts who was said to have fashioned man on a potter's wheel. Rams sacred to the god were mummified, and the sarcophagus of one, with mummy, is in the **museum**. This is a verandahed old house on high ground overlooking the ruins and set in well-kept gardens. On view are a golden bust of Khnum with brown peaceful eyes, and an assortment of jewellery, pots, granite statues of island governors, weapons, bronze mirrors and beautiful slate palettes for cosmetics in the form of fish, birds, buffalo and hippopotamus — all of them local finds dating from the predynastic through Byzantine periods, and labelled in English and Arabic.

The greatest pleasure of the island, however, is to follow the pathways which wander off through the fields and luxuriant palms to the three **Nubian-speaking villages** of the island. The houses are pale yellow or brilliant blue, the eyes of the young girls alluringly black. A brass woman's hand serves as a door knocker, a ring on one finger. Some doorways are carved with crocodiles at the foot, fish in the middle and a man on top, the woman's hand between fish and man, a statement of ideal proximities. The Kaaba, the sacred black cube at Mecca, is painted on some housefronts to show that its owner has been on the hajj, and sometimes to show how he got there a boat will be added, or fancifully a single-engined propeller plane with open cockpit, or more likely a wide-bodied chartered jet.

Those who have been to Mecca

At the north end of the island is that big hotel again, behind a 3-metre high cordon sanitaire, erected I first thought to keep the Nubians out, but on second thought almost certainly to keep the air-conditioned people in.

Botanical Gardens

On the way to **Kitchener's Island**, Aswan disappears behind Elephantine Island and you could be almost anywhere along the Nile, except that few stretches of the river are as lovely as this. Kitchener was presented with the island when he was Consul-General in Egypt and here he indulged his passion for flowers, ordering plants from India and all over the Middle and Far East. You should allow a guide to attach himself to you; he will skip about like one of Peter Pan's boys amongst the trees and plants in his sandals and galabiyya, picking leaves, flowers and fruits and crushing these in his fingers for you to smell, awakening all the pungency and variety of your surroundings. The island attracts birds of remarkable pattern and colour, and at the south end there is the odd sight of hundreds of white ducks paddling about in a closed-off cove, a research station for duck breeding.

The Noble Tombs

The noble tombs are on the west bank of the Nile opposite the north ends of Elephantine and Kitchener. They are modest structures, mostly dating from the end of the Old Kingdom through the First Intermediate Period and the Middle Kingdom.

Ascending steps from the landing stage, you come to the tombs numbered from south to north. The first of interest are **Nos. 25 and 26, the tombs of Mekhu and his son Sabni**. These are of the VI Dynasty, a period of decline, and are crude both in construction and decoration; it is the entrance (blocked) of No. 26 that is noteworthy, for an inscription on it states that Sabni, governor of Elephantine, mounted an expedition against the Nubians who had killed his father; that he recovered the body which was then mummified by embalmers sent by the Pharaoh; and that Sabni went to Memphis to thank him and offer presents. Apart from instancing an occasion of Yebu's military role on Egypt's southern border, the inscription shows how much importance was attached to the outpost by Memphis. **Tomb No. 31 of Sirenput,** also a governor, and son of Satet-Hotep, is one of the largest and best preserved. It was constructed in the XII Dynasty, the apogee of the Middle Kingdom, when Egypt extended its power beyond the Second Cataract. Paintings of Sirenput alongside Osiris statues of the deceased in the corridor, and in the recess of the second chamber, are delicately executed and still vivid. The unnumbered **tomb of Heka-ib**, immediately to the north of No. 35, was only cleared in 1947. It has a handsome facade with two columns and inside good reliefs depicting fishing, hunting and bulls fighting. **No. 36** is the **tomb of Sirenput**, son of Sat-tjeni, and is about 60 years earlier than No. 31, but also XII Dynasty. A limestone doorway leads to a six-columned courtyard decorated with the makings of a contented afterlife: a large figure of the deceased followed by his sandal-bearer and two dogs; another of his bow-bearer, dog and three sons; and others of fishing, women bringing flowers and two men gambling.

Magnificent view

The summit of the hill is crowned with the **Kubbet el Hawa**, the shrine of a local sheikh and holy man, and commands a magnificent view of the Nile Valley, the cataract and the desert that more than compensates for the difficult climb. A path runs from here across the desert to St Simeon, about 45 minutes by foot.

The Mausoleum of the Aga Khan

An easier way of reaching St Simeon is by landing below the Mausoleum of the Aga Khan. The walk from here is about 20 minutes, though it may be possible to hire a donkey or preferably a camel. But first you should visit the mausoleum, principally for the view, built above the Aga Khan's white *villa* where until his death in 1957 he spent the winter months and where the Begum still does. Apart from its beauty, I have heard a story that he associated himself with the spot after he found a cure here for his leg trouble by immersing himself up to the waist in the sand. The restrained proportions and the granite and sandstone of the domed mausoleum are entirely in keeping with the surroundings. The tomb within is of white Carrara marble. Each morning in winter the Begum lays a red rose on the tomb, and the ritual is taken over in summer by the gardener. There is another story that one July not a single rose was to be found in Egypt and on six successive days a red rose was flown in by private plane from Paris.

The Aga Khan is spiritual leader of the Ismailis, a Shi'ite sect (as were the Fatimids) centred on India but with large communities in East Africa and elsewhere. Aga Khan III, buried here, had a fondness for horses and was of such wealth that on his diamond jubilee in 1945 he was weighed in diamonds. His playboy son Ali predeceased him, and he was succeeded by his more earnest grandson Karim, Aga Khan IV.

Fortress of God

The **Monastery of St Simeon** (in Arabic, Deir Amba Samaan) with its towers and walls looms like a Byzantine fortress on a ridge at the head of a desert valley once cultivated with fields and gardens down to the Nile. Founded much earlier but largely built in the 8th C, it is the finest example of an original Christian monastery in Egypt, and is highly evocative. Little is known of St Simeon — he was not the Stylite — but the death, perhaps martyrdom, in 304 of Bishop Hadra occasioned the founding. The Copts base their calendar from that year. The bishop's tomb may have been here, a pilgrims' rest and monastery growing up afterwards. The monastery actively survived into the Middle Ages, but in 1321, 11 churches were destroyed by the Arabs in Aswan, the St Simeon monks were killed or driven out, and though the monastery was left intact it remained abandoned thereafter.

Christian city in the desert

St Simeon was built on a grand scale, with dressed stone walls 10 metres high. A small city lay within the walls, with cells for 300 resident monks and dormitories for several hundred pilgrims, as well as bakeries and workshops to support the community. The hills and desert roundabout offered solitude and godly communion for probably thousands of monks and hermits.

The lower storeys of the monastery are stone; the upper are mud brick and it is these that have most fallen into decay or vanished altogether. You enter the *portal*, and before you, on a height, is the three-storey *keep*, open to the sky, cells on either side of the long corridors. Stucco seems to have been applied throughout the monastery, and on it, in the apses of the *basilica* to your left, are badly damaged paintings. There is a Christ Pantokrator in the central apse; on the sides, the faces of saints have been cut out. Names are carved right into the paintings by Arabs and tourists alike — it is not only time that has taken its toll. The monastery has never been systematically excavated, nor has there been any reconstruction: it is largely a confusion of vaults, staircases, walls, workshops and quarters. From the tops of the *walls* there is a glimpse of Aswan, of green, but around 350 of the other degrees there is only the desert sea, luridly red at sundown. Yet there is an evening breeze, and amidst the gardens and within the shadow of the towering walls it must have been cool. It is strange to wander round these arches, vaults and apses of familiar shape and significance; and even before the Arabs came it must have been like that, this comforting bastion against the fierce landscape.

Women and camels

On the way back, my camel was grunting and snorting and emitting high-pitched complaints, and with the Nubian chiding and crying at her, it was like a dialogue, a dialogue of those inarticulations of a man and woman in bed. I would guess that there is an extensive woman-as-camel (or vice versa) folklore in the East.

Sailing on the Nile

By now you have become addicted to sailing in a felucca on the Nile, and the only cure is to have more of it. The longer journey upstream to the island of **Sehel** is recommended. The current is against you but the prevailing wind is in your favour and the gaff is extended upwards giving great height and grace to the sail. Sehel is just below the *First Cataract*, and even at the north end the boat is shoved about by turbulent whirlpools. Hawks hovering above the cliffs wheel and dive for fish.

The First Cataract

St Simeon: Christian bastion in the desert

You land on the east side and walk southwards over the sands to a granite outcrop streaked with bird droppings and covered with *inscriptions* from the IV Dynasty to the Ptolemaic period. Up top and towards the south is one of the most interesting (No. 81), Ptolemaic in date but depicting Zoser and the god Khnum. The inscription relates to a famine lasting seven years through Zoser's reign. Zoser asks the governor of Aswan why the Nile has not flooded and is told that is in the power of Khnum to whom Zoser then erects a temple. From here there is a *view* of the rocks and swirling waters of the cataract, but the pounding Nile and foam passed into history with the construction of the British dam. It is cool as you sail upon the river, though the sun can be dangerous; on the island there is no mistaking its ferocity. You need to be well shod, for the sand and piles of rock are blisteringly hot. A *Nubian village* lies off to the west and here you can enter a house and enjoy a refreshing cup of mint tea. The walls are thick and insulating, and the barrelled or domed roof reflects the heat at every angle; it is very cool inside.

The felucca tacks back down the Nile, taking advantage of the current. The round trip to Sehel is about 3 hours. The boatmen drink directly from the Nile, pointing out that there is no bilharzia above Esna and certainly not in the middle of the river where the current flows swiftly. It is said that to drink from the Nile is to ensure your return, so I drank: a fresh and slightly organic taste. Nor, with bilharzia no nearer than Esna and the crocodiles held at bay by the High Dam, could I resist plunging into the river altogether and opening my eyes on the almost impenetrably green water. Afterwards, you smell like the Nile, but a shower admits you once again onto the terrace of the Old Cataract. Just as they are designed to catch the slightest breeze, so in the last faint blue of sunset the felucca sails catch that glimmer of light off the horizon, and like crescent moons glide among the rocks in the Nile below.

Drinking from the Nile

Outlying Sights

Early another morning you are collected by your hired car and are driven round the outlying sights. A road leading off the roundabout by the public gardens turns south towards the **Fatimid cemetery** with its domed mausolea of holy figures, some local, others — such as Sayyida Zeinab, Ali's daughter and granddaughter of the Prophet — more widely revered. A turning to the left brings you to the **ancient granite quarries** and the *unfinished obelisk*. Roughly dressed and cut nearly free from the surrounding bedrock, in its finished state it would have weighed over one million kilograms (2.3 million pounds) and would have been the largest piece of stone handled in history. But work stopped after a flaw was discovered in the stone.

Back on the road south and 5 kms from town you come to the old **Aswan Dam**, built by the British between 1898 and 1902. The road passes over it and across the cataract; the water swirls round the jagged stones, plays white, but has lost its boil. The height of the dam was twice raised to increase irrigation and its hydroelectric capacity was multiplied, but

The Low and High Dams

Egypt's fast growing population and the need both further to increase her cultivable land area and to provide vast new supplies of power for a necessary industrialisation programme led to work beginning in the mid-1960s on the High Dam 6 kms upriver. The road linking the two runs through disturbed desert on the west bank, a giant disused sand pit it seems; you cannot imagine that this is the shore of an uncharted sand ocean going on forever. Numerous electricity pylons add to the impression of it being a manmade litter ground. At the west approach to the dam there is a giant lotus-shaped monument commemorating Russian-Egyptian co-operation. The police here take the opportunity to check your papers and impose a charge.

The High Dam

The High Dam has commanded world attention. Its construction became a political issue between East and West. Its sheer size, its effect on the economic potential of the country, and the sudden attention it forced on the Nubian antiquities threatened by the rising waters of Lake Nasser, have all been extraordinary.

The dam was completed in 1971 and since then the water contained by it has reached a height of 182 metres and has backed up 500 kms, deep into the Sudan. Evaporation from the artificial lake amounts to 5000 million cubic metres annually (about seven percent of the lake's volume) and is causing unusual clouds and haze in the surrounding area, and even occasional rain. But the lake also retains the silt that once renewed Egypt's fields. Chemical fertiliser plants running off the dam's hydroelectric power are filling that gap, while it is estimated that in 500 years' time the silt will have filled the lake. By then, however, some other means of water conservation may have become available, or the wasteland to the south may have reverted to the lushness of long distant millenia. The water table beneath the Sahara has already risen noticeably as far away as Algeria.

Downstream, Egypt's cultivable land area has increased by 30 percent, while the High Dam's dynamos have doubled the country's supply of electricity. The drought that has brought starvation to Ethiopia and the Sudan has seen the Nile fall to its lowest level in 350 years, and the same scenes of famine would have been repeated in Egypt had it not been for the High Dam. The British dam regulated the flow of the Nile during the course of the year; the High Dam can store surplus water over a number of years, balancing low floods against high and ensuring up to three harvests a year. The god Khnum has answered Zoser's prayer.

The structure that achieves this contains the equivalent in material of 17 pyramids the size of the Great Pyramid of Cheops, and enough metal has been used in its gates, sluices and power plant to build 15 Eiffel Towers. The *road* runs across the top back to the east bank. In merely driving along, somehow the hugeness of the enterprise is lost upon you, and because it is not ancient, and because it is functional and it works, it is easy not to be impressed. It is even possible for some to complain that it was not worth the drowning of so many Nubian monuments. The same was said when the British built their dam, to which Churchill replied: 'This offering of 1500 millions of cubic feet of water to Hathor by the Wise Men of the West is the most cruel, the most wicked and the most senseless sacrifice ever offered on the altar of a false religion. The state must struggle and the people starve, in order that the professors may exult and the tourists find some place to scratch their names'.

'The most cruel, the most wicked and the most senseless sacrifice'

Some feeling for the controlled energy of the place is realised at the *viewing platform* over to the eastern end of the dam. The green water rises in eddies, like large bursting bubbles from somewhere below the visible tops of the sluices. The generators hum as the river is put through its paces. Scores of lesser pylons flick currents of electricity towards the larger pylons striding across the desert, and bound by thick cables this energy is delivered into Egypt. Downstream, the Nile slips its harness and runs free beneath a glassy surface.

New Kalabsha

On the island of New Kalabsha immediately upriver from the High Dam and towards the west bank, you can see the **Temple of Kalabsha**, built during the reign of Augustus to the familiar blueprint of his Ptolemaic predecessors. Considering the effort that went into saving the temple from drowning at its original site 50 kms further into Nubia, little encouragement is given to visiting this stone-by-stone reconstruction. Three permissions and a motorboat full of passengers are required before a local travel agency will contemplate the undertaking. A German team removed the temple here, and as a reward the west pylon was presented to the Berlin Museum. As the temple was being dismantled, evidence of earlier structures dating from the time of Amenophis II (XVII Dyn) and Ptolemy IX was found. Considered to rank second only to Abu Simbel as the finest monument south of Philae and enjoying a harmony of proportion, nevertheless the temple was never completely adorned with reliefs and inscriptions, and the reliefs are generally of poor workmanship. Dedicated to Mandulis, a Nubian god associated with Isis, the Kalabsha temple later became a Christian church. Its greatest delight for the visitor is the spectacular view from its roof across the vast blue of Lake Nasser.

Also on the island are the **Kiosk of Qirtasi**, a Ptolemaic edifice from 40 kms upriver, and the **Temple of Bayt al-Wali** rescued from near the original site of the Kalabsha temple. Bayt al-Wali is Arabic for House of the Governor, and the temple was built by the Viceroy of Kush for Ramses II.

Philae: Island of Isis

Before the construction of the British dam, you could winter at Aswan and visit the Temple of Isis standing proud on its sacred island. But the dam all but submerged the temple for half the year, during the winter at that, and Philae became a name only, hardly a place to visit. Yet there was romance in that visit, and perverse though it may seem to say it, a romance, once established, far greater than any satisfaction

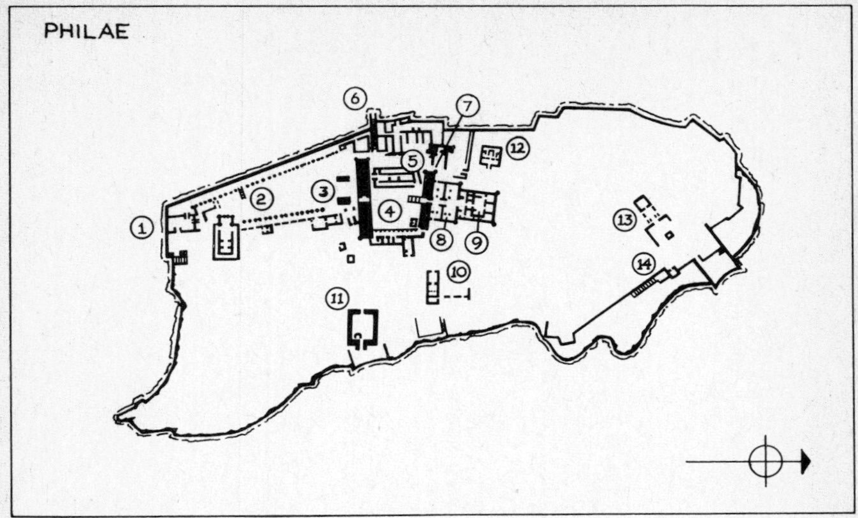

1. Vestibule of Nectanebos I
2. Outer temple court
3. First Pylon
4. Central court of the Temple of Isis
5. Birth House
6. Nilometer
7. Second Pylon
8. Pronaos
9. Naos and Sanctuary
10. Temple of Hathor
11. Kiosk of Trajan
12. Temple of Harendotes
13. Temple of Augustus
14. Roman Gate

gained from seeing Philae raised again on new and profane ground. In *Daniel Martin*, John Fowles records the experience many travellers have enjoyed this century: 'Then they drove to see the temple of Philae; a long row out into the lake, followed by the slow gondola-like tour round the submerged columns, shadowy shafts in the translucent green water. An exquisite light shimmered and danced on the parts that rose into the air. They and the guide were rowed by two old men, with scrawny wrists and mummified bare feet. Every so often, on the long haul, the pair would break into a strange question-and-answer boating-chant, half sung, half spoken. Work on transporting the temple to its new site, the guide proudly told them, would begin within the next few months; very soon sunken Philae would be abusimbelized. They didn't argue with him, but voted it a vulgarity, the whole project, over lunch'.

Saving the temple

The annual rise and fall of the Nile, elevated behind the British dam, slowly wore on the inscriptions and reliefs of the temple and eventually, though perhaps after only hundreds of years, would have brought the whole thing down. But then the High Dam was built and Philae, between the two, was permanently almost completely submerged, and worse, where it rose just clear of the river, suffered swift daily tide-like movements that would have destroyed the temple far sooner. With Hathor doubly gratified, it has now been the turn of professors and tourists to avenge Churchill's words. Whether Isis would have preferred drowning to the new *son et lumiere* is unknown.

Touring the new island

Now Philae has been reconstructed on the nearby island of Agilquiyyah, which has been carved and sliced to replicate the original island, so that it is 450 metres long and 150 metres across, with the blunt nose and truncated tail of a primitive fish. The **Temple of Isis** has been arranged along the dorsal position, the lesser temples placed elsewhere, all corresponding as nearly as possible to their previous relationship. The site was opened to the public in 1980.

The logical starting point for a tour is the *Vestibule of Nectanebos I* (XXX Dyn) at the southwest corner of the island. The temple it once led to was washed away by the Nile, but this vestibule was rebuilt by Ptolemy II Philadelphos. Nearly every other monument on the island dates from the Ptolemaic and Roman periods, and Herodotus, who visited Elephantine c.450 BC, seems to have found no reason to make any mention of Philae, though it is probable that older temples stood on the island then. Northwards extends the *outer temple court*, the first pylon of the Temple of Isis at its far end, colonnades on either side. The East Colonnade is unfinished, with many of the columns only rough-hewn; the West Colonnade follows the shoreline, its columns bearing reliefs of Tiberius offering gifts to the gods, the capitals of varying plant motifs, no two alike.

The *First Pylon*, 18 metres high, 45 metres wide, consists of two massive towers with a gateway between them. The towers were begun by Ptolemy II Philadelphus and completed by Euergetes I, though the decorations were carried out over a long period. On the front of the right or eastern tower, Ptolemy XII Neos Dionysos is shown in the traditional pharaonic pose of seizing his enemies by the hair, about to bash their brains out with a club; Isis, Hathor and the falcon-headed Horus of Edfu look on placidly. Above and to the right, Neos Dionysos offers the crowns of Upper and Lower Egypt to Horus the child. On the left or western tower, Neos Dionysos is again sacrificially braining his foes while above he appears before Unnefer (the name given to Osiris after his resurrection) and Isis, and before Isis and Harsiesis, a form of Horus. The reliefs have been severely damaged by the Copts. The vertical grooves on the towers were for holding flagstaffs. The *main gateway* was built earlier by Nectanebos and bears reliefs of him as well as Coptic crosses and, as you pass through, a French inscription on the right commemmorating the victory of General Desaix over the Mamelukes in 1799 ('an VII de la République').

The gateway through the First Pylon admits to the *forecourt* of the temple, with the colonnaded quarters of the priests to the right, the *Birth House* to the left. The birth house became an essential feature of Ptolemaic temples, its purpose similar to Hatshepsut's depiction at Deir el Bahri of her divine birth.

The cult of Osiris

There, Hatshepsut justified her temporal rule by proclaiming her descent from Amun-Re; with the spread of the Osiris cult until under the Ptolemies it became the universal religion of Egypt, each Pharaoh legitimised his accession by demonstrating his descent from Horus, first Pharoah and prime lawgiver in the land. There are many strands to the Osiris legend, and many accretions to the story and levels of meaning. Osiris, son of Re, was a king who ruled and was greatly loved in distant times. Isis was his sister and wife, Seth his brother. When Seth killed Osiris and dismembered his body, Isis searched out the pieces and put them together again, wondrously restoring Osiris to life in the underworld where he reigned as judge and king. Isis' son Horus was secretly raised to manhood in Lower Egypt and after a long and desperate struggle overcame Seth and established order over all Egypt. Historically, this may recall the subjection of the south by the north in pre-dynastic times. Mystically, Horus is the incarnation of his father, while Isis is the agent of both resurrection and reincarnation. Celebration of the rites relating to the legend, and in particular to the birth of Horus, took place at these birth houses, the Pharaoh proclaiming his legitimacy through his involvement in them. The Birth House at Philae is surrounded on four sides by colonnades and round their walls and columns are reliefs and inscriptions dating from Euergetes II, Neos Dionysos, Augustus and Tiberius. In the last (northernmost) chamber within are reliefs of Horus as a falcon in the marshes, and Isis suckling Horus in the marshes of the Delta. On the west shore of the island, beyond the Birth House, is a nilometer.

The *Second Pylon* is at an angle to the first and not quite so large. Again, Neos Dionysos is shown before the deities, this time offering animal sacrifices and incense; the reliefs on the eastern tower are better preserved than those on the western. Shallow steps lead to the *gateway* between the two. Figures here of Euergetes II and deities are greatly defaced; on the right there is an inscription to Bishop Theodoros, in whose name, most likely, much of the defacement occurred. It is testimony to the sheer quantity of antiquities in Egypt that through 4000 or more years, with one pharaoh defacing the work of another, Christians defacing the work of pagans, Moslems defacing the work of Christians and tourists defacing the work of everybody, there still remains so much to be defaced by those who can find the time and excuse for doing so.

It is through the Second Pylon that you enter the *pronaos* of the Temple of Isis proper. Pharaohs might have justified themselves at the Birth House, but this would have been the all-important goal of select pilgrims not only from Egypt but from all over the Mediterranean right through to the mid-6th C AD. For Isis was the hinge upon which the Osiris legend hung, and through her suffering and her joy the goddess offered an emotive identification so powerful and satisfying that she became identified too with all other goddesses of the Mediterranean, whom she finally absorbed. Isis was the Goddess of Ten Thousand Names, Shelter and Heaven to All Mankind, the House of Life, the Great Mother of All Gods and Nature, Victorious over Fate, the Promise of Immortality, Sexuality and Purity, the Glory of Women — when all else failed, she still could save. She was passionately worshipped by men and women alike. Cleopatra deliberately identified

The cult of Isis

herself with Isis, and called herself the New Isis, casting Antony as Dionysos, the Greek equivalent of Osiris, so that on earth they affected the already existing cosmological bond. Christianity, with its male-oriented antecedents in the Judaic and Greek religions, may never have given the prominence it did to the Virgin Mary had not a figure been needed to absorb in turn the great popularity and success of the rival Isis cult. It was a rivalry that continued late in the Christian era. In spite of the edicts of the Roman Emperor Theodosius I, which succeeded in terminating the Olympic Games after a thousand years in the 4th C AD, pagan Philae continued as a centre of Isis worship till the reign of Justinian in the 6th C, while further into Nubia the worship of Isis probably persisted until the Arab Islamic conquest.

The walls of the pronaos are covered both outside and inside with reliefs of Ptolemies (Philadelphus, Euergetes II, etc) and Roman emperors (Augustus, Tiberius, Antoninus) performing the customary ceremonies in the guise of pharaohs. Christian services were celebrated in the court and pronaos, of which the numerous Coptic crosses chiselled in the walls are memorials. In the doorway of a room to the right is another Greek inscription to Bishop Theodoros, claiming credit for 'this good work'.

Three antechambers lead through the naos to the *Sanctuary* with two small windows and a pedestal on which stood the sacred boat with the image of Isis. To the west of the first antechamber entered, a staircase runs up to the roof and to the *Osiris chambers* with fine reliefs of mourning for Osiris. Flaubert commented: 'In one of the upper rooms, scenes of embalming: in the corner to the right a woman on her knees lamenting, her arms raised in despair; here the artist's observation cuts through the ritual of the conventional form'.

Back at the bottom of the stairway, a door in the west wall of the naos opens onto *Hadrian's Gateway*. The most interesting relief is on the north wall of the vestibule and depicts the source of the Nile: the Nile god, entwined by a serpent, pours water from two jars. This relates to the ancient belief that the source of the Nile was at the First Cataract. The waters so swirled and seemed to flow in different directions that it was thought the river rose here from underground, flowing north to the Mediterranean and south into Africa. The belief hinged, as most beliefs do, on laziness and the desire not to spoil a good story: the most cursory examination of the river's flow at any point south of the First Cataract would have revealed, as no doubt it did reveal a thousand times, that the Nile always flows north. Herodotus, who enjoyed a good story himself, nevertheless dismissed the notion expressed in this relief, traced the northerly flow of the Nile back deep into Africa, and even reported a theory, based almost certainly on lost knowledge, that the source of the Nile, and the cause of its floods, lay in distant snowfalls — a theory he rejected (though 2000 or so years later it was proved right) because he could not imagine high snow mountains somewhere in the hot interior of Africa.

Speculations on the source of the Nile

Off to the east of the Second Pylon is the **Temple of Hathor**, comparable to the Greek Aphrodite despite the usual

Dahabeah moored under Trajan's Kiosk: 19th C photo of the original Philae

convention of cow's ears, built by Ptolemy VI Philometor and Euergetes II. The colonnade was decorated during the reign of Augustus with amusing carvings of music and drinking — apes dancing and one playing a lute, dwarfish Bes beating a tambourine, while Augustus offers a festal crown to Isis. To the south stands the unfinished **Kiosk of Trajan**, a rectangular building of 14 columns with beautifully carved floral capitals. On the only two screen walls between the columns to have been completed are scenes of the Emperor Trajan offering incense and wine to Isis, Osiris and Horus. The elegance of the kiosk has made it the characteristic symbol of the island.

PRACTICAL INFORMATION

ACCOMMODATION

Like Luxor, Aswan's high season is from October through May and it would be best then to make reservations in advance if you are choosy. Summer can be slack, however, though the heat should not deter you — it is a dry heat, and there is air conditioning if you want it. See the *Background* chapter under *Accommodation* for general information, also for rates.

Note that late in 1984 the Grand Hotel on the corniche burnt down. Whether it will be rebuilt, and to what standard, I do not know. It was a ramshackle old place, with cavernous rooms and an air of much-faded glory — back in the 1920s Baedeker singled it out, along with the Cataract, for star rating. Wagon-lits and Eastmar had offices in the arcade along the front; I do not know where they have gone since the fire.

Cataract, Sharia Abtal el Tahrir, at the south end of the corniche. Tel: 3576 (for the Old Cataract) and 367395 (for the New Cataract). Telex: 92720 ASCTE UN (for both). Like Luxor's Winter Palace, this is now 2 hotels, the New Cataract and the Old Cataract (both 5-star). The Old stands apart, on higher ground, with the most magnificent view in Aswan, and for my money is the finest place to stay in Egypt. The Old has recently been refurbished and is now entirely air-conditioned. Its outstanding amenity is its terrace; the New has shops, bank, a hairdresser, etc, and there is an Olympic-size pool for all Cataract guests. Whether staying at the Old or the New, insist on a Nile-side room. Alas, guests at the Old Cataract must dine at the New (half-board is compulsory year-round) in a dull restaurant with poor service and indifferent food.

Aswan Oberoi (5-star), on Elephantine Island. Tel: 762835. Telex: 92120 OBEROI UN. Owned by the same company as the Mena House at the Pyramids, this modern and slightly tacky hotel looks like an airport control tower rising absurdly from the north end of the island. I wish this, rather than the Grand, had burnt down. It is reached by regular ferries designed like ancient Egyptian royal barges (free for guests and the curious alike). Deplorable though its concrete monumentality is, the Oberoi offers some fine views, particularly westwards at sundown from the rear terrace across to Kitchener's Island. There are a bank, bookshop, hairdresser, cafe, nightclub, pool, boutiques and other trappings. Egyptair has a branch here.

Amun (4-star), Amun Island. Tel: 22555. Telex 92720 ASCTE UN. The island is beautifully and peacefully situated just south of Elephantine and is reached by launches by the public gardens near the Egyptair office. Half board is compulsory year-round, though here the food is better than at most members of the Egyptian Hotel Company chain; there is also a bar. The verandah and rooms overlook the gardens and Nile. All rooms have bathrooms and air conditioning.

Abu Simbel (2-star), Corniche el Nil. Tel: 22888. Telex: 92720 ASCTE UN. You come to this hotel soon after reaching the corniche from the train station; it is surrounded by tree-shaded gardens. The bar and restaurant are over the lobby and have a view of the Nile — only Continental breakfast is compulsory. Most of the rooms have only curtained-off bathrooms, though for a bit more you get a wall. All rooms are simple, some are air-conditioned.

Philae (2-star), Corniche el Nil. Tel: 2117. This is further south along the corniche from the Abu Simbel Hotel. There is a bar and better than average restaurant — only Continental breakfast is compulsory. All rooms have bathrooms, a few have air conditioning. The place is simple and clean.

Abu Chieleb (1-star), Sharia Abbas Farid, just behind the corniche. Tel: 23051. A decent place for its category.

Aswan's **youth hostel** is on Sharia Abtal el Tahrir (Tel: 2313) at its station end — in a hot and crummy part of town away from the corniche. Walk 1 block from the station, turn left and then proceed half a block: it is on your right.

EATING PLACES AND ENTERTAINMENT

Apart from the **Philae** and **Oberoi** hotels, both of which have good food for their price range, there are several Egyptian restaurants along the corniche, tables outside. Better than these, however, is **El Masri**, tucked away in the centre of town just off the main market street, Sharia Abtal el Tahrir. Ask and you will be directed.

Both the **Kalabsha** and **Oberoi** hotels

have nightclubs with Western and Nubian music, the Oberoi usually having a belly dancer too. In winter, the **Aswan Cultural Centre**, between the Abu Simbel and Philae hotels, presents exciting Nubian dancing.

Non-residents can swim in the **Cataract hotels' pool** for LE2.

SHOPPING

The **Aswan Cultural Centre**, on the corniche between the Philae and Abu Simbel hotels, sells Nubian handicrafts. A block of two back from the river, however, Sharia Abtal el Tahrir is Aswan's sinuous market street, the best **bazaar** outside Cairo, with an atmosphere still and an array of goods suggesting trade with Africa deeper south. Woven blankets and rugs are particularly good here and cheaper than elsewhere in Egypt; also there is ivory, ebony, spices, galabiyyas and everything else conceivable. As you wander along, have a glass of pressed cane juice. At the northern end there are several shops selling delightfully kitsch post cards.

OF INTEREST

On **Elephantine Island** is the museum, admission LE1, open winter from 9am to 2pm daily, 10am to 2pm Sundays; in summer (1 May–31 October) from 8.30am to 1pm daily, 8.30am to 11am Fridays, and 10am to 1pm Sundays. There is also the nilometer, the site of the ancient town of Yebu, and the pleasant walk through Nubian villages. Small ferries cross to the island from the corniche (about 20PT return trip). You cannot get to the rest of Elephantine from the Oberoi compound at the north end of the island.

To reach the **west bank** of the Nile for the Mausoleum of the Aga Khan, St Simeon's Monastery and the tombs of the nobles, and to reach Kitchener's Island, you must hire a felucca by the public gardens across from the Egyptair office, or below the bluff at the Old Cataract Hotel. Expect to pay (after bargaining) LE5 for 2 hours, LE10 for half a day — these include keeping the felucca waiting while you go off exploring. Your bargaining position will be stronger if you do not seek a felucca by the Old Cataract and if it is summer.

Once at the west bank you can proceed by foot, donkey or camel. Camel is best and will cost, for example, no more than LE3 for the jaunt to St Simeon's and back. Donkeys are less. There is a camel and donkey corral as you land below the mausoleum. (Entry fees for nobles' tombs, St Simeon, LE1 each.)

Groups, including a few of you together, may benefit by making all your felucca and camel hire arrangements through an agent. I recommend Wagons-lits, formerly in the arcade of the Grand Hotel which has burnt down — you will have to discover where they are now.

A visit to the granite **quarry**, the **old Aswan Dam** and the **new High Dam**, as well as a trip out to **Philae**, can be done in a morning starting early. The day before, you should go to Wagons-lits and arrange for a car. If they know of other people interested, they will put together a small group which can share the cost. This should work out at around LE10 per head. Or for Philae take a taxi (no more than LE7), then the boat (about LE5) — and divide this among 3–4 people. Philae entry is LE3. The High Dam (60PT) is a 10-minute walk from Sadd el Ali train station. The **Kalabsha temple** is difficult to visit: a group of at least 20 is necessary to justify revving up the motorboat which departs from the High Dam; also 3 permissions are required. The whole thing is a headache to agents and they do not bother except with ready-made groups.

Other expeditions, like a morning's or afternoon's **sail along the Nile to Sehel** in a felucca, or a **drive to Kom Ombo and Edfu**, are best arranged through an agent like Wagons-lits. They can assure you of a good price and reliability. The cost of a felluca or taxi should be divided among the number of people going. A local bus (from behind the Abu Simbel Hotel) will take you near Kom Ombo temple (2-km walk, or ride in a pick-up truck).

Some boatment will offer to sail you downriver to Kom Ombo or beyond, and some agents have refurbished old steamers for journeys to Luxor at far less the price of the Hilton and Sheraton behemoths (see *Travel* below).

The only way to reach **Abu Simbel** is to fly from Cairo, Luxor or Aswan. You should reserve a seat at the earliest opportunity, but it is always worthwhile trying even at the last moment. I was told in Cairo that all seats for Abu Simbel were booked up a week in advance; I asked again at the Egyptair office in Aswan and was given a seat for the following day. I have heard, though cannot confirm it, that Egyptair always holds back 10% of its seats for counter sales on the last day or so — on all flights, not just those to Abu Simbel. It is better to go in the morning when the sun is full on the temple facades.

Unless you can show that you have made a booking at the Nefertiti Hotel at Abu Simbel, Egyptair will often insist that you fly back from Abu Simbel on the same day — an obstacle that anyone wanting to sack out at the temples in their sleeping bag should be on the look out for. A 2-hour stay at Abu Simbel is sufficient; the flight takes 25 minutes, though check-in at Aswan is anywhere from 1 to 1½ hours before the flight, which is usually late anyway. In short, allow 5 hours for the trip.

TRAVEL

The best source of **information** and advice on travel and much else is **Wagons-lits**. This used to be on the corniche at the Grand Hotel which has burnt down — so look for its new location. **Thomas Cook** has an office in the Aswan Oberoi.

The **train station** is at the north end of town, several blocks back from the corniche. A taxi from the station to, say, one of the Cataract hotels should cost around LE1 on the meter at most, though an unmetered taxi or carriage will cost more.

Egyptair is at the south end of the corniche, also at the Aswan Oberoi.

For a **car with driver** to **Kom Ombo** and **Edfu**, also onwards to **Esna** and **Luxor**, make arrangements through Wagons-lits. By way of example, one-way or return to Kom Ombo will cost about LE14. This is divided amongst the passengers. Or go by **service (shared) taxi**: their depot is by the Abu Simbel Hotel on the corniche and the day's ride to Kom Ombo, Edfu, Esna and Luxor, requiring a change of taxis each time, should cost around LE1 per leg. There is also a **local bus** (from behind the Abu Simbel Hotel) to near Kom Ombo (2 kms).

The most enjoyable way of visiting places between Aswan and Luxor is by **felucca**. See *Background* chapter. Among 4 people or so, it can work out quite reasonably. Hire through or at least consult with Wagons-lits.

To reach the **Sudan**, either you can **fly from Cairo or from Aswan**. Or you can **sail from Aswan** (in fact from Sadd el Ali, the High Dam). The voyage lasts for 2 nights up the length of Lake Nasser to Wadi Halfa on the border. Departure from Sadd el Ali is at 4pm on Mondays and Thursdays, arrival at Wadi Halfa is on the third day at 8am. A connecting train to Khartoum departs at 4.40pm. In fact, these schedules are for the amusement of those enchanted by such things: the boat may not leave on time; it will almost certainly arrive at Wadi Halfa late; the train will wait, however, but instead of taking the scheduled 24 hours to Khartoum is more likely to take 36 hours.

Before you will be sold a boat ticket, you must have a visa for the Sudan and must offer proof that you are paying in Egyptian pounds bought officially (ie must show a bank receipt). First and second class tickets must be bought in Cairo (see *Background* chapter). Third class tickets can be bought at the **Nile Company for River Transport** — it is on a street off the corniche; ask for directions — or on the quayside at Sadd el Ali.

If the boat makes good time, you will pass Abu Simbel just as the sun goes down on the second night out; more likely you will not get even that glimpse. There are no stops between Sadd el Ali and Wadi Halfa, and food availability on board is erratic; bring your own. The boat is a paddle steamer with a barge tied alongside. Deck (third) class means sleeping in the lower metal deck of the barge; it can get very cold at night and a sleeping bag is essential. Deck class also gets crowded, so get to the boat as early as possible.

There is a train from Aswan to Sadd el Ali; take one leaving around noon to allow plenty of time for customs and passport formalities. Also, you can take a taxi for several Egyptian pounds.

Once at Wadi Halfa, you continue to **Khartoum** by first, second or third class train. Air conditioning is in first class only. Second class is bearable; third is uncomfortable and usually extremely crowded, passengers often riding on the roof (which, incidentally, is very cold at night).

ABU SIMBEL

Before the crowds

Originally, the rock-temples of Abu Simbel stared from sandstone cliffs which rose like gigantic pylons over the narrow Nile. In 1812, John Lewis Burckhardt, the first European since classical times to visit Abu Simbel, was not immediately impressed; he had come upon the cliffs from above, and only as he gained the river and turned upstream was he struck by the four colossal statues of Ramses II. 'Could the sand be cleared away,' he said, 'a vast temple would be discovered.' The sand was repeatedly cleared away during the 19th C. There is a remarkable photograph taken in 1850 by Maxime du Camp, Flaubert's travelling companion, of the sand rising over the faces of the two right-hand colossi. On Holy Thursday, Flaubert noted, 'We begin clearing operations, to disengage the chin of one of the exterior colossi'. It was only later in the century, with the coming of the British, that Abu Simbel and so many other monuments were properly cleared. Then, usually by Cook's steamer, tourists came. Laid bare in all their glory, and enhanced by the unique and striking beauty of the setting, the temples at Abu Simbel excited the enthusiasm of early visitors. Baedeker allowed himself a large adjective: they 'are among the most stupendous monuments of ancient Egyptian architecture'; and he went on to say: 'the temples produce a very grand effect by moonlight or at sunrise. The interior of the great temple is illuminated at night by electricity provided from the steamer'. Those were the days.

Jetting there

There is no road or railroad to Abu Simbel, tourist steamers no longer make the voyage, and the Sudan ferry, if it does not actually sink enroute, usually passes at night and never lands. You must fly. The pilot may swoop back and forth before the temples so that first, unlike Burckhardt, you see the facades. But the colossi are small from the air, and further lose all advantage of proportion by having to outstare the vastness of Lake Nasser. Once the plane lands, you bumble along a desert road by bus, disembark behind the artifical mounds, tread round to the front, gaze upon Ramses in quadruplicate, and say, 'So what'. That is what I said, anyway, though the journey itself, and the phoniness of the climax, were in their way worthwhile.

The flight is a mixture of sensations: orbiting round the moon; going on a school outing. The latter because you know everyone else on board is going exactly where you are going, will stay as long as you are staying, will look at what you are looking at, and that you will appear in a thousand of their photographs and they on a roll of yours. The former because the landscape enroute is spectacularly alien, a rippling sand plateau interrupted by sharpened buttes, perhaps the cores of eroded ancient volcanoes which later from ground level will occasionally look like pyramids; and Lake Nasser, peculiar and varying in its colours, a giant drifting oil slick upon the desert sea.

Rescuing the Temples

As the waters of Lake Nasser rose during the mid-1960s, the original site of the temples was protected momentarily behind a coffer dam while the friable sandstone was injected with synthetic resin and then hand-sawn into 1050 blocks. The first block was cut in spring 1965; by autumn 1967, block had been replaced upon block at the new site 210 metres from the old one and 61 metres higher up. The $42 million operation was organised and funded by UNESCO. The temples were saved, the dam was breached, and the sacred site, which had known human activity since prehistoric times, was swallowed by the lake.

Spirit of place

There is such a thing as spirit of place. That place lies behind you and below you somewhere beneath the waters as you stand facing the colossi of Ramses. The reconstruction has been impeccable; you knock your knuckles against Ramses' foot and are assured it is stone, not plaster; you look for the filled-in joins in the torsos but cannot detect them; and if you are there at dawn you will see that the sun's rays fall flat upon the pharaonic faces and, if the temple door is open, penetrate to the innermost sanctuary. Everything is as it was before, except that it is here and not where it used to be, and that greatly weakens the force of the new Abu Simbel. The genius of the place lay in working with the living rock, the temple facades set into cliff faces seemingly prepared by nature for the purpose, the colossi of Ramses at the south temple, those of Nefertari at the north temple, seeming to step out from the mountain, liberated from the imprisoning rock by the divine force of the rising sun. But when the cliffs are themselves reconstructions, that dramatic relationship between architecture and topography, and that mystical emergence of man from nature, is lost. To have left those ancient and powerful links intact would have meant surrendering the temples to the waters. Instead, it was decided to save the body and lose the soul. We now examine the carcass.

Touring the Temples

The temples stand on the west bank of the lake, the more southerly *Temple of Re-Harakhte*, with its colossi of Ramses II, facing east, the smaller and more northerly *Temple of Hathor*, with its colossi of Nefertari, Ramses' wife, angled slightly towards the south. Before the lake, the temples overlooked a bend in the Nile and must have dominated the landscape. This in part explains their purpose. Travellers into Africa would first have seen the imposing colossi of Ramses, a proud spur to Egyptians, a warning of Egypt's might to any fractious Nubians. On the return, Hathor, in the guise of Nefertari, would welcome Egyptians and Nubians alike to the embrace of a great civilisation. Also, the temples would have served as a convenient store for the gold and other riches exacted from Nubia as tribute, just as nearly a thousand years later the Parthenon served as the Athenian treasury. But the political and strongbox functions of Abu Simbel would have relied greatly on the religious character of the temples, and that the architects addressed themselves to religious symbolism of magnificent scale and quality there can be no doubt.

Purpose of the temples

The left-hand colossus of Ramses II

You come first upon the **Temple of Re-Herakhte**, its trapezoidal *facade* crowned by a corvetto cornice surmounted by dog-headed creatures worshipping the rising sun. The falcon-headed sun god stands within the niche above the entrance door. Arranged in pairs on either side of the entrance are the four enthroned *colossi of Ramses* wearing the double crown. Each figure is 20 metres high, taller than the Colossi of Memnon at Thebes, and hewn from the cliff face. Between and beside the massive legs are smaller figures of members of the royal family. The feet and legs of the colossi are crudely carved, as though deliberately inchoate, but the work grows finer up through the torsos (the head and torso of the second colossus from the left fell sometime in the past and has been left that way), and the heads are excellently executed. This is most true of the first head on the left, of which Burckhardt remarked, 'a most expressive, youthful countenance, approaching nearer to the Grecian model of beauty than that of any ancient Egyptian figure I have seen'. The sides of the thrones on either side of the entrance are decorated with Nile gods symbolically uniting Egypt, while below are fettered prisoners: those to the left, black Africans; those to the right, Syrians.

Colossi of Ramses

Entering the temple, the first room is the *Hypostyle Hall*, corresponding to an open court with covered colonnades. There are four pillars on either side, against which and facing the central aisle are 10-metre high *Osiris-type figures of Ramses*, though this is Ramses alive, not dead, in an athletic near-nudity showing a process of heroisation at work. The best is the fourth figure in the north row. Heroic martial deeds are depicted in *sunk relief around the walls*. If you face the entrance you will see on the left (north) entrance wall a vigorous account of the battle of Kadesh in the fifth year of Ramses' reign. It was a battle Ramses endlessly boasted about, and boast he needed to do as it was no more than a Pyrrhic victory. Ramses cut himself out of a Hittite trap, but he failed to take Kadesh. Above Ramses is a vulture, and behind him his ka, who acted as guardian angel in the struggle. On the right (north) entrance wall a corresponding scene shows Ramses in the presence of Amun-Re, to whom the king appealed at his most desperate moment: 'What ails thee, my father Amun? [Amun was absorbed in Amun-Re.] Is it a father's part to ignore his son? Have I done anything without thee, do I not walk and halt at they bidding? I have not disobeyed any course commanded by thee... What careth thy heart, O Amun, for these Asiatics so vile and ignorant of God?... What will men say if even a little thing befall him who bends himself to thy counsel?'

Poem of Pentaur

Facing again the interior, the left (south) wall of the hall bears an epic masterpiece depicting (below the top five reliefs showing Pharaoh making offerings to the gods) Pharaoh in his chariot storming a Syrian fortress, at centre Pharaoh piercing a Libyan with his lance, and to the right Pharaoh's triumphal return from battle with black captives. On the opposite (north) wall are further scenes from the Hittite campaign while on the rear wall Ramses is shown leading Hittite and black captives. *Lateral chambers* leading off from this top end of the Hypostyle Hall were probably used for storing the Nubian tribute.

In the next *hall of four pillars*, reliefs on the left (south) wall show Ramses and Nefertari before the sacred boat of Amun, and on the opposite (north) wall a similar scene before the boat of Re-Herakhte. Three doors lead from here into a transverse chamber from which in turn three doors lead off, the central one into the *Sanctuary*. Four seated mutilated figures are carved out of the rear wall: Ptah, god of Memphis, Amun, god of Thebes, the divinised Ramses, and Re-Harakhte, god of Heliopolis. Before them is a stone block on which would have rested the sacred boat. The symbolism is one of unity, the Pharaoh and gods of Egypt's three greatest cities as one; but there is also Ramses as the living and visible god, perhaps again to awe the Nubians. The entire temple leads to this central message: Ramses as conqueror, hero and then god, the awesome progression enhanced by the heightened perspective of ever-smaller chambers, ever-smaller doorways, and at the dawns when the sun rose exactly opposite the temple, a brilliant shaft of light pointing to the sacred boat and Ramses with his fellow gods in the sanctuary. Leaving the temple you should stand before the facade again, before the entrance with its falcon-headed sun god, and imagine that effect.

The power of Allah

You now walk on to the Temple of Hathor. On the edge of the forecourt there are some trees and welcome shade. While I was last here, and perhaps now too, there was a low rectangle beneath these trees, hardly more than an outline on the ground with a gap at one end, a niche at the other. It was a mosque, just broad enough for two prostrate figures, so great a contrast to the massive temples, so great a witness to the immanence and power of Allah.

The **Temple of Hathor** is secondary and complementary to the larger Temple of Re-Harakhte, and in some ways more symbolically satisfying. Hathor was wife to the sun god during his day's passage and mother to his rebirth. As Ramses is identified with the god of the first temple, so his wife Nefertari is identified with the goddess of this, and so god, goddess, Pharaoh and wife are each mated with one another at Abu Simbel. The *facade* is again a pylon, though the cavetto cornice has fallen. A series of buttresses rise into the cliff, and between them six *colossal statues* of Ramses and Nefertari. You should get up close to them. There is here the uncanny impression that they are emerging from the rock, that they are forming and will at any moment stride out towards the sunrise. The royal children stand knee-high in the shadows.

Inside the *Hypostyle Hall* with its crudely carved heads of Hathor on the six pillars, turn to examine the entrance wall.

Delightful Nefertari

Ramses is smiting his enemies; Nefertari's hands are raised, perhaps as part of the ritual, though she seems to be seeking to moderate the fury of Pharaoh. In any case, she cuts a delightful figure, a slender form in flowing dress, appealing, graceful, dignified. The side walls show Ramses before various gods, while the rear wall shows Nefertari before Hathor (left) and before Mut (right). Three doors lead to a *transverse chamber*. On either side is a further chamber above the entrances to which are Hathor's cow in her boat. In the *Sanctuary* there is the startling sight of the divine cow emerging from the rear rock wall, a suggestion of the world beyond where her milk brings life to the souls of the dead.

A surprising cow

By now you are parched and you discover a small door leading into a rock face to the right of Re-Harakhti's temple. The atmosphere is suddenly air-conditioned and there is a man selling cold drinks and post cards. You climb some stairs at the back and with even more surprise than seeing a cow coming at you from a stone wall you enter a vast echoic *dome*. It is the bubble that surmounts the major temple and over which fill has been dumped and shaped to recreate the contour of the original bluff. A walkway runs right round the inside where there are abandoned displays and sheets of data explaining how it was all done. There is much to be said for this bubble. It is the one thing at Abu Simbel that is real.

The bubble of reality

PRACTICAL INFORMATION

See the *Aswan* chapter for notes on getting to Abu Simbel.

Tickets for the temples cost LE6 and include the busride from the airport and back. You are offered a guided tour round the site.

Accommodation is at the **Nefertiti** (3-star). Enquire at the Tourist Information Office in Aswan for booking details — reservations are a necessity. The hotel is halfway between the airport and the temples, in other words in the middle of nowhere. The only excuse for staying here is if you want more time to see Abu Simbel. Rooms are air-conditioned; half-board is compulsory; there is a pool and tennis courts.

The alternative is to bring a sleeping bag and without making yourself too conspicuous to sack out right at the temples. It can get very windy, but the dawn is magnificent.

THE WESTERN DESERT

Egypt is a land of pairs — arranged as opposites, as complementaries, as identities. There is this life and the afterlife; the river and the sky; the cultivated land and the desert; and there is the desert and the sea. It is the desert and the sea, described in this and the following chapter, that bound Egypt, protect it, preserve it, sometimes suddenly change it, and with the Nile determine its fortunes.

The deserts and the sea have always provided Egypt with her security, but have provided her conquerors with avenues of attack. It has generally been the forces of the West that have come by sea or at least secured themselves by Mediterranean routes of supply. Alexander marched into Egypt from Gaza, but founded his city by the sea, his Ptolemaic successors governing from Alexandria. The Crusaders landed repeatedly at Damietta. The French and British came by sea and prized Egypt less for herself than for her strategic position on the route to India. They underlined this by building and operating the Suez Canal, and as recently as 1956 fought in vain along with Israel to keep it under their control. The Germans attacked across the desert and met defeat at El Alamein, one of the most important battles of the Second World War; they had come in tanks to break British naval power in the Mediterranean, and that naval power broke them in turn.

In its effects, the greatest desert attack on Egypt came in AD 640–1 when Amr swept across the sands under the banner of Islam. He had with him only 3500 men.

Alexander's Journey to Siwa

There is the strange story of Alexander's visit in 331 BC to Siwa, an oasis in the Western Desert, 550 kms from Cairo as the crow flies, 300 kms from the sea. After founding Alexandria, he made the long and dangerous journey, attended only by a small number of men, to consult the Oracle of Ammon, a ram-headed Libyan god associated with Egyptian Amun and Greek Zeus. Only twice in Alexander's career did his route diverge from strategic dictates; the first time he went to Troy, the site of his hero Achilles' glory; the second he went to Siwa.

The ram-headed god

Writers ancient and modern have adduced a variety of reasons why Alexander should have made the journey, but there is the recurring theme that he went to seek confirmation that he was the son of Zeus. Alexander himself never explained his motive, nor did he ever reveal what he had asked the oracle, nor what he had been told, though from that time on he was shown on coins with the horns of a ram.

Before entering Egypt, Alexander had defeated Darius at the battle of Issus, appropriating the fleeing King's 365 concubines. After Egypt, Alexander would strike at the heart of the Persian Empire, march to the Indus, and appropriate the world. In doing so, he would combine East and West, and the journey to Siwa may have been an early example of this policy of amalgam. Alexander the son of Ammon; the son of Amun; the son of Zeus. It is a usefully embracing pedigree for a young man on the threshold of universal domination.

Even today on an asphalt road the journey to Siwa takes eight hours or more from **Mersa Matruh** on the coast. Enough petrol must be taken for the return journey and an ample supply of water too, for the wells along the way may have dried up and in any case are reserved for emergencies. At least two cars should travel together so that one can go for assistance in the event of a breakdown. (As this is a sensitive military area near the Libyan border, prior permission is required from Cairo or the frontier police at Mersa Matruh. It can also be possible, with permission, to hire a private plane for the journey.)

Alexander and his guides and companions took eight days to cover the distance from the coast, getting lost in a sandstorm and after four days exhausting their water; then clouds gathered and a sudden storm broke, 'not without the help of the gods', and they were able to refill their leather water-bottles. They travelled by night along a chain of hills, their way rising and falling through valley after valley and into a final pass which wound down a ravine to the sandy plains beyond. In this pass, beneath the light of the moon and desert stars, the ground was covered with shells which reflected the moonbeams till the whole road sparkled. Bayle St John, a 19th C traveller, followed Alexander's route and described it at this point: 'A gorge black as Erebus lies across the path, and on the right stands a huge pile of rocks, looking like the fortifications of some vast fabulous city... There were yawning gateways flanked by bastions of tremendous altitude; there were towers and pyramids and crescents and domes and dizzy pinnacles and majestic crenellated heights, all invested with unearthly grandeur by the magic beams of the moon but exhibiting, in wide breaches and indescribable ruin, that they had been battered and undermined by the hurricane, the thunderbolt, the winter torrent and all the mighty artillery of time'.

A landscape blasted by 'all the mighty artillery of time'

Here Alexander lost his way again, but was rescued by a pair of crows, some writers say also by a pair of talking snakes, who set him on the proper track. Bayle St John also saw crows here, and the valley is still known to the Berbers of the region as the Pass of the Crow.

Arrival at Siwa

Gazelles are seen along the way, until the last blinding 15 kms of whitened sand and land hardened with natural salt; and then suddenly there is the **Siwa oasis**, palms and fruit trees, streams and meadow grasses, quail and falcons, and the remains of the Temple of Ammon. For both Alexander and the people of the oasis, the sudden arrival must have been momentous. Alexander had survived the phantasms and perils of the desert and was lucky to be alive; the natives had never seen a pharaoh, but here was a Macedonian conqueror. Desert caravans and the occasional pilgrim were its only link with the outside world, and after the oasis was visited by Pausanias in AD 160, it was not visited by a European again until 1792. It local customs, including homosexuality to the point of all-male marriage, survived into this century, and the

Veiled bedouin earlier this century

language spoken by its population of 5000 is as often Berber as Arabic. There is a feeling of the Sahara, of the African land mass; Egypt is distant, though Siwa's dates and olives find their way around the country and have the reputation for being the finest. Women still live secluded lives, kept often indoors, emerging wearing the veil and long robes. But their heads, their necks, their arms and legs are decorated in enormous amounts of silver jewellery, some sold at Khan el Khalili in Cairo. Amidst these unusual and gradually vanishing scenes, and innovations and new building, the old village of Siwa, its mosques and houses built of mud brick with blank and windowless facades, contributes still to the mood of isolation.

The scant remains of the *Temple of Ammon* are on the hill of Aghurmi to the east. Alexander entered into the innermost shrine, a small room about 3 metres wide and 6 metres long, and put his questions directly to the god. As at Kom Ombo in Upper Egypt you can still see here — can see more than Alexander knew — the means by which the god replied: a narrow passage ran behind the right-hand wall and was linked to the shrine by a series of small holes. Through these the priest could speak as though the god were answering in person. But it was on the temple steps, as Alexander entered or departed, that the words which came to establish Alexander's divinity were spoken. Accounts and interpretations differ. Alexander had come to Siwa via Memphis and Alexandria, and the priest in welcoming him may simply have called him 'son of Amun', that is 'Pharaoh', and this translated into Greek would have been 'son of Zeus'. Another story is that the priest, who would not have known much Greek, addressed Alexander as 'my boy', but saying *'o paidios'* for *'o paidion'*. To Alexander and his Macedonians this would have sounded like the two words *'pai dios'*, 'son of Zeus'. In any case, Greeks attached great significance to slips of the tongue, so even if they realised the error it would happily have been taken as a truth. What is historically important is not what was said that day, but what was believed in the four years between Siwa and the Indus, and it is true that Alexander did come as close as any mortal might to being the son of Zeus.

Alexander's divinity

The Inner Oases of the Western Desert

A road something over 1000 kms in length loops far out into the Western Desert from Giza, at first southwest to Bahariya and Farafra oases, continuing southeast to Dakhla oasis and then due east to Kharga oasis, finally turning northeast to join the Nile Valley near Assiut. The distance between each stage is about 200 kms, except between Giza and Bahariya where the distance is about 350 kms. The journey can be done by car, but sufficient water and petrol should be taken to cover any emergency. There are also buses and trucks. Kharga is served by air from Cairo. Travel permits are not required but you must register with the police at each oasis. Kharga and Dakhla, being closest to the Nile Valley, have been under greater control by the central authority and this is reflected in the number of monuments and relative prosperity of these areas. These last two are best visited (if travelling overland) from Assiut which can easily be reached by express train from Cairo or Luxor.

Ninety-three percent of Egypt lies on either side of the Valley and the Delta and overwhelmingly this is desert wasteland. No more than one percent of the country's population inhabits these regions, and the oases, found only in the Western Desert, are home to the majority. The four inner oases mark the line of a prehistoric branch of the Nile and in 1958 the government decided to bring this area back to life to create a New Valley in parallel with the present Nile Valley. Power stations, factories, packing plants and housing estates have been built and the intention is to extend Egypt's agricultural land by many thousands of square kilometres. For the most part, however, the way of life remains simple and traditional, and the oases are hardly visited by tourists for whom in any case there are few facilities.

The New Valley

The ancient Egyptians were in full control of **Kharga oasis** from the XVIII Dynasty; it was an area of exceptional fertility, and the Greeks and Romans called it the Great Oasis. Decline set in during the Middle Ages, though Kharga remained an important centre on the Darb al-Arbain, the Forty Days Road named for the time it took camel caravans to reach the Nile from Darfur in the Sudan. Today attempts are being made to raise the water table and wells, some of them 1.5 kms deep, have been drilled. The water is estimated to have been in the ground 25,000 years, the time it has taken to percolate through from Lake Chad. The New Valley project has proved more difficult and costly than anticipated, and the intended mass transfer of population, mostly landless fellahin from the Delta and the 'old' Valley, too ambitious. Nevertheless, at Kharga oasis there is a population of around 20,000, model villages have been built, new roads laid, electricity (which often blacks out) installed. Kharga is not the most romantic of the oases, but it is the easiest to get to and there is much of interest roundabout.

In the town itself is a *museum* containing finds ranging from VI Dynasty stelae to 12 C Islamic pottery from Dakhla and Kharga. Just to the north of Kharga, on the west side of the Assiut road, lie the ruins of the *ancient town of Hibis*. The site has not been excavated except for the central *Temple of Amun*, dedicated to the god by Darius I, he whose soldiers met defeat at Marathon and whose namesake Alexander would thrash 150 years later. It has been reconstructed and makes a picturesque scene amidst groves of date palm, in contrast to the edge of desert situation of so many temples along the Nile. On a ridge one kilometre north is the Christian *Necropolis of al-Baqawat*. The mud brick mausolea, some surmounted by domes, were painted inside with biblical themes, a few well preserved.

It is a four-hour journey from Kharga to Dakhla with spectacular scenery enroute — cliffs, wadis and crescent dunes. The dunes in the northern and western parts of the desert form in long continuous ridges or 'swords' (*seif*), but here in the southeast are the crescent (or *barchan*) dunes — the two are never found together. The barchan is a remarkable phenomenon, weighing up to 450 million kilos, standing perhaps 30 metres high and advancing forward in the direction of its horns which may be as much as 365 metres apart. The two widely separated horns always remain exactly level with one another, and the dune keeps its simple crescent shape intact with extraordinary persistence even while it is on the move, and while it is passing over such large obstacles as rocks, small hillocks and villages. Why it forms at all, why it never degenerates into a seif dune, is unknown; it is an organism existing in a slow elementary way, and there is evidence that it is capable of a sort of reproduction whereby baby dunes are formed in the open a hundred metres or so downwind of the horn of a fully grown parent.

The sex life of sand dunes

The most beautiful oasis

Dakhla oasis is visited for the sheer beauty of the place, its peace, its pleasant walks and the kind-heartedness of its people. For this reason it is enough to arrive at **Mut**, one of the two main towns of the oasis, and sit around in the spacious central square. There are a few ruins in the area but you need not trouble yourself with these; every other building in Mut contains a coffee house where men sit playing backgammon and smoke waterpipes and the muezzin wails to the sudden Saharan darkness from his crenellated mosque. There are springs nearby at **Mut Talata**, one above blood temperature, the other a little cooler, where you can join the local people for a pitch-dark wallow under the desert stars. Still within the oasis, 27 kms to the west, is the other principal town, **al-Qasr**. This is the original fortified settlement, silent and ageless, where the Mamelukes rebuilt the main *mosque* on Ayyubid foundations and its misshapen domes rise over low mud brick and white plaster houses. A kilometre southwest of al-Qasr there is a *Roman cemetery*, and 2 kms further, at **Deir al-Hagar**, there is picturesque ruined *Roman temple* dedicated to Amun, Mut and Khonsu, the Theban Triad.

Farafra is the smallest of the major oases but is set within one of the largest depressions in the Western desert, marked by a gradual descent as you enter from the south but steep cliffs along the northwest rim. The limestone landscape dazzles, and much of the depression is filled with blown sand which here forms seif dunes. The one small town, of mud brick, stands on an island rising out of the surrounding desert flatness. There are good hot springs, and gardens and olive groves.

Entering **Bahariya oasis** from the south there are the ruins of a *Coptic church* at **al-Hayz**. The dunes are blackened with stones containing ferrous oxides. Yet in this near rainless environment, dates especially, but also rice, maize, wheat, olives, grapes and apricots flourish. The administrative centre is **Bawiti**, a village of white-walled houses decorated with patterns in blue and red. A ridge to the southwest, *Qarat al-Farargi* (Ridge of the Chicken Merchant), is drilled with galleries of bird burials, mostly hawks and ibises, from the XXVI Dynasty to Roman times — the locals imagined they were chicken bones.

Monasteries of the Wadi Natrum

The early Christian churches in Old Cairo have already been

Christendom's first monasteries

mentioned, but the soul of Christian Egypt is in the desert. In *Desert Pilgrimage,* James Wellard makes the extraordinary assertion that 'beyond the green belt of the river, both on the west towards Libya and on the east towards Arabia and north towards Palestine, lies an Egypt which has influenced the course of history far more than the pharaohs'. Egypt was one of the earliest strongholds of Christianity, its believers persecuted terribly by the Romans, especially under Diocletian in 303, so that thousands of Christians retreated into the desert where they lived in caves or founded the first monasteries. 'O Desert, bright with the flowers of Christ! O Solitude, whence come the stones of which the Apocalypse, the city of the Great King, is built! O Wilderness, gladdened with God's special presence! What keeps you in the world? How long shall gloomy roofs oppress you? Oh, that I could behold the desert, lovelier to me than any city' (St Jerome).

Wellard's assertion seems extraordinary to us only because mysticism is no longer in fashion and monasticism outdated, its achievments in defining Christian thought and in

Iphlogios: monk's habit and canvas shoes

harbouring and extending learning overlooked or devalued in our secular age. St Jerome was in fact a visitor, in 385, to the monasteries of the Wadi Natrun, over 100 at one time, now only four, but among the oldest and holiest shrines of Christendom. You can visit these monasteries today — they lie just west of the Desert Road about halfway between Cairo and Alexandria.

The Wadi Natrun is a valley, in part cultivated, extending southeast to northwest for 40 kms, with a width of 8 to 10 kms. It lies below sea level and takes its name from its salt lakes which dry up in summer, leaving a deposit of sodium carbonate (natron), once used in mummification and glass making. The monasteries look like fortresses, as they were intended to be, in defence against Bedouin attacks. Until recently inhabited by a declining population of preponderantly old men, Coptic monasticism is experiencing something of a revival and there are now many young monks, dressed head to ankle in black robes, their hoods embroidered with white stars, sometimes a pair of tennis shoes incongruously completing the costume. Full beards and dark eyes, soft footfalls and quiet certainty, impress powerfully as they show you round their fortified man-made oases. From among the monks of the Wadi Natrun is chosen the Coptic Pope, who at present is Shenouda III, 117th Successor to St Mark the Apostle.

Getting to the monasteries

From Cairo, the Desert Road is gained by turning off the Pyramind Road just before the Mena House Hotel. A *rest house* (95 kms) about halfway to Alexandria marks the point where you turn left into the wadi. By car, the journey can be made in half a day, or the visit can be made enroute to Alexandria. Of course before the building of the road in 1917 the monasteries were in the middle of nowhere.

You drive into the valley, passing through the village of **Bir Hooker**, and come to a sign indicating the Monasteries of St Bishoi (Deir Amba Bishoi) and the Syrians (Deir el Suriani). The road is paved all the way to Bishoi, and Suriani is only a short distance over the sands. From Bishoi the road continues to the Monastery of St Makarios (Deir Abu Maqar) at the southern extremity of the wadi (though the easiest way to reach Maqar is to turn off the Desert Road 13 kms before the rest house, a signposted track leading 8 kms into the desert). The northernmost Monastery of Baramous (Deir el Baramus) still keeps its distance from the world across a long trek of sand.

All Egypt's monasteries are coenobitic, that is food and possessions are shared and the monks submit absolutely to the authority of the 'householder', as the Copts call their abbot. The monasteries of the Wadi Natrun were all founded during the 4th C, though to varying degrees their structures date from the 8th C, being restorations and fortifications following Bedouin attacks. St Bishoi founded two of these monasteries, the one bearing his name and the Suriani. The shrine and body of the saint are in **Deir Amba Bishoi**, indeed the body lies uncorrupted and unwithered beneath a dusty

Shaking hands with St Bishoi

red cloth, though unless the saint reaches out his arm to shake your hand (apparently a not uncommon courtesy extended to true believers), you will not be allowed to check for yourself. This was one of the rewards bestowed upon Bishoi for having washed Christ's feet when the Saviour appeared before him. He was also permitted to drink the water afterwards. Next to him lies the body of Paul of Tamweh, who achieved a reputation for sanctity after committing suicide seven times. Otherwise the monastery is unremarkable, with much new building and an air of administrative bustle.

Though lacking in illustrious corpses, **Deir el Suriani** is altogether a better place. It is in fact the most interesting of the four. Once inside its high forbidding walls (alas, women are not allowed), there is an atmosphere of serenity which you regret having to leave. There are several small domed churches, courtyards and gardens, and also tall bell towers with comforting bongs. Here Iphlogios with merry eyes showed me around: entering the Chapel of the Virgin, he opened a casket full of relics — Mary Magdalene's hair, somebody else's teeth, I could not remember them all as he went on and on. Then in a cave, now abutting the chapel, I saw the very place where Bishoi chained himself upright by the hair and did not sleep for four days until he saw Christ and washed His feet. You can imagine my delight — but I am being serious, as serious as Iphlogios, for these monasteries are strange and wonderful places, holding out against time, against the desert, against Islam; they are themselves miracles, and the least surprising (but most confirming) thing about them is that they should be storehouses for the fantastic.

The hair of Mary Magdalene

Deir Abu Maqar has suffered most from Bedouin pillaging and destruction and consequently is the poorest of the four. Apart from portions of the saint's church, little remains of its earliest past, architecturally or decoratively, though it does possess what the monks would regard as far greater treasures. A disproportionate number of Coptic popes came from Maqar and many are interred in the monastery, while beneath the floor of the saint's church are the remains of the Forty-Nine Martyrs, monks slain by Bedouins in 444. Recently a crypt was found containing what some claim to be the remains of John the Baptist. Against this, Mary Magdalene's hair or even the uncorrupted body of the man who drank from Christ's foot bath pale.

What is left of John the Baptist

Deir el Baramus to the north across the sands is difficult to get to. Its isolation has had a paradoxcial effect. On the one hand, its small number of monks have allowed themselves a greater degree of comfort then elsewhere and live in rooms instead of cells. Yet its remoteness attracts hermits to its environs where they live in self-dug caves. Indeed, Shenoudi's immediate predecessor, Kyrillos VI, spent ten years in a cave nearby as an 'athlete of Christ'. For those wishing to stay overnight at Wadi Natrun, Baramous could be the best choice for a feeling of both the wilderness and the fold. Out here in the desert what had seemed absurd in Old Cairo, those macabre relics as vessels for a putrefying mysticism and a faith in retreat, comes close to comprehension. As all life-giving as the Nile seems to be, one cannot understand Egypt without taking account of the void.

Athletes of Christ

The City of St Menes

Further along the Desert Road to Alexandria, at Bir Abu Hush, a turning (west) is signposted in English and Arabic for the Monastery of St Menes. Or from Alexandria you most easily reach Abu Mina, as it is called, by following the coast road to Abusir, turning left inland for Burg el Arab, then east for Bahig. Across the railway lines a dirt road, sometimes faintly paved, always dusty, leads to the site which soon hoves into view on account of the large modern *Coptic monastery* with its two belfry towers. Built in 1959, the relics of St Menes were transferred here three years later. The monastery sits within high stone walls, its buildings concrete and ugly though luridly decorated inside.

Menas was a young Egyptian officer who was martyred in 296 during his service with the Roman army in Asia Minor because he would not abandon Christ. When his legion moved back into Egypt his friends brought his ashes with them, but at this spot the camel carrying the burden refused to go further. Menes was buried and forgotten, but later a shepherd noticed that a sick lamb that crossed the spot became well. Then a sick princess was healed. The remains were exhumed and a church built (350) over the grave. The church was incorporated into the great Basilica of the Emperor Arcadius, added at the beginning of the 5th C, and soon houses, walls and cemeteries were built, a city in the desert. The secret of this rapid growth was water; there were springs in the limestone that have since dried up. But in its heyday the cult was carried by caravans across the deserts (Menas is always shown between two camels) and extended throughout the Mediteranean, pilgrims coming from as far as Italy and France for 'the beautiful water of St Menas that drives away pain'. Souvenirs of these pilgrims' visits, little earthenware flasks with the saint depicted between the camels, have been found all over Europe and Africa.

Vineyards in the desert

As the water gave out, the city declined, though in the 11th C the Arab geographer El Mekri could still describe 'superb and beautifully constructed palaces' and 'the Cathedral of St Menes, an enormous building ornamented with statues and the most beautiful mosaics ... Over the church is a dome covered with paintings which, they say, represent the angels ... The whole countryside round about is planted with fruit trees which produce excellent fruit and there are also many vines which are cultivated for wine' — this when water was already scarce. A century later, when the wells finally did dry up, the city and its vineyards simply disappeared beneath the sands. For nearly a thousand years El Mekri's description was regarded as the fantasy of an oriental geographer, until, in 1905, the site was excavated almost single-handedly by Monsignor Kaufmann.

Since then Menes has enjoyed a revival. In 1943, the Coptic Pope Christopher II issued an encyclical letter ascribing the saving of Egypt from invasion at the Battle of El Alamein to 'the prayers to God of the holy and glorious martyr Menas, the wonderworker of Egypt' — which was something else Rommel never counted on. Menes has been, in fact, a very practical saint. A paralytic man and a dumb woman both happened to implore his help at the same time. During the night, the saint came to the man in a vision and said, 'Don't be afraid, but fasten your lips to the dumb woman's. Then get into bed with her and you will be cured'. Although astonished, the paralytic followed instructions: the dumb woman awoke and screamed; the paralytic, alarmed at being caught, fled.

Miracle of the dumb woman and paralytic man

The site is amidst slight mounds and clearings a few hundred metres beyond the monastery. The ground is littered with fragments of marble paving, granite and basalt columns and shards. The foundations of the primitive church and the encompassing basilica are clear, though little rises to any height.

The *crypt* in which St Menes was buried is down a marble staircase in the original *church* which is incorporated into the portico of the *Basilica of Arcadius*. A *baptistry*, octagonal within a square, its walls standing to 14 metres with a font in the central courtyard, is to the west. North of the basilica are the *hospice* and *sacred baths* with hot and cold cisterns. Surrounding the whole area are the remains of the *pilgrims' town*. Most of the artefacts and decorations found during excavations can now be seen at the Graeco-Roman Museum in Alexandria.

To the Mediterranean

From the City of St Menes it is worth following the country roads northwards to the sea. Southwest of Bahig is the model village of **Burg el Arab**, built by an Englishman early this century like a miniature medieval Italian town, circular and fortified. Hard by the carpet factory outside the walls the President of Egypt has a villa. The village is on a rise and beyond it to the north runs another, the extension of that same limestone ridge on which Alexandria stands. Between the two is **Lake Mariout** (ancient Mareotis), expiring here at its western extremity in marshes, brilliant with wildflowers in spring. As the road crosses the lake bed you may notice (right) traces of the *causeway* that connected ancient **Taposiris** with the desert. Its name is preserved in the modren **Abusir**; its ruins are indifferent — except for its tower and its temple.

Crossing Lake Mariout

Taposiris was contemporary with Alexandria, though little is known about it. Like Alexandria it worshipped Osiris, and on the limestone ridge stand the enclosure walls of its *Temple of Osiris*. The actual temple has disappeared, but the walls are impressive and there are gate-towers to climb for fine views over the delicate greens of the Mariut marshes to the south and to the north the sea astonishingly turquoise, a burning blue against the burning white of coastal sand. A few hundred metres to the east a solitary tower (*Burg el Arab*, the Arab tower) is in fact a *Ptolemaic lighthouse* rising in three stages of honeyed stone, one of a chain that stretched from the Alexandrian Pharos all down the North African coast to Cyrene. It was modelled on its gigantic contemporary, but only one-tenth its size.

Below, on the littoral, there are plans to build a holiday complex which will ruin the place forever.

Along the Mediterranean Coast

West from Alexandria at 106 kms is **El Alamein**, scene of that series of battles which from July to November 1942 halted Rommel's thrust to the Delta and reversed the tide of war in northern Africa. On 1 July as the Afrika Korps arrived at Alamein, the British fleet left Alexandria and withdrew through the Suez Canal into the Red Sea; clouds of smoke rose from the chimneys of the British military headquarters in Cairo as their files were hastily burned; Cairenes, certain that the British were fleeing Egypt, besieged the railway station in a rush to get away; and the outside world took it to mean that Britain had lost the Middle East. But Rommel was over extended, his men exhausted, and the majority of his supplies consigned by the British Navy to the bottom of the sea.

The battles of Alamein

General Auchinleck cooly gauged the situation. 'On 17 July 1942, Auchinleck had won a historic battle. It had been as desperate, difficult and gallant as Wellington's repulse of Napoleon at Waterloo ... He saved the Middle East, with all that this implied for the general course of the war. It was the turning point' (General J F C Fuller). Later, Montgomery took command of the Eighth Army: 'a man of dynamic personality and of supreme self-confidence ... a past-master in showmanship and publicity; audacious in his utterances and cautious in his actions ... He was the right man in the right place at the right moment' (Fuller), and during 23 October-5 November decisively defeated the Germans and put Rommel on the run. Within little more than six months the Germans and Italians were cleared from Africa altogether.

There is a *museum* at Alamain, with tanks, heavy artillery and other debris left behind after the battles, while to the east of the town is the starkly beautiful *British Cemetery*.

Beautiful beaches

The drive along the coastline is startling, the desert on the left, broad scallops of fine white sand beaches on the right and the brilliant turquoise of the Mediterranean beyond. There is no transition, just sharp jumps in colour and texture. The road is good all the way to Mersa Matruh (291 kms from Alexandria), the beaches beautiful, cooled by sea breezes and still only occasionally developed — though the Egyptian government is aware of their tourist potential and has drawn up plans. At present there are modest resort facilites at **Sidi Abdel Rahman** (20 kms past El Alamein), where there are a hotel, villas and camping, as well as *cenotaphs to the Italian and German war dead*, and at **Mersa Matruh**, with a number of hotels along the corniche, and *Rommel's Cave*, a hideout of the Desert Fox, now a museum containing, *inter alia*, Rommel's own armoury, donated by his son.

PRACTICAL INFORMATION

THE OASES

The poor relations between Libya and Egypt find **Siwa** within a restricted zone, off-limits to foreigners. It is worth enquiring, though, whether the situation has eased.

There are no restrictions on travel to the **inner oases** of Kharga, Dakhla, Farafra and Bahariya, though foreigners should register with the police on arrival at each oasis (a formality) and obtain police permission for travel between Farafra and Bahariya (again a formality).

Bahariya is accessible by daily bus from Midan Giza, Cairo, or by car, turning off the Fayyum road after a few kilometres. There is a very simple rest house at **Biwiti**, nicely kept and surrounded by a pleasant garden and verandah. Bring your own food.

Farafra is accessible by truck (irregular) from Bawiti. There is a very basic rest house. Women can stay with local families, but not men.

Dakhla can be reached from Farafra by truck (irregular), though a bus service is contemplated. But both Dakhla and Kharga are most easily reached from Assuit: there is a regular bus service. There is also a once-weekly direct bus from Cairo via Assuit. Also mini-buses and share taxis ply between Kharga and Dakhla. There is a rest house in the centre of **Mut** where the bus stops, and there is a very attractive one at **Mut Talata** (camping site also) where pools have been constructed at the spring. Mut Talata is reached by taxi or van in 5 minutes; or it is a 40-minute walk. Neither rest house supplies food, but there are 2 restaurants in Mut. The meat is excellent due to the amount of grain grown in the oasis.

Note that there is a tourist tax of LE4 at Dakhla and Kharga, notionally for entrance to the sites at these oases.

There is a daily bus to **Kharga** from Assiut. It departs at 7am from the bus station to the left of the railway station as you come out. The journey takes 5 hours with a break mid-way, and the bus is perfectly comfortable. Be at the bus early as it soon fills up. There is a 2-star hotel, the El Kharga Oasis, near the entrance to the oasis (Tel: El Wadi el Guedid 4500), with pleasant staff. Further in (turn left at the first traffic lights and look by the church) are the (in summer) oppressively hot metal prefab New Valley Tourist Houses.

Egyptair flies to Kharga (New Valley) twice a week from Cairo.

WADI NATRUN

Though permission is no longer required from the Coptic Patriarchate to visit the monasteries here, it might pay to enquire nevertheless — one or more might be closed, for example, and it would be best to advise the church if you are travelling with a large number of people. The Patriarchate is at the new Cathedral of St Mark, 222 Sharia Ramses, in the Abbasia district of Cairo, a 15-minute walk or short taxi ride northeast of the Cairo railway station at Midan Ramses.

Note that Suriani is closed to women.

The monasteries are just off the Cairo-Alexandria Desert Road, with access from the Rest House (3-star); Tel: Wadi Natrun 3451; telex 93865 NABI UN), 90 kms from either city. Buses frequently travel between Cairo and Alexandria; at the Rest House you can walk (long) or hire a taxi. Or you can jump in a share taxi at either city. There are no organised tours to Wadi Natrun, though perhaps arrangements for a car and driver could be made through Thomas Cook.

CITY OF ST MENES AND ABUSIR

In addition to the information given in the main text, there is also a train from Alexandria to Bahig, but this takes ages. A car for St Menes and Abusir would be best; for Abusir only you might be able to catch a bus at Alexandria.

ALAMEIN AND WEST TO MERSA MATRUH

A train runs along the coast, though a bus or car would be preferable. To Alamein, Misr Limousines quote around LE100 from Cairo, LE50 from Alexandria, which if shared amongst several might be bearable. Thomas Cook in Alexandria does a full-day tour to **Alamein** and **Sidi Abdel Rahman**. There are 1- and 2-star hotels at **Mersa Matruh**, and there is a hotel and camping site at Alamein. Misr Travel in Alexandria can help with accommodation along the coast, also with transport.

THE CANAL, THE RED SEA AND SINAI

In days gone by, many visitors to Egypt were no more than passers-through the Suez Canal, disembarking from their ship at one end, racing to Cairo to see the Pyramids, then racing back to board ship as it reached the other end of the canal. Today, the process is reversed and visitors who have flown into Cairo will sometimes take a day-trip to the canal to watch the ships sail through.

The Suez Canal

The ancient canal

The idea of a Suez canal is by no means a modern conception. The earliest authenticated attempt to connect the Red Sea with the Nile, and thereby with the Mediterranean, was made by Necho (XXVI Dyn). Herodotus says that 120,000 Egyptians perished while engaged in the work which was abandoned when an oracle warned that only the Persians would profit by it. And indeed it was Darius I (he of Marathon) who completed it a century later, c.500 BC. Tradition, however, reports a canal as early as the reign of Tuthmosis III (XVIII Dyn). Darius' canal (which ran from the Red Sea to the Great Bitter Lakes and then westwards to Bubastis, modern Zagazig) was maintained by the Ptolmies and improved by Trajan. It was later restored by Amr, the Arab conqueror of Egypt, in order to supply Arabia with corn, but was abandoned 100 years later to starve out Medina which had risen in revolt against the Caliph. The Venetians, the Ottomans and the French under Louis XIV all contemplated its renewal. It was during Napoleon's sojourn that for the first time a canal was proposed direct from the Red Sea to the Mediterranean, but his engineer wrongly calculated a difference of 10 metres between their two levels and the plan was dropped.

Construction of the modern canal

At its narrowest, the **Isthmus of Suez** is 144 kms long and apart from dividing the two seas is also the divide between Africa and Asia. The present canal, at 167 kms, is the third longest in the world and the longest without locks. Its construction is owed to Ferdinand de Lesseps, formerly French consul in Cairo, who obtained a *firman* from the Khedive Said (whence Port Said) granting a concession to run 99 years after the canal's completion. Work began in 1859, two-thirds of the finance coming from private investors, one-third from the new Khedive, Ismail (after whom Ismailia was named). Twenty thousand Egyptians dug the canal and many thousands died from cholera and accidents. The official opening took place on 17 November 1869 amidst much fanfare, the Empress Eugénie the principal attraction after the ditch itself. The expense of the canal contributed largely to Ismail's bankruptcy, his shares purchased by the British government in 1875, and Egypt falling under the authority, in effect, of British and French bankers. It was this event which led Ismail to speak the words which serve as an ironic commentary on the significance of the canal: 'My country is no longer in Africa; we are now part of Europe. It is therefore natural for us to abandon our former ways and to adopt a new system adapted to our social conditions'.

The Suez Canal crisis

Nasser's nationalisation of the Suez Canal Company in July 1956 was a reaction to the continued manipulation of Egypt by the West. Nasser wanted to build a new dam at Aswan which would increase farming land by one-third, and went to Britain, France and the United States for loans. These were refused because of Nasser's willingness to deal with both East and West. Nationalisation was intended to prevent canal revenue from draining to the West; instead it would help finance the High Dam. In response, Israel, France and Britain invaded Egypt in October, Sir Anthony Eden for one deluding himself that Egypt's legitimate rejection of imperialism was no more than a replay of Hitler's reoccupation of the Rhineland. World opinion was outraged and the invaders were forced to withdraw. Nasser was left with both the canal and a considerable moral victory.

The Six Day War in 1967 closed the canal for eight years. This time the British, French and American governments proved more cooperative and aided in its dredging. But meanwhile the canal towns were impoverished by the closure and devastated by Israeli shelling, Suez even being entirely evacuated.

In 1975 President Sadat officially re-opened the canal. As many as 90 ships pass through every 24 hours with an average transit time of 15 hours. They carry with them 14 per cent of the world's trade. There are plans to double the canal's width, and the Egyptian-Israeli peace has permitted the canal cities to get back on their feet.

Visiting the canal towns

From Cairo the most direct route to Ismailia is across the desert (128 kms), though in one direction it is worth taking the slower road via Bilbeis, following the course of the Ismailia Canal through well-cultivated countryside for fascinating glimpses of Delta life. About 50 kms along the desert road is **Medinet Ramadan** (Ramadan City), one of the new desert cities intended to relieve the capital's overpopulation. It is a good example of the inanity of city planners. Where traditional architecture would be cheap, familiar and insulating against the fierce heat, here amidst the desolate expanse are pointless highrises. One knows that the lifts will break down, the air conditioners will fail, and these poor pioneers will have to sweat their way to the uppermost storeys, there to roast alive in their oven-like rooms. Further along, on the right, a *tank monument* indicates the furthest advance of the Israeli counterattack during the 1973 war. Now outside Ismailia where the eucalyptus begin there is the Sixth October Restaurant, a breakfast halt for the Cairo to Tel Aviv bus.

Along the main street through **Ismailia**, Sharia Mohammed Ali, where Sharia Ahmed Orabi runs down from the train station, is *De Lesseps' house*, a small villa now encompassed by a larger one used as a government rest house — you will have to talk your way in through the side entrance. His carriage is in the garden, and one small room contains his effects — a bed, desk, cross and picture of the Empress Eugénie. In the entrance hall bookshelves there is a complete *Description*, that famous survey of Egypt published by Napoleon's savants. Ismailia stands on the edge of Lake Timsa and the canal, and in these favoured waterside quarters are the suburban villas of a tropical England. Here amongst the neat gardens, the clean and silent streets, drawn shutters keep time at bay, as though the English were still inside, drinking tea and gin. There is a *museum* among these streets, designed like a Ptolemaic temple. On the canal is a *swimming club* with refreshments, a sand beach and the opportunity to dodge the passing supertankers for a swim to Asia and back. A plume of black smoke rises from behind a ridge of sand, then you see the bridge of a ship and slowly its vast form slides into view; the constant procession is hypnotic.

Swimming across the canal

Only when looking across the canal at the steep sand embankments on the other side do you realise what a bold achievement it was for the Egyptians to have overrun the Israeli positions in 1973. Even with surprise and meticulous preparation it would seem suicide. I was told a story here, that the Egyptians had ordered from America powerful water cannon for the Cairo fire department. The Bar Lev line was least well defended at those points where the embankments were steepest, and against these sand slopes the Egyptians trained their hoses, carving gullies up which they scrambled.

Port Said, 80 kms from Ismailia at the north end of the canal, flourishes owing to its status as a duty free port. Visitors arriving from inland must show their passports. It is very much a canal city with a plain grid pattern, though there is a touch of the picturesque along Sharia el Gumhuriya where there are many beautiful old wooden buildings with balconies dating from the last century and reminiscent of the French Quarter in New Orleans. Perhaps the most famous building, known to many sea travellers, is the *Suez Canal Building* on Sharia Filastin, its two-storey gleaming white colonnade crowned with three brilliant green domes. There is good swimming along its Mediterranean beaches. But it is the furthest of the canal towns from Cairo and not really worth the trek.

Suez is at the southern end of the canal and like Ismailia is easily reached from Cairo (134 kms, or from Ismailia 88 kms). It was the worst affected by the 1967 and 1973 wars and the sporadic shelling in between; three-quarters of the town was razed and has since been rebuilt. Suez is now an industrial centre producing cement, fertiliser and petrochemicals. It offers very good views of ships passing through the canal and also more distant views of Sanai stretching away to the south. **Ain Sukhna**, 55 kms down the coast of the Gulf of Suez, is being developed as a beach resort, the nearest to Cairo.

Along the Red Sea Coast

Superb beaches

From Suez to Mersa Alam, hundreds of kilometres of beautiful and deserted sand beaches wind along the red-hued flanks of the Eastern Desert plateau where it falls into the Red Sea. Numberless coves and bays provide ideal camping terrain, and the resorts of Ain Sukhna (above) and Hurghada

Sunbathing along the Suez Canal

(below) provide complete facilities. There is a road the entire distance, and there is also a road across the Eastern Desert from Qena, north of Luxor, to Port Safaga, south of Hurghada.

The **Monastery of St Anthony** is 130 kms south from Suez and then 45 kms west into the Eastern Desert. It is the largest of the Coptic monasteries, more like a village with streets but surrounded by high walls and strikingly positioned beneath the cliffs of Mt Kalalah. There are several churches, decorated with frescoes; the oldest structure in the monastery is the *Church of St Anthony* built over the saint's tomb by his disciples. Up the cliff face at an elevation of 680 metres, and 276 metres above the monastery, is *St Anthony's cave* where he kept himself apart from his pursuing disciples. The climb is worth it for the superb view, but a monk should be taken as guide.

Animal loving saint

St Anthony came here in 294, accompanying a caravan bound for the Red Sea, to escape the growing number of disciples who had joined him at his hermit's tomb along the Nile. He was born the son of a village merchant, but at 20 took literally a sermon heard in church: 'If though wilt be perfect, go and sell all thou hast'. In his cave on Mt Kalalah, high above the world, his only companions the wild animals he treated as God's creatures, he lived out the remainder of his 105 years, dying in 356. (Perhaps we should not be surprised that these men who endured the extremes of the desert and lived only on beans did generally live to be very old. Comforts kill.) He did not escape fame, however, and apart from the foretaste of St Francis 800 years later, became spiritual father of such great figures of the early Church as Jerome and Augustine of Hippo.

Skin divers' paradise

Between the mountains and a sea of electric blue, the dusty fishermen's town of **Hurghada** (395 kms from Suez or 214 kms from Qena on the Nile) is the modest centre of the Red Sea region, with oil derricks nearby and a marine biology station. But 5 kms south a cluster of international hotels around a protected bay emphasise Hurghada's development as a beach, skin diving and sport fishing resort. Despite near-daily flights from Cairo, it is still a fairly quiet, unfrequented place of lovely white sand beaches scattered with delicate shells, of crystalline waters, coral islands, hot sun and relieving breezes — though winter and early spring can be very cool. There is a wide variety of aquatic sports, with lessons available for the uninitiated; some entertainment; and a *marine museum* with a huge collection of brilliantly coloured fish, Red Sea sharks and rare manatees. Also you can go on excursions to the *porphyry quarries* of the Eastern Desert where the Romans hewed so much of that magnificent red stone (at terrible human cost) for the adornment of their basilicas, baths and private houses.

Sinai

Development of the peninsula

The Israelis completed their withdrawal from the Sinai peninsula in April 1982 and Cairo ministries quickly unleashed scores of plans for the rapid exploitation of this least developed part of Egypt. The good news is that some of this development is going ahead — and that most of it certainly will not for a long time yet.

The present population of Sinai is around 200,000, almost all Bedouin; the government hopes to settle two million immigrants here from the overpopulated Nile Valley by the year 2000. Foreign experts doubt that Sinai will more than double in population by the end of the century. Al Arish on the Mediterranean coast and El Tor on the Gulf of Suez are the new administrative centres of north and south Sinai; urban development is being concentrated here. Coal, manganese, and offshore oil and gas are intended to provide the industrial base, while fishing and agriculture are also being encouraged. But all this requires heavy capital investment; it is cheaper and quicker to attract tourism and along the Gulf of Aqaba at Sharm el Sheikh, Dahab and Nuweiba the Egyptians have ready-made resort facilities purchased from the evacuating Israelis to build on. These pinpoints of activity around the three coasts of the Sinai triangle, and the attraction of St Catherine's Monastery in the southern interior, are helping to make the peninsula more accessible to travellers without spoiling what remains for the most part one of the least touched parts of the world.

But still remote

The Mediterranean coast of Sinai is set to become the Egyptian Riviera for overland travellers between Cairo and Tel Aviv. At **El Arish** the beach is excellent and there are several new resort complexes as well as more modest hotels and restaurants to offer comfort to the passerby.

St Anthony's: Coptic monastery in the Red Sea hills

Scuba diving

Along the coast of the Gulf of Aqaba there is a bus between **Taba** (right next door to Eilat in Israel) and **Sharm el Sheikh** near the tip of the peninsula. It makes the return journey daily so that you can set off from either end, spend a few hours at **Nuweiba** or **Dahab**, and return. The Gulf of Aqaba has some of the best scuba diving in the world, and the landscape is majestic, inhabited only by wild camels and Bedouin encampments.

St Catherine's Monastery is 250 kms southeast of Suez towards the tip of Sinai and is surrounded by a dramatic array of bare stone mountains, marvellous for walking, and where the way of life of the Bedouins has remained unchanged for centuries. The site is traditionally that where God manifested himself to Moses in the burning bush; that and a supply of holy oil from Catherine's corpse (see Old Cairo) have had pilgrims, or tourists, coming here ever since 400. The monastery, however, is Greek Orthodox and not Coptic. A chapel erected by St Helena, mother of the Emperor Constantine, already stood on the site when Justinian, urged on by his formidale harlot-actress wife Theodora (Procopius said she had made love through every orifice of her body), built a fortified monastery here in 527. Apart from its fortifications, it has survived marauding Bedouins because Moslems revere Moses as one of their prophets, and because of its close connections in the Middle Ages with Europe, particularly France where the cult of St Catherine was especially strong. With sometimes hundreds of visitors on any one day of the year, it grew wealthy and was never lost to the Western world in the way that the desert monasteries of the Copts were. It has continued a success, at least as a tourist attraction, but for that reason and its dwindling number of monks and its electric lighting and thrumming generator (gifts of the British army before pulling out of the Canal Zone) it lacks the unworldly atmosphere of Egypt's other monasteries.

The Burning Bush

The principal attractions are the *Basilica of Justinian* with its 6th C Byzantine mosaic in the apse and its Chapel of the Burning Bush, the most sacred spot in the monastery; the *Old Refectory*, used by Western pilgrims and covered with their graffiti from the 14th to 16th C; the *Library* with one of the richest monastic collections in the world and a museum of Byzantine ikons; and in the garden the *Charnel House*, the skulls of monks piled high on one side, their limbs on the other. The monks are first buried and after ten years exhumed. But unburied was St Stephen, who died in 580 while sitting in a chair, his head in his hands — he is still there, at the entrance, looking rather dry.

PRACTICAL INFORMATION

THE CANAL

Port Said, Ismailia and Suez have never been much of a tourist attraction; their *raison d'etre* has been the canal and their facilities have matched this purpose.

If going to Port Said, take your **passport**.

Buses depart from Midan el Tahrir in Cairo, **trains** from the Midan Ramses station.

Accommodation in Port Said includes: **Etap Motel** (4-star), on the corniche. Tel: 8823. Telex: 54175 PDS UN. The motel overlooks both the sea and the canal. All rooms have a refrigerator, TV and bathroom. Prices are well below usual 4-star rates.
Abu Simbel (2-star), 15 Sharia Gumhuriya. Tel: 21590. A clean and quiet family hotel, the double rooms face the street and have balconies, TVs and refrigerators, while the singles face a back alley and are without these.
Regent (1-star), 27 Sharia Gumhuriya. Tel: 23802. Like the Abu Simbel, the Regent is situated on Sharia Gumhuriya which runs parallel to the canal, though a couple of blocks back from it.

There is also the **Nasr Youth Hostel**, Sharia el Amin.

Accommodation in Ismailia includes: **Etap** (4-star), Forsan Island. Tel: 22220. Telex: 63038 UN. A large hotel waiting for something big to happen in Ismailia. Pool, tennis courts, supper club entertainments; air-conditioned rooms with colour TV.
Nefertari (2-star), 41 Sharia Sultan Hussein. Tel: 2822. Rooms are clean and cool, all have balconies.
El Salam (2-star), Sharia el Geish, near Midan el Gumhuriya. Tel: 24401. A new, very clean hotel on a pleasant tree-lined street, and with a fairly good restaurant.

Accommodation in Suez includes: **Beau Rivage** (2-star), 32 Sharia Saad Zaghloul. Tel: 3885. This is a hotel/motel.
Bel-Air, Sharia Saad Zaghloul. Tel: 3711. A no-star place, but decent rooms and restaurant; a few rooms have baths and those along the front have balconies.

THE RED SEA

The **road** from Suez to Hurghada is in a bad state in parts, though buses do the run between Cairo and Hurghada in about 8 hours. Signposting can be a problem; the route is not always as clear as it seems on the map.

The **Monastery of St Anthony** is Coptic; it offers overnight accommodation (no meals), but you must first apply to the Coptic Patriarchate in Cairo (see *Practical Information* for *The Western Desert* chapter).

Known as *Ghardaka* in Arabic, the one-time fishing village of **Hurghada** is being developed as the main resort along the Red Sea coast. You can drive along the wild, undeveloped coastline from Suez or across the Eastern Desert from Qena (you reach the Red Sea at Port Safaga, no facilities, no shade, one flash hotel). The usual approach is by Egyptair flight from Cairo. The resort centres on the **Sheraton** (4-star), though it is in need of some sprucing up. Tel: 40779. Telex: 92750 SHRGA UN. And centres too on the **Magawish Tourist Village** (4-star), a series of bungalows by the sea run by Club Méditerranée. Tel: (Cairo) 914972. Telex: 93152 CMHUR UN. Bookings can be made through Misr Travel, the owners. The newest place is **Gifton Village** (3-star), a number of limestone chalets, each with 24 rooms containing bath and shower. There is a fully equipped diving centre run by German experts. Visits to nearby islands and into the Sinai desert can be organised. It opened early in 1985, and as of going to press you should reserve through Spring Tours, 65 Sharia el Gumhuriya, Cairo. Tel: 910873. Telex: 93766.

SINAI

Air Sinai flies from Cairo to El Arish in northern Sinai, and to Sharm el Sheikh and St Catherine's Monastery in the south. **Buses** leave daily from Midan Ahmed Helmy in Cairo for El Arish and for Sharm el Sheikh. There are buses too from Suez for St Catherine's, and **tours** from Cairo organised by Istrabus, 44 Sharia Talaat Harb (Tel: 747342) and Spring Tours, 65 Sharia Gumhuriya (Tel: 910873; telex: 93766 SPITO UN), among others.

In **El Arish** there are a number of decent no-star hotels, especially along Sharia 26 July. There is also the new Oberoi El Arish (4-star) — reservations through other Oberoi hotels. This is a resort in itself, with many facilities including a pool and its own beach.

In **Sharm el Sheikh** there is a youth hostel and Cliff Top Village (2-star; Tel: Cairo 770200; telex 94002 OHTEG UN) amongst others. At **Naama Beach**, 8 kms distant, there are a couple of 3-star hotels and a campsite.

Dahab and **Nuweiba**, along the Gulf of Aqaba, also have a 3-star hotel each. At **Taba**, on the border with Israel, is the Sonesta Beach Hotel, ultra-luxurious, though there is some doubt as to which country it is in.

For information on southern Sinai resorts, contact Sinai Hotels and Diving Clubs, 32 Sharia Sabri Abu Alam, Cairo. Tel: 770200. Telex: 94002 OHTEG UN.

There is a 2-star hotel, the El Salam, at **St Catherine's Monastery**, and a new hotel, the St Catherine, not yet classified, but probably 2-star as well.

THE DELTA

Politically, economically and culturally, the Delta has played no less an important role from the earliest times to the present that has Upper Egypt, yet it almost entirely lacks the historical survivals of the deserts and the Valley. Where the aridity and limited cultivation of the south has preserved the past, the fanning Nile and its irrigation channels, some Mediterranean rainfall and the consequent rich earth of the north have all but obliterated it. This imposes some distortion on our apprehension of Egyptian history, for it was the Delta that was cosmopolitan, influenced and often settled by peoples beyond Egypt's borders, while it was and still is Upper Egypt that has been provincial. Provincialism and orthodoxy, however, go hand in hand, and when reaching the pitch of zealotry they can become a moulding force — from Upper Egypt came the impetus for the unification of Egypt, as came also the expression in stone, as pyramids and titanic temples, of the nomad's confrontation with the cosmos. We see one and forget the other.

Reasons for the lack of concrete history

Where the Delta did build in limestone and granite, these blocks had to be brought great distances from the deserts and the Valley. It was common already in pharaonic times for the stone of earlier structures to be re-used in later ones rather than to go to the far-off quarries for more. The disassembling of the past was even more intense during the Middle Ages when the Delta people would plunder ancient buildings, burning the limestone in their kilns and using the granite for foundations or grinding stones. Right up until recent decades the sebakhin (mentioned at Medinet el Fayyum) would work the tells (or *koms*, to use the particularly Egyptian word for those great mounds of debris marking the sites of ancient settlements) for fertiliser, so that some that were 10 metres high in Napoleon's time are near-level today. In any case, mud brick was more often used, and where these remains have been excavated, they have immediately begun to suffer weathering. Finds from the famous sites of the Delta have been taken away to the museums of Cairo, Alexandria or abroad, and what remains *in situ* does no justice to their historical renown.

Nevertheless, the Delta knew greatness, and during the first millenium BC it dominated the affairs of Egypt. The XXI Dynasty came from Tanis; the XXII Dynasty was founded at Bubastis; the XXIII Dynasty came also from Tanis; the XXIV, XXVI and XXVIII Dynasties all came from Sais.

These and other places both within the Delta and nearby can be visited enroute to Alexandria from Cairo, or in some cases most conveniently by using Alexandria as your base for excursions. There is a good railway service linking Cairo with Zagazig (for Ismailia) and Cairo with Alexandria, with stops along the way, while there are numerous good paved roads. The alternative to the Cairo-Alexandria Desert Road is the shorter though more heavily trafficked main road through

Visiting the Delta

the Delta via Benha, Tanta and Damanhur, paralleling the railway.

Whatever one's interest in the ancient sites, there is the fascination of a drive or train ride through the Delta landscape — its extraordinary flatness and vast fields of cotton, rice and maize; buffalo with sleek oily coats and down-turned horns like large floppy ears, grazing or ploughing or turning wheels for grinding or pumping; also sheep, donkeys, camels, and huge dovecotes like Cambodian temples. High clouds blow in from the Mediterranean, a reminder that here in the north during the winter months it is advisable to have a raincoat, and along the coast a warm sweater for evening breezes throughout the year. And spectacle though it is to see a tanker seemingly plough through the desert at Suez, it is enchanting to see the sails of feluccas billow across fields furrowed with canals — the effect of Norman church towers at stages across the watery flatness of the Suffolk landscape.

Ancient Sites in the Eastern Delta

An excursion from Cairo around the eastern Delta, which could be combined with the Suez Canal, or which otherwise could be a roundabout way of reaching Alexandria, would take in **Zagazig** (85 kms from Cairo) for ancient Bubastis and **San el Hagar** (159 kms from Cairo) for ancient Tanis.

Though Zagazig was founded only in the 1820s, 3 kms south on the road to Bilbeis you can see the site of **Bubastis**

Rice fields in the Delta

(known today as Tell Basta), one of the most ancient cities in Egypt. Bubastis means House of the goddess Bastet, represented as a lioness, later as a graceful domestic cat, and the most impressive feature of the site is the remains of her *temple*, begun by Cheops and Chephren (IV Dyn), altered by Ramses II (IXX Dyn) and given its final form by the Pharaohs of the XXII Dynasty, who resided here. Of all the temples of Egypt, Herodotus said this gave the greatest pleasure to look at, both for its own merits but also because the city all round it had been raised to a higher level, so you could look down upon it where it stood amidst shade trees on almost an island formed by two embracing canals which stopped short without meeting.

Flashers

A licentious festival was held here: 'They come in barges, men and women together, a great number in each boat; on the way, some of the women keep up a continual clatter with castinets and some of the men play flutes, while the rest, both men and women, sing and clap their hands. Whenever they pass a town on the riverbank, they bring the barge close inshore, some of the women continuing to act as I have said, while others shout abuse at the women of the place or start dancing, or stand up and hitch up their skirts. When they reach Bubastis they celebrate the festival with elaborate sacrifices, and more wine is consumed than during all the rest of the year. The numbers that meet there, are, according to a native report, as many as 700,000 men and women'.

Nearby are *underground galleries* for the burial of cats, where many fine bronzes of cats or of Bastet have been found.

Affliction of the Hebrews

The site of **Tanis** at San el Hagar is a huge kom, 3.5 kms from north to south, 1.5 kms broad and rising to 35 metres above sea level. A number of excavations since 1825 have still only turned up a small portion of the whole, revealing structural remains from the XXI Dynasty through Ptolemaic times. But also a great quantity of stone, originally statues, stelae, carvings and blocks from the time of Ramses II and frequently bearing his cartouche, have been found incorporated into later buildings or littered about. It is argued by Pierre Montet, who excavated here from 1927 to 1956, that this was Ramses, named after the great Pharaoh, where the Hebrews suffered their afflictions as recorded in the Bible, and where later in the XX Dynasty a conflict between the people of the south who worshipped Amun and those of the east who worshipped Seth, led to the destruction and then rebuilding of the city. The site is a *walled compound* enclosing a sacred lake, several temples, a royal necropolis and much Ramessid statuary and carving; you should climb the *hill* to the east for an overall view of the mostly still buried city.

Damietta and the Crusades

Dumyat, as Damietta is known in Arabic, is at the mouth of the eastern branch of the Nile, 126 kms from Cairo and 70 kms along the coast from Port Said. It is a thriving port and industrial centre, and has some interesting old town houses like those at Rosetta (Rashid), but it is not worth travelling very far out of your way to see. Its history during the Crusades, however, deserves mention (also see Cairo, *To the*

Northern Walls chapter). Damietta's heyday was before the revival of Alexandria and the opening of the Suez Canal when it was a prosperous Arab trading city. Its fame rests in its struggle against the Crusaders, those vandalising European mercenaries who sacked the Christian city of Constantinople and slaughtered the inhabitants of Jerusalem. Damietta was taken in 1218, principally by Germans, and abandoned again in 1221, but not before its townspeople were sold into slavery. Its inhabitants fled when in 1249 St Louis landed nearby, but Damietta was returned to Egypt a year later as part of St Louis' ransom. It was these experiences which helped turn a religiously tolerant Egypt, with a still substantial Christian population, against Christianity both without and within. Even so, it says something for Egypt's underlying moderation, and the tenacity of its Coptic population, that it is the only country in northern Africa where Christianity has survived.

St Francis and the Sultan

One of those amongst the besiegers of Damietta in 1218 was St Francis, and his story here illustrates the abysmal ignorance of European Christianity in its medieval encounters with the country that had been, after all, one of the most important nurturers of that religion. Seeing that the attack was at first going badly, despite the fact that the Christians had God on their side, not to mention a papal legate at the head of their ranks, St Francis courageously crossed the enemy lines to confront the Sultan Kamil in person. He informed the Sultan that he had come to convert him and his people to the religion of Jesus, apparently unaware that Kamil was surrounded with Coptic advisors and fully familiar with the Christian faith. St Francis offered to enter a fiery furnace on the condition that should he come out alive, Kamil and his people would embrace Christianity. The Sultan replied to the saint with a lesson in humanity and common sense, saying that gamblings with one's life was not a valid proof of one's god, and saw St Francis on his way with oriental courtesy and lavish gifts.

Ancient Sites in the Western Delta

So little remains of antiquity in the western Delta that it is not worth visiting except as a passerby to Alexandria.

Sais is to the northwest of Tanta; once a royal capital, it was sacred to the goddess Neith who protected the embalmed bodies and entrails of the dead and is often depicted on sarcophagi and at the entrances to tombs. **Buto** lies to the east of Desuk and is most conveniently reached via Damanhur; its deity was the cobra goddess Wadjet, represented as the uraeus on the pharaonic crown. Hellenistic **Naukratis** is a level and desolate patch of ground to the left of the Tanta-Damanhur road. Damanhur stands on the site of the Roman **Hermopolis Parva**, no remains of its past surviving.

Rosetta (Rashid in Arabic) and Abu Qir (ancient Canopus) are covered later as excursions from Alexandria.

PRACTICAL INFORMATON

There is almost no **accommodation** above the no-star category in the Delta. At **Tanta** there is the Arafa (3-star), by the train station (Tel: 26952) — and that is it, unless you go to the Mediterranean resorts of **Ras el Bar** (numerous 1-star hotels) or **Gamassa** (3-star Amoun, Tel: 76; and lesser hotels).

Ras el Bar is beyond Damietta to which you take the train and then continue by bus; there are also direct buses from Cairo. Gamassa is to the west, reached by train to Mansura or Shirbin, then bus, or direct bus from Cairo. Both are beautiful and quiet, coastal rather than Delta in character.

ALEXANDRIA: CAPITAL OF MEMORY

Alexandrian facades have the same dull brown colour as those of Cairo. Possibly a little lighter, the rooftops almost white and gleaming in the morning sun. Instead of brushed by desert sand, frosted perhaps by the salt air of the Mediterranean. When open to the sea, playing a role in the broader life of the Mediterranean, receiving into her the Greeks, the Jews and others, the milieu has been intoxicating and Alexandria has thrived. But like the desert, the Arabs encroached upon the sea, they stood with their backs to it, and Alexandria (in Arabic, Iskandariya) withered. The meteorological fact of the prevailing northern breeze driving the sea against the rocks along the Corniche reminds you of the city's past and possibilities.

The founding of Alexandria

When Alexander the Great entered Egypt in November 332 BC he marched straight to Memphis. But early in 331 he sailed northwards down the Nile, as though one last time to gaze upon the uncertain Hellenic sea, and on the site of a small fishing village made his most lasting contribution to civilisation. He did not stay long enough to see a single building erected, and instead made his mysterious visit to Siwa and then back across the desert to Memphis before committing his life to the conquest of Asia. Eight years later, at the age of 33, he was dead. His body was brought to Memphis but the priests refused it, saying, 'Do not settle him here, but at the city he built at Rhakotis, for wherever this body must lie the city will be uneasy, disturbed with wars and battles'. So he descended the Nile again, wrapped in gold and enclosed in a coffin of glass, and he was buried at the centre of Alexandria, by her great crossroads, to be her civic hero and tutelary god. Memphis has slipped into the mud; Alexandria after many battles survives.

Once flying to Egypt it was nighttime and all below was black. I did not know if it was the Mediterranean or the desert. And then the captain said that we had crossed the coast, were approaching Cairo over the Western Desert, and that to the left you could see Alexandria. And there she was, far away, bright with lights — and unmistakable. No other city in the world has such an unmistakable and enduring form. Amr or Cleopatra could have recognised her, and perhaps even Alexander himself: the island of Pharos attached to Rhakotis by the causeway that has silted up.

The causeway, now a thickened neck of land, joins two limestone ridges running parallel to the coast. The inner ridge holds Alexandria fixed against the shifting alluvium of Egypt; the outer breaks the waves and gives Alexandria her harbours. It is a unique feature in Egypt, and Alexandria, never wholly Egyptian, yearns for the wider vistas of the Mediterranean.

On the edge of two worlds

Immortal in form, ambiguous in her situation, Alexandria is a curiously drifting city. Memories were stirred a few years ago by a wedding near the crossroads where Alexander was buried. The ground opened beneath the bride and she was never seen again. For all the commonplace surface of the modern town, Alexandria is haunted by the past. If more survived it would haunt you less. Unlike Rome or Athens with their monuments extant, Alexandria is all intimation: *here* (some spot) is where Alexander lay entombed; *here* Cleopatra committed suicide; *here* the Library, the Serapeum, etc... and there is nothing physically there — a stone, a broken column, an unsuspected chamber, but nothing substantial to root her phantom personages to their place, and they wander through Alexandria's streets, intruding on your waking thoughts.

History of the City

The Ptolemaic dynasty

When Alexander died, one of his Macedonian generals made Egypt his portion of the divided empire and Alexandria his capital, ruling as Ptolemy I Soter, and founding a dynasty that was to end with the suicide of Cleopatra VI — 'It is well done and fitting for a princess/Descended of so many royal kings.' Under Cleopatra and Antony, the city very nearly supplanted Rome which both strategically and culturally was Alexandria's inferior.

During the reign of the Ptolemies Alexandria became a resort of artists and scholars, and was outstanding particularly in its mathematicians and scientists, Euclid and Eratosthenes most notable amongst them. Claudius Ptolemy, the astronomer, lived during the Roman period when philosophy also flourished. Eratosthenes (see Aswan) determined the circumference and diameter of the Earth, while Claudius Ptolemy less accurately proclaimed the revolution of the universe round the Earth. The first was forgotten; the second received the blessing of the medieval Church which threatened Galileo with the stake for presuming to correct the error. Here between desert and sea philosophers struggled with the problems of the universe in a way that the earlier Egyptians never admitted, though unlike some of their predecessors in Greece never doubting the existence of God.

Christianity and the persecutions of Diocletian

It was Alexandria which raised Christianity, until then addressed to the poor and unlearned in Palestine, to the level of philosophy, and Egypt which provided it with many of its images: the resurrection of Osiris; Isis with Horus her child — we can recognise these in Christ and the Virgin, while the pharaonic *ankh* appears unaltered on some early Christian tombstones as a looped cross and slightly altered on others as a cross with a handle. These early Christians suffered heavily for their faith: Diocletian (early 4th C) demolished all churches, demoted all Christian officials and enslaved the rest, also killing 60 a day over five years, according to the Coptic Church. It was this persecution which caused the great flight into the desert, the founding of the first monasteries. 'The desert so swarmed with monks that their chaunts and hymns by day and by night made the whole country one church of God', wrote a contemporary.

It was Diocletian who divided the Roman Empire into four administrative regions, an emperor each for East and West, each emperor assisted by a caesar; and it was Diocletian who began the Caesaropapism, albeit in pagan form, that later marked the rule of the Christian Emperors of Byzantium. His persecutions made such an impression on the Egyptian Church that it dates its calendar from the Era of the Martyrs. It is understandable that in Egypt this struggle between Christianity and paganism should have given rise to a kind of nationalism — indeed Copt means Egyptian — and that it should have continued even after the Emperors at Constantinople were Christians themselves, for whatever the religion of the Empire, it was still a foreign (now Greek) oppressor.

The monophysite controversy

It was this undercurrent of nationalism that fuelled an otherwise seemingly abstruse debate on the nature of Christ. The Alexandrian theologians had decided that though born of Mary, the man in Christ had been entirely absorbed into the divine. Christ had one nature, the divine, and the adherents of this view were monophysites. However at Chalcedon (conveniently across the Bosphorus from Constantinople) it was decided in 451 that Christ had two natures, unmixed and unchangeable but at the same time indistinguishable and inseparable — this is the view of the Western Church to this day, just as the Copts are monophysites and so heretics in the Western view. The issue may not seem terribly important, or even comprehensible, and really it was more a slogan by which two political groupings denounced one another, but it

Alexandria: the breeze licks sudden plumes of water against the corniche

was the device by which Christian Egypt was lost to the world.

The Arabs welcomed

The hatred between Constantinople and Alexandria was so intense that when in 641 the Arab general Amr rode into Egypt with his 3500 Bedouin horsemen, the Alexandrians signed an armistice and in the following year admitted him into their city as a lesser evil than the evacuating Greeks. The city was still recognisably that of its glorious past; colonnades of marble lined Amr's triumph along the Canopic Way; the Tomb of Alexander rose to his left, the Pharos to his right. Amr reported back to the Caliph in Arabia: 'I have taken a city of which I can only say that it contains 4000 palaces, 4000 baths, 400 theatres, 1200 greengrocers and 40,000 Jews'. E M Forster writes: 'There was nothing studied in this indifference. The Arabs could not realise the value of their prize. They knew that Allah had given them a large and strong city. They could not know that there was no other like it in the world, that the science of Greece had planned it, that it had been the intellectual birthplace of Christianity. Legends of a dim Alexander, a dimmer Cleopatra, might move in their minds, but they had not the historical sense, they could never realise what had happened on this spot nor how inevitably the city of the double harbour should have arisen between the lake and the sea. And so though they had no intention of destroying her, they destroyed her, as a child might a watch. She never functioned again for over 1000 years'.

In fact, and it must be held to their eternal credit, the Arabs did absorb much of what Alexandria offered, creating with its help a civilisation for many centuries incomparably more beautiful, more intelligent, more humane than existed in Europe, storehousing, adding to and then passing on to the world the learning of the ancients. But Alexandria herself did suffer, and eventually Egypt too relapsed. By the time Napoleon landed Alexandria was no more than a fishing village once again. What brought her back to life was the construction of the Mahmudiya Canal by Mohammed Ali, giving her access to the vital Egyptian hinterland, and bringing Egypt again face to face with the Mediterranean. During the 19th C the Greeks returned and the Jews, and also came the French, the English, the Italians, and all of central Alexandria and the coast stretching out to Montaza was a European town. 'Alexandria was the foremost port of Egypt, and a hive of activity for the country's cotton brokers... with wide streets flanked by palms and flame trees, large gardens, stylish villas, neat new buildings, and above all, room to breathe. Life was easy. Labour was cheap. Nothing was impossible, especially when it involved one's comfort' (as Jacqueline Carol remembers in her appropriately titled *Cocktails and Camels*).

The modern city

Post-war and post-Suez nationalism meant the ejection of the Jews, Greeks and other foreigners and for some years the Arabs were again in possession of no more than a skeleton, a city 'clinging to the minds of old men like traces of perfume upon a sleeve: Alexandria, the capital of Memory' (Lawrence Durrell, *Justine*).

There is a nostalgia about the city, but also lately something of her former sparkle. Alexandrian women are attractive and often smartly dressed. They are of a wide range of colour and beauty, reflecting a cosmopolitan ancestry. At restaurants, cafés, patisseries — Alexandria has a reputation for the best food in Egypt — you are often served by women (almost unheard of in Upper Egypt and not all that common in Cairo), and they are pleasant, self-assured, chatty, even flirtatious. (There is much to be said for judging a place by the rapport you can have with the opposite sex.) Alexandria is cleaner, less congested than Cairo, not desperate. There are slums, but on the whole the city does not have Cairo's problems. There is a sense of well-being; Alexandrians stream about the streets late into the night, shopping or simply walking, sitting at cafés talking. And there is the breeze that licks sudden plumes of water against the Corniche and carries an Aegean tang and freshness into Africa. This much has not changed since Alexander ordered his Greek metropolis to be built on this Egyptian shore.

Orientation

The old Turkish quarter

That part of Alexandria which juts out into the Mediterranean is the old, rundown and interesting area called **El Anfushi**. But this was once the island of Pharos, and prophetically it was a Greek who gave a first account of it: 'There is an island in the surging sea, which they call Pharos, lying off Egypt' (The *Odyssey*); it was here that Menelaus was becalmed on his way home from Troy. Towards the western tip of the headland is the Ras el Tin Palace; at the eastern tip Fort Qaytbay, which stands on the foundations, indeed is part built, of Alexandria's ancient lighthouse which gave its name, Pharos, to lighthouses everywhere and was one of the Seven Wonders of the World.

The island was connected to the mainland by a causeway 7 stades long, the Heptastadion. Silting has made it a permanent broad neck of land. Along this neck runs Sharia Faransa (Rue de France). This runs south into **Midan el Tahrir**, the former Place Mohammed Ali; at the southern end of the midan was, approximately, the former mainland coastline and the fishing village of Rhakotis.

The harbours

To either side of the Heptastadion were the two ancient harbours, the Eunostos or Harbour of Safe Return to the west, the Great Harbour to the east. Their roles have been reversed in modern times; Mohammed Ali developed the **Western Harbour** for commerce and it can be difficult to get to for all its docks and warehouses, but under the Ptolemies it was the less important of the two. The **Eastern Harbour** makes a graceful sweep and with its long **corniche**, Sharia 26 July, is the most pleasing attraction of the city. Fort Qaytbay marks the tip of its northern arm; the lesser promontory of **Silsileh**, hardly developed but for a military compound, forms its eastern arm. From Silsileh westwards ran the palace of the Ptolemies where Cleopatra killed herself.

Midan Saad Zaghloul is between the Ramleh tram station and the corniche. Here Cleopatra began the Caesareum in honour of Antony and Octavian finished it in honour of himself. Two obelisks here, the famous 'Cleopatra's Needles', are now on London's Embankment and in New York's Central Park. In the midan is a statue of Saad Zaghloul, a nationalist leader who after the First World War negotiated the British withdrawal from Egypt, though they maintained a military presence in the Canal Zone. Another nationalist leader was the fellah officer Arabi who in 1882 led an uprising against the British. British warships retaliated by devastating Alexandria. Where Arabi failed, Nasser later triumphed. Arabi is remembered by a square in downtown Cairo and in Alexandria by **Midan Orabi** which extends from Midan el Tahrir to the corniche.

Shopping and tourist facilities

The Hotel Cecil stands on the west side of Midan Saad Zaghloul, and the streets to the south of the midan and between it and Midan el Tahrir form the central shopping district of Alexandria. The most fashionable street is Sharia Salah-Salem, formerly Rue Chérif Pasha, running southeast out of Midan el Tahrir. Also in this area, and around the Ramleh tram station, as well as along Sharia Horreya, are many airline offices and travel agencies.

Sharia Nebi Danyal runs nearly north to south through this area, at its southern end running into **Midan el Gumhuriya** with the train station for Cairo. About halfway along its length, Nebi Danyal intersects a street called Sharia el Mitwalli to the west, Sharia Horreya to the east. Nebi Danyal was anciently the Street of the Soma and the east-west street was the famous Canopic Way. Their intersection was once the crossroads of the world, and here was Alexander's tomb. To the west the Canopic Way left the city through the Gate of the Moon, to the east through the Gate of the Sun — by which Amr entered in triumph, Antony in final defeat after his last resistance against Octavian outside the walls. A poem by Constantine Cavafy (1863–1933), translated by George Valassopoulos, describes this moment as the god Hercules, whom Antony loved and who loved him, was heard passing away from Alexandria in mysterious music and song. It is called 'The God Abandons Antony'.

When at the hour of midnight
an invisible choir is suddenly heard passing
with exquisite music, with voices —
Do not lament your fortune that at last subsides,
your life's work that has failed, your schemes that have proved illusions.
But like a man prepared, like a brave man,
bid farewell to her, to Alexandria who is departing.
Above all, do not delude yourself, do not say that it is a dream,
that your ear was mistaken,
Do not condescend to such empty hopes.
Like a man for long prepared, like a brave man,
like to the man who was worthy of such a city,
go to the window firmly,
and listen with emotion,
but not with the prayers and complaints of the coward
(Ah! supreme rapture!)

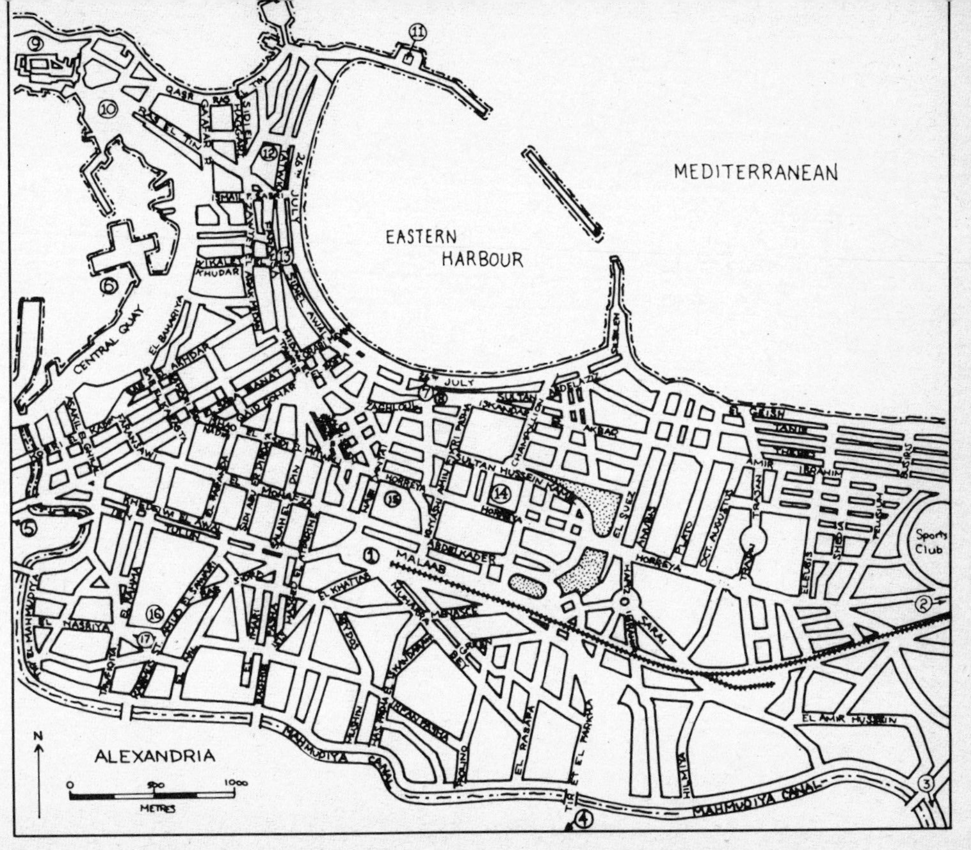

1. Midan el Gumhuriya and Misr Station (for Cairo)
2. Sidi Gabir Station for Cairo and Abu Qir)
3. Delta Road to Cairo
4. Desert Road to Cairo
5. Road to Alamein and Mersa Matruh
6. Passenger ships (Venice, Piraeus, etc.)
7. Midan Saad Zaghloul
8. Ramleh Tram Station
9. Ras el Tin Palace
10. Anfushi Tombs
11. Fort Qaytbay (site of Pharos)
12. Abu el Abbas Mosque
13. Terbana Mosque
14. Graeco-Roman Museum
15. Kom el Dikka
16. Pompey's Pillar
17. Catacombs of Kom el Shogafa

listen to the notes, to the exquisite instruments of the mystic choir,
and bid farewell to her, to Alexandria whom you are losing.

Eastwards Still within the vanished lines of the ancient walls, further east along Sharia Horreya and then a short way down a road to the left is the Graeco-Roman Museum, while at this point but to the right of Horreya are the Ptolemaic and Roman ruins being excavated at Kom el Dikka. The modern city extends 16 kms eastwards in a string of beach suburbs to **Montazah**, a former summer residence of the royal family, with vast gardens and good swimming nearby.

Southwest To the far southwest of the city, near the **Mahmudiya Canal**, is Pompey's Column and the Catacombs of Kom el Shogafa.

While this outline might already suggest a number of casual strolls through the city or excursions beyond, detailed itineraries are set out in the following chapter.

PRACTICAL INFORMATION

ACCOMMODATION

Montazah Sheraton (5-star), Montazah. Tel: 968550. Telex: 54706 MONSH UN. New (1981) and overlooking the Mediterranean, with its own beach and a heated swimming pool. Restaurant, café, nightclub; tennis and golf by arrangement. Rooms have colour TV and balconies. The great disadvantage for those who want to get the feel of Alexandria is that the hotel is nowhere near the centre of the city (16 kms).

Salamlek (4-star), Montazah. Tel: 860585. Telex: 65813 UN. Set in the grounds of the royal palace and indeed once itself a royal pavilion, the Salamlek has a commanding view of the sea (spoiled only by the 5-star Palestine, a dump, to one side). Rooms are not air-conditioned, but that is not necessary in Alexandria; all rooms have baths. Half board is compulsory in summer. Like the Sheraton it is a long way from town.

Cecil (4-star), Midan Saad Zaghloul. Tel: 807532. Telex: 54358 CECIL UN. This is my favourite hotel in Alexandria and something of an institution. Make sure you have a room commanding the magnificent view over the Eastern Harbour. From your balcony you watch the Mediterranean splash against the corniche; you see the site of the Pharos on the breakwater in the distance, and off to the right on the Silsileh headland, imagine the palace of the Ptolemies. The Cecil figures often in Durrell's *Alexandria Quartet* and he himself stayed here when he first came to the city. A Moorish pile in the centre of town, with large rooms, private baths and TVs, it is also a bit bare and frayed now. There is a restaurant (half board compulsory, the food indifferent), a bar (Monty's), a tea lounge, casino, bank and an Avis desk.

Windsor Palace (4-star), 17 Sharia el Shohada. Tel: 808700. Two blocks west of the Cecil along the corniche, though the entrance is on a side street, the Windsor is of similar vintage. There is an agreeable pavement café out front.

Metropole (3-star), 52 Sharia Saad Zaghloul. Tel: 21467. Telex: 54350 METRO UN. Recently modernised, this is another of Alexandria's period hotels — this one owned by a Greek who has remained in the city. Most rooms with bath. Restaurant, bar, coffee shop; half board compulsory in summer.

Admiral (2-star), 24 Sharia Amin Fakhry. Tel: 805343. Telex: 32388 UN. Well located near the Ramleh tram terminus near Midan Saad Zaghloul. Restaurant, bar, café, nightclub; air-conditioned rooms.

Leroy (1-star), 25 Sharia Talaat Harb. Tel: 960608. The hotel occupies the top 3 floors of a 7-storey building; the rooms are large and high, solidly furnished, with views over the city's rooftops — an especially superb view from the top floor restaurant. Recommended.

There is a **youth hostel** on Sharia Port Said, at Chatby. Tel: 75459.

EATING AND ENTERTAINMENT

Alexandria has a reputation for good food, particularly seafood. Not fancy, but with character and good fish, try the **Restaurant** (= Estiatorion in Greek) **Denis** on Rue Ebn Bassan, a short street running north off Midan Ramleh (Olympic Airways on the corner) to the corniche. Where this street meets the corniche, a few blocks east of Midan Saad Zaghloul, is the **Mustafa Darwish Restaurant**. If the night is warm and not too breezy it is agreeable to sit outside: fish, chicken, Egyptian meat dishes, an unsolicited variety of taheena, salad, pickles and onions. For dessert you should not miss the Mohallabiya Darwish: fruit in thick fluffy cream with cherry sauce.

Here, one night: a woman positioned herself before my table, juggled two flaming torches and extinguished them both in her mouth. Then she put a can of benzine to her lips, applied the torch and breathed out a ferocious blast of flame. I was astounded and laughed, but looking around saw all the Arabs poker-faced. None of them gave so much as a piastre. In Egypt you can toil in the hot wet fields of the Delta for a lifetime, or breath fire along the Alexandrian corniche: it makes no difference, you are not noticed. The woman's assistant was her tawny-skinned, blonde-haired daughter, 4 years old at the most, who refuelled and relit the torches — and suddenly, accidentally, knocked over the benzine. She shrank like a child who had opened the wrong sluice and flooded the year's crop with water and mud.

Here, one afternoon: a baboon with slim waist, red arse, a lead around his full mane, walked along the corniche, his owner clutching a tambourine. They walked with purpose, as though to an appointment. Broad hot daylight.

For a Greek meal, try the **Taverna Diamantakis**, on the south side of Midan Ramleh; fried and grilled fish, squid or shellfish, all ordered by weight, and Greek salads. You could make the long drive out to Abu Qir for a seafood meal at the **Zephyrion** overlooking the sea.

Or south from Midan Ramleh, at 40 Sharia Safiya Zaghloul, there is the **Santa Lucia**, usually a lively place. Or along Sharia Salah Salem, just as you reach Midan el Tahrir, on your right is Sharia el Borsa, and at No. 1 is the **Union**, one of the famous places of the past, very quiet now, spectral to dine here.

Alexandria has many cafés, patisseries, confiseries, glaceries, etc: here are some of the best and most interesting:

Athineos, on Midan Ramleh, full of mirrors, was one of Cavafy's favourite haunts. Diagonally across, where Sharia Safiya Zaghloul runs into Midan Saad Zaghloul, is the **Trianon**. (Above it was the Third Circle of Irrigation where Cavafy worked; if you are interested therefore in tracing the limits of this man's physical world you need only walk the short distance from the Trianon up Sharia Safiya Zaghloul and then right into Estanbul for Sharia Sharm el Sheikh — about 700 paces. Forster observed Cavafy waiting at the corner, 'standing at a slight angle to the universe'.) Up Safiya Zaghloul, on the right just before Santa Lucia, is the **Billiards Palace**, a café and billiards hall combined, where a few old Greeks hang out and where the poet would pick up young boys. Where Safiya Zaghloul crosses Sharia Horreya you will find **Pastroudis**, another old Greek place — coffee, tea, a selection of pastries; there is a restaurant here too.

You would expect Alexandria to have quite a nightlife. It does not. Belly dancing is almost unknown here: the **Miramar**, at 234 Sharia 26 July (the corniche), may be the only place with an oriental show. There is the **Crazy Horse** nightclub by Athineos on Midan Ramleh, and on the ninth floor of the Admiral Hotel there is the **Calvados** disco. But also you should wander around Midan Ramleh, and up Safiya Zaghloul, keeping an ear out for the sound of a Greek bazouki, the rough, wailing, loud rembetika music, the smashing of plates, as Iskandariya closes in all around.

The *Eyptian Gazette* and Saturday's *Eyptian Mail* carry entertainment listings for Alexandria. Advertisements for clubs, etc, will be found in the free booklet *Alexandria Night and Day*, available at hotels and the Tourist Information Office.

OF INTEREST

Much of what there is to see in Alexandria can be reached on foot, and visiting mosques or standing at a street corner imagining that it was once the crossroads of the world is free and depends little, if at all, on hours of opening.

The Graeco-Roman Museum, off Sharia Horreya, LE1, students 50PT. It is open year-round from 9am to 4pm daily except Fridays when it closes from 12.30

to 2pm.

Nearby is **Kom el Dikka**, the site of excavations into Alexandria's Ptolemaic and Roman, and indeed Moslem, past. Entrance is from Sharia Nebi Danyal and costs LE1; hours are from 9am to 4pm daily. You are free to wander about the Roman amphitheatre and to glimpse down into the Ptolemaic excavations. To get down to Cleopatra's street-level may depend on the state of digging and could require a nod from an attendant, or an illicit sense of adventure.

The Greek Consulate, 63 Sharia Iskandar el Akbar (ie Alexander the Great Street, of course), recreates on its top floor **Cavafy's apartment**: his desk, books, some interesting photos, etc. They keep consular hours, and it might be a good idea to phone them first to make sure they are open: 38454.

To get to Anfushi to see the tombs there and Fort Qaytbay, take tram 4 or 5 from Midan Orabi or bus 6 or 83 from Midan Ramleh. The **Anfushi Tombs** have no strict hours of opening, though the keeper is usually there from 10am and the fee is a few piastres of baksheesh. **Fort Qaytbay** can be entered at any time of day, but its inner keep, where the musuem is, opens only from 9am to 3pm daily except Fridays when it closes from 11.30 to 1.30. There is a small fee.

Pompey's Pillar and the site of the **Serapeum** is reached by tram 2 from Misr Station (the main railway station), tram 5 from Midan Orabi, or buses 9 or 14 from Midan Ramleh. The area is open from 9am to 4pm, admission 50PT. Nearby are the **Catacombs of Kom el Shogafa**, same hours, same fee as Pompey's Pillar.

To reach **Montazah**, you can take the 20 bus from either Midan Orabi or Midan Ramleh, also the 28 bus from Midan Orabi or Misr Station. There is a modest entry fee for the grounds; the beach is additional. The grounds are open from 7am to sunset — unless of course your hotel is here.

The easiest way of getting to **Abu Qir** and **Rosetta** (Rashid) is by car. However, you can take a bus to Abu Qir: the No. 28 from Midan Orabi or the 29 from Misr Station or Sidi Gabir. The train to Rosetta (from Sidi Gabir) is not recommended.

INFORMATION

The principal **Tourist Information Office** is in Midan Saad Zaghloul (Tel: 807985), on the same side as the Cecil Hotel. There is a branch at the port (800100). For the Tourist Police, Tel: 60000. Information can also be obtained at travel agencies and hotels.

You should pick up a copy of the free booklet *Alexandria Night and Day* at any of these places. As with the Cairo version, it contains hotel listings, addresses and phone numbers of various ministries and consulates, advertisements for restaurants, entertainments and travel agencies, and some travel information (city trams and buses, trains to Cairo, etc). It includes, too, an inadequate map of the city.

TRAVEL

Alexandria is a compact city and much of it can be covered **on foot**. There is a good system of **trams** and **buses**, their principal termini being Midan Orabi, Midan Ramleh and Misr Station. Fares are first and second class, most journeys costing 2PT and 3PT depending on class and distance. From downtown to Montazah you will pay about 5PT to 7PT.

Taxis, which are orange and black, are inexpensive — especially as you are more likely to pay the metered fare than in Cairo. A car, with or without driver, can be hired from **Avis**, at the Hotel Cecil in Midan Saad Zaghloul (Tel: 807532 and 807055).

Tours can be arranged through Thomas Cook, Menatours and others.

Travel Agents in Alexandria are located in or not far from Midan Saad Zaghloul and include:

De Castro and Co, 33 Sharia Salah Salem (Tel: 35770). Agents for Adriatica shipping lines (to Piraeus and Venice).

Eastmar, 16 Sharia Salah Salem (Tel: 808130). All tourist services, plus operators of their own Nile cruises.

Menatours, Midan Saad Zaghloul, next to the Cecil Hotel (Tel: 809676). For sightseeing tours around Alexandria and vicinity.

Misr Travel, 33 Sharia Salah Salem. (Tel: 29617). The Egyptian state travel agency, helpful with all accommodation and travel arrangements.

Thomas Cook, 15 Midan Saad Zaghloul — in fact Midan Ramleh, where the trams terminate (Tel: 27830). All travel arrangements, tours, travellers cheques.

Alexandria is not served internationally by air, but a number of **airlines** have offices in the city. For information on **sailings**, see the *Background* chapter and also consult one of the agents above.

Egyptair, 19 Midan Saad Zaghloul (Tel: 20778), flies to Cairo. A good **bus service to Cairo** via the Desert Road departs from Midan Saad Zaghloul; its booking office near the Cecil Hotel. The main **railway**

station, Mahattat Misr, is at Midan el Gumhuriya, at the south end of Sharia Nebi Danyal. This is where you get the train to Cairo (see *Background* chapter for timetables). There is a secondary station, Sidi Gabir, in the eastern part of the city which serves Abu Qir and Rosetta, though Cairo trains stop here too. Another way of covering long distances is by **service** (or **shared**) **taxi**; try for these at Midan Saad Zaghloul and Midan Orabi.

OTHER THINGS

The chief attraction of Alexandria for some is its **beaches**; the No. 20 bus runs from Midan Orabi and Midan Ramleh all the way along the corniche to Montazah and Maamura, as do convoys of service taxis. Also the **breeze** off the Mediterranean makes Alexandria a desirable place to be during summer. But as soon as the sun goes down, it can get chilly, and in winter it can be both chilly and rainy during the day. So when going about Alexandria, dress accordingly. (A bright, brisk winter's day in Alexandria can be the most beautiful time to be here.)

There is a **post office** at Midan Ramleh.

To exchange money, go to the banks at the Cecil or Sheraton Montazah hotels, or to Thomas Cook.

For **medical care**, ask at your hotel. Also the Tourist Police or your consulate can advise. Recommended is the **University Hospital** in Chatby (Tel: 25952).

The **Tourist Police** can be reached through the Tourist Information Office, or direct by dialling 60000, 25977 or 807611. For **urgent help** of any sort, telephone 123.

For a city so famous in literature it is remarkable that Alexandria possesses few **bookshops** these days. Feeble best is the **Al-Ahram**, 10 Sharia Horreya, on the corner of Sharia Nebi Danyal. It has French- and English-language paperbacks, guides and newspapers.

DISCOVERING ALEXANDRIA

'If a man make a pilgrimage round Alexandria in the morning, God will make for him a golden crown, set with pearls, perfumed with musk and camphor, and shining from the East to the West' (Ibn Duqmaq). Today even the most determined seer of sights will be able to catch the evening train back to Cairo. A Roman odeon, Pompey's Pillar, the tombs at Kom el Shogafa; these and a medieval fortress squatting on the foundations of the Pharos lighthouse are the principal but paltry remains of Alexandria's resplendent past. Some will see nothing in her. Others will voyage through the phantom city and listen to her voices and her music.

The Crossroads

From Midan Saad Zaghloul you should walk south along Sharia Nebi Danyal and where it meets Sharia Horreya you should pause. This is the **crossroads of the city**, and has been for more than 2300 years. From east to west ran the Canopic Way (Horreya), from the Gate of the Sun to the Gate of the Moon. From north to south ran the Street of the Soma (Nebi Danyal). Standing on this rather ordinary-looking corner you might need this description by Achilles Tatius, a 5th C bishop, to assist your imagination: 'The first thing one noticed in entering Alexandria by the Gate of the Sun was the beauty of the city. A range of columns went from one end of it to the other. Advancing down them, I came in time to the place that bears the name of Alexander, and there could see the other half of the town, which was equally beautiful. For just as the colonnades stretched ahead of me, so did other colonnades now appear at right angles to them'.

Continue south along Sharia Nebi Danyal till you are nearly at the large square before the train station. On the right is a mosque set back from the street and with *four antique columns* serving as gate posts. This is the typical way you encounter the past, if you encounter it tangibly at all, in Alexandria — a dwindling number of remnants used in building after successive building, their original purpose only to be guessed at. It is possible that the Mouseion once stood here and that these columns once adorned its facade. Founded by Ptolemy Soter, the Museion was the great intellectual accomplishment of his dynasty, a vast complex of lecture halls, laboratories, observatories, a library, a dining hall, a park and a zoo. It was like a university, except that the scholars, scientists and literary men it supported were under no obligation to teach. It would have been here that Euclid and Eratosthenes worked.

The Museion

Directly opposite is the **Mosque of Nebi Danyal** (popularly believed to be the tomb of the prophet Daniel but in fact named for Mohammed Danyal al-Maridi, a venerated sheikh who died in 1407) on the site of Alexander's tomb, the Soma, where he and some of the Ptolemies lay. (Its entrance is set back from the street, nearly hidden between two buildings.) If you go in you can gaze down upon a *crypt* where Daniel and an

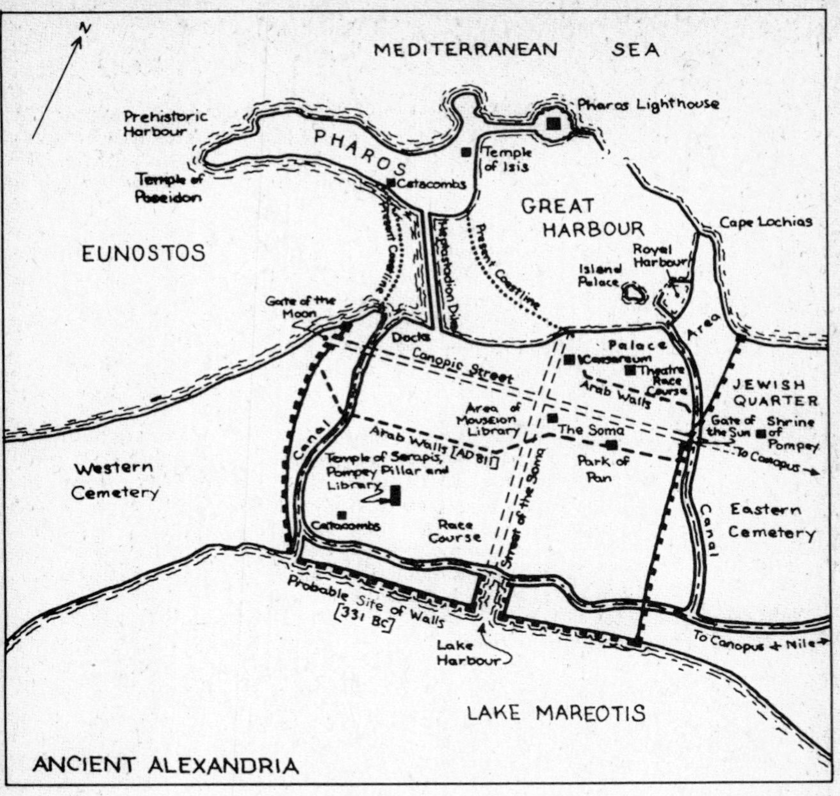

uncertain figure called Lukman the Wise lie. It is easy to imagine a still deeper crypt where Alexander himself still lies, for the cellars and foundations of the mosque have never been properly examined. The body is thought to have been destroyed in city riots of the late 3rd C AD, but in the absence of any certain knowledge rumour has flourished. In 1850 a dragoman from the Russian Consulate said that down in the cellars through a hole in a wooden door he saw 'a human body in a sort of glass cage with a diadem on its head and half bowed on a sort of elevation or throne. A quantity of books or papyrus were scattered around'. Suetonius tells a good story of Octavian's (later Augustus) visit here: 'When Alexander's sarcophagus was brought from its shrine, Augustus gazed at the body, then laid a crown of gold on its case and scattered some flowers to pay his respects. When they asked if he would like to see Ptolemy too, "I wished to see a king,' he replied, 'I did not wish to see corpses".

Alexander's tomb

In *The Alexandria Quartet*, Lawrence Durrell refers to 'the city's exemplars — Cavafy, Alexander, Cleopatra and the rest', giving pride of place to the poet who inspired E M Forster and Durrell himself to discover the dream-city

Constantine Cavafy

Alexandria. Cavafy lived nearby, at **10 Rue Lepsius** as it was early this century, now 4 Sharia Sharm el Sheikh — typical of Alexandria to disguise the whereabouts of even this part of her past. You get there by returning north across Sharia Horreya (in Forster's time the Rue Rosette, in Durrell's the Rue Fuad) and taking the second right into Sharia Sultan Hussein (also called Sharia Estanbul). Off this street to the right is first a foot-alley, then a narrow street which is Cavafy's.

Here the literary apotheosis of Alexandria began. On the second floor of what is now the Pension Amir but was once a more impressive building, Constantine Cavafy passed the years of his poetic maturity. A dusty plaque in Arabic and Greek reads, 'In this house for the last 25 years of his life lived the Alexandrian poet Constantine Cavafy (1863–1933)'. (Cavafy's apartment has been recreated as a **museum** on the top floor of the Greek Consulate, 63 Sharia Iskandar el Akbar.)

E M Forster

Forster first met Cavafy in 1917: 'It never occurred to him that I might like his work or even understand it... and I remember the delight to us both, one dusky evening in his flat, when it appeared that I was "following". When he was pleased he would jump and light a candle, and then another candle and he would cut cigarettes in half and light them and bring offerings of mastica with little bits of bread and cheese, and his talk would sway over the Mediterranean world and over much of the world within.' In *Pharos and Pharillon* and *Alexandria: a History and a Guide,* Forster introduced Cavafy to the English-speaking world. Years later Forster remarked, 'I did a little to spread his fame. It was about the best thing I did'.

On the ground floor of 10 Rue Lepsius was a brothel. 'Poor things!' Cavafy said to a friend who had accompanied him to his door one night. 'One must be sorry for them. They receive some disgusting people, some monsters, but' — and here his voice took on a deep, ardent tone — 'they receive some angels, some angels!' His English friends called the street the 'Rue Clapsius', though indeed the entire quarter was ill-famed. Cavafy satisfied his homosexuality by picking up boys in the cafés along the Rue Missala (now Sharia Safiya Zaghloul) — his favourite haunt, the Billiards Palace, survives still. With the Greek Hospital opposite and the patriarchal church round the corner, Cavafy was fond of saying, 'Where could I live better? Below, the brothel caters for the flesh. And there is the church which forgives sin. And there is the hospital where we die'. He did die in that hospital, his funeral service took place at St Saba, and his body buried in the Greek Cemetery at Chatby.

Lawrence Durrell's Alexandria

'Radiating out like the arms of a starfish from the axis of the founder's tomb' (*Clea*), the streets of this part of the city housed most of Durrell's characters. Darley and Pombal shared a flat in the Rue Nebi Daniel; Clea's studio was in the Rue St Saba; Justine and Nessim lived in a town house set back from the Rue Fuad — and Balthazar lived in the Rue Lepsius, in 'the worm-eaten room with the cane chair which creaked all night, and where once the old poet of the city had recited "The Barbarians"' (*Clea*). The Cervoni's house, where

Glass and mirrors at Athineos: another favourite haunt of Cavafy's

at the carnival ball Narouz drove a hat pin through Toto de Brunel's skull, thinking he was killing Justine, was not far from the Greek Patriarchate; both Cohen and Melissa died in the Greek Hospital; and you can still visit Pastroudis a little east down Sharia Horreya by Kom el Dikka where Darley and Nessim, and Balthazar for an arak, would gather.

Along the Canopic Way

It is pleasant to sit at Pastroudis, an old Greek place, with a drink, a coffee, a rich pastry — there is also a restaurant — and let time pass. It is on a triangular block on the south side of Sharia Horreya, one block east of Sharia Nebi Danyal. The excavations at **Kom el Dikka** lie immediately to the south. It is likely that a great deal of Alexandria's past could be uncovered, and the work here, begun by the Polish Centre of Mediterranean Archaeology in 1959, marks a start. Layers of *Moslem tombs* were found, dating from the 9th to 11th C, and a large complex of 3rd C *Roman baths*. The spur to further and intensive excavation came in 1964 with the unearthing of a small *Roman odeon*, a covered theatre for musical performances, with seating for 700 to 800. Inscriptions suggest it was used also for wrestling contests. It is pretty, the area around it landscaped, which is all very well, but it possesses none of the excitement of an excavation in progress.

That is provided by the deep broad trenches still being dug to the northeast of the Odeon. The dusty walls of the

Unearthing the ancient city

trenches are layered with extraordinary amounts of potsherds, and as you peer down several metres from the surface of the kom you can see substantial stone walls and the remains of brick houses. Best of all is to climb down. You walk along a *Ptolemaic street* lined with shopfronts. If Cleopatra ever went shopping, then here you can say to yourself is where Cleopatra walked. It is a sensation of immediacy rare to Alexandria.

A few streets further east along Sharia Horreya the Rue de la Musée (Sharia el Mathaf) on your left runs along the entrance to the **Graeco-Roman Museum** (see below).

But continuing east you come, after nearly a kilometre, to the **Shallalat Gardens**. Here stood the Gate of the Sun, while remaining still are ruined segments of the *Arab wall* (north side of gardens). About 3 kms southeast, by the Mahmudiya Canal, are a series of gardens. The northernmost is the **Zoo**;

Gardens

in the middle are the **Nouzha Gardens**, originally planted for the Khedive Ismail with specimen trees; the southernmost are the **Antoniadis Gardens**, early this century the grounds of a wealthy Greek family, rather formal and planted with statues. In the area of these gardens Amr and his cavalry camped before entering the city.

The Graeco-Roman Museum

Not far from Kom el Dikka, heading east along Sharia Horreya and turning north (left) into the Rue de la Musée (Sharia Mathaf), is the Graeco-Roman Museum which fills the historical gap between the Egyptian Museum in Cairo and the Coptic Museum in Old Cairo. The rooms are numbered but the exhibits are not always numbered, or their numbers are hard to find. Nor is everything labelled, though usually the most important exhibits are, but not always. Furthermore, there has been some rearranging recently. In short, take what follows with a sense of adventure. The museum could be greatly improved by maps, plans, models, etc, showing the development of the city. Nevertheless, it is fascinating as it is, and pleasant.

You enter a *vestibule* with a statue of Nike (26019) carved from several marble blocks. It is probably Roman, 2nd C AD, based on a Hellenistic model. Until 1950 it was part of the flotsam of the city, lying on a site just off Sharia Horreya. Modern Alexandria troubles little about its past. There is also a cast of the Rosetta Stone. The original is in the British Museum.

Now turning left into *Room 6*, there are masks which were placed over the faces of the Roman dead before burial and afterwards hung about the house as mementoes. There is also a fine black granite statue of the Apis bull, erected at the time of Hadrian and found towards the end of the last century at Pompey's Pillar. Behind this is a magnificent statue of Serapis (22158), a great jolly fellow like Dickens' Ghost of Christmas Past.

The cult of Serapis

Serapis was the only god ever successfully made by a modern man. Egyptians at Memphis had worshipped Osiris in his Apis form as Osorapis; Ptolemy I combined this deity with Dionysos and made what was in effect a new god. The

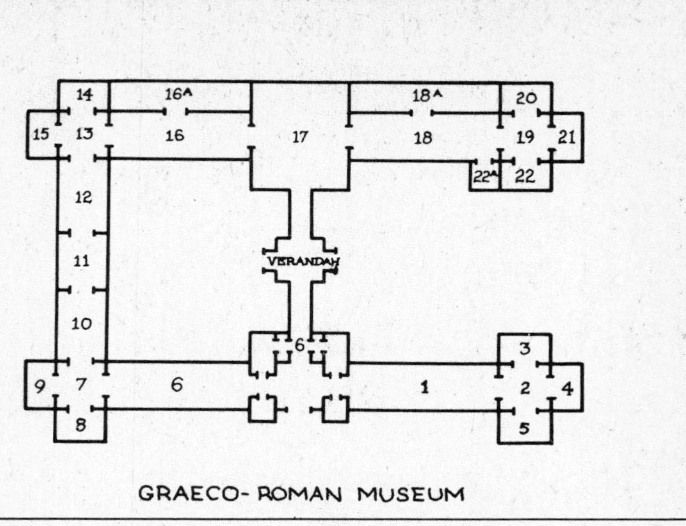

intention, probably, was to unite Greeks and Egyptians in a common worship, but the Egyptians would not accept him and he became the Greek god of Alexandria. His cult statue (this is a contemporary copy) of white marble was painted blue, its gilt head and jewelled eyes gleaming from the darkened recess of its shrine, the Alexandrian Serapeum, which stood near Pompey's Pillar. His worship spread throughout the Aegean, his cult established at Athens and particularly at Delos, though he was venerated as far away as India. His importance can be gauged by the fact that when Bishop Theophilos destroyed the Serapeum and its statue in 391, it was taken by the world as the definitive triumph of Christianity.

Cleopatra identified herself with Isis, that still greater deity, and so naturally, and with useful effect, Antony was identified with her consort Serapis, or at least with Dionysos. This may have assisted Roman propagandists (from whom Shakespeare took his cue) in depicting Antony as a debauched Bacchic figure — more a measure of Roman methods and philistine contempt for Greek culture (and fear of Antony's alliance with Greek Alexandria) than any true reflection on Antony the man. Romans admired and copied *things* Greek, but Greeks themselves, and those like Antony who immersed themselves with genuine understanding in Greek culture, were despised. There was a ready Roman audience for a 'scheming' and 'treacherous' Cleopatra, a 'cowardly' and 'besotted' Antony, and history, particularly the Battle of Actium, was easily distorted to provide proof for the slanders.

Room 7 has a statue of a Hyksos pharaoh (Second Intermediate Period) at the centre. It was appropriated by Ramses II and on its shoulder appears Ramses' daughter

Hout-Ma-Ra, traditionally the princess who found Moses in the bullrushes. On the left between Room 7 and 8 is a Hathoric capital (476) of black basalt dating from the Ptolemaic period.

Room 8 contains five mummy cases and includes two Roman mummies with painted portraits, elaborate diamond-pattern wrapping and, in one instance, a glimpse of Roman toes.

Crocodile cult

At the centre of *Room 9* is a wooden stretcher bearing a mummified crocodile. The room illustrates, the Ptolemies in their Egyptian aspect, and here it is crocodile worship in the Fayyum. There are the remains of the chapel (19678–81) of a crocodile god with the wooden door of the first pylon and the coffin and beir of the sacred animal (2nd C BC). The entire chapel has been reconstructed in the north garden of the museum. There is also a Heliopolitan bas-relief (380) from over the door of a tomb, the deceased on the left amidst delicately carved scenes of rejoicing: an old harpist singing and accompanied by a girl on a drum and by two others who clap their hands. To the right, a man prepares a drink; then two dancing girls.

Room 10 is a collection of small objects of the pharaonic period. Most strange is the mummy of a baby. Apart from its smallness, no concession is made to its babyness, eg the face mask is the usual stereotype. Also here, in the far right corner, is a headless, sensuous, magnificent piece, a fragment of black granite breast (3221). It is similar to a statue of Queen Arsinoë, wife of Ptolemy II Philadelphus, in the Vatican.

Room 11 has objects in which the Greek and Egyptian influences mingle — never very well. There are some curious blocks with footprints, votive offerings to Isis and Serapis.

At the centre of *Room 12* is a dull statue of Marcus Aurelius; a sea-worn head of Alexander in pink granite is on the right-hand shelf. Both of these were found in Alexandria, the Aurelius along the Canopic Way.

Rooms 13 and 14 contain miscellaneous sculptures and architectural fragments.

Room 15 too contains architectural elements, and decorations; at the centre is a portion of wall with a painted scene (27029) of oxen turning a *sakiyeh* or waterwheel, a Greek work from a tomb.

Room 16 is devoted to sculpture. There is a limestone head of another Serapis (3917) on a shelf to the left. Against the wall at the far end is the repulsive Mithras (24407), sun god of the Persians, his worship introduced into the Roman Empire during the 1st C BC. This statue comes from near Minya. He is lion-headed, cloven-hoofed and winged, with hairy legs, and is draped with snakes.

Hellenistic sculpture

In *Room 16A* are the finest pieces of Hellenistic sculpture in the museum. In a case on the left is a small white marble head of Alexander (3402); the nose and torso are restorations. The larger torsos at the left end of the room are particularly impressive: a seated woman with a standing girl (14942); two unclothed male torsos (3923 and 3925); and a female torso (3924) wearing a light tunic.

In *Room 17* is the largest known statue (5934) carved from a monolithic block of porphyry; some authorities say he is

Diocletian, others that he is Christ Pantokrator — about as wide a split as you could hope for. Among the six marble sarcophagi is one (17927) showing the sleeping Ariadne surprised by Dionysos on Naxos.

Funerary objects

Room 18 has pottery, terracotta and funerary urns. In the far left corner is an urn (16152) from the Chatby necropolis which still retains its wreath of artificial flowers, bright green and gold (4th C BC). The terracottas on the right wall, from the Fayyum, are stupid and vulgar.

But in *Room 18A* are perhaps the finest objects in the museum: miniature Tanagra terracotta figures of great delicacy and charm. These come from Alexandrian cemeteries, late 4th to early 2nd C, and occur only in tombs of children, adolescents or young women. In Case K, note the child on a man's shoulder (9205); but the best are the figurines of women in Case L, full of detail and dignity. These works were prompted by the sadness of death in youth; they are entirely sincere and noble, and they live.

Rooms 19, 20 and 21 contain terracottas and pottery; in *Room 20* there is a caseload of bronze wreaths, their flowers gilded. These are ugly and were probably more ugly at the time, but they are impressive for being so old.

Room 22 displays tenth-rate Hellenistic material from excavations at Canopus.

The Treasure Room

Finally in this gallery, there is the *Treasure Room*. There is a collection of Ptolemaic coins. The most beautiful items are the torso of Aphrodite (24042) in silver and the silver gilt goblet (24201) decorated with cupids gathering grapes. The most important, however, are the foundation plaques (8357–66 and 9431–40) in gold, silver, bronze, Nile mud, green faience and opaque glass, carved with Greek and hieroglyphic inscriptions, each recording Ptolemy III's dedication of the Temple of Serapis. Only when these were found in 1943–5 was it established with certainty that the Serapeum had stood on the plateau where Pompey's Pillar stands.

Tomb and chapel reconstructions

You can now walk back towards the entrance, visiting the gardens via the verandah. The *South Garden* has reconstructions of two rock-cut tombs. One (21004) of the 3rd C BC contains a sarcophagus in the form of a bed. The other (20986) of the 1st C AD has an arched entrance with shell decoration in relief. In the *North Garden* is the reconstruction of the three pylons and chapel of the crocodile god whose furnishings have already been seen in Room 9.

Re-entering the building, you pass through *Room G* with a number of white marble statues from a private sanctuary of the 2nd C AD dedicated to Isis.

Christian antiquities

Room 1 contains Christian antiquities. There is the surprising sight of a Christian mummy. Note the cross painted at the neck. There are also many objects from the city of St Menas. On the left wall, in Cases G and G1, are the little souvenir flasks once filled with spring water and taken by departing pilgrims all over the Christian world. Note the motif of St Menas between two camels. There is a bas-relief of the saint which is a crude copy of the one that stood in his desert shrine. And near Case N are two absurd reliefs from the Christian era of Leda and the swan — in one of them she holds an egg.

Rooms 4 and 5 have Christian tapestry fragments on their walls.

In *Room 3*, in painted stucco, are Christian designs and saints from the Alexandria vicinity.

At the centre of *Room 3* is a Christian capital.

The Heptastadion

From Midan Saad Zaghloul you should walk south again along Nebi Danyal and turn right at the ancient crossroads into the western extension of Sharia Horreya, called Sharia el Mitwalli. A block along and leading diagonally off to the right is Sharia Salah-Salem, formerly Rue Chérif Pasha, once Alexandria's most fashionable shopping street but not as smart as it was. Nothing in Alexandria is.

At No. 30 on the right is the National Bank of Egypt, once the Banco di Roma (the wolf of Rome can still be seen over the left doorway). A modified **copy of the Palazzo Farnese** in Rome, Forster thought this the finest building in the city. During the Second World War the British Information Office was lodged round the side and in a letter to Henry Miller, Lawrence Durrell wrote: 'I am in charge of a goodish-sized office of war-propaganda here, trying to usher in the new washboard world which our demented peoples are trying "to forge in blood and iron". It's tiring work. However, it's an office full of beautiful girls, and Alexandria is, after Hollywood, fuller of beautiful women than any place else. Incomparably more beautiful than Athens or Paris; the mixture Coptic, Jewish, Syrian, Egyptian, Moroccan, Spanish gives you slant dark eyes, olive freckled skin, hawk lips and noses, and a temperament like a bomb.

At the end of Sharia Salah-Salem, on the left as it issues into Midan el Tahrir, was the Bourse, once housing the Cotton Exchange. 'The howls and cries that may be heard here of a morning proceed not from a menagerie but from the wealthy merchants of Alexandria as they buy and sell' (Forster). It was set alight and gutted during food riots in 1977 and has since been demolished.

European eclipse

Midan el Tahrir (Liberation Square) was formerly Place Mohammed Ali and laid out by him in 1830 as the centre of his new city. Once attractively planted with trees and gardens, it now roars with traffic and is filled with fumes. This was the European centre of the city, flanked on the left (west) by the Mixed Tribunals which mediated between foreigners and natives (these are now the **Law Courts**), and on the right (east) by the Anglican **Church of St Mark**, commemorating inside the British regiments which saw action against Arabi. At the centre of the square is a fine **equestrian statue of Mohammed Ali**. In Ptolemaic times all this was under the sea.

In the wake of political fortune the streets of Alexandria have suffered many changes in name. The locals however are usually a revolution behind and so the old Rue de France (Arabised into Sharia Faransa) which starts at the northeast end of Midan el Tahrir is still familiarly known as such. If some general, sheikh or politican has appropriated the street, he has so far failed to impress either me or the neighbourhood with his name.

Here you are walking along the Heptastadion through what is very much an Egyptian quarter of the city, often picturesque. There are several mosques along the way; the most interesting is the **Terbana Mosque**, dating from 1684. Its exterior is pale yellow except for its high doorway of brick, painted red and black in Delta Style (there is much more of this at Rosetta), with occasional courses of wood and a Kufic inscription: 'There is no God but God' and 'Mohammed is the Prophet of God'.

Before going in, have a look at the entrance to the cellars round the left-hand side of the building. The columns are ancient. Now go up the steps of the main entrance, arriving at an open air terrace with two great Corinthian columns of granite. The entire building seems to have been made out of Alexandria's antique past; there are more ancient columns propping up the interior and painted gloss white. You will probably be shown round, the gloss paint and similar refurbishments pointed out with pride. Tiles decorate this upstairs entrance to the mosque, but they are in a bad state, the enamel dropping off, but fine where they survive. There are excellent tiles too in the mihrab inside, predominantly blue, though some green; the larger tiles with white daisies are inferior modern work.

Alexandrian pastiche

As you continue north along Sharia Faransa from the Terbana and cross a main intersection, the street becomes narrower and winding with several overhanging balconies in the Turkish style. This is landfall for the island of Pharos. Continue north along Sharia Tatwig; it runs into a square dominated by the large **Mosque of Abu el Abbas Moursi**. It was built in 1943 but stands on the site of a 1767 mosque built by Algerians over the tomb of the 13th C saint. At the end of the square where two tall palm trees rise is the little Mosque of Sidi Daoud with his tomb. This was the main square of the Turkish town, the reduced settlement, its population 4000, to which Alexandria had shrunk when Napoleon landed in 1798. Between the Abu el Abbas Mosque and the harbour is the **Bouseiri Mosque**, its own square illuminated with white lights visible from anywhere along the corniche at night. From this mosque there is a view of Fort Qaytbay and fishing boats, their nets stretched along the harbour wall.

The Turkish town

To the Pharos

From the old Turkish quarter, first follow Sharia Ras el Tin westwards to the **Tombs of Anfushi** near the end of the tram line. These are Ptolemaic, their decorations principally Greek but with Egyptian elements. They have been cut into the limestone ridge that was the island of Pharos; there are four of them, arranged in pairs, each pair sharing an atrium. Their walls are painted to simulate marble, or alabaster blocks, or tiles; archaeologists call this the First Pompeian Style, with all the shoddiness that suggests. In the tomb furthest to the right are scenes of a felucca and a warship of the sort Cleopatra may have sailed in to Actium. The keeper rubs the felucca with his moistened thumb to show that it will not come off — it does not, but is covered with smudgy thumb prints. Also in this tomb are Greek scribblings left by a workman of the period named Diodoros, who immortalises his friend Antiphiles. How innocent these ancients were in their graffiti; we know by what signs our present period would instantly be recognised by archaeologists of the future. The attempt in all these tombs of simulated materials is poor. They are very much bourgeois tombs; their inhabitants paid the going rate for an eternity of tastelessness.

Farouk's abdication

Further towards the western tip is the **Palace of Ras el Tin**, built by Mohammed Ali, though altered this century. Here on 26 July 1952 King Farouk abdicated and sailed away to Italy aboard his yacht. It is now the Admiralty headquarters. You cannot get in.

Now walk eastwards along the seafront towards **Fort Qaytbay**. There is a poor beach and a fish market enroute. The fort is at the end of a breakwater and has been restored since the British shelling in 1882. It was built in 1480 by Sultan Qaytbay on the site and partly from fragments of the Pharos lighthouse, the wonder of the ancient world.

The Pharos was built during the reign of Ptolemy Philadelphus, its architect Sostratus, an Asiatic Greek. 'The sensation it caused was tremendous. It appealed both to the sense of beauty and to the taste for science — an appeal typical of the age. Poets and engineers combined to praise it. Just as the Parthenon had been identified with Athens and St Peter's was to be identified with Rome, so, to the imagination of contemporaries, the Pharos became Alexandria and Alexandria became the Pharos. Never, in the history of architecture, has a secular building been thus worshipped and taken on a spiritual life of its own. It beaconed to the imagination, not only to ships at sea, and long after its light was extinguished memories of it glowed in the minds of men' (Forster).

One of the Seven Wonders of the Ancient World

The Pharos exceeded 125 metres in height and might possibly have touched 150 metres. Its square bottom storey was pierced with many windows and contained perhaps 300 rooms where the mechanics and attendants were housed. A double spiral ascent ran through the centre and hydraulic machinery was used for raising fuel to the top. At its cornice was an inscription by which Sostratos dedicated the Pharos 'to the Saviour Gods; for sailors', the gods being Castor and Pollux who protected mariners, but an allusion to Ptolemy Soter and Berenice, whose worship their son Philadelphus was promoting. Above this was an octagonal second storey, then a circular third storey, and finally the lantern.

The workings of the lantern were mysterious. Visitors spoke of a mirror, perhaps of polished steel for reflecting the sun by day, the fire by night; though others described it as made of glass or transparent stone, and declared that a man sitting under it could see ships at sea that were invisible to the naked eye. It might have been a lens, and it is not at all impossible that Alexandrian mathematicians did discover the lens and that their discovery was lost and forgotten when the Pharos fell.

The Pharos retained its form and functions up to the Arab

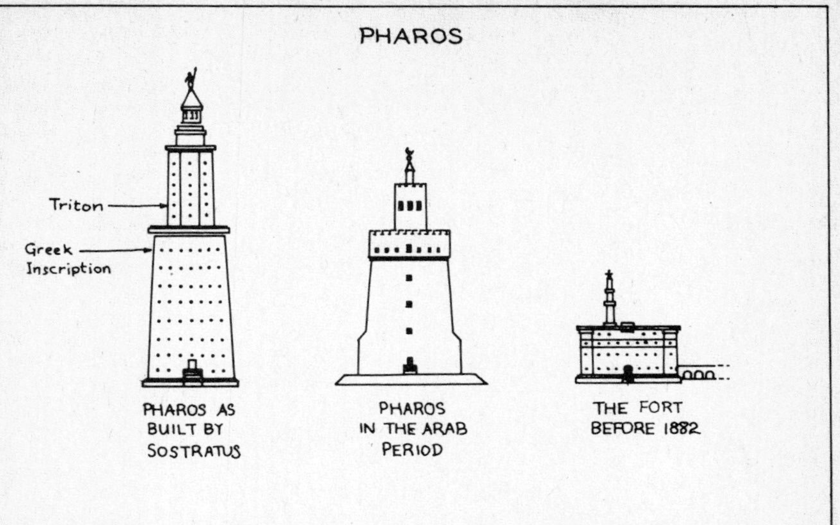

conquest in 641. About 700 the lantern fell, and perhaps at the same time but certainly soon after the two top storeys fell also — the tale is that the Byzantine Emperor, frustrated in his ambitions against Egypt because of the early detection of his ships, put it about that the Pharos stood upon Alexander's treasure, whereupon the Caliph commenced demolition. The first storey survived intact and Ibn Tulun restored the octagonal storey around 880, but an earthquake around 1100 destroyed his work and its place was taken by a mosque. Finally the bottom storey was ruined by a final earthquake in the 14th C. Interestingly, the four stages of the Pharos — square, octagon, round and summit — are exactly reproduced in the minaret of Qaytbay's Mausoleum in Cairo's City of the Dead.

Traces of the Pharos

Here on this promontory, Qaytbay built in part at least from the debris of the Pharos and you can see where bits of it have been incorporated into his structure. The *enclosure walls* describe an irregular pentagon and as you approach, with the open sea to your left, you can make out some granite and marble columns in the northwest section. The seawall of the Pharos probably diverged slightly from the present walls and where these meet the sea it laps over what might have been ancient foundations. It can be difficult to peer too closely at some parts of the fort as within the enclosure there are anti-aircraft emplacements and barracks, and the armed soldiers will have little comprehension of your antiquarian curiosity. Nevertheless there are numerous column sections in the facade of the *keep*, and at its entrance are five great monolithic pillars of red Aswan granite. Inside is the **Naval Museum**.

While approaching the fort along the causeway you passed the **Hydrobiological Museum** and the **Marine Life Institute** (aquarium) — and missed nothing.

To Rhakotis

Acropolis of the Ptolemies

What Alexander flattened he in this case immortalised. Who would know of this obscure Egyptian fishing village had his town planners not built upon it the capital of the Hellenistic world? To reach what was once the citadel of Rhakotis, later the acropolis of the Ptolemies, you must today travel about 1.5 kms southwest from the Corniche, perhaps along Sharias Salah al-Din and Amud el Sawari, in any case through less salubrious parts of the city where impressions in paint, in mud, of children's hands against the walls of squalid streets avert the evil eye.

The Ptolemies built a *Temple of Serapis* here which incorporated a *Library* established by Cleopatra; some tunnels in the rock with crypts and niches and a few marble pillars are all that remain. The destruction was wrought, originally, in 391 when the Patriarch Theophilos led a mob against them in the final triumph of Christianity. Paganism was overthrown, as was learning. The belief that the older 'mother' Library, part of the Museion, was burnt when Julius Caesar fought to maintain himself in the city is now discredited.

Also on this hill stood a *Temple of Isis*, of which still less is to be seen. There is a *statue of Isis Pharia* standing 8 metres tall, found near the site of the Pharos, and two granite *sphinxes*. But the landmark attraction is **Pompey's Pillar**, wrongly named such by the Crusaders; it was raised in honour of Diocletian. The column is 30 metres high and has a circumference of 9 metres; it is of pink Aswan granite and is entirely uninteresting. I have preferred watching Egyptians catching pigeons here. An orange beetle is used to bait a small wire trap hidden in the dry powdery soil.

A Roman Forest Lawn

A short distance south are the **Catacombs of Kom el Shogafa**, the largest Roman funerary complex in Egypt and run by a syndicate for the benefit of non-Christians. The catacombs date from the 2nd C AD and are decorated in a curious blend of classical and Egyptian styles. They are a sort of underground Forest Lawn.

The catacombs are on three levels, the lowest usually flooded and inaccessible. A winding staircase leads up to a *rotunda* encircled by chambers with sarcophagi and niches for funerary urns. The large room to the left was the *banqueting hall* where relatives of the deceased saw him out with a feast. The table in the middle, probably of wood, has disappeared, but cut out of the limestone are the three couches where they reclined on mattresses.

From the rotunda a stairway goes down to the second level. You are now at the *central tomb*. The decorations are composite, not to say weird. Bearded serpents adorn the vestibule wall at the entrance to the inner chamber. Each holds the suggestive pine cone of Dionysos and the serpent wand of Hermes, and also wears the double crown of Upper and Lower Egypt, while above them are Medusas in round shields. In the *tomb chamber proper* are three large sarcophagi, cut out from the rock. Their lids do not open, for the bodies would have been introduced from the passage which runs right round the chamber with accommodation for 300 mummies. In the niche over each sarcophagus is a relief in Egyptian style. Turning around and

Guardian gnomes

facing the entrance, on either side of the door are two extraordinary figures. On the right is Anubis, with a dog's head, but dressed up as a Roman soldier, with sword, lance and shield; on the left is Sobek who, despite being a crocodile, is also shoved into a military costume, with cloak and spear. 'Perhaps the queer couple were meant to guard the tomb, but one must not read too much into them or into anything here — the workmen employed were only concerned to turn out a room that should look suitable for death, and judged by this standard they have succeeded' (Forster).

East to Rosetta

Beaches

There are numerous public beaches along the city's seafront between the Eastern Harbour and Montazah — Chatby, Sporting, Ibrahimiya, Cleopatra, Stanley, Glym, San Stefano (also a private beach, small fee, belonging to the hotel of that name), Sidi Bishr, Miami, Asfara and Mandara; the public beaches are free but usually crowded and often dirty. There are better beaches at Montazah and nearby.

At **Montazah** is the former summer residence of the royal family. Farouk was there when the 1952 coup occurred in Cairo — he fled to Ras el Tin. The *palace* was built in Turko-Florentine style by the Khedive Abbas II around the turn of the century; he also built the *Salamlek* nearby, overlooking a cove, in the style of a chalet for his Austrian mistress. These are set within extensive grounds (fee), planted with pines imported from Europe and palms.

Fishermen at Rosetta, where the Nile flows into the sea

The next bay east is Maamoura with a long fine beach (fee). In the distance you can see the long limestone spur running out to Abu Qir.

Battle of the Nile

Abu Qir (or Aboukir), 24 kms east of Alexandria, is most famous for the two battles fought here in 1798 and 1799. The first was the Battle of the Nile at which Nelson surprised Napoleon's anchored fleet and over the course of two days (1 and 2 August) annihilated it. Though still in control of the country, Napoleon was cut off from France by sea and eventually had to abandon his army and his dreams of Eastern dominion. The circumstances were similar to Antony's at Actium, except that Napoleon's star was still rising. A year later, in July, he personally commanded a battle here against a Turkish force of 15,000 landed by British ships. Napoleon had raced down from Cairo with Kléber and Murat, and with 10,000 men, mostly cavalry, drove the Turks back into the sea, drowning a third of them. That same year he returned to France and overthrew the Directory.

Today Abu Qir is built-up and unattractive, though Alexandrians will drive here for its good seafood restaurants. Nearby is the site of ancient **Canopus**, once one of the most important cities in Egypt owing to its position on the Canopic mouth of the Nile, since dried up. There is little to see. Hadrian liked to stay here, and tried to recreate its pleasures in the garden of the Villa Hadriana at Tivoli, near Rome.

The excursion to Abu Qir (which could be skipped) and on to Rosetta will take about half a day. **Rosetta** (Rashid) is 63 kms from Alexandria and stands on the western branch of the Nile near the sea. Its name is associated most famously in the West with the discovery here of the Rosetta Stone, inscribed in ancient hieroglyphs, demotic Egyptian and Greek, enabling the eventual decipherment of the pharaonic language by Champollion. It is testimony to Napoleon's expedition, which included numerous savants and a well-informed soldiery, that when a Captain Bourchard was shown the stone, turned up by one of his men while restoring Fort Rashid, he immediately recognised its significance.

The Rosetta Stone

The town is visited, however, for other reasons. Founded in the 9th C, it flourished while Alexandria faded and declined again as modern Alexandria prospered. It reached its apogee in the 17th and 18th C, when it was the most important port in Egypt, and there are still some fine houses dating from this period, built in red and black brick, their facades decorated in the Delta Style illustrated, though not nearly so well, by the Terbana Mosque in Alexandria. Many, too, incorporate ancient stones and columns, and have delicately carved mashrabiyyas. The oldest and finest of these is the *House of Ali el Fatairi*, 17th C, just off the main street which runs south, parallel with the Nile, from the train station. This street is fascinating in itself, a market for much of the way, covered by awnings. Other houses are the *Arab Keli*, 18th C, now a museum; and *El Amaciali*, early 19th C. At the bottom of the main street is the most important building in town, the *Mosque of Zaghloul*. This is really two mosques, the eastern one smartly painted white, arcades with handsome arches running round a glaring courtyard. The western one, founded in 1600, is

Fine Delta architecture

more interesting however, partly because it is under a few feet of water and crumbling but mostly for its wonderful forest of columns, as though rising out of a swamp.

Rosetta makes an interesting footnote to Alexandria's history. Its fortunes were built on the default of the greater city. The coast of Egypt here is delta, the shifting sediment of a senseless river. Rosetta can have no sea harbour, the limestone ridges that created the two great harbours of Alexandria do not continue eastward of Abu Qir. Alexander saw this potential, that his city could hold its own against land and sea. When the broad political will is there, Alexandria is willing. She can afford to wait.

Leaving Rosetta by the north, numerous high chimneys mark brickworks along the Nile. Here at the very end of the river its mud is still pressed into service. A few kilometres along there is a spit of land, the river washing mud up on one side, the sea washing sand up on the other. At the very point there is a small yellow mosque; inside I saw two men praying. The sea and the river are rising up through its foundations, curling the paint off its walls, the whole thing disintegrating and tipping towards that line where the blue steady Nile is pounded by the light green waves of the Mediterranean.

The mosque at the end of the Nile

A soldier came up to me: 'Have you come to save the land from the sea?' It seems that since the building of the Aswan Dam the river hardly lays down silt and has stopped pushing the Delta out into the Mediterranean. Those waves were nibbling away at Egypt at the rate of several feet a year. The mosque will soon tumble and be drowned. The soldier was like some pathetic Canute, stationed at the northern limit of his country to guard its retreat.

Ecologists come, I suppose, sent by international organisations, and offer him some comfort. I said nothing, and with an idiot's fascination I stood there watching the Mediterranean grow impercepitably larger.

PRACTICAL INFORMATION

See the *Practical Information* section at the end of the *Alexandria: Capital of Memory* chapter.

For those who can manage only an **abbreviated itinerary**: take a carriage to the Cecil and having taken a room overlooking the corniche, sit on the balcony looking out over the harbour and try to resurrect in your mind's eye the city that was. Perhaps have a coffee at the Trianon, and then follow the walk recommended along Sharia Salah Salem and across Midan el Tahrir so that you follow Sharia Faransa (the old Rue de France) to Anfushi and the Fortress of Qaytbay. Alexandria is less a city you come to for seeing specific sights than a place you might just fall in love with. Reading Durrell, Forster and Cavafy helps: the architecture of Alexandria is found in the words written about her.

PLACE INDEX

The following index is in two parts, the first covering Cairo, the second covering the rest of Egypt.

Note that the Arabic prefixes *el* and *al* have not been taken into account for the purpose of alphabetisation.

MAP AND PLAN INDEX

The following index is arranged alphabetically by place, ie sites at *Abydos* first, at *Thebes* last.

NOTES

NOTES

NOTES

NOTES

NOTES

NOTES

NOTES